THE ECONOMICS OF OFFSETS

Studies in Defence Economics

Edited by Keith Hartley and Nicholas Hooper, Centre for Defence Economics, University of York, UK.

This monograph series adopts a wide definition of defence economics to cover all aspects of the political economy of defence, disarmament and peace.

This book is part of a series. The publishers will accept continuation orders which may be cancelled at any time and which provide for automatic billing and shipping of each title in the series upon publication. Please write for details.

The Economics of Offsets
Defence Procurement and Countertrade

Edited by

Stephen Martin
The Centre for Defence Economics
University of York, UK

Routledge
Taylor & Francis Group

LONDON AND NEW YORK

Published 2007 by Routledge
2 Park Square, Milton Park, Abingdon, Oxfordshire OX14 4RN
711 Third Avenue, New York, NY 10017

First issued in paperback 2014

Routledge is an imprint of the Taylor and Francis Group, an informa business

British Library Cataloguing in Publication Data

Economics of Offsets: Defence Procurement and
    Countertrade. — (Studies in Defence
    Economics, ISSN 1062–046X; Vol. 4)
    I. Martin, Stephen   II. Series
    382

ISBN 13: 978-3-7186-5782-7(hbk)
ISBN 13: 978-1-138-00221-0 (pbk)

Publisher's Note
The publisher has gone to great lengths to ensure the quality of this reprint but points out that some imperfections in the original may be apparent

Contents

Acknowledgements

The preparation of this volume was funded by the Economic and Social Research Council (R000233146). The editor would like to thank all those who have assisted in the publication of this book. Thanks are due to Professor Keith Hartley, who read and commented upon the manuscript, and to Roberta Blackburn and Margaret Cafferky, who provided excellent secretarial and editorial assistance in the final stages of publication.

List of Contributors

Abdulla M Al-Ghrair, BS King Faisal Air Academy, MDA Cranfield, Brigadier General, Royal Saudi Air Force, pilot. His research interests include economic offsets, Saudization and conflict resolution.

Nicholas Antonakis has a PhD in Defence Economics from the University of Athens. He is an expert economist in the Greek Ministry of Industry, Energy and Technology. His research interests include the determinants and growth effects of military expenditure, and the structure and performance of defence industries.

Dean Cheng has worked for several years as a researcher and writer on Asian defence and foreign affairs. He is completing his dissertation, which examines Asian perceptions of the United States and Japan in the post-World War II era. He lives in Washington, DC.

Michael Chinworth is the Senior Analyst of Asian Technology for The Analytic Sciences Corporation of Arlington, Virginia. He has published widely on the technological capabilities of the Far East, including Inside Japan's Defence: Economics, Technology and Strategy (published by Brassey's (US) in 1992). He writes a monthly column on Asian science, technology and business trends in Automotive Engineering (published by SAE International)

Dr James Fergusson is the Deputy Director of the Centre for Defence and Security Studies at the University of Manitoba, Winnipeg, Canada. He has written extensively on issues related to Canadian defence industrial policy and practices, and is currently examining the defence industrial implications of Canadian participation in Ballistic Missile Defence.

Peter Hall has a long standing research interest in industry economics and, in particular, in the economics of technological innovation. This culminated in his book Innovation, Economics and Evolution, published in 1994, which has also led to specialist work in defence industry economics. He has recently been one of the leaders of a major government inquiry into R&D activity and policy in Australia.

Keith Hartley is Professor of Economics and Director of the Centre for Defence Economics, University of York. He has continuing research interests in defence economics, including procurement policy, the Single European Market for defence equipment and various aspects of disarmament.

Jean-Paul Hébert has a PhD in economic theory and is a member of the Defence Sociology group in the Ecole des hautes Études en Sciences Sociales (GSD/EIIESS, Paris). He is a specialist on the French armaments industry and his latest book is Production d'Armement, Mutation du Système Français, Editions de la Documentation Française, Paris, 1995.

Nick Hooper is currently Deputy Director of the Centre for Defence Economics at the University of York. Previous appointments included Industrial Development Analyst for Aramco from 1982 to 1985. His current research interests include defence industries, procurement policy and industrial and manpower adjustment to reductions in military expenditure.

Dr Stephen Martin is a Research Fellow in the Centre for Defence Economics at the University of York. His current research interests include the economics of defence procurement and the impact of privatisation on corporate performance.

Stefan Markowski is the convenor of the postgraduate Management Studies Program for the Australian Defence Force Academy at the University of New South Wales in Canberra. His research interests include applied microeconomics, in particular defence economics, and operations and logistics management. He has also been retained by a wide range of private and public sector clients, including the Australian Defence Organisation, as an economic and management consultant.

Keith Maskus is an Associate Professor of Economics at the University of Colorado (Boulder). He received his PhD from the University of Michigan in 1981. His research interests lie in empirical modelling of trade theories and in aspects of multilateral trade policy. Recently he has devoted considerable attention to the economics of international differences in intellectual property rights regimes.

Ron Matthews is a senior lecturer in economic and financial management at the School of Defence Management, Cranfield University. He has research interests in technological offsets and defence industrialisation and is the author of numerous articles on these related subjects. He is also the co-editor of a recent book, entitled Japan's Military Renaissance, published by Macmillan.

Maison Miscavage is the Projects Coordinator at International Technology Sourcing Inc. His responsibilities include project research and structuring, as well as competitive analysis. He also takes a special interest in Russia and FSU affairs.

Dr Jordi Molas-Gallart is an economist working as a Research Fellow at the Science Policy Research Unit, University of Sussex. His doctoral dissertation, Military Production and Innovation in Spain, has been published by Harwood Academic Publishers.

Alon Redlich is the President of International Technology Sourcing Inc (ITS), a Chicago-based company engaged in the development and implementation of off-set strategies. Mr Redlich and the ITS team serve as strategic planning and business development advisors to numerous Fortune 100 companies. He is currently focusing on initiatives in Russia, India, Israel and the UAE.

Dr Wally Struys is head of the Department of Economics and Management and Professor of Economics at the Royal Military Academy (Brussels). His research activities and publications lay mainly in the field of Defence Economics. He participates in several working groups dealing with defence matters in NATO, WEU and UE. He is a founding member of the International Defence Economics Association (IDEA).

Bernard Udis is a Professor of Economics at the University of Colorado (Boulder). He was awarded the PhD degree by Princeton University in 1959. Interests cover defense economics, labour economics, industrial policy, technology transfer and international economic policy. His most recent research examines the costs and benefits of offsets in defence trade and the possible role of Japan in a future military technical revolution.

Chapter 1

Introduction and Overview

Stephen Martin
Centre for Defence Economics,
University of York, UK

1.1 Context

Defence procurement can take a number of forms. From indigenous projects, through shared development and production, licensed production and offsets, to an off-the-shelf purchase of a foreign design. Each form of procurement offers the purchaser a different degree of industrial involvement with the development and production of the system being acquired. At one end of the spectrum lie off-the-shelf purchases of a foreign system: these yield neither development nor production work for the domestic defence industrial base (DIB). At the other extreme lies indigenous development and production where all work is allocated to domestic firms. Between these two extremes are procurement options where work is shared between vendor and purchaser.

When purchasing defence equipment, vote-sensitive governments face some difficult choices. Indigenous development and production will, theoretically, provide an independent capability, the required equipment, as well as the most benefit for the domestic economy in terms of jobs and technology acquisition. However, this is also likely to be the most expensive option. An off-the-shelf purchase might involve compromise over the system's capability and will generate little domestic economic benefit. Moreover, there is always the risk that a vendor will not be willing/able to deliver further supplies as and when these are required. Yet this is likely to be the cheapest procurement option.

The ever-increasing costliness of defence equipment, limited defence budgets, as well as concerns about unemployment levels and the competitiveness of domestic industry, have all encouraged many states to eschew both indigenous development and off-the-shelf purchases. Instead, governments have favoured procurement forms which yield benefits for the domestic economy as well as being less costly than an indigenous programme. One option, which has been pursued by the larger Western European nations, has been to collaborate in the development and production of new equipment.[1] This has been particularly common for aerospace products, such as aircraft and missiles, where collaboration, by eliminating the duplication of costly R&D, can offer substantial savings over an indigenous programme.[2]

1

For some products, collaboration is not possible (e.g. where no other state has a similar requirement) or is considered too costly relative to the usually much cheaper off-the-shelf import option. However, imports typically bring few industrial benefits to the purchaser's economy. As a compromise, many countries have sought other procurement methods which ensure that each major defence procurement contract placed with a foreign supplier also provides substantial industrial benefits for the purchasing nation. These benefits are often discussed under the umbrella term 'offsets'. To the uninitiated, this can be confusing because the term 'offset' is also used to describe one particular form of industrial benefit. In this book, the broad definition of offset is adopted and this is taken to include the following forms of industrial benefit: co-production, licensed production, direct offset and indirect offset.

Licensed production occurs where the purchaser obtains a share of the production work for its own order and, sometimes, for its own exports to third parties. The licence may cover the manufacture of the entire item or only specified parts. Sometimes the licence only covers final assembly. Both Italy (Agusta) and the UK (Westland) have frequently purchased licences to produce American-designed helicopters.

Similar to licensed production is co-production, where the nation buying a foreign design is given a share in manufacturing work for its own order, the designer's order, and orders from third parties. For example, the General Dynamics F-16 European co-production contract in 1975 was based on sharing the manufacture of a 998 aircraft programme. The European consortium, which ordered 348 aircraft, was allocated work on the following basis: ten per cent of the initial US order (650 aircraft), forty per cent of their own order and fifteen per cent of export sales to other countries. Exports were estimated at 500 units and achievement of this figure would have meant that the Europeans would have obtained manufacturing business to the value of 80 per cent of their total order, namely 279 aircraft.[3]

While both co-production and licensed production provide employment and technological benefits for the domestic economy, the establishment of an indigenous production line is a costly business. As defence budgets have been cut and unemployment has risen, purchasers have sought a less costly form of procurement which still generates work for the domestic economy. Typically, this obliges the foreign vendor and its sub-contractors to buy goods and services over and above what it would have bought from firms in the purchaser's economy. This offset is usually some percentage of the contract price and a time period is often set for its fulfilment. Restrictions are usually imposed on the type of goods eligible for inclusion towards the offset, and certain types of work (e.g.

R&D) might be weighted more heavily than other purchases (e.g. off-the-shelf purchases of manufactured goods). These offsets might be for items to go into the equipment that the purchasing state's defence ministry is buying, in which case they are known as direct offset, or for items totally unrelated to the actual equipment being purchased, which is termed indirect offset. If the industrial base in the country purchasing the equipment is relatively small and underdeveloped, there may be few goods that can be purchased and thus inward investment might constitute the major component of any offset programme (e.g. as in the recent Al Yamamah sale of military aircraft by British Aerospace to Saudi Arabia).

Drawing hard and fast boundaries around the forms of work-sharing is not always either useful or easy. For example, there are obvious similarities between the licensed production of an aircraft part which is to be included in the aircraft to be purchased, and the production of the same part which is eligible towards a vendor's (direct) offset obligation: in both cases the work is placed with the domestic manufacturer. There are, of course, also differences: the direct offset implies that domestic manufacturer already had access to the necessary technology whereas licensed production implies the transfer of new technology to the manufacturer.

1.2   The Need for a Comparative Volume

All governments purchase defence equipment and it is, therefore, hardly surprising that over 130 countries have some form of offset policy.[4] Although commonplace, offset requirements vary considerably from one country to another (e.g. in terms of the type expenditure that is offset eligible). Moreover, states vary in terms of how long they have had an offset requirement and thus some policy differences will reflect their different experiences. Other policy differences will reflect different objectives (e.g. an emphasis on production or R&D work). This international diversity makes for an interesting comparative study.

Furthermore, as a specialism, economists have long neglected defence matters although the level of resources devoted to defence spending and indeed offsets is such as to warrant a substantially increased research effort. Certainly, there are very few economic evaluations of offset programs, not least because of the considerable problems associated with such an exercise. First, there is little, if any, routinely published data. Hence the analyst is reliant on the goodwill of those in industry and government to discuss such matters. Second, offsets are big business and are thus commercially sensitive. In an era of high unemployment, vote conscious governments are sensitive to the charge of spending large amounts of tax-payers' money on products that generate few domestic jobs. One response to this is to cite the number of jobs created by offset work. Nevertheless, governments remain vulnerable to criticism of the efficacy of their offsets policy which is thus a politically sensitive issue. Third, those involved with offsets in both industry and government have vested interests. Consequently, it is sometimes difficult to disentangle fact from fiction. One of the advantages of a comparative volume is that, although the effect of offsets might be rather difficult to elucidate for any individual country, taken together, the experience of a number of states might more clearly reveal a number of common themes.

Finally, as defence budgets are cut and competition in the industry increases, offsets are likely to become more rather than less important. Firms will seek to compete for contracts by offering increasingly attractive offset packages and purchasers will increasingly demand domestic benefits for their defence expenditures. Thus a sound knowledge of the cost and impact of offsets becomes even more critical.

1.3   The Approach

The original aim of this volume was to provide an authoritative account of offset policy and experience across a representative cross-section of countries. The achievement of this objective was constrained by the availability of economists who were willing and able to write on offsets. However, an even more binding constraint proved to be the availability of appropriate information and, in particular, data on the cost and impact of offsets.

With regard to giving and receiving offset work, each country can be allocated to one of three groups. First, there is the USA that largely exports equipment and thus only gives offset. The chapter on this country examines the development of US offset policy over the past two decades. Second, there is the small number of states that both import and export armaments and thus who both give and receive offset work. France, Germany and the UK are three countries that fall into this category, two of which provide case studies for this book. Finally, there is the large number of states that largely import defence equipment and who thus typically only receive offset work.

The last group of countries offers a wide choice of case studies and an attempt has been made to select a representative sample in terms of geographical location, industrial base and defence policy. Four countries with a well-developed defence industry were selected: Australia, Belgium, Canada and Switzerland. Even within this group, however, there is a considerable diversity of offset experience and policy. In Belgium and Canada, for example, there are strong regional issues so that the Federal government is as concerned with the geographical distribution as well as the level of offset work. Similarly, the group is far from homogenous in terms of defence policy. Canada can, for example, free-ride on the USA for its defence while Switzerland pursues a policy of independent neutrality.

Two other European states were selected, both with developing defence industries. Greece provides an interesting case study because the Turkish invasion of Cyprus in 1974 prompted a re-evaluation of the importance of its indigenous defence capabilities. Similarly, over the past two decades, Spain has been seeking to modernise its defence forces and both nations have attempted to use offsets to improve their defence industrial bases. In addition, both countries have made substantial defence purchases and their respective offset policies have changed markedly from one purchase to another. This suggests that their experience can offer useful insights into the operation and effectiveness of offset programmes.

From the Far East, three countries are studied: Japan, South Korea and Taiwan. All three are similar in the sense that their offset policy has emphasised technology transfer rather than merely production work. Consequently, their preferred offset option has been to licence produce US-designed aerospace products. However, this is a particularly costly option and one which the US government has become increasingly reluctant to permit for fears that its competitive advantage in aerospace will disappear as these transfers create new competitors in world markets.

From the Middle East there are chapters on Israel and Saudi Arabia. The Israeli chapter is unique in the sense that it is written by practitioners rather than academics. The authors work for *International Technology Sourcing (ITS),* a US-based firm that specialises in identifying offset opportunities that are mutually beneficial to both the client country and the defence contractor. ITS has recently completed an offset campaign in Israel, and the authors discuss their experiences there. Three very large defence purchases over the past decade and a shift in offset policy make Saudi Arabia an interesting case study. In addition, the Saudi emphasis in its offset policy is not on providing work for domestic industry (which is very small) but rather on encouraging western companies to form joint ventures with Saudi partners to reduce the economy's dependence on oil. Like Japan, South Korea and Taiwan, the emphasis is on technology transfer but in the Saudi case this is neither focused on the aerospace industry nor does it involve the licensed production of the item being procured.

Obvious gaps in this study are the omission of any countries from either South America or Africa. These were areas where the availability of authors constraint bit particularly hard.

1.4   Overview

Chapter 2 provides a theoretical and empirical overview of offsets associated with both civil and military purchases. This should enable the reader to place each of the subsequent country studies within the wider context of reciprocal sales agreements as a whole.

Stefan Markowski and Peter Hall (Chapter 3) provide an interesting historical perspective on, and critical evaluation of, Australian offset policy. Their chapter also admirably demonstrates the terminological minefield that bedevils any international comparative discussion of offsets! As noted above, offset can either be used as an umbrella term for several forms of work-sharing or as a form of work-sharing in its own right. With regard to the latter usage, typically two forms of offset are distinguished, direct and indirect offset. In Australia, the term offset refers to indirect offset whilst the Australian equivalent of direct offset is known as 'local content' (which is not discussed). The authors argue that:

- (indirect) offsets are not costless;
- the purchaser should seek quotes for various levels of offset;
- the evidence suggests that (indirect) offsets have had limited success in either enhancing the DIB or improving the competitiveness of Australian firms in world markets.

Hence Markowski and Hall welcome the very recent policy changes whereby (indirect) offsets become a mechanism of "last resort". However, this should not be interpreted as signalling the demise of offsets in Australia. For as indirect offset is being downplayed, local content (direct offset) "will have an increasing impact on programs, with the emphasis on the use of local prime contractors".[5]

Jim Fergusson (Chapter 5) argues that, for the student of defence matters, Canada provides an interesting case study. Security considerations are notably absent from defence-industrial policy deliberations, not least because there is an implicit understanding that, if attacked, the US would defend its weaker neighbour, and so competition between industrial and economic benefits is to the fore. One consequence of this has been that offsets have served to improve Canada's technological capability and unemployment record but at the cost of its military capability. Again, semantics are important. Officially, Canada does not have an offset policy but rather a requirement for industrial and regional benefits; in other words, offsets by another name. Unlike Australia, political issues in Canada frequently have a strong regional theme and thus the successful vendor will have ensured the appropriate regional distribution of offsets. However, industry is concentrated in central Canada and this makes it difficult to place work with existing factories elsewhere. Moreover, the establishment of a new capability is costly and, without export markets, such capacity becomes dependent on domestic orders, thus constraining future procurement decisions. It is also interesting to note that both Canada and Australia have had a formal offset requirement for over two decades and that both have moved away from indirect and towards direct offset as their preferred policy.

Another country where regional considerations play an important role is Belgium. Like the Canadian case, this aspect of Belgian offset policy does not appear to be particularly successful in an industrial or economic sense but a political necessity. Wally Struys (Chapter 4) argues that overcapacity has been and remains one of the major problems facing the Belgian defence industry and that offsets, far from encouraging rationalisation, have served to keep inefficient producers in business and to create additional capacity albeit in industrially deprived regions. Struys argues that Belgian offsets have not been free goods and that their additional cost has reduced the purchasing power of the defence budget. Again, offsets help to maintain the defence industrial base but only in the short term. Firms become dependent on offset work, which constrains future procurement choices and masks industrial shortcomings. Struys argues that there is a need to integrate offsets in to industrial development policy as a whole and to focus on sustainable long-term goals rather than more immediate short-term objectives.

Alon Redlich and Maison Miscavage (Chapter 15) provide a practitioner's viewpoint. They argue that offsets should be seen as an opportunity rather than a burden, and that with a co-operative rather than adversarial attitude, offsets can prove beneficial to both the client country and the defence contractor. In addition to their general remarks on offsets, which (reassuringly) are very much in line with those made by academics elsewhere in the book, the authors discuss their recent campaign in Israel and indicate how a company, such as ITS, identifies mutually beneficial offset opportunities. Like several other countries, Israeli offset policy encourages foreign and Israeli firms to establish very close, long-term working relationships in an attempt to improve global market access for domestic goods. Consequently, short-term, one-off deals play a very small role in the Israeli offset environment.

Much of the discussion of offsets is plagued by a lack of relevant information. Stephen Martin and Keith Hartley (Chapter 13) outline and discuss the results of two industrial surveys: one looks at incoming offset work while the other examines the impact of offsets associated with UK defence exports. These will be of interest as the survey responses provide a rare insight into the employment, technology and competitive impact of offsets. The studies suggest that although, financially, offsets involve considerable sums, in practical terms their impact is, for the UK at least, much less significant. For example, the $1.5bn offset associated with the UK's purchase of AWACS aircraft is thought to have generated 4804 person-years of work for UK industry while £450m of export offset 'cost' the UK 1105 employee-years of work. It is also interesting to note that the survey evidence suggests that offsets *do* cost more than an equivalent off-the-shelf purchase and, not surprisingly, that vendors seek to include most of this premium in the selling price. Once it is acknowledged that offsets are not free, it then seems sensible that the benefits associated with offset should be carefully documented. Offsets can be viewed as an instrument of industrial policy and whether this tool is the most cost-effective way to achieve policy objectives needs careful examination. At the time of writing, however, this is not the UK's approach, although elsewhere offsets are part of a wider industrial policy.

Abdullah Al-Ghrair and Nick Hooper (Chapter 9) argue that in Saudi Arabia offset policy can be viewed as an extension of its industrial policy. Offset is not about encouraging the vendor to purchase more domestically manufactured goods — the Saudi industrial base is simply too small to absorb the required amount of work. Instead, the objective is to reduce the economy's dependence on oil by encouraging the growth of other industrial sectors through the establishment of international joint ventures. These joint ventures typically comprise a Saudi partner, the firm that owns the relevant technology, and (often), the firm with the offset obligation. The latter typically contributes equity capital as well as knowledge of the type of ventures sought by the Saudi authorities and the personal contacts and local expertise necessary to facilitate the establishment of a new venture in the Kingdom. Most of these joint ventures are not in the defence field. This latter aspect of current policy is in marked contrast to the earliest developments associated with the Peace Shield offset. Here, Boeing established factories for the repair and maintenance of, *inter alia*, the AWACS aircraft, but these facilities were unable to secure sufficient additional work to justify their construction. The Saudi response to this was to continue to seek international joint ventures as a way of introducing new technologies into the economy but to move away from defence and into other sectors where demand is more substantial and the prospects for market growth more attractive. The emphasis is much more on offset as a means to long-term viability rather than as a short-term stop-gap to meet a deficiency of demand.

There can be few countries where offsets have made a greater contribution to economic and industrial development than Japan. Seeking control over its technological destiny, Japan required a local ability to research, innovate, design and manufacture. Hence offsets have taken the form of licensed production. These offsets have not been cheap but the Japanese government has been willing to pay the necessary premium for the associated benefits such as stimulating local industry and improving the security of supply. Michael Chinworth and Ron Matthews (Chapter 9) argue that the US has been willing to transfer technologies and thus to risk the development of new competitors for several reasons. First, US firms receive substantial royalty payments. Second, such transfers improve the strength of an ally against any potential Soviet threat. Third, if the US did not grant the relevant licences, it is likely that the Japanese would turn to the Europeans and thus acquire similar technologies, but from US competitors. This policy has yielded a strong, technologically advanced, and increasingly self-reliant defence industrial base. Although Japan's defence budget is likely to be increasingly squeezed in the foreseeable future, and the defence environment has changed considerably, the commitment to domestic defence production and hence offset is likely to continue unabated.

Michael Chinworth and Dean Cheng (Chapter 10) argue that technology transfer has also driven offset demands in both South Korea and Taiwan. With the announcement of the Nixon doctrine in 1970 and the subsequent reduction of US forces from the Asian region, both countries sought to develop an indigenous defence industrial capacity which was seen as essential to guarantee their territorial integrity. Also, the increased sophistication of their defence industries was viewed as a way of injecting advanced technologies into the economy as a whole. For the US, arms sales with offsets served to strengthen diplomatic and military ties; this was particularly important after the Nixon doctrine when many in the region feared an imminent American withdrawal and the destabilising consequences that would follow. With the end of the Cold War, the US has become more concerned about the economic consequences of offsets and, in particular, fears that such packages contribute to the growth of potential competitors. The lessons of past technology transfers to Japan remain! However, the authors argue that both South Korea and Taiwan are unlikely to be able to exploit these transfers to the extent that Japan was able to do. First, because South Korea and Taiwan are attempting to develop their economies from a far lower technological level than that which faced Japan at the end of the Second World War and second, that this technological deficiency is exacerbated by human resource constraints. Moreover, Japan benefitted from a far more liberal trade and technology transfer environment than either South Korea or Taiwan, due partly to the Western experience with Japan. Consequently, even if offsets do transfer technologies it is unlikely that either economy will be able to exploit such transfers to the extent that Japan was able to do so.

Jordi Molas-Gallart (Chapter 11) looks at the development of Spanish offset policy over the past decade. The author examines the $1.5bn offset, to be met over a ten-year period, associated with the purchase, in 1984, of 72 F-15 fighter aircraft. The objective for the offset was to improve the industrial and technolog-ical base, particularly in the defence sector, and to increase the political accept-ability of spending such a large sum on a foreign product when domestic unemployment levels were relatively high (20%). At the beginning of the 1980s Spain's NATO membership was still pending and thus she was absent from various major international arms co-operation fora. The author argues that it was only through the purchase of foreign defence equipment that Spain could attempt to upgrade the technological level of its defence industries. Particular emphasis was given to aerospace, materials, avionics and simulators. If placing work with Spanish firms was more expensive for McDonnell than using its usual suppliers, then the Spanish government was willing to pay for this and set aside $100m for this purpose.

As McDonnell-Douglas' annual obligation grew, fulfilling the offset became more and more difficult. Molas-Gallart identifies several reasons for this. In principle, offsets could be in any area of technological development but this allowed the authorities to establish sectoral and regional priorities. McDonnell submitted hundreds of projects for offset approval and the authorities, as so often happens in other countries, were faced with the problem of deciding whether each proposal met the conditions required to be a genuine offset. Proposed transactions had to result in a net increase for Spanish exports to the US. Once a project was accepted, the Management Office then had the other familiar problem of calculating its "offset value", which involved, amongst other things, estimating the growth in normal trade flows that the new offset caused, and the associated Spanish value added. By the early 1990s, McDonnell-Douglas was finding it difficult to meet its annual obligations, not least because the global recession was making it increasingly difficult to find new markets for Spanish products.

According to Gallart, these problems with the F-18 offset prompted a shift in policy. Rather than seek offset, Spain sought direct participation in the devel-opment and production programme for the modernisation of its AV-8B Harriers. Although the amount of business generated is similar, joint development and production allows the tasks that Spanish industry will undertake to be defined in advance of any final procurement decisions whereas offsets are agreed after the procurement decision. Moreover, with joint development there is no need to oversee offset applications.

At the same time there has been a policy to use acquisition programmes to draw foreign partners into domestic companies. The idea here is that with an equity interest in the profitability of the Spanish partner, the foreign company will be more willing to share its technological and marketing skills. Moreover, with offset the vendor's interest in placing work with Spanish firms is likely to decline once it has fulfilled its obligation. With an equity interest, however, it is hoped that this will lead foreign firms to take longer term view although there is of course nothing to stop them from selling their shareholding, although such investments might assist US manufacturers to win other (European) orders.

Spain is not the only country to move away from one form of offset and towards other forms of cooperation, particularly joint ventures. A similar trend is revealed in Nicholas Antonakis' paper (Chapter 7) on Greece. The Turkish invasion of Cyprus in 1974 and the continuing territorial disputes between the two countries, focused attention on the need to modernise Greece's defence as well as to improve the domestic defence capability to minimise Greece's foreign dependent and vulnerability in wartime. However, a formal offset package did not come into being until a decade later with the purchase of 40 Mirage 2000 aircraft from Dassault. For this offset, valued at some 80% of the purchase price, co-production and investment projects, technology transfers, the promotion of Greek exports as well as the development of tourism, were all acceptable for offset credit. Unfortunately, there is no publicly available information on the success or otherwise of this package.

However, the offset agreement which accompanied the purchase of 40 F-16C from the USA, signed almost three years later, was rather different. This led to the formation of the Greek Investment Development Company (GIDC), owned jointly by the Greek government and three US companies, General Dynamics, General Electric and Westinghouse. The GIDC will undertake investment projects, mainly for the production of high technology goods, it will ease and facilitate the transfer of technology to Greek firms and it will promote the export of Greek industrial products in new foreign markets. In addition, the offset is said to involve the co-production of air frame and engine parts to the value of $100m. Similarly, two other major offset purchases — for four Meko-200 frigates and the upgrading of the Kanaris directional firing system on Harpoon missiles — focused on the Greek production of parts or the entire product, either for the equipment being purchased by the Greeks or for export to third parties.

As in the Spanish case, there seems to have been a move away from offsets from any part of the Greek economy and towards those directly associated with the equipment being purchased. And at the same time, the formation of the GIDC joint venture seems to parallel Spanish attempts to draw foreign firms into the domestic economy as a way gaining access to new technological, production and marketing skills.

Few studies outline in more detail the various forms that offset can take better than Jean-Paul Hébert's examination of French exports (Chapter 6). Hébert defines offset in a broad way and includes such transactions as barter, the simultaneous counter-purchase of specific goods, the counter-purchase of unspecified industrial products and services to a specific value, technology transfers and the provision of favourable financial loans. Hébert argues that offsets have become an important competitive tool in the armaments market and cites several deals where the offset package proved decisive in the choice of which product to purchase. He concludes that as defence budgets are cut and suppliers chase fewer and smaller orders this aspect of the competitive process is likely to become more rather than less important.

Bernard Udis' case study of the Swiss F-5 purchase (Chapter 12) is an interesting one because it involves a number of issues which arise with many offsets. Previously, the Swiss had licensed produced foreign designs but by the 1970s this procurement method had become prohibitively expensive. Direct and indirect offsets offered the opportunity to buy the aircraft required and at the same time to compensate the defence industrial base for not licence producing the aircraft domestically. For both vendor and purchaser this was one of the early offsets of its type and, as might be expected, both sides were involved in a learning process. Swiss industry expected automatically to win contracts from US firms and found the administrative hurdles of selling to the US military difficult to overcome. The vendors, Northrop and General Electric, were finding it difficult to identify quickly Swiss firms with the necessary cost and quality characteristics. As is often the case with technologically advanced countries, the Swiss wanted the offset not so much to provide jobs or to improve the balance of payments, as to assist firms that would have received orders had the aircraft been produced in Switzerland. And as is often the case, there was the by now common debate concerning which sales occurred as a result of the offset and which reflected established business relations. Udis' chapter also sheds some light on other issues associated with offset. He notes that the US vendors continued to place work with Swiss firms after the obligation had been fulfilled although, as Udis notes, this was partly because such purchases could be banked as offset credit. Swiss industry is still producing parts for F-5s and Udis argues that technological spinoffs from the offset increased the possibility of Swiss participation in joint European projects. The Swiss recognise that there is a cost premium to pay for offsets but consider that a figure of up to 10 per cent is reasonable for a well-designed offset program, and have sought offset on all major purchases since the F-5.

US industry, with a vast trade surplus in defence equipment, incurs more offset obligations than any other country and, given some of the alleged effects of offsets, this has (not surprisingly) led to calls for the US Congress to limit the offsets that US firms can offer. However, as Bernard Udis and Keith Maskus

(Chapter 14) point out, offsets were not always viewed in such a negative light. In the aftermath of the Second World War and the development of the Cold War in the 1950s and 1960s, the US encouraged the Europeans to licence produce US equipment to strengthen NATO's defence both directly and via the improvements this brought to the European's defence industrial base. In the 1970s, however, the Europeans began to want more than just state-of-the-art equipment from their defence expenditure on US-designed systems. Additional concerns, such as the balance of payments, technology transfer, and domestic employment levels, became prominent. At the same time, concerns grew in the US at the impact that these offsets were having on the domestic defence industrial base, particularly the transfer of technologies which, it was feared, would allow foreign manufacturers to catch up with US firms and then compete with them in world markets. Japan's success in the automobile and consumer electronics fields only served to illustrate the potential dangers.

US prime contractors, of course, would prefer not to give offset but are forced to do so by competitive pressure. Moreover, whilst US firms would like to see offset demands fall, Congressional limitations on what US firms can offer suppliers would be of no help; purchasers would simply take their custom to other manufacturers whose governments impose no such limits on outgoing offsets. Indeed, US primes have to adopt a rather schizophrenic attitude towards offsets: to get sales firms must emphasise the positive impact that offsets will have on the purchaser's economy, whilst at the same time telling Congress that the negative effect on the US economy will be relatively trivial. Recognising the futility of unilateral limits on the offsets that US firms can offer, the US has sought NATO-wide agreement on the gradual elimination of offsets and a more open market for weapons. However, the existence of an implicit US offset requirement that all major weapons systems purchased by the US should have a North American source, and the existence of various other measures (such as the Buy American Act), suggest that the US is not the bastion of free trade in defence equipment that it would have its allies believe! Hence, offsets are likely to persist as a feature of defence purchases for many years to come.

Endnotes

1. Hartley K. and Martin S., International Collaboration in Aerospace, **Science and Public Policy**, 1990, vol. 17, no. 3, pp. 143–151.

2. Hartley K. and Martin S., Evaluating Collaborative Programmes, **Defence Economics**, 1993, vol. 4, no. 2, pp. 195–211.

3. Hartley K., **NATO Arms Co-Operation**, London, George Allen & Unwin, 1983.

4. Wood D., Australian Defence Offsets Program, **Proceedings of Defence Offsets Seminar**, Canberra: Department of Defence, 1992.

5. DoD, **Australian Industry Involvement (AII): Draft Guidelines**, Canberra: Department of Defence, September 1993, p. 2.

Chapter 2

Countertrade and Offsets
An Overview of the Theory and Evidence

Stephen Martin
Centre for Defence Economics
University of York, UK

2.1   Introduction

Offsets — where the vendor agrees to undertake some reciprocal transaction over and above that associated with a purely cash transaction — are not confined to military sales. However, where the purchase of *civil* goods gives rise to this reciprocity, this phenomenon is typically known as countertrade. Moreover, just as there are various forms of offset associated with defence purchases, there are various types of countertrade connected with the procurement of civil goods and services. Although the focus of this book is on offsets, the reader should be aware of the parallel and at times overlapping literature on countertrade not least because research in one area can inform developments in the other.

The purpose of this chapter is to outline the various forms of countertrade, evaluate the economic theories that have been proposed to account for this phenomenon, and to review the literature dealing with empirical work. With this background, the reader should be able to place the subsequent discussion on defence offsets within the wider context of reciprocal sales agreements as a whole. To put these issues into context further, the chapter concludes with a parallel overview of offsets.

2.2   Countertrade — Definitions

Although countertrade is a global phenomenon, different countries use different terms to describe the same practices and, as a result, no internationally consistent use of terms has emerged. Understandably, the literature on countertrade is also troubled by this lack of a consistent lexicon and thus any discussion of the topic has to be preceded by a definition of terms.

Pure **barter** involves the simultaneous exchange of one product for another.[1] Most barter is accomplished via government-to-government transactions through a series of barter exchanges that are consolidated into a **clearing arrangement.**[2] Both parties agree to purchase a specified (usually equal) value of goods and services from each other over a given period. Each country establishes an account that is debited when ever one country imports from another. At the end of the specified period, imbalances are cleared through the transfer of goods or hard currency payments. The introduction of the clearing arrangement facilitates the non-instantaneous settlement of barter transactions. If the debtor country has a shortage of hard currency and the creditor does not want repaying in goods, the creditor can sell, at a discount, its 'credits' to a **switch trader** who will use these credits to purchase goods from the debtor nation. These will then be sold in world markets.[3]

With the possible exception of the final settlement, none of the barter transactions mentioned above involve the use of any currency. Under a **counterpurchase** deal, the (usually western) exporter will agree to take goods and services, from a shopping list and at prices established by the importer, to the value of the initial export. In this countertrade transaction, however, hard currency is involved in the form of two parallel contracts: one for the sale of the initial export, and one for the purchase of goods and services from the importer's shopping list. Similar to counterpurchase transactions are **buy-back** deals. Once again, the exporter agrees to purchase goods from the importer. However, in this case the exporter transfers technology (usually embodied in plant and equipment) and agrees to purchase a proportion of the plant's output over a specified period. As with counterpurchase deals, there are usually two parallel hard currency transactions. First, the importer borrows the hard currency and uses this to pay the exporter for the plant. The importer of the plant then uses the proceeds of the sale of the output (obtained in whole or in part from the vendor of the equipment) to repay the hard currency which was borrowed to purchase the equipment.

Having defined terms, many authors go on to discuss the quantitative importance of countertrade in total world trade. Unfortunately, trade statistics do not differentiate between direct sale and transfer of goods under any form of reciprocity. In addition, no national government requires firms to report data on these types of transactions. Thus only approximate estimates of this form of trade are possible.[4] Moreover, this is one area where countertrade and offsets are often lumped together.

The growth in countertrade and offsets can be illustrated by noting the number of countries that typically demand such reciprocal trading arrangements. In 1972, 15 primarily centrally planned economies (CPEs) mandated countertrade, with 27 in 1979 (with the addition of some Central and South American states), and 67 in 1983 (although the latter figure rises to 88 if countries that request offsets are included.[5] By 1992, a total of 130 countries had some form of countertrade/offset policy.[6]

The OECD estimated that in 1983 countertrade accounted for a maximum of around $80 billion, or some 5 per cent of world exports.[7] This is one of the most frequently cited figures in the literature although other, much larger, estimates exist. Bilateral clearing arrangements are excluded from this estimate. The OECD values this annual trade at $130 billion and thus if this is added to the earlier figure of $80 billion, then countertrade accounts for just over 13 per cent of world trade. Many other estimates of the importance of countertrade in world trade in the mid-1980s exist. Korth argues that GATT estimates of 8 per cent of world trade for countertrade are conservative, suggesting a level ranging from 5 per cent to 20 per cent, possibly higher.[8] The UK's Department of Trade and Industry reports that estimates vary, with a general belief that the actual proportion lies between 10 and 15 per cent of world trade[9] and UNCTAD estimates that countertrade accounts for at least 15 per cent of world trade.[10] For an even larger figure, Hammond cites James P. Moore Jr, Deputy Assistant Secretary for Trade Information and Analysis, who, in testimony before the US House Subcommittee on Economic Stabilisation, alleged that 'a significant number of government and non-government experts and observers estimate that countertrade accounted for between 20 and 30 per cent of the roughly $2 trillion of total world trade in 1983'.[11] Basically, precise figures are not available.

2.3 Countertrade — Economic Motives

Identifying and evaluating the reasons for countertrade fill more than a few pages in the literature. Before plunging into such an exercise, the reader might find the following, highly stylised, overview useful. Since the 1960s, the CPEs of Eastern Europe had frequently demanded countertrade when dealing with Western companies.[12] Towards the end of the 1970s, a few newly industrialised countries (NICs) and less developed countries (LDCs) began to make similar demands and, by the mid-1980s, this trickle had become a torrent with some form of countertrade almost *de rigeur* for the completion of any Western export sale in the East or South.

As countertrade grew, so too did the literature on the subject; most of this can be divided into one of two categories. First, and for those practitioners actually involved with countertrade, there were the guides to the successful negotiation and undertaking of countertrade deals. These publications often outlined various countries countertrade requirements.[13] Second, and for a rather different audience (the academic community), there were countless papers, particularly in the early 1980s, drawing the reader's attention to this relatively new form of trade. These papers would usually discuss possible reasons for this growth and whether and to what extent government-mandated countertrade was the appropriate policy response to the supposed conditions that had given birth to this phenomenon.

Within the academic literature, several distinct themes can be identified. First, there is the very hostile view which tends to emanate from multi-national organisations such as GATT, the IMF and the OECD, which views countertrade as a threat to those (typically western exporters) who have such requirements foisted upon them. In addition, this activity is also portrayed as being harmful at the global level.[14] The argument is that, because of its bilateral nature, countertrade has the effect of reducing trade to the level of the country with the lowest export capability. Moreover, such bilateralism runs counter to the spirit of an open and multi-lateral system of international trade as embodied in the GATT.[15] In addition, the need to balance trade at the microeconomic level (that is for each deal or firm) will have a more pronounced limiting effect than an equilibrium set at the macro-economic level.[16]

Second, and often espoused by the same authors, there is the view that those governments that mandate countertrade are ill-informed/irrational because there is little that countertrade can achieve and that, as a result, those who pursue such policies are misguided.[17] A variant of this argument is that although these transactions might appear advantageous in the short-term they are likely to perpetuate the existing distortions that have given rise to the need for countertrade in the first place. There is also the argument that countries resort to countertrade as a way of avoiding (more politically harmful) structural adjustments, which are typically stipulated by the IMF as a condition for further lending.[18]

Third, there is a growing group of commentators that cautions against immediate opposition to all countertrade transactions. Typically, these authors suggest that the costs and benefits of each transaction need to be evaluated and that there can be no necessary presumption that all countertrade is inefficient.[19]

Finally, there are those who see the various forms of countertrade as a rational response to the costliness of effecting some types of transaction along the more conventional cash-for-goods lines,[20] while Caves and Marin develop a model of barter/counterpurchase that offers benefits to both parties in a rational-actor model.[21] According to proponents of these views, countertrade is the optimal way to structure transactions in certain circumstances and is to be preferred to the more conventional cash-for-goods approach. It is also worth noting that in some parts of the literature the reasons for these reciprocal arrangements are discussed as if the various types of countertrade form a homogeneous whole. However, this level of generalisation looks particularly costly as other work suggests that the different forms of countertrade grow out of different trading conditions.[22]

Before moving on, let us remind ourselves that the major issue when examining the reasons for countertrade is to explain why a, say, CPE importer would make its purchase of goods from, say, a western exporter, conditional upon a reciprocal purchase by the initial exporter of CPE goods, rather than sell the goods direct on world markets. Various hypotheses have been advanced and these are now examined.

2.3.1 Easing foreign exchange shortages (all forms of countertrade)

One of the reasons often advanced for government-mandated countertrade is that it protects the often small foreign exchange reserves held by various East European states, NICs and LDCs. Indeed, many accounts of official countertrade requirements cite this motive as one of the reasons for the existence of such a policy.[23] However, critics argue that 'it is ... unlikely that countries resort to countertrade because of shortages of foreign currencies and, if they do, they are likely to be disappointed'.[24] To illustrate their argument, Mirus and Yeung structure their discussion around two widely accepted ways of defining the current account:

1. current account = exports-imports + net services
2. current account = saving by the private sector + saving by the public sector-investment

The authors argue that, in this context, expression (1) is not particularly useful as all it reveals is that a countertrade transaction, with exports by definition equal to imports, has no impact on the current account. This is clearly true. However, Mirus and Yeung do not explicitly outline what would have happened in the absence of the countertrade transaction although, implicitly, the assumption is that no trade takes place. In both cases, the current account is identical, although with countertrade imports are higher than they would otherwise have been. If another alternative scenario is adopted, that in both cases imports are at their higher level, then with countertrade the current account is improved by the volume of exports that the policy brings about. It is, presumably, for this reason that many countries expect and believe that mandated countertrade conserves foreign exchange (i.e. that the policy generates additional exports). Of course, if the initial exporter can dispose of these goods then it is not clear why the producer cannot do so directly, rather than via a countertrade requirement. Instead, Mirus and Yeung focus on expression (2) and consider how countertrade (in the forms of counterpurchase, buy-back and barter) might affect those factors, such as the level of income, the rate of interest, the cost of capital, and the rate of profit, which determine the national level of savings and investment, and, ultimately, the current account. The authors conclude that countertrade is likely to have little net impact on the balance of trade.

Rather curiously, in another paper the same authors argue '... that foreign exchange shortage or rationing and other forms of capital control can explain some countertrade ...'.[25] Their argument is that, where foreign exchange is rationed in the importer's country, a Western exporter might accept payment in terms of a commodity in order to move the deal forward in time and to reduce the uncertainty of whether the necessary exchange will be available to facilitate the transaction.

More interestingly, Mirus and Yeung also consider the situation of a country which has a high external debt and a shortage of foreign exchange, which is being denied further hard currency loans. In these circumstances, and with export earnings earmarked for debt service, it might be possible to increase imports if countertrade exports are able to escape the attention of international creditors seeking repayment. As the authors acknowledge, this scenario depends on the asymmetrical treatment of countertrade exports (compared with other exports), and requires that either countertrade escapes the creditors' audit or that creditors are naïve. Mirus and Yeung believe that these conditions are '... not applicable to too many situations'[26] but other commentators find evidence to support this hypothesis.[27]

Banks notes that there are two rationales for countertrade where there is an over-valued currency and foreign exchange controls.[28] First, local firms can continue trading when they exhausted their allocation of foreign exchange. Second, the terms of exchange can be adjusted to a more mutually agreeable rate for the particular transaction. This is equivalent to a selective devaluation or the establishment of multiple exchange rates.[29]

2.3.2 Dumping, price cutting and price discrimination (barter/ counterpurchase)

One clear attraction of countertrade is its reduced transparency relative to cash-based transactions. If, for example, international agreements attempt to fix prices above their world market-clearing levels, producers will have an incentive to dispose of their surplus production by under-cutting the agreed price. Barter offers the opportunity to dispose of export surpluses, typically of primary commodities, without having to state explicitly the price of the good and thus risk the charge of threatening the cartel's existence. Similarly, many industrial countries subsidize their agricultural sectors, with support prices above market-clearing levels. To avoid having to acquire and store the surplus production, governments can dispose and have disposed of this stock on world markets at subsidised prices. Again, barter can obscure the price at which this stock is being sold, thus reducing the possibility of a complaint to GATT.[30] It has also been argued that barter can assist market segmentation, directing lower-priced sales to more price-elastic or low-income markets but it is not clear why this capability is specific to barter.[31] Indeed, Caves and Marin discuss the role that both barter *and* counterpurchase can play in facilitating price discrimination and their findings provide some support for this hypothesis.[32] (This study is discussed in more detail below.)

2.3.3 Economising on search/transaction costs in the international marketing of products (barter/counterpurchase)

Many commentators have suggested that counterpurchase enables participants to:

a. sell goods, which, because of their poor quality would not normally be sold in export markets; and
b. to increase exports of other goods through access to new markets.

Banks for example, argues that unless the Western firm is very large and diversified, it will usually sell counterpurchase goods at a discount to a specialist trading company rather than use the goods itself.[33] This raises the issue of why the producer does not purchase the marketing expertise of the specialist trading agencies direct rather than via the Western firm.

Mirus and Yeung argue that a barter transaction might facilitate the disposal of a *temporary* excess supply of a good with lower search and transactions costs than if the sale went directly through the market.[34] Typically, additional exports would incur extra search and transaction costs for the manufacturer. The argument is that, by using the Western firm's superior marketing knowledge for this one-off transaction, the manufacturer can dispose of the countertraded goods more efficiently than if it attempted to do this itself or via a marketing agent.

Various authors have argued that counterpurchase can be used as a device to reduce the risks and costs of arranging the international marketing of products.[35] Hennart's argument is particularly interesting, suggesting as it does that independent distributors might be reluctant to make the transaction-specific investments necessary for the successful distribution of products in foreign countries, because distributors fear being "held up" by manufacturers once the investments are made. One solution to this problem, that of vertical integration of manufacturing and trading, is not available in countries that limit incoming FDI. By restricting imports to those from suppliers who take back and market their products, counterpurchase requirements can encourage suppliers to make manufacturer-specific marketing investments that would not otherwise be undertaken.

2.3.4 Signalling product quality (buy-back)

Murrell argues that buy-back can reduce problems that arise when the quality of, say, East European products is unknown or the country has a poor reputation with regard to quality.[36] If the country wants to sell higher quality goods in the West, it must signal that these products are of a better quality than it normally produces. Murrell suggests that the use of the Western firm's capital equipment, and the distribution of the resulting product by the Western firm, both signal that the quality of these products is better than normal. This arrangement increases the price at which the output can be sold in the West, and thus the value of the western firm's capital equipment.

2.3.5 Information asymmetries in technology markets (buy-back)

One of the major forms of countertrade is buy-back where an exporter (often a Western firm) will supply and construct an entire plant and, in addition, provide start-up training and supervision of maintenance and production. The exporter will also agree to buy a proportion of the output of the new plant over a period of years, often to the same value as the value of the initial export of capital. The question arises, of course, as to why either party should wish to link the purchase of the resulting output to the original sale of the capital equipment.

Very simply, the argument is that as the importer of capital does not know the value of the equipment *ex ante*, there is the potential for the exporting Western firm to sell outdated technology. By requiring the firm to purchase the resulting output, the seller who supplies old technology will be faced with the disposal of inferior outputs. Thus there is an incentive for the capital exporter to supply a technology which produces output that can be readily sold in world markets.[37] Although this encourages the supply of the appropriate technology, there is still the problem that the supplier might attempt to overcharge the purchaser although the existence of rival suppliers would, of course, ameliorate this hazard.

Mirus and Yeung examine this issue in some detail.[38] They assume that the capital/technology package produces a good with a distinct quality dimension which is determined by the quality of the technology package. The price of the package depends on its quality which is unobservable *ex ante* to the recipient but is, of course, known to the supplier. The information asymmetry encourages the technology supplier to overstate the quality of the capital that is being supplied. One possible solution, that of internalising the transaction by encouraging the supplier to establish their own factory, is ruled out as the recipient wants ownership of the output (i.e. FDI is prohibited). Consequently, no simple market exchange might occur as there is no way of verifying the price and quality of the capital/technology package.

If the recipient's concern was only for the project's profits then a profit-sharing contract would solve the problem. If the quality (price) of the capital is too low (high), then profits (having deducted the cost of capital), and hence the supplier's revenue, will be adversely affected. Thus there is less incentive for the supplier to overcharge for the capital it is supplying. However, the local agent might want a particular quality of technology and, the assumption is that the latest technology is sought. Mirus and Yeung argue that if quantity and quality are substitutes from the supplier's point of view, then by offering the supplier a fixed quantity of output for a specified number of years, the recipient has a means to influence the supplier's provision of quality.

Buy-back is also an incentive contract where a firm provides a production facility in return for some of the output for further use in its own production. The assumption is that the output is production process-specific, so that other firms could not easily use this intermediate good in their own production processes. It is also assumed that the initial exporter would find it difficult to secure a replacement for the input. Mirus and Yeung quote the example of the construction by Volkswagen of an engine production plant in what was the GDR.

Again, FDI is assumed to be prohibited, and the putty-clay nature of the project gives rise to a time inconsistency problem. As the sole purchaser of the output, the technology supplier has the incentive to depress monopsonistically the price of the output. Similarly, the purchaser of the technology might attempt to inflate monopolistically the price of the plant's output. In the extreme case, it is possible that no plant might be built. A contract specified in terms of prices would still suffer from a problem of double information asymmetry. First, the value of the output is much better known to the technology supplier than it is to the technology recipient and thus the former has an incentive to understate the value of the output. The supplier can also inflate the value of management and production services. At the same time, the lack of a competitive factor market in the CPE puts the technology supplier at an information disadvantage with respect to the productivity of local participation and might fear that the local partner will inflate their factor costs.

A contract specified in physical quantities overcomes the problem of quantity-quality substitution mentioned above and thus satisfies the recipient's desire for state-of-the-art technology. However, even where quality is not an issue, a quantity contract will conceivably induce the supplier to reveal his valuation of the product by furnishing technology to the extent that the marginal revenue from extra technology is equated to its marginal cost. Similarly the recipient has no incentive to waste labour resources. In this way, 'the counter-trade contract … overcomes difficulties that … prevent a market solution'.[39]

Chan and Hoy find an explanation for buy-back in a similar environment.[40] In their model, the host country prohibits foreign direct investment (FDI) and the multinational corporation (MNC) possesses a knowledge-based production process that requires skilled labour or information which the host country does not possess. The host cannot write legally enforceable contracts for the acquisition of a specified quality level of the MNC's production process. A joint venture would be one way to proceed, but either party might shirk if it is not the full residual claimant to the profits generated by the production facility. The authors show that a sharing rule for output or revenues as well as an enforceable set of minimum standards requirements on some inputs ameliorate the tendency to shirk. Hence buy-back and minimum standards for inputs yield a second-best outcome where the first-best (FDI) is prohibited by fiat.

Finally, Marin and Schnitzer have recently suggested that counterpurchase, in addition to buy-back, can be used to overcome information asymmetries associated with the export of technology.[41] In their model, the firm in the developed country (DC) is seeking to export capital goods to a CPE/LDC. As usual, the firm might be tempted to undersupply quality and blame adverse circumstances in the LDC/CPE. The LDC/CPE lacks creditworthiness because of a large outstanding debt and thus its purchase cannot be financed by a loan from an international bank. Hence the vendor is unsure as to whether it will actually be paid. Marin and Schnitzer suggest that the existence of a second deal which is tied to the first, deters cheating on quality and defaulting on the payment for the initial export as either action would jeopardise the second transaction. However, this argument would seem to depend on the assumption that the second deal is profitable to both parties, which might not always be the case.

2.3.6 The absence of long-term futures/forward markets and the reduction of uncertainty concerning the level of exports (all forms of countertrade)

Banks argues that one of the handicaps faced by the CPEs is the absence of any self-equilibrating mechanism to ensure that the values of exports, imports and capital flows balance. One attraction of countertrade is that it is a balancing device.[42] To fulfil production objectives, certain items must be imported from, say, the West. Unfortunately, the demand for exports cannot be easily planned but should exports fail and further credit not be forthcoming, imports must be reduced with severe consequences for domestic production. Countertrade, by reducing the uncertainty associated with the trade balance, reduces the potential for the disruption of the CPEs. Hennart discusses this motivation in terms of risk shifting.[43] He argues that countertrade substitutes for missing forward markets by ensuring that any outlay of foreign exchange will be balanced by future inflows.

Along similar lines, Amann and Marin view counterpurchase '... as a second-best outcome in the absence of complete risk and futures markets'.[44] The authors construct a model in which a firm in a western industrialised country wants to export to a CPE or a LDC. The potential exporter faces an entry barrier in this market and, consequently, is willing to reward the CPE for its assistance to overcome this barrier. Facing a tight foreign exchange budget constraint, the CPE/LDC is very risk averse when choosing which goods to produce for future exports. Ideally, futures markets, by guaranteeing the price at which the CPE can sell its product, would enable the CPE/LDC to eliminate all risk associated with the CPE's future foreign exchange earnings, thus making the present foreign exchange constraint look less binding. However, such markets do not exist and so the DC's market entry depends on its willingness to provide such a private futures market in the form of a commitment to purchase at a future date the products produced by the CPE. The DC is willing to do this to gain market entry and because it is (assumed to be) less risk averse than the CPE (the latter point reflecting the fact that a firm in market economy can more easily spread risk than a CPE which has far fewer risk absorbing institutions).

Mirus and Yeung argue that buy-back might occur where a firm, with a specific advantage in mining and processing, wants guaranteed access to a raw material, yet there is no forward market and backward integration via FDI is impossible or prohibitively expensive.[45] For the owner of the resources that prohibits FDI, countertrade might be preferred to market sales where there are costs of market penetration and uncertainty concerning future sales. Basically, the buy-back contract establishes a forward market where none previously existed.

This review by no means exhausts the reasons why governments might impose a mandatory countertrade policy. For example, some of the other motives might be political. Yoffie argues that countertrade requirements can be used to disguise a government- sponsored austerity program.[46] A severe countertrade requirement leads to a decline in imports which the Third World government can blame on foreign corporations for failing to export (although Yoffie's argument seems to ignore the fact that the IMF is usually behind such austerity programs). Nevertheless, the most frequently quoted hypotheses for countertrade have been discussed. Some of these represent a first-best response to excessive transaction costs which might otherwise preclude the possibility of trade (e.g. by using counterpurchase where manufacturer-specific marketing investments are necessary). Others are clearly second-best responses where the first-best alternative is prohibited by government policy (e.g. where FDI is ruled out as a solution to information asymmetries associated with international technology transfers).

This is not to suggest that all countertrade can be justified as the optimal response to a particular set of trading conditions. Rather, that there might be circumstances where various forms of mandated reciprocity are superior to the more conventional cash-for-goods transaction and that, as a result, an unqualified hostility to countertrade is wholly inappropriate.

2.4   Countertrade — Empirical Overview

Despite the plethora of academic papers that appeared in the early 1980s, describing the various forms and growth of countertrade, it was not until the end of the decade that any substantive empirical work began to appear. This was not particularly surprising given the lack of readily available statistics and the fact that, as a result, any empirical work would be particularly labour intensive. Jones and Jagoe compiled a database of 1,350 reported countertrade deals signed between 1980–87 where at least one of the partners was a Third World country.[47] The authors used their data to provide an overview of countertrade trends. Their report runs to over 130 pages and the following paragraphs can only provide the briefest glimpse of the wealth of information that they presented.

Jones and Jagoe reported a rapid increase in the annual number of deals signed to 1985, with a slight decline in the following two years. This was mirrored by an increase in the number of developing counties actually involved in doing deals at any particular time. OECD countries provided the partner in 45 per cent of all deals while the Eastern bloc was a partner in 21 per cent, and other developing countries were involved in the remaining 34 per cent of deals. Their database also recorded the goods traded and the authors expected to find the developing countries exporting raw materials, foodstuffs and energy products (basic commodities) while importing capital equipment and manufactures. This pattern was largely confirmed by the data but an interesting trend emerged in the pattern of exports. Whereas foodstuffs accounted for 60 per cent of product observations in the 1980–1983 period, this had declined to 37 per cent in the 1984–87 period, and the importance of the manufactures had similarly increased. The authors interpreted this an indicating that developing countries had some success persuading countertrade partners to accept more manufactured goods, although it could also be interpreted as indicating that developing countries were simply manufacturing more, or manufacturing goods that they did not previously make. With regard to imports, agricultural commodities were again the most important category, with 25 per cent of product observations, although manufactures come a close second with 24 per cent. Also noted was the rapid increase in the import of construction projects. In the first half of the study period, six instances of this type of import were recorded, whereas in the second half this figure soared to 101 cases.

Jones and Jagoe also examined the types of goods traded with each type of partner. In North/South trade, 71 per cent of developing country exports were basic commodities while 72 per cent of their imports from OECD countries were of capital equipment, manufactures and construction projects. Foodstuffs and raw materials accounted for 66 per cent of developing country exports to the Eastern bloc while in return developing countries received capital equipment, manufactures and construction projects, and these accounted for 76 per cent of imports. Agricultural products were the single most important group of commodities in South/South trade, accounting for 37 per cent of observations. Where available, the database also recorded the value of the transaction. Just over one-half of the 1,350 deals had a value attached to them, with the average being $143 million. The authors consider this a surprisingly high figure and note that if 56 'mega-deals' (worth over $500 million each) are omitted, then the average falls to $57 million.

Although the Jones and Jagoe report provides a wealth of information about countertrade involving developing countries, it is unfortunate that they were only able to classify 21 per cent of the deals in their database according to the form of countertrade. Almost 79 per cent of transactions were allocated to a residual category which included barter, counterpurchase, and other unspecified transactions. In addition, little attempt was made to use the data to test hypotheses about the causes of countertrade. Nevertheless, the authors expressed scepticism about the idea that the export of basic commodities (such as coffee, cocoa and rubber) with a countertrade requirement confers any real advantage. The report argued that the underlying causes of countertrade in the 1980s (such as lack of foreign exchange, limited access to conventional trade finance facilities, depressed commodity prices and deepening debt) are likely to remain and thus that countertrade is likely to persist. However, the authors conclude by noting that little is known about the costs and benefits of countertrade policies and that, as a result, there is an urgent need to evaluate such policies.

It can be argued, quite reasonably, that Jones and Jagoe's work does not provide a global overview of countertrade as the focus is on deals involving Third World countries. Hveem's work makes good this deficiency by studying 1,071 countertrade contracts signed over the (somewhat shorter) period, 1985–88.[48] Like Jones and Jagoe, Hveem's database consists of countertrade agreements drawn largely from the countertrade press. Fortunately, the two studies are broadly consistent with regard to their coverage and definition of countertrade terms, although, for example, Jones and Jagoe include bilateral clearing arrangements which Hveem excludes. Unfortunately, the two studies adopt different categorisations of the variables used to analyse the data (e.g. geographical groupings) and this makes it difficult to compare their results directly.

Hveem's data confirm the idea that countertrade is no longer an East-West phenomenon with this particular geographical configuration accounting for only 22 per cent of all deals. South-West trade is involved with 32 per cent of all transactions while East-South contracts provided 15% of all deals. Interestingly, the second largest geographical trade pattern was intra-South trade with 24% of deals.

Also of interest is the distribution of deals according to the particular form of countertrade. Counterpurchase accounted for 54 per cent of all transactions with buy-backs at 23 per cent and barter deals at 9 per cent.[49] The types of goods traded primarily consisted of industrial equipment (the most frequent), manufactures, basic commodities, infrastructure, and energy products. When the value (rather than the number) of the products was taken into account, however, the picture changed dramatically with energy and military equipment the top two products. The issue of whether countertrade 'works' is complex and not really addressed. Nevertheless, the Hveem paper is a substantial one and, as with the Jones and Jagoe paper, only a flavour of its contents has been presented here. The reader seeking more detail should consult the original work.

In a rather different vein, Lecraw uses data on 211 countertrade deals undertaken by 152 firms in the US, Canada, and Japan to test various hypotheses about the factors that contribute to the success of a countertrade transactions *from the perspective of the Western exporter*.[50] For each deal, the Western firm was asked to indicate on a scale of 1 (low) to 10 (high), the success of the countertrade arrangement and the strength of various characteristics of the exported product, the exporter, the importer, and the importing country. These characteristics included such factors as: export product quality, the number of direct competitors, the stage in product life-cycle, the product's price relative to the competitor's price, non-tariff barriers to export and so on. These factors were then used as independent variables to explain the respondents' evaluation of the success of the transaction.

Lecraw's model was able to explain just over one-half of the variance in the dependent variable and suggests that:

'Countertrade can be beneficial for large firms with extensive trade operations for large, complex products, firms that are vertically integrated or can accommodate countertrade take-backs, and for firms that trade with countries with inappropriate exchange rates, rationed foreign exchange and import restrictions whose importers are relatively inexperienced in assessing technology or in export marketing'.[51]

Although providing useful information on those factors that contribute to a successful countertrade deal, Lecraw's contribution would be considerably enhanced if he had been able to perform a similar analysis *from the perspective of the importer*. After all, the issue is less why Western exporters (albeit often reluctantly) agree to countertrade, but rather why importers mandate some form of reciprocity rather than selling their goods for cash.

The third study of publicly reported countertrade deals was by Hennart who analysed 1,277 countertrade transactions detailed in the weekly newsletter *'Countertrade Outlook'* over the period June 1983 to December 1986.[52] Although much of his material came from the same source as that used by Hveem,[53] and their study periods had a two-year overlap, Hennart's paper provides an interesting contribution to as it attempts to use the available data to test the various hypotheses concerning reasons for the use of countertrade. Interestingly, Hennart found evidence to support the hypothesis that different forms of countertrade have different motives.

Hennart's database consisted of 694 clearing arrangements, 171 barter deals, 298 counterpurchase transactions, 71 buy-backs, and 43 offsets. Countries were allocated to one of five groups (developed nations, OPEC members, CPEs, middle-income counties and low-income countries). Hennart found that OPEC and developing countries imposed more counterpurchases, CPEs more buy-backs, and developed and middle-income developing countries (MIDCs) more offsets, than would be anticipated if there was no relationship between country group and form of countertrade.

Hennart also found that the most common form of barter involved two MIDCs and noted that this was consistent with the view that barter is used to avoid the repayment of external debt. Barter was prevalent between developed countries and MIDCs, and between MIDCs and CPEs. The author interpreted the absence of barter between OPEC members and between developed countries as evidence that this form of countertrade was used to bypass international cartels and commodity agreements.

Hennart found that counterpurchase was largely imposed by OPEC, MIDCs and CPEs on developed countries, while buy-backs were largely an East-West phenomenon. Offsets involved developed countries selling to developed countries, OPEC members and MIDCs. More generally, the data supported the established idea that countertrade was rife in North-South and East-West trade but, given the widespread involvement of MIDCs, it also suggested that South-South trade was important.

Hennart's study also identified the broad type of good involved in the countertrade transaction. For CPEs, the proportion of barter, counterpurchase, and buy-back sales that were manufactures was higher than the proportion manufactures in their overall trade. However, the evidence did not support Murrell's hypothesis that buy-back deals would be more likely to involve manufactures than barter and counterpurchase (because product quality is more variable in manufactures than in food, raw materials, and fuels).

For OPEC members, 76 per cent of barter deals involved fuels while 11 per cent involved manufactures. For counterpurchase transactions, however, the proportions are reversed with 51 per cent involving manufactures and 10 per cent with fuels. Hennart argues that this confirms the different motivations behind these two forms of countertrade: that barter is used to undercut cartel prices while counterpurchase is used to penetrate new export markets.

For all developing countries, barters are heavily concentrated in raw materials (the very products typically supported by cartels), while counterpurchases are largely manufactures (which is consistent with the view that counterpurchase is a marketing tool for differentiated products). Hennart also grouped all countries according to whether their credit rating was above or below the median value and found that those in the below-median group accounted for 9 per cent of world trade, 16 per cent of buy-back deals, 25 per cent of counterpurchase transactions and 38 per cent of barter deals. This implies a strong inverse relationship between credit-worthiness and the propensity to barter, supporting the hypothesis that barter is used to secure imports rather than repay debt. Hennart also found that 80 per cent of all buy-backs were imposed by countries with very high or high barriers on incoming FDI and that this percentage is statistically significantly different from the percentage of world trade captured by these countries (15 per cent). Similarly, support for the idea that counterpurchases are substitutes for vertical integration between manufacturing and distribution was forthcoming: 65 per cent of all counterpurchase contracts were imposed by countries with very high or high barriers to incoming FDI, a percentage significantly greater than their share of world trade.

Finally, consider the study by Caves and Marin.[54] These authors develop a model of a barter/counterpurchase transaction where an exporter is seeking to sell a differentiated product to a state-ministry which, in turn, is seeking to export a product which is not normally exported. The quality of the latter good can be verified at a price, and a competitive industry of trading houses exists which will verify quality of goods and locate buyers for non-standard products. The state-ministry cannot resell the exporter's goods. This has the effect of making price discrimination feasible and '... stands in for the subtle ways in which countertrade facilitates discrimination ... [such as] the effective price paid for the export good is obscure to third parties'.[55]

Given this model, the authors derive a series of testable hypotheses which are evaluated using a database of 230 completed countertrade agreements from Viennese firms active in countertrade. Two-third of all agreements occurred in 1986 and 1987. Over 86 per cent of the countertrade partners were CPEs and, in

94 per cent of cases the exporter was a Western industrialised nation. Just under 77 per cent of the transactions were counterpurchase deals, 12 per cent were buy-backs, and 11 per cent were barter.

On the basis of their model and empirical evidence, Caves and Marin conclude that some countertrade is a result of price discrimination by the exporter although this '... model is enveloped by a more general model of countertrade as a device to bargain with an exporter who asks a price higher than its marginal cost'.[56] However, the authors do note that 'countertrade can offer some partners least-cost access to Western markets, as when the Western exporter can use the partner's goods directly' and caution that the model's explanatory power is not large, '... leaving ample room for the hypotheses that countertrade develops from non-convertible currencies or provides partners only the illusion of benefit'.[57]

2.5   Offsets — Definitions

Much of the discussion about the motives for countertrade assumes that at least one of the participants is a CPE/NIC/LDC and that any Western involvement will be as a potential exporter. When studying offsets, the military counterpart of countertrade, this characterisation is no longer valid. Indeed, whereas CPEs led the demand for countertrade, it was the industrialised nations of western Europe that initiated offsets when buying (US) defence equipment.

First, though, some definitions. Just as there are various forms of countertrade and no universally accepted definitions, so different categories of offset are distinguished, and different authors use the same term in different ways. The US Office of Management and Budget (OMB) has conducted more work on offsets than most other organisations and, for this reason, their terminology and definitions are given below.[58]

Offsets — A range of industrial and commercial compensation practices required as a condition of the purchase of defense articles and/or defence services. The various types of offset are defined as follows:

a. **Co-production** — Overseas production based upon government-to-government agreement that permits a foreign government or producer to acquire the technical information to manufacture all or part of a U.S. origin defence article.
b. **Licensed Production** — Overseas production of a U.S. origin defence article based upon transfer of technical information under direct commercial arrangements between a U.S. firm and a foreign government or producer.
c. **Sub-contractor Production** — Overseas production of a part or component of a U.S. origin defence article. The subcontract does not necessarily

involve licence or technical information and is usually a direct commercial arrangement between the U.S. firm and a foreign producer.

d. **Overseas Investment** — Investment arising from the offset agreement, taking the form of capital invested to establish or expand a subsidiary or joint venture in the foreign country.

e. **Technology Transfer** — Transfer of technology that occurs as a result of an offset agreement and that may take the form of: research and development conducted abroad; technical assistance provided to subsidiary or joint venture of overseas investment; or other activities under direct commercial arrangement between a U.S. firm and a foreign entity.

f. **Countertrade**

   i.   **Barter** — A one-time transfer only, bound under a single contract that specifies the exchange of selected goods or services for another of equivalent value.

   ii. **Counterpurchase** — An agreement by the initial exporter to buy (or to find a buyer for) a specified value of goods (often stated as a percentage of the value of the original export) from the original importer during a specified time period.

   iii. **Buy-back** — An agreement by the original exporter to accept as full or partial repayment products derived from the original exported product (e.g. a turnkey facility; machinery).

Several points are worthy of note about these definitions. First, the distinction between co-production and licensed production turns on whether the agreement is government-to-government or U.S. firm-to-government and *not* on the division of production between the US firm and the foreign buyer (compare this with the more conventional definitions given in chapter 1). Second, co-production and licensed production are included under the offset umbrella, although the Aerospace Industries Association of America (AIAA) argues that these forms of work-sharing are irrelevant to any discussion of offsets.[59] The AAIA's argument is that these transactions are no more offset-related than, say, the establishment of a U.S.-licensed electronics operation in Hong Kong. Third, that the standard forms of civil reciprocity are included under the usual countertrade heading, and that the conventional three-way distinction (between barter, counterpurchase and buy-back) is made. Reciprocal purchases of foreign-made civil goods would, of course, be included under the counterpurchase category. Finally, this categorisation does not readily lend itself to the differentiation of direct and indirect offsets, which characterises much of the literature. For example, sub-contractor production would be split between direct and indirect offset e.g. the production of components for the equipment actually being imported would be direct offset whereas production for equipment for export to third parties would be indirect offset.

Data on the quantitative importance of offsets is scarce. As is the case for countertrade, no multi-national agency is responsible for the collection of these data, and only the U.S. government has sought information about offsets from industry. However, as the U.S. has been the largest western exporter of arms, accounting for two-thirds of all non-CPE arms exports over the period 1987–91[60] an analysis of this data set is likely to prove invaluable. Unfortunately though, the data only go back to 1980.

Before examining this data set, and to provide some insight into post-World War II procurement trends, this author put together a database on purchases of defence equipment by the EU12 over the forty-year period 1950–1990, which involved some form of offset. Here, three types of offset were distinguished: co-production, licensed production and indirect/direct offset (for definitions see chapter 1). This exercise drew on three data sources. Since 1973, SIPRI have published an annual register of the licensed production of foreign designed major weapons. Although this includes a number of sales dating from the previous decade, coverage of the immediate post-1945 period has been improved by drawing on the list of major system programmes collated by researchers working at the RAND Corporation.[61] This covers the licensed production of all major US defence equipment since 1945. The third source is Todd and Humble who provide information on the licensed production of aero-engines, a topic which both of the other sources neglect.[62] The only area where the database might be deficient concerns work-sharing agreements involving the production of European-designed equipment in the 1950s. However, such contracts are unlikely to have been that important quantitatively and thus their omission will not significantly distort the analysis (not least because in the 1950s there were substantial direct transfers of US-produced military equipment to bolster western defences against the Soviet threat). Nevertheless, as the database is unlikely to be free from error, the analysis concentrates on broad trends rather than the minutiae of individual projects. Moreover, a broad brush approach is far less vulnerable to the exclusion of a few relevant projects, the inclusion of a subsequently cancelled order, or to debates over the appropriate classification of a contract (e.g. licensed production or offset). The focus on EU12 procurement (rather than that of all countries), can be justified on two grounds. First, the data collection exercise is considerably reduced and, more importantly, it is well-known that western governments led the way in demanding offsets with their defence purchases.[63]

The evidence, summarised in Table 1, suggests that there has been a marked increase in the number of arms purchases by EU states involving some form of production work-sharing. Co-production and offsets are relatively new phenomena, commencing in the 1970s, with offsets exhibiting a considerable growth in popularity in the 1980s. The paucity of work-sharing deals in the 1950s reflects the substantial direct transfer of US military equipment. By 1960, European industry had recovered from the ravages of the war and direct transfers were being replaced by the licensed production of US equipment e.g. the F-86 and F-104 fighters, the M113 Armoured Personnel Carrier, and a number of utility helicopters. Widespread European prosperity meant that governments were able and willing to pay the cost premium associated with licensed production for the technology transfer and other associated benefits.

Table 1: EU12 Work-Sharing Contracts by Date of Contract[64]

Years	Number of Contracts			
	Licensed Production	Co-production	Offsets	Total
1950–59	14	1	0	15
1960–69	34	0	0	34
1970–79	43	10	6	59
1980–89	48	8	26	82
Unspecified	22	0	0	22
Total	161	19	32	212

By the early 1970s, the economic climate was far less favourable. Moreover, state-of-the-art defence goods were becoming increasingly costly and licensed production was becoming a luxury few were willing to indulge. Nevertheless, when spending large sums of tax-payers' money, governments wanted more than just defence equipment: jobs, technology, an enhanced DIB, foreign exchange, and political support for such expenditures were also valued. Offsets offered, or at least seemed to offer, all of these.[65]

Table 2 reveals the distribution of these work-sharing contracts according to the type of product being purchased. As with collaborative projects, the dominance of aerospace (aircraft, aero-engines and missiles) is apparent and with this sector accounting for 82 per cent of all work-sharing contracts.[66] Although a few contracts for the higher technology and more costly land and sea systems have involved work-sharing (e.g. for frigates and MBTs), EU states have largely sought work-sharing arrangements when buying costly aerospace products.

Table 2: EC Work-Sharing Contracts by Product Purchased, 1950–89

	Number of Contracts			
	Licensed Production	**Co-production**	**Offsets**	**Total**
Aircraft	78	6	19	103
Missiles	50	12	9	71
Land	19	1	3	23
Sea	14	0	1	15
Total	161	19	32	212

Source: As for Table 1

Udis and Maskus argue that several characteristics of the aerospace sector make it a suitable target for industrial policy. First, defence purchases from this sector typically involve high-value contracts and thus have the potential to generate considerable economic activity. Second, the goods purchased often embody highly advanced technologies which might generate spillovers that could improve productivity elsewhere in the economy. Moreover, aerospace industries are highly concentrated and governments might use their purchasing power in an attempt to appropriate for domestic industry a share of the available economic rent. And because offsets are usually negotiated with firms that subcontract work for the design and production of components, it is feasible for the prime to re-direct substantial amounts of work to suppliers in the purchaser's economy.[67]

France, the former FRG, and the UK have been the most active participants in collaborative procurement programmes.[68] However, Table 3 reveals that this is not the case for purchases where it is production work that is shared. In this case Italy is the purchaser with by far the largest percentage (25 per cent) of work-sharing contracts and with about one-half of this number of contracts each come a group of five countries: Belgium, the former FRG, the Netherlands, Spain, and the UK. Then come Greece and France each responsible for 7 per cent of the total number of work-sharing contracts.

This distribution of work-sharing programmes between the EU12 reflects differences in their defence industrial base. France, the former FRG and the UK, with relatively large defence budgets, have been willing and able to support a large advanced technology defence industrial base involved in an extensive range of air, land and sea systems. The ever-increasing real cost of high technology has encouraged them to share the development and production costs associated with

THE ECONOMICS OF OFFSETS

Table 3: EC Work-Sharing Contracts by Purchasing Country, 1950–89

	Number of Contracts				
	Co-production	**Licensed Production**	**Offsets**	**Total Work Sharing**	**(%)**
Belgium	4	16	4	24	11
Denmark	2	6	1	9	4
France	0	12	3	15	7
FRG	5	16	2	23	11
Greece	1	10	4	15	7
Italy	1	49	2	52	25
Netherlands	4	16	2	22	10
Portugal	0	4	1	5	2
Spain	1	13	8	22	10
UK	1	19	5	25	12
Total EU12	19	161	32	212	100

Source: As for Table 1

the most expensive projects. Other countries such as Belgium, the Netherlands and Greece, have much smaller defence budgets and are unwilling to pay for the privilege of sharing the development bill for new products. Rather, they prefer to 'buy' manufacturing jobs and technology for their domestic industry through licensed production. Italy falls between these two groups both in terms of the size of its defence budget and its preference between development and production work. Although there have been far fewer offsets than contracts involving the licensed production of foreign equipment, this instrument of industrial policy has been (and is) widely used throughout the EU and, according to Table 3, this is largely irrespective of the purchaser's technological capability.

Having examined which EU countries typically demand a work-sharing agreement for their equipment purchases, let us consider Table 4 which reveals those nations that have been the vendors in these sales. Not surprisingly, a large majority (69 per cent) of work-sharing deals involve the production of US-designed equipment; British French, and German equipment accounts for a further 22 per cent of work-sharing deals. The remaining 9 per cent of agreements relate to the purchase of equipment from 12 other countries. One other interesting point to note from Table 4 is that while US-designed products have accounted for over 73 per cent of the number of sales involving licensed production this figure falls to 28 per cent for offset sales. Of course, an analysis by the value, rather than the number of sales, might offer a different picture but what evidence there is does suggest that as far as work-sharing deals are concerned, EU suppliers of final equipment are increasing their share of the market at the expense of US suppliers but they are also incurring a major share of offset commitments.

Table 4: EC Work-Sharing Contracts by Selling Country, 1950–89

Vendor	Number of Contracts				
	Licensed Production	**Co-production**	**Offsets**	**Total**	**(%)**
USA	118	18	9	145	68.4
France	15	—	8	23	10.9
UK	9	—	5	14	6.6
FRG	6	—	4	10	4.7
Others	13	1	6	20	9.4
Total	161	19	32	212	100

Source:　As for Table 1

This overview of work-sharing associated with defence procurement has revealed a rapid growth of offsets in the 1980s and that this growth has involved the EU states as purchasers and, in some cases, as providers of defence equipment. It has, however, provided little insight into the economic arguments for offsets and it is to these that we now turn.

2.6　Offsets — Economic Motives

2.6.1　Oligopolies, second-best outcomes and capturing economic rent

Neoclassical economic theory stresses the advantages of exchanging money for goods through conventional markets. However, as mentioned above, purchases of aerospace goods provide multi-dimensional benefits (e.g. security, jobs, technology) that might not be amenable to a single efficiency criterion. Consequently, the establishment of a mutually satisfactory bargain might be enhanced if the dimensions of the bargaining problem are increased (e.g. price and offset terms). Typically, the marginal rates of substitution of the parties will differ across the various dimensions of the transaction and such differences can be exploited to their joint advantage. Moreover, the market for high technology aerospace products is characterised by oligopoly and thus a rationale exists for bargaining to restore the flexibility of prices where they are not usually varied to meet changing market conditions. Furthermore, the existence of oligopolistic distortions could be cited to justify the use of industrial policy to achieve a second-best outcome or in an attempt to capture, for domestic citizens, some of the economic rent that such imperfect markets generate.

Economic rent is any payment to an input greater than the most it could earn in its next most lucrative use. In a competitive economy, the argument is that the existence of rent will attract new entrants and that any rent will be competed away. However, Krugman suggests that the existence of a steep learning curve might, for example, make entry look unprofitable yet existing firms might be enjoying abnormal profits. If these industries also happen to be important trading sectors, such as the aerospace industry, then there is a theoretical case for strategic government participation in an attempt to capture some of this rent for domestic citizens when purchasing foreign aerospace products.[69] However, the practical difficulties associated with the successful execution of such a policy are substantial (e.g. the promotion of the interests of one strategic sector might have an adverse effect on other sectors). Reviewing this literature, Udis and Maskus conclude that '... offsets have relatively limited usefulness as tools of strategic trade policy'.[70]

2.6.2 Technology transfer and spillovers

Often, governments seek the transfer of new technologies into the domestic economy, and offsets, where for example the vendor agrees to establish a local plant, do just this. Eventually, the new technologies will diffuse throughout the economy, stimulating economic growth. The economic justification for this form of government intervention is straightforward. An individual firm will purchase technology up to the point where marginal cost equals marginal benefit. However, because the technology ultimately diffuses throughout the economy, the benefits to society exceed the benefits to the firm. Thus individual firms under-invest in technology as, when formulating their investment levels, they ignore the benefits that accrue to others from their own investment decisions. Of course, this does not necessarily mean that offsets are the best way to acquire technology. However, Udis and Maskus suggest that offsets might be a more efficient way of acquiring technology than a straightforward purchase. Their argument is that with a direct purchase the buyer bears all the risks associated with the failure of the technology. When the technology transfer is part of a larger contract, however, this risk is shifted to the vendor who, in an attempt to protect his reputation, will have a greater incentive to transfer successfully the technology for fear that failure will tarnish his reputation for the provision of the entire system.

2.6.3 The infant-industry argument

Governments often want to enhance their defence industrial base to improve their military capabilities. Where learning and scale economies are important for unit production costs, a certain level of sales might be necessary to achieve international competitiveness. By encouraging foreign suppliers to place work with domestic manufacturers, in addition to that which would have occurred in the absence of the offset, the domestic government is in effect protecting this industry. However, the volume of work placed might be such that domestic industry becomes internationally competitive, moves down the learning curve and, once established, has no need for further protection.[71] Of course, to the extent that other countries have their own offset requirements, which might draw work away from domestic firms, then there will be a need for the initial exporter to be allowed to bank offset credits, once it has fulfilled its initial obligation, to encourage it to continue place work with domestic manufacturers.

2.6.4 Offsets as a form of market entry/overcoming protectionism

The size of some domestic markets, such as that in the US, might generate sufficient competition among sub-contractors that primes feel no need to consider overseas suppliers. In this case, by forcing, say, US primes to consider UK suppliers, offsets help to get UK firms onto the bidders list. Of course, UK suppliers will only win contracts to the extent that they are competitive with their American rivals. In this instance, offsets can be interpreted as assisting the entry of UK firms into US markets and/or as reducing the protection that the size of the US market offers domestic sub-contractors against foreign competitors.[72]

2.6.5 Offsets as a form of employment and regional policy

As happens in the market for technology, the divergence between private and social costs, and between private and social benefits, can also be used to justify government intervention in the labour market. If someone would otherwise be unemployed, then the social cost of hiring this person will be markedly less than the private cost (which is equal to the wage rate plus employer taxes). Consequently, from society's point of view, firms will employ too few people and thus a role emerges for government policy to offer the appropriate incentives (e.g. labour subsidies) to remedy this situation (although critics of this argument would point out that such subsidies have to be funded through higher taxes, which reduces spending and thus employment in other areas of the economy). By encouraging foreign firms to buy more from, say, the domestic aerospace industry, government is effectively subsidizing employment in this sector. Similarly, some countries require a specific regional distribution of offset work and this is clearly a form of regional policy as it encourages firms to locate economic activity in specific geographical areas. Whether offsets are the most cost effective way of achieving these objectives remains a moot point but, in principle, it should be possible to compare the cost per offset-generated job with the cost per job through a regional employment subsidy.

2.7   Offsets — Political Objectives.

Procurement choices, particularly those involving large sums of taxpayers' money, are made in the political market place where various interest groups seek to influence decision-makers. In this situation, arguments about economic efficiency can be swamped or hijacked by those who want offsets to be used to reward favoured interest groups (e.g. a particular industry or region) by providing hidden subsidies to local firms.

Governments can also cite the alleged economic benefits of offsets as justification for spending large sums of taxpayers' money on foreign rather than domestic products. In this case though, offsets are trade creating, in the sense that they facilitate international transactions which would otherwise have been (politically) impossible. Once again, offsets help to overcome protectionist sentiment.

If the defence industrial base is relatively weak so that there is no indigenous capability, the alleged jobs and technology benefits of offsets might facilitate the purchase of defence equipment which would otherwise have been politically impossible, or if possible, at a much reduced level.

Offsets can also assist the establishment of a DIB which might be valued for the improved security of supply it offers, as well as reducing the support costs over the life of the system compared with the provision of such services by the original supplier.[73]

Finally, offsets might be used to reduce the adverse impact on the balance of payments of a large defence purchase, particularly where the purchaser is seeking to maintain a fixed exchange rate.[74]

2.8   Offsets — Empirical Overview

Before any evaluation of offsets can be made, basic information on the costs and benefits of these policies are essential. Unfortunately, this is rarely available and, as a result, the economic literature on offsets is not particularly extensive. Moreover, that which does exist mirrors the literature on countertrade in the sense that it largely comprises papers which describe the various forms of offset, illustrate the growth of this form of reciprocity, and then discuss one or two deals in more depth. Rarely is there any evaluation of either how much the offset cost (compared with an off-the-shelf sale) or any quantitative estimate of the benefits forthcoming (e.g. in terms of the technology transferred, or the number of jobs generated).

One exception to this general rule is the fascinating series of reports published by the US Office of Management and Budget in the late 1980s. The US, of course, is largely an exporter of arms and thus it is not concerned with the cost premium that importers pay for offsets. Nevertheless, some Congressmen are concerned at the impact that offsets are having on American employment levels, the DIB, US international competitiveness and international trade. Consequently, before moving on to the country studies, the reader might find that the following summary of one OMB report provides some interesting background material.[75]

In the late summer and fall of 1988, the OMB sent a questionnaire on offsets in military exports to 52 of the top 100 DoD contractors. This mandatory survey covered all contracts signed over the eight-year period, 1980–87, and responses covered 90 per cent of all US military exports for the years 1980–85.[76] For the 8 years covered by the survey, contracts with offset agreements totalled $34.8 billion and involved 30 countries. The offset agreements associated with these contracts were valued at $19.9 billion, or 57 per cent of the value of the sales. The size of individual offsets varied considerably, from 5 to 175 per cent, with three countries (Spain, Switzerland and the UK) having an offset ratio greater than 100 per cent. Canada, Spain, EPG, UK, Turkey, Israel and Australia had all signed contracts that gave rise to offset commitments from US suppliers in excess of $1 billion. The survey also found that for about one-half of the value of the offset obligations, the types of goods and services to be provided were not precisely defined at the time the contract was signed. Where mention was made of the types of goods to be purchased, most of the value was to be accounted for by manufactures, largely aircraft engines and engine parts, other aircraft parts and equipment, electronic components, and radar and related navigational equipment.[77] To implement their offset agreements, firms were allowed, on average, 11 years, although this period ranged from 6 years to 21 years. Hence only about 50 per cent of the offset obligations had been implemented by the end of 1987. Of these implementations, about 31 per cent were direct and 61 per cent indirect. Subcontractor production accounted for over 50 per cent of direct offsets while subcontractor production and countertrade accounted for almost all indirect offsets. These implementations can also be disaggregated by the type of firm that fulfilled them. US prime contractors accounted for 60 per cent while US subcontractors accounted for another 37 per cent of these implementations.[78]

The Act requiring the production of the report specifically asked those responsible to consider the impact of offsets in military exports on defence preparedness, industrial competitiveness, employment, and international trade. As the OMB report points out:

'The greatest barrier to analysis of military offsets is the difficulty of determining an appropriate baseline for comparative analysis. Unless we have some idea of how affected industries would differ in the absence of offsets, it is difficult to answer any question along the lines of "How much higher (or lower) would exports (or employment, profits, etc.) be without offsets?".[79]

For example, if US companies ceased offering offsets whilst their competitors continued to do so, US firms might lose sales that they would otherwise have won. Even if the assumption is that US firms would still have won the contract, countries might be willing to spend more on foreign-designed defence goods accompanied with an offset, and that without such reciprocity, sales of US-designed defence goods would be lower and, in the case of NATO, its defence would be weaker.

2.8.1 Defence preparedness

The OMB report contends that by facilitating the sale of US equipment, offsets contribute to RSI within NATO. In addition, by enhancing the DIB of NATO members, offsets contribute to their ability to produce US systems overseas. Another indicator of the impact of offsets on defence preparedness is their impact on the principal sectors of the economy supporting national defence. Using data gathered in an earlier survey of US exports, the OMB found that defence export sales, net of their associated offsets, increased real output of the top 30 defence-related industries by over $6 billion over the period 1980–84. Thus the report concludes that '... defence exports net of offsets provide economic benefits that strengthen US defence preparedness'.[80]

Of some Congressional concern is the impact of offsets on subcontractors. As the report points out, foreign sourcing can increase competition and thus lower defence costs. In addition, with aerospace as the largest component of defence, it might anticipated that if the DIB effects of offset were significant, then these would be apparent in the aerospace industry. However, the AIAA reports that all tiers of the industry continue to show this is a leading sector of the US economy, with a trade surplus of $16 billion in 1987, whilst most other sectors show a trade deficit.

2.8.2 Industrial competitiveness

While the US trade balance has gone from a position of equilibrium in 1973 to a deficit of $170 billion in 1987, the aerospace trade balance has improved from $4 billion to $16 billion. Thus offsets do not appear to have had an immediate and obvious negative impact on industrial competitiveness in this sector. However, co-production and licensed production can transfer technologies and establish new competitors, and the OMB reports that there is some evidence that sub-contracting has caused some firms not to expand or to contract their capacity. Nevertheless, without an offset, the US prime contractor might not have won the contract. The report suggests that while offset-related sales contribute to the marginal income of defence firms, the health of the industry depends primarily on US government purchases. In spite of substantial budget cuts in the early 1990s this is still likely to be true, although export sales might now be of more importance than they were in the 1980s.

2.8.3 Employment

The OMB report on the employment effect of offsets comes to the, perhaps somewhat counter-intuitive conclusion that, if anything, offsets increase domestic US employment opportunities compared with identical sales without any offset. The report assumes that the initial sale would have been made without the offset and it estimates, first, the employment effect of the sale *without the offset* and then the adverse employment effect of the offset. For offset implementations over the period 1980–84, the OMB puts the first figure at 89,750 employee-years and the latter at 28,400 employee-years. However, this is not the end of the matter. The report argues that '... there can be no foreign sales, over the long run, without "offsetting" purchases (imports), whether or not these purchases are linked directly to the sales as they are in the case of offsets'.[81] In other words, over the long run, the US trade balance must be zero. For the purpose of their report, the OMB assumes that imports equal exports over the five-year period 1980–84, and the authors calculate the employment impact of:

a. the extra imports necessary to ensure that the value of the initial export equals the offset plus residual imports; and
b. the imports necessary to match the export without the offset.

In this scenario, the net effect of the offset is to increase the number of employee-years of work for US industry by 1,372. Basically, those industries that lose sales because of offsets are less labour-intensive than those other industries whose products are imported to ensure that the trade balance is zero.

It is pointed out by the OMB that, although offsets have little effect on the level of employment, their inefficiency is reflected in their effect on the distribution of employment across industries. The report reveals that, relative to normal trade, offsets tend to shift workers from activities in which they have a comparative advantage to those where they have a comparative disadvantage.

2.9   Concluding Remarks

This chapter has provided an overview of countertrade theory and evidence. There has also been a discussion of the economic arguments for offsets and a summary of one of the very few detailed studies of their impact. Unavoidably, many of the themes that have already been identified will emerge again in the following chapters. Nevertheless, having absorbed this overview, the reader who is unfamiliar with the area should now be able to view each of the country studies within the wider context of the debate about offsets.

Endnotes

1. Korth, C.M., (ed.), **International Countertrade,** Quorum Books, New York, 1987, p. 2.

2. Rubin, S., **The Business Manager's Guide to Barter, Offset and Countertrade**, Economist Intelligence Unit, London, 1986, p. 15.

3. Weigand, R.E., **International Trade Without Money**, *Harvard Business Review*, November-December 1977, p. 30.

4. de Miramon, T., **Countertrade: A Modernized Barter System**, *The OECD Observer*, No.114, January 1982, pp. 12–15.

5. Liesch, P.W., **Government Mandated Countertrade**, Avebury, Aldershot, 1991, p. 4.

6. Wood, D., **Australian Defence Offsets Programme.** Proceedings of Defence Offsets Seminar, Department of Defence, Canberra.

7. de Miramon, J., **Countertrade: An Illusory Solution**, *The OECD Observer*, No. 124, May 1985, pp. 24–29.

8. Korth, *op. cit.*

9. Department of Trade and Industry, **Countertrade**, DTI, London, 1989 p. 1.

10. United Nations Conference on Trade and Development**, Trade and Development Report**, New York: United Nations, 1986, p. 79.

11. Hammond, G.T., **Countertrade, Offsets and Barter**, *International Political Economy*, London: Pinter, 1990, pp. 10–11.

12. Yoffie, D.B., **Profiting from Countertrade**, *Harvard Business Review*, May-June 1984, pp. 8–16.

13. See, for example: Alexandrides, C.G., and Bowers, B.L., **Countertrade**, John Wiley, New York, 1985; C. Brown and R. Franklin, **Countertrade: Paying in Goods and Services**, Longman, London, 1994; S. Rubin, *op. cit.*

14. de Miramon, 1982, *op. cit.*

15. Wülker-Mirbach, M., **New Trends in Countertrade**, *The OECD Observer*, No. 163, April-May 1990, pp. 13–16.

16. de Miramon, 1985, *op. cit.*

17. See, for example: G. Banks, **The Economics and Politics of Counter-trade**. *The World Economy,* 1983, pp. 159–182; J. Dizard, **The Explosion of International Barter**, *Fortune Magazine*, 7 February 1983, pp. 88–95.

18. de Miramon, 1985, *op. cit.*

19. See, for example: Hammond, *op. cit.*; Liesch, *op. cit.;* M. Thorpe, **Economic Motivations and the Development of Countertrade**, Working Paper 90.07, School of Economics and Finance, Curtain University of Technology; B. Udis, and K. Maskus, 1991, **Offsets as industrial policy: lessons from aerospace**, *Defence Economics*, vol. 2, no. 2, pp. 151–164.

20. Hennart, J.F., **The Transaction Cost Rationale for Countertrade**, *Journal of Law Economics and Organisation*, vol. 5, 1989, pp. 127–153.

21. Caves, R. and Marin, D., **Countertrade Transactions Theory and Evidence**, *Economic Journal*, 102, 1992, pp. 1171–1183.

22. For example by Hennart, 1989, *op. cit.*, and by R. Mirus, and B. Yeung, **Buy-Back International Trade: A Rationale**, *Wettwirtschorftliches Archiv,* 122, 1986, pp. 371–374.

23. See, for example, Rubin, *op. cit.*

24. Mirus, R. and Yeung, B., **Countertrade and Foreign Exchange Shortages: A Preliminary Assessment**, *Wettwirtschortliches Archiv*, 122, 1986, p. 543.

25. Mirus, R. and Yeung, B., **Economic Incentives for Countertrade**, *Journal of International Business*, 1986, vol. 17, p. 35.

26. Mirus, R. and Yeung, B., **Countertrade and Foreign Exchange Shortages**, 1986, *op. cit.* p. 542.

27. For example, Hennart, 1989, *op. cit.*

28. Banks, G., *op. cit.*, p. 165.

29. See also Tschoegl, A., **Modern Barter**, *Lloyds Bank Review*, 1985, pp. 32–40.

30. Banks, G., **Constrained Markets, 'Surplus' Commodities and International Barter**, *Kyklos*, 38, 1985, pp. 249–267.

31. *Ibid.*, p. 255.

32. Caves and Marin, *op. cit.*

33. Banks, *op. cit.*

34. Mirus and Yeung, **Economic Incentives for Countertrade**, *op. cit.*, p. 36.

35. For example, Mirus and Yeung, *ibid.*, Hennart, 1986, *op. cit.*, and Hennart, 1989, *op. cit.*

36. Murrell, P., **Product Quality, Market Signalling and the Development of East-West Trade**, *Economic Inquiry*, 20, 1982, pp. 589–683.

37. Hennart, J.F., **Some Empirical Dimensions of Countertrade**, *Journal of International Business Studies*, 1990, p. 252.

38. Mirus and Yeung, **Buy-Back in International Trade**, *op. cit.*

39. Mirus and Yeung, **Economic Incentives for Countertrade**, *op. cit.*, p. 34.

40. Chan, R. and Hoy, M., **East-West Joint Ventures and Buy-Back Contracts**, *Journal of International Economics*, 30, 1991, pp. 331–343.

41. Marin, D. and Schnitzer, M., **Tying Trade Flows: A Theory of Countertrade**, Centre for Economic Policy Research, London, Discussion Paper No. 946.

42. Banks, 1983, *op. cit.*

43. Hennart, 1989, *op. cit.*, pp. 247–248.

44. Amann, E. and Marin, D., **Risk-Sharing in International Trade: An Analysis of Countertrade**, *Journal of Industrial Economics*, 42, 1994, pp. 63–77.

45. Mirus and Yeung, **Economic Incentives for Countertrade**, *op. cit.*, p. 30.

46. Yoffie, *op. cit.*, p. 9.

47. Jones, S.F. and Jagoe, A., **Third World Countertrade**, Produce Studies Ltd, Newbury, 1988.

48. Hveem, H., **Countertrade: The Global Perspective**, Institute of Political Science, University of Oslo, 1989.

49. This is similar to the distribution of countertrade deals reported by D. Lecraw, **The Management of Countertrade Factors Influencing Success,** *Journal of International Business Studies,* 20, 1989, pp. 41–59.

50. *Ibid.*

51. *Ibid.*, p. 57.

52. Hennart, 1990, *op. cit.*

53. Hveem, *op. cit.*

54. Caves and Marin, *op. cit.*

55. *Ibid.*, p. 1172.

56. *Ibid.*, p. 1182.

57. *Ibid.*, p. 1183.

58. OMB, **Offsets in Military Exports**, Office of Management and Budget, Executive Office of the President, Washington DC, 1988, p. 128.

59. Aerospace Industries Association of America, **Views of the AIAA on a US Government Policy on Offsets related to Military Exports**, AIAA, Washington DC, 1990, p. 2.

60. SIPRI Yearbook 1992: **World Armaments and Disarmaments**, Oxford University Press.

61. Rich, M., Stanley, W., Birkler, J. and Hesse, M., **Multinational Co-Production of Military Aerospace Systems**, Rand Corporation, Santa Monica, 1981.

62. Todd, D. and Humble, R., **World Aerospace: An International Survey**, Croon Helm, London, 1987.

63. Neuman, S.G., **Co-Production, Barter and Countertrade: Offsets in the International Arms Market**, *Orbis*, 29, 1985, p. 183–213.

64. Calculated from: Rich *et al*, *op. cit.*; SIPRI Yearbook (various issues); and Todd and Humble, *op. cit.*

65. Udis, B., **Offsets in Defence Trade: Costs and Benefits**, Mimeo, University of Colorado at Boulder, 1994.

66. Hartley, K. and Martin, S., **International Collaboration in Aerospace**, *Science and Public Policy*, 17, 1990, pp. 143–151.

67. Udis and Maskus, *op. cit.*, p. 153.

68. Martin, S., **Economic Collaboration and European Security** in S. Kirby and N. Hooper (eds.) *The Cost of Peace: Assessing Europe's Security Options*, Harwood Academic Publishers, Reading, 1991.

69. Krugman, P.R., **Industrial Organization and International Trade**, National Bureau of Economic Research, Working Paper 1957, Cambridge, Massachusetts.

70. Udis, Maskus, *op. cit.*, p.156.

71. See Liesch, *op. cit.*, p. 78 and Udis, *op. cit.*.

72. Udis, *op. cit.*

73. *Ibid.*

74. Weida, W., **Paying for Weapons: Politics and Economics of Countertrade and Offsets**. Frost and Sullivan, New York, 1985; L.G.B. Wett, **Military Ofsets**, *National Defense*, March 1984, pp. 20–23.

75. OMB, *op. cit.*

76. *Ibid.*, p. 7.

77. *Ibid.*, p. 8.

78. *Ibid.*, p. 21.

79. *Ibid.*, p. 35.

80. *Ibid.*, p. 37.

81. *Ibid.*, p. 52.

Chapter 3

The Defence Offsets Policy in Australia

Stefan Markowski and Peter Hall
Australia Defence Force Academy
University of New South Wales, Canberra

3.1 Introduction

For the past two decades, compensatory contracting arrangements have been applied by most nations in the procurement of defence materiel. In principle, these arrangements are "designed to 'offset' the cost of procuring expensive weapons on the part of the buyer through the recovery of hard currency, employment creation in the buyer country, support of the buyer's industrial base and, significantly, technology transfer from seller to buyer".[1] This paper is concerned with the Australian Defence Offsets Programs (ADOP). The overall aim of the ADOP has been "to provide access for Australian industry to advanced technology, skills and overseas markets to as to help establish internationally competitive industries within Australia".[2]

Australia presents a very interesting case for a student of defence economics. It is a well developed economy which maintains a modern force structure at a relatively low share of GDP. In gross terms Australia's defence budget is about the same as those of some medium size European countries. Whilst Australia maintains a special relationship with the USA, its defence doctrine is that of self-reliance and, thus, the development of industrial capability to support the Australian Defence Force (ADF) rather than attain self-sufficiency in weapons manufacture and logistic support.

When Australian offsets arrangements were originally set up in the early 1970s, they were aimed primarily at overseas suppliers of military and aerospace equipment, requiring them to place work with Australian industry to develop local defence-oriented manufacturing and support capabilities. The scheme was subsequently expanded to include a wider range of high technology manufactures (see below). From 1986 until the end of 1992, Defence offsets were a mandatory countertrade requirement applied by Australian Defence to achieve such objectives as the attainment of certain technological, manufacturing or service support capability, pump priming of new activities, and so on. An offsets obligation was deemed to arise whenever the imported content of a Defence contract had a value of at least AUS$2.5 million. From 1993, following the 1992 Review of Defence Policy for Industry, Defence is to reduce its reliance on "less focused mechanisms such as offsets" applying them only as a measure of last resort (see below).[3]

Clearly, joint transactions involving packages of goods and services including specific countertrade arrangements could be negotiated between Defence and overseas contractors if the mandatory ADOP did not exist. What is therefore the rationale for the mandatory ADOP as opposed to a world in which Defence and contractors could freely negotiate the most appropriate and advantageous packages of goods and services?

We argue in the final section of this paper that there is no good reason for a mandatory offsets scheme and that the mandatory version of the ADOP could only ever offer any potential advantage if Defence were incapable of or uninterested in pursuing the best possible contractual arrangements. In a world in which Defence had identified its needs and negotiated hard and freely with potential contractors, a mandatory scheme would have nothing extra to offer. Such arrangements merely shift the initiative away from the purchaser and give suppliers scope for opportunism at the expense of the buyer. First, however, we present a brief sketch of the history of Australian offsets, Defence and civil (Section 2). This is followed by an evaluation of offsets programs (Section 3).

To set the context for an assessment of the significance and the likely impact of Defence offsets, it is useful to refer to the Defence of Australia, 1987 White Paper,[4] which outlines the current rationale for Australian industry involvement in the Government requirement for defence self reliance:

"The capacity to maintain, repair, modify and adapt defence equipment to the Australian environment, independently of overseas sources, is of fundamental importance to our combat effectiveness in all levels of conflict. This requires Australian involvement in design, development and production to acquire the necessary detailed knowledge, skills and facilities. Through such work local industry can make an important contribution to the sustained operational effectiveness of our forces in combat."[5]

Hence it has been the Government's policy "to encourage the widest possible cost-effective involvement of Australian industry in defence work" ... including circumstances whereby ... "cost and delivery time penalties (incurred by Australian industry involvement) ... must be justified for each item in terms of their contribution to independent supply and support compared with alternatives."[6]

3.2 Brief History of Australian Offsets Programs

3.2.1 Early Developments

The development of Australian offsets programs has been largely associated with the procurement of military equipment. In the late 1950s, substantial quantities of defence materiel were purchased from the USA and it was felt at the time that some form of reciprocal purchasing was desirable to encourage and support the development of Australia's defence-related industries. In 1958, a US military mission was invited to visit Australia to assess the country's defence-related industrial capabilities. The mission concluded that Australian defence industries would not be able to supply US Defence requirements or comply with American standards.

During the Vietnam War a further effort was made to create opportunities for Australian industry to bid for US Defence contracts. This met with a limited response from Australian manufacturers as many of their order books were full and firms were reluctant to invest or innovate to respond to American Defence requirements. Many companies felt that the continuity of US orders could not be assured even if Australian firms attained US military standards. Nevertheless, efforts to make Australian manufacturers more import competitive and export oriented continued through the 1960s.[7]

In 1968, a high ranking Australian mission visited the US to discuss the practicalities of increasing American Defence procurements from Australia. As a result, semi-annual Procurement Liaison Meetings (PLMs) between the two countries were initiated to develop a joint programme for increased Australian industry involvement in US Defence procurement. The real problem in achieving this was finding suitable Australian tenderers: there was no lack of potential sub-contracting offers from American defence contractors. In 1969, an Australian mission visited the US to assess and report on opportunities for Australian industry in US Defence procurement. It was during the mission's discussions with US DOD officials that the possibility of Australian Government using its leverage, as major purchaser of American equipment, to seek 'offsets' (reciprocal purchases) as a condition of buying became a serious option.[8]

In 1970, following the mission's recommendations, the Ministers for Trade & Industry, Supply and Defence established the first 'offsets program' under the banner of the Australian Industry Participation Program (AIPP). The purpose of the AIPP was to obtain offsetting work for Australian industry when major purchases were made overseas. The Program sought to develop and sustain Australian defence-related industrial capabilities, and industry generally, through the diffusion of new and improved technologies.

The original Program covered purchases of military and civilian aircraft and the label of "Offsets Program" was attached to both elements together. Initially its operation was the responsibility of a standing Inter Departmental Committee (IDC) consisting of the Departments of Trade and Industry (in the chair), Supply (responsible for the Program's day-to-day operations) and Defence. Although the odium of any failure of the policy was to be borne primarily by the Trade

Department, the Program kept all defence purchasing and associated offset orders or sub-contracting within the hands of Defence.[9] However, as rules associated with the Program were not very clear, confusion ensued as to what 'offsets' were — offsetting purchases from Australia by the supplying country (i.e., countertrade) or increased local content in producing the contracted goods (i.e., forced sub-contracts). Subsequent changes in the administration of the AIPP added to the apparent confusion. A key point is that the original Program specified neither that offsets were to be mandatory nor desirable levels of offsets that should be sought. In a nutshell, contractors were expected to do 'their best' in identifying the scope for agreed offsets and in discharging offsets obligations. This became known as the 'best endeavours' basis for offsets compliance.

Two examples drawn from the 1970s serve to indicate how offsets evolved as they were put to work in this period. First, in 1973, following the Australian commitment to purchase the FFG ships, the Australian and US Departments of Defence negotiated offset arrangements under which the US DOD and industry agreed to meet an offset objective of up to 25 per cent of the value of a major Australian order. Those American firms that benefited most from Australian order were to carry the initial and primary burden of offset implementation. US Defence procurement from Australian sources was normally to be competitive, that is, subject to satisfactory performance, quality and delivery requirements while costs were not to exceed those of comparable US items or other foreign items eligible for award.

Second, the New Tactical Fighter (NTF) program started in 1977 led Defence to reconsider in depth the nature of appropriate industrial involvement. Its analysis led to the publication of Guidance Paper released to the contenders for supply of the NTF in November 1978. The paper explained that offset work would be one element of a two part industry program and would comprise activity to a value of at least 30% of the imported content of project costs. Preferred work for offset purposes was production for export of NTF components but other types of offset were also acceptable. Many of the offset opportunities suggested by the Guidance Paper were to appear in later years in official documentation describing the operation of the scheme.[10]

3.2.2   The 1984 Inglis Review

In 1984, Committee of Review on Offsets was set up under the chairmanship of Sir Brian Inglis (the Inglis Review). It undertook a comprehensive review of the Offsets Program and attempted to make an assessment of its costs and benefits. It found the existing objectives set for the Offsets Program to be very general and equally applicable to a range of other industry initiatives. It therefore sought to formulate new objectives to identify the Program's specific mission.[11]

The Review found it difficult to make precise quantitative assessments of the costs and benefits of the Program. It identified transaction costs to the Commonwealth and businesses concerned and noted that price premia (reflecting the cost of anticipated offsets requirements) might have been factored into purchases. The perceived benefits were associated with enhanced access to overseas markets and technologies. Despite the intangible nature of benefits and poor data on costs, the Review concluded that there were net benefits from the Program.

The Review was also very critical of the administration of the Offsets Program and made 24 recommendations, many of which were reflected in a revamped Offsets Program which came into effect in March 1986.

3.2.3   The Post-1986 Programs

The new program formalised the division between civil and defence offsets and provided written guidelines for the administration of both program components. The broad objective of the Program was to bring to Australian industry advanced technology, skills and capabilities to assist in the establishment of internationally competitive industries in Australia and support defence industry capability objectives. The first goal applied to Civil Offsets and the second to Defence. Priority was to be given to offsets incorporating direct transfer of advanced technology and training, R&D conducted by Australian industry or research institutions and the participation of local enterprise in design and related work.[12]

On a broader front, the Government's response to the Inglis recommendations produced a more targeted policy of industry assistance. As a result, the Defence program of industry support moved away from the AIPP and was replaced by the Australian Industry Involvement (AII). The AII was defined as a program of activity put in place by an overseas contractor and comprised two elements: Defence Designated and Assisted Work (Designated Work) and Defence Offsets. In special cases, the AII responsibility was placed on the Australian prime contractor, e.g., the Collins Submarine Project. This allowed the prime contractor to maximise local content and through this establish the through life support capabilities in support of the ADF.[13] Both programs were also consistent with the general policy of preference for Australian- and New Zealand-made goods and services.

The most radical aspect of the new Offsets Program was its departure from the 'best endeavours' approach and the explicit adoption of mandatory offsets arrangements for all Government purchases which exceeded AUS$2.5 million with an imported content of at least 30 per cent. It appears that the arrangements related to the New Tactical Fighter program had already moved a long way in this direction, however, as early as 1978.[14]

The offsets obligation of foreign companies was set at 30 per cent of the imported content of contracts. Acceptable activities were defined as activities of technological significance including but not restricted to manufacturing, software development, research and development, design and development, technology transfer and certain types of training undertaken by overseas suppliers as a result of attracting or anticipating an offsets obligation. There was a strong emphasis on long term viability and international competitiveness. New production initiated as a result of offsets was expected to be sustained after the fulfilment of prime contractors' offsets obligations. Multiplier incentives were used for the first time to give particular encouragement to the provision of offsets in the form of R&D and approved training expenditures. These activities were credited at three times their nominal value for offsets purposes. The Program also stipulated that offsets obligations should not result in any price increase for goods and services procured by the Commonwealth, i.e., primary contracts subject to offset obligations should not be 'padded' in the anticipation of offsets requirements.

Until 1986, Defence contract conditions were specified and designated work and offsets obligations were secured in contract. One problem with securing the obligation in contract was that where the period for completion of the industry program was longer than that needed to complete the contract, there was no legal mechanism to enforce compliance with the industry program. This was overcome by developing Project Deeds which were legally enforceable and were separate from the contract. Credit Deeds were also developed to encourage contractors to put in place long term industry programs whether or not they had offsets obligations. Credits could then be used to discharge existing or future offsets obligations whilst suppliers could establish long term industry programs that were commercially viable.

When the 1986 combined Defence-civil guidelines were introduced, it was envisaged that they would soon be reviewed to smooth out various teething problems. The guidelines were reviewed in 1988 when it was agreed that, due to the growing disparity of the civil and defence programs, separate guidelines should be promulgated. Accordingly, separate Civil offsets guidelines were published in 1988 and Defence offsets guidelines in 1989. The scope of the AII was also widened to include Australian Production, in addition to Designated Work and Offsets. The 1988–92 AII and Defence Offsets Programs are described in the following section.

3.2.4   1988–1992 Australian Industry Involvement Program

The 1988–89 Defence Offsets Program is a part of the revised Australian Industry Involvement (AII) Program. This comprises a broader program of production work, research and development or enhancement of Australian technology or industrial capability, arranged by a prime contractor or sub-contractor for delivery by an Australian company.[15] Maximising competitive Australian value-added is a major AII objective and the level of Australian production offered by a prospective contractor is an important factor in the evaluation of each proposal.[16] The AII Program comprises:

- Australian Production; and/or
- Designated Work; and/or
- Defence Offsets.

Australian Production "means direct participation in a contract for procurement of supplies and/or services by Australian manufacturing industry. It includes the provision of goods and services conjointly of that industry and is referred to as the 'level' or 'value' of Australian Production".[17] The goods and services under consideration are deliverables under the contract for supplies and the 'level' or 'value' is used in the calculation of any Defence Offsets obligation arising from a contract placed with an overseas supplier. These goods and services are not acceptable as Offsets. (Indeed, the terminology under the program has now changed and Australian Production is now called 'local content', which at once makes it clear why such activity is not acceptable as offsets.)

Designated Work comprises "those work activities of defence and/or strategic significance undertaken by Australian firms, where the activity involves the Department of Defence paying a cost premium which has been mutually agreed with the Contractor".[18] Designated Work involves a cost premium and is therefore not acceptable for consideration as meeting any part of the Defence Offsets obligation arising from the purchase. In calculating the level of Offsets obligation, the mutually agreed premium involved in Designated Work, is not included as Australian Production and in the calculation of the 'level' or 'value' of AII. In contradistinction to Offsets, Designated Work benefits from explicit funding assistance. For example, in the F/A-18 Project, the Designated Work requirement increased the overall project cost by about 15 per cent.[19]

Defence Offsets are "activities of defence and technological significance which are directed to Australian industry by an overseas supplier as a result of receiving an order" ... "for goods and/or services from the Department of Defence".[20] The Defence Offsets obligation of an overseas supplier is seen as a commitment to generate a program of activities in Australia. This commitment is required whenever the imported content of a contract has a value of at least AUS$A2.5m. Offsets are to be provided at a rate of 30 per cent of the value of the imported content.

The following example from the Guidelines[21] shows different components of the AII Program:

		AUS$ million
a.	Prime contract value (including premium)	10.5
b.	Level of Australian Production	2.0
c.	Level of Designated Work (excluding premium)	4.0
d.	Level of premium	0.5
e.	Level of imported content $[(a) - (b+c+d)]$	4.0
f.	Offsets obligation $[30\%$ of $(e)]$	1.2
g.	Level of AII $[(b) + (c) + (f)]$	7.2

In this example, the level of AII is 72 per cent of prime contract value excluding the Designated Work premium. The level of AII in Defence capital equipment contracts reached 70 per cent in 1989–90. Of this some 60.5 per cent was accounted for by Australian Production and Designated Work and about 9.5 per cent was secured as Offsets.[22]

The new civil guidelines included Partnership for Development Agreements, aimed primarily at the information technology industries, a Pre-qualified Supplier Scheme, a new category of investment Offsets, the inclusion of some insurance activities as eligible Offsets activity and increased emphasis on service industries. The Program was directed at "developing internationally competitive, technology intensive industries by bringing into Australia advanced technologies, skills, research and investment and encouraging overseas companies to establish Australia as a research and development and manufacturing base for exports to the South East Asian and Pacific region".[23]

3.2.5   Defence Offsets Program

The 1988–92 Defence Offsets Program is an expanded and tighter version of the 1986 Program. The earlier guidelines were largely rewritten to remove a number of ambiguities resulting from poorly drafted rules and, in some cases, the unclear intent of the previous scheme. Some of the most significant changes between the old and new guidelines are noted below. However, the new Program retains the mandatory character and the basic logic of the previous system.

The objectives of the Defence Offsets Program are stated to be improvement in the capability of defence industries to maintain and adapt military equipment, provide munitions and spares and develop technology to meet the longer term needs of the ADF. To be acceptable as offsets, activities proposed by overseas suppliers must meet four criteria:

a.   **commercial viability**: the offset must be likely to lead to activities which are internationally competitive, in terms of price, quality and delivery, and also commercially viable on a sustained basis without further subsidy from the Commonwealth or State Governments;

b. **price**: goods and services procured by Defence when offsets apply must not be more highly-priced than they would have been in the absence of the Offsets Program;

c. **technology**: offset activities must be at least as 'sophisticated' technologically as the goods/services procured from overseas but not necessarily directly related to such goods and/or services; and

d. **new work**: offsets must involve an addition to or extension of the activities already undertaken by the overseas supplier in Australia. More specifically, they must be activities which meet any of the following:

    i. are new to individual Australian firms or which improve existing capabilities and which would not otherwise be undertaken in Australia,

    ii. result in local research, design, development, production or support activities which would not otherwise have been undertaken in Australia,

    iii. open up markets overseas new to Australian products and/or services.

Generally, Defence requires that approved offsets are related to the provision of specialised support in Australia for the maintenance of the equipment being purchased and which contributes to self reliance. The normal after sales customer support, distribution or marketing activities, which form the part of the normal commercial activities undertaken by the supplier in Australia, are not acceptable as offsets.[24]

The threshold for offsets purposes was increased to AUS$2.5 million of the *imported content* as suggested by the Inglis Review. Under the previous definition, offsets were often sought against contracts as low as AUS$2.5 million in value with import content of AUS$0.75 million resulting in very small but administratively costly offsets obligations.[25] Also, the new guidelines permit the application of a range of multipliers (×1, ×1.5, ×2 and ×3), the particular one chosen depending on the nature of offsets-related activity. The multiplier used is based on the priority ranking of the project to the Defence Department, and is no longer related to specific offset activities.

Since 1986, Defence has sought compensation for non-performance of the agreed offsets programs by means of pre-agreed Liquidated Damages. Under the revised Program, these are to be specified in the Contract or Deed. Under the 1986 Guidelines, Australian prime contracts could be made liable for contingent liabilities, such as liquidated damages, on behalf of their foreign sub-contractors. The new Guidelines make an Australian prime contractor responsible only for ensuring that its foreign sub-contractors enter into satisfactory arrangements (by means of a sub-contract or a Deed) with the Commonwealth. The facilities for transferring offsets obligations from one contractor to another have been removed. The list of activities suitable for offsets has been revised, e.g., part production and gifts and donations were removed from the list and hire/lease agreements incorporated under the revised Guidelines.

3.2.6 Winding Down of Offsets Programs

The winding down of the Civil Offsets Program was announced in the March 1991 Economic Statement. Following the Statement, the shift of civil industry policy away from offsets has been accelerated as:

- offsets were abolished for automotive purchases;
- aerospace offsets were replaced by long term Memoranda of Understanding (MOUs). These commit overseas contractors to give Australian companies equal opportunities to bid for work. There are no sanctions in the event of non-compliance apart from a threat to revert to the case-by-case accounting of offsets; and
- information technology and tele-communications acquisitions were covered by Partnership for Development arrangements and Fixed Term Arrangements for 'non-partners'.

Following the 1992 Review of Defence Policy for Industry (the Price Review), Defence decided to reduce "its reliance on less focused mechanisms such as offsets in support of Australian industry involvement." ... "As a rule, however, specific Australian Industry Involvement objectives will be achieved best by more focused provisions within contracts, ensuring continuing capabilities in areas of importance. Defence offsets will remain as a last resort but will have to address high priority capability requirements set out in the proposed industry capability planning statements."[26]

3.3   Evaluation of the Australian Defence Offsets Program

Data on the operation of Offsets programs are incomplete (especially in the early years) and, on the occasions they have been collated, sometimes cover only Defence and sometimes both Defence and civil offsets. The main sources used here are Bureau of Industry Economics (BIE), Purcell, Howe and Dunne.[27] We present the available information in three sub-sections. First, we report figures related to the operation of the combined Civil-Defence Program between 1970 and 1984. This is based on data submitted to the Inglis Review as reported by the BIE.[28] Second, we consider data on Defence-related offsets during the period 1973/74–1990/91.[29] Third, we report data on Defence offsets in the 1980s and 1990s.[30]

Defence offsets performance can be assessed in terms of dollar values and acquittal rates or in terms of their success in meeting specified objectives. Analysis of the first kind is presented in 3.3.1. In principle, this should be a relatively unambiguous type of assessment. However, the available data is not very consistent and conclusions may vary depending on which source of information is used. The more controversial performance criteria in terms of value to Defence and the wider community in terms of program objectives are reviewed in 3.3.2.

3.3.1   Offsets Obligations and Acquittal Rates

3.3.1.1   The Combined Program 1970–1984

Table 1 contains an overview of civil and Defence offsets 1970–84 and shows that offsets commitments comprised 21.8 per cent of the value of contracts in relation to which offsets might have been sought.

Table 1: Summary of Offsets Program Performance 1970–1984

	Contract value AUS$m	Contract value for offsets purposes[a] AUS$m	Offsets commitment[b] AUS$m	Offsets achievement[c] AUS$m	Offsets completed[d] AUS$m
Civil	3058	2971	632	450	331
Defence	3845	2971	876[e]	252[e]	223[e]
Total	6903	5942	1508	702	554

Notes:
a. This is defined as the total contract value less the value of all Australian local content included in the contract for other than providing approved offsets.
b. This represents the value of offsets which prime contractors are committed to provide over an agreed period of time. The status of this commitment varied considerably between purchases, depending on the form of the contract and/or side agreement. In some cases, the prime contractor had agreed only to satisfy the offsets commitment on a 'best endeavours' basis.
c. This comprises orders placed by overseas companies for offsets work in Australia plus the value of technology transfers and other eligible activities.
d. This is the value of offsets orders and other activities actually completed by Australian industry.
e. This includes an unknown proportion of subsidised "designated defence work" which is not classified as offsets.

Source: BIE[31]

The table relating to both components of the program shows the low level of offsets delivered (orders placed) of AUS$702 million relative to offsets obligated (AUS$1,508 million) in the period 1970–84. This discrepancy was seen in the early 1980s as the major failure of the 'best endeavours' policy.

Table 2 shows offsets commitments and achievements by country. Of these commitments, worth AUS$1,508 million in current prices, the large majority (78.2 per cent) were borne by US contractors followed by UK (9.7 per cent), Federal Republic of Germany (4.6 per cent), Japan (3.4 per cent) and France (3.2 per cent).

Table 3 shows the industry distribution of offsets for the same period. The main area targeted by the Program was the aerospace industry (65 per cent of overall contract value, 53 per cent of offset obligations and 46 per cent of orders issued). Some 13 Australian firms undertook about 60 per cent of offsets work with Hawker de Havilland accounting for one third of offsets orders issued.

The local parts content of offsets related purchases was estimated at 25 per cent of offsets achieved (15 per cent for civil offsets). Local production of parts incorporated into international aerospace sales was about 50 per cent of offsets and technology transfer about ten per cent.[33]

Table 2: Offsets Commitments and Achievements by Country 1970–1984

Country	Commitments AUS$m	Achievements AUS$m
United States	1180	437
United Kingdom	146	131
FR Germany	70	48
Japan	51	24
France	48	49[a]
Other	13	13
Total	1508	702

Note:

a. Indicates that some companies have accumulated offsets credits in excess of the total commitments of all companies.

Source: BIE[32]

Table 3: Offsets Program Performance by Industry 1970–1984

(a)	Contract value for offsets purposes AUS$m (b)	Offsets commitment AUS$m (c)	Percentage commitment (c/b) % (d)	Offsets achievement (orders issued) AUS$m (e)	Percentage achievement (e/c) % (f)
Civil Aerospace	1945.4	340.3	17.5	238.2	70.0
Defence Aerospace	2011.3	590.6	29.4	138.7	23.5
Civil Shipbuilding	100.0	30.0	30.0	0.6	2.0
Defence Shipbuilding	620.3	154.3	24.9	27.4	17.8
Civil Vehicles and associated equipment	7.4	2.2	29.7	0.7	31.8
Military Vehicles and associated equipment	164.0	75.1	45.8	56.6	75.4
Telecommunications and radar equipment	570.0	166.6	29.2	126.8	76.1
Computing equipment	326.1	91.2	28.0	28.2	90.1
Machine tools	8.0	2.2	27.5	0.3	13.6
Earth moving equipment	0.8	0.2	30.0	0.2	67.0
Miscel. electrical and electronic equipment	104.7	31.8	30.4	10.7	33.6
Miscel. mechanical equipment	63.6	19.1	30.0	18.8	98.4
Miscel. industry and business machines	20.4	4.3	21.1	1.2	27.9
Total Defence	2971.0	876.4	29.5	252.0	28.8
Total Civil	2971.0	631.5	21.3	450.4	71.3
Grand Totals	5942.0	1507.9	25.4	702.4	46.6

Note: See Table 1 for definitions of terms. Percentages are based on unrounded figures.

Source: BIE[36]

3.3.1.2   Defence Offsets Between 1973/74 and 1990/91

Dunne analysed data relating to 254 major defence equipment contracts with AIPP/AII implications signed between 1973/74 and 1990/91.[34] At 1991 prices, these contracts were worth AUS$21,168 million, had an import content of AUS$10,124 million (an average of 48 per cent of the value of each contract), and generated offsets obligations of $3,568 million, of which 62 per cent had been met by 1991. Local production created by the Defence offsets policy was worth 0.25 per cent of all merchandise imports and 0.04 per cent of national output during this 17 year period.

By country of origin, over half (52 per cent) of contracts examined were placed in the USA and accounted for 40 per cent of the value of all projects analysed. Contracts placed in Australia comprised 45 per cent of aggregate project value but only 20 per cent of all projects. By contract value, France (5.1 per cent), West Germany (3.3 per cent) and the UK (2.6 per cent) trailed far behind and Japan (0.2 per cent) was the only Asian nation represented.

As for obligations and acquittals, offsets obligations by 1991 had been fully or more than fully discharged in only 37 per cent of the 254 projects Dunne examined. Over half of the projects were incomplete at the time of analysis but of those which were complete, less than 100 per cent of offsets obligations had been met in almost a third of cases and in 17 per cent of cases, no obligations at all had been discharged.

3.3.1.3   Defence Offsets in the 1980s and 1990s

Purcell analysed the value of Australian industry work secured under the Defence Offsets Program between 1 January 1986 and June 1990.[35] This was estimated at about AUS$855 million. The value of offsets obligations fluctuated from year to year with fluctuations in capital procurement. In 1988/89, the value of contracts involving offsets was AUS$96.1 million and new offsets obligations amounted to AUS$25.8 million. The corresponding figures for 1989/90 were AUS$3,914 million and AUS$346 million respectively, reflecting the impact of the ANZAC Ship Project. Tables 4–6 contain tabulated data on offsets obligations and local content in the 1980s and 1990s.

Table 4: 1990–91 Offsets Obligations and Industry-related Defence Spending

	Per cent	AUS $bn[1]
Defence budget	100	9.0
of which industry related expenditure	39	3.5
● local content	28	2.5
● imported content	11	1.0
Offsets	2	0.18

Note: [1]Rounded figures

Source: Purcell[37]

Table 5: Defence Spending with Industry: Local Content Achievement

	Early 1980s (per cent)	Early 1990s (per cent)
● Capital equipment	30	65
● Repair and maintenance	75	85–95
● Replacement equipment and spares	75	75
● All spending with Australian industry	45	70

Source: Purcell[38]

Table 6: Real Defence Spending on Capital Equipment and Offsets Obligations 1980–81 to 1989–90

Annual averages in constant 1991 prices		
	AUS$bn	Change in AUS$m
● Defence budget	8.5	+125
● Spending on capital equipment	2.0	+80
● Imported capital equipment	1.2	–15
● Offsets obligations	0.37	–4

Source: Purcell[39]

The relationship between offsets obligations and the relevant ('industry-related') defence spending in 1990/91 is shown in Table 4. This assumes offsets obligations to be about 18 per cent of the imported content of 'industry-related' goods and services, i.e., the gross value of offset obligations (30 per cent) reduced to take into account purchases below the AUS$2.5 million (imported content) threshold and the multiplier rebates. Overall, the 'net offsets obligations' are equivalent to some two per cent of the total budget and seven per cent of the local content.

Since the mid-1970s, the local content in Defence equipment procurement, measured in real dollars, has increased considerably (from an initially small base). Table 5 shows high levels of local content achieved in the 1990s and Table 6 shows the implications of rising local content in projects for offsets obligations. The latter table shows a declining trend in imports and therefore offsets. Also, with the growing share of local content in capital procurement, the current level of offsets obligations is well below the average for the 1980s.

The large decline in the share of the imported content of capital equipment in the 1980s, and, thus, the illustrated decline in the value of offsets obligations, reflects the impact of a small number of relatively large, by Australian standards, projects with high local content. As commitments to these large projects account for over 60 per cent of the current Five Year Defence Plan funding, it is unlikely that the imported content of Defence purchases will continue to decline rapidly in the 1990s. In view of Australia's dependence on imported technology, the retention of the 60–70 per cent local content ratio over the next decade would represent a considerable achievement for the home industry.

Purcell notes that the presently available time series of offsets obligations and acquittals are not readily amenable to statistical analysis.[40] In particular, the year-on-year variations have been large and difficult to interpret. Nevertheless, using the available statistics, Purcell estimates that in the decade to 1989–90, it is estimated that the 'raw' (historic) value of contracts with Australian Industry Involvement was AUS$13 billion. Leaving aside considerations of the value for money (in terms of Defence priorities) and the timeliness of offsets acquittals, the 'raw value' of offsets obligations was AUS$2 billion during that period and acquittals AUS$825 million — yielding an acquittal rate of over 40 per cent.

Despite the difficulty of tracking offsets acquittals relative to obligations, Howe shows there was an improvement in the acquittal rate between 1970–80 and 1980–86.[41] This is not surprising, considering the steps which were taken to tighten offsets arrangements. For the period 1986–92, historic data are likely to offer only an imprecise indication of the acquittal rate achieved because of imperfections in our knowledge of the lag structure involved. Anecdotal evidence, however, suggests it will have risen.

Table 7 contains the most up to date estimates of offsets obligations and available at the time of writing. The table shows the 'raw value' of pre-January 1986 offsets obligations (AUS$956 million) to be some 31 per cent of the corresponding imported content of projects (AUS$3,090 million). The 'raw' offsets achievement rate appears to be 94 per cent. Whilst some offsets obligations have not been acquitted, others were exceeded and some offsets credits were earned. For the post January 1986 period, offsets obligations (AUS$1,393 million) were about 38 per cent of the corresponding imported content of projects (AUS$3,710 million). By mid 1993, some 29 per cent of the post-January 1986 offsets obligations have been achieved. The overall 'raw' acquittal rate (pre and post 1986) is about 56 per cent. This appears to be significantly higher than the earlier estimates reported above.

Table 7: Offset Obligations and Achievements

	AUS$million					
Financial Year Totals[1,2]	**Contract Value**	**Aust. Content**	**AIPP or AII in Contracts[4]**	**Imported Content Value**	**Offsets Obligations**	**Offsets Achieved**
to 30 Jun 80	954.629	0.000	163.083	481.606	163.083	148.912
1980/81	155.081	0.000	24.478	28.935	24.478	29.895
1981/82 (F/A-18 Project)	2,510.064	0.678	800.733	2,151.358	557.631	492.775
1982/83	140.172	0.920	47.867	61.269	46.947	62.662
1983/84	105.087	0.000	31.260	19.372	31.260	31.804
1984/85	111.663	0.000	37.277	79.915	37.277	44.658
to 31 Dec 85	313.955	17.976	143.230	267.555	95.425	89.238
Grand Totals for Contracts, Pre 1 Jan 86	4,290.651	19.574	1,247.928	3,090.010	956.101	899.944
01 Jan 86–30 Jun 86	889.419	16.927	249.188	510.517	195.259	94.641
1986/87 (Submarine Project)[3]	3,328.545	1,955.570	2,723.866	875.218	287.604	153.216
1987/88	653.686	420.528	453.403	270.809	27.375	21.139
1988/89	363.094	22.490	136.960	282.191	111.078	88.961
1989/90 (Frigate Project)	3,908.221	2,799.313	4,108.469	1,063.358	560.453	40.041
1990/91	1,134.554	578.658	724.452	469.844	143.693	7.529
1991/92	171.336	58.104	79.207	81.716	21.103	3.267
1992/93	187.101	51.294	97.745	156.220	46.451	0.000
Grand Totals for Contracts Post 1 Jan 86	1,0635.956	5,902.884	8,573.290	3,709.873	1,393.016	408.794

Notes:
1. Totals include projects where offsets are not required
2. Some project details not available
3. No offsets against submarine platform
4. AIPP pre 1 January 1986 and AII post 1 January 1986 (see Section 3.2)

Source: Unpublished figures. Defence Industry Committee Report 1993.[43]

3.3.2 Offsets Performance and Offsets Policy Criteria

To measure the perceived value of offsets, Howe identified 1386 tasks undertaken between 1970 and 1992,[42] and sought expert advice on their perceived worth to Defence or the community at large in terms of:

a.   level of contribution to the through-life support of the parent equipment;
b.   technology transfer effects;
c.   degree of "national benefit", i.e., benefits from offsets obligations flowing not to Defence but the wider community;
d.   formal training implications;
e.   relatedness to the parent project; and
f.   R&D implications.

On performance criteria (a)–(c) weights were allocated on a scale of 1 (lowest) to 5; on (d)–(f) simple Yes/No answers were sought. To derive a very rough indication of trends, the full period was divided into two 1970–1986 (997 tasks) and 1986–1992 (389 tasks).

The results are considered from two angles: first the proportion of all offsets tasks which were considered to have made any positive contribution in terms of given criteria; second, the level (low, medium or high) at which offsets which made such a contribution were perceived to have been effective. (The second angle could only be taken in relation to criteria (a)–(c)).

From the first angle, the two attributes of offsets which were perceived to have occurred at positive levels with greatest frequency in 1970–1986 were "national benefit" and "relatedness to project", 77 and 84 per cent respectively. These two were also the only attributes to show declines in frequency between the earlier and later (1986–92) periods, to 48 and 74 per cent respectively. The perceived positive incidence of all other attributes of offsets thus increased, through-life support from 58 to 62 per cent, technology transfer from 20 to 56 per cent, tasks involving training from 5 to 20 per cent and those involving R&D scoring below ten per cent in both sub-periods.

From the second angle it is striking that, whatever the attribute chosen, the value of offsets when positive has nevertheless been perceived to be predominantly low. This was true in both sub-periods for technological transfer and national benefit dimensions and markedly so for through-life support in the earlier sub-period. Since 1986 however, the through-life support aspect of offsets has come to be dominantly medium- and high- valued.

Putting both first and second perspectives together:

a.   the generally low level of national benefit reaped from offsets reflects the perception that they have done little to enhance Australia's export potential;
b.   over half of the offset tasks have contributed little or no strategic benefit to Defence self-reliance;
c.   over three quarters of tasks have little or no value in terms of transferring technology (a very low return on investment in technology transfer).

Leaving aside for a moment the actual cost of offsets requirements to the portfolio or the taxpayer, Howe's analysis cast doubts on the utility of offsets outcomes to Defence ("strategic benefit to Defence self-reliance"). The analysis also casts doubt on the value of external benefit of Defence offsets to the community at large. Further, "national benefits", which are not a requirement of the Defence Offsets Program (external benefits) may be obtained in lieu of Defence-related benefits.

In sum, benefits (to Defence) from the Offsets Program "remain somewhat indistinct".[44] Offsets proposals have largely been driven by suppliers rather than initiated on the basis of well defined ADF support requirements and reporting of achievements is not mandated by either contractor or Defence. The supplier predominance even extends into the structuring of some project reporting systems.[45] Also, there has been a lack of clarity about which of the offsets criteria are primary and those which are enabling. "Current thinking is that critical capabilities which must be provided in country are the proper province of project deliverables whereas sustaining beyond the life of a project might be encouraged by separate arrangements".[46] Key issues that must be addressed here concern the supportability of capability proposals on strategic grounds, the extent of industry's capability to provide the required level of support, and the extent to which Defence may use its leverage in negotiating the prime contract to secure priority capabilities in industry.[47]

The shift away from civil offsets and their replacement by Partnerships in Development, Long Term Agreements and Import Facilitation Programs suggests that in the absence of offsets there may in any case be a basis for procurement leverage on suppliers to demonstrate their commitment to the Australian market.[48] The key issue here is that any procurement mechanism used should be customer- rather than supplier-driven. This means that the policy focus should be on the identification of support priorities for Australian industry and flexibility in procurement to maximise the customer benefit rather than the application of mandatory provisions such as the 1988 ADOP scheme.

If offsets were a 'free good' as stipulated in 1989 Guidelines, any positive benefit accruing to Defence on the taxpayer could be regarded as a bonus. For example, from the calculations presented in Table 5, Purcell concludes that offsets resulted in "the budget add on" of two per cent in 1990–91.[49] Thus, "it can be seen that there is a 'free good' to Defence" and, by implication, the table demonstrates "why offsets are potentially so useful to Defence".[50]

This appears to be a classic case of the 'free lunch' fallacy. Under the 1989 Guidelines, offsets are meant to be provided at no extra cost to Defence, they are thus assumed to be a 'free good'. The relevant question that has not been asked in this case is this: what would have been the total cost of goods and services obtained under the 'imported content' plus obligated offsets (in the illustrated case AUS$2.5 bn.) in the absence of the mandatory offsets scheme? If, in lieu of the mandatory offsets obligations, Defence were able to negotiate price discounts on the imported content and pay for the offsets goods and services separately, it is not unlikely that the total cost of the two separate packages could be less than AUS$2.5 billion spent on the combined package. In such a case, the apparent 'free lunch' of AUS$0.18 billion may obscure a real loss to the taxpayer from forgoing price discounts on the imported content which might have exceeded AUS$0.18 billion. It is only if it can be demonstrated that the opportunity cost of the mandatory offsets scheme to Defence is less than AUS$0.18 billion that it could be argued that "offsets are potentially so useful to Defence" All that is presupposes that the value of offsets to the ADF is at least equal their obligated value — an assertion that remains to be validated.

The administration of offsets also results in costs to Defence. Howe estimates that administrative monitoring costs alone for the offsets scheme run to at least AUS$1.5 million per year. Other cost may be imposed on Defence by contractors.[51]

What the above examples show, even if offsets are entirely free to Defence, which is certainly not the case, the purpose of all policy is to raise the level of social net benefit which is found by looking at impacts on both costs and benefits. Thus, acquiring something 'free' if it generates only modest or negligible net benefits may compare unfavourable with acquiring instead something at a positive cost (if the net benefits are more substantial).

The international trade policy aspects of the ADOP is also important in determining procurement policies. Whilst some recent major acquisitions of platforms have been of European origin, the USA continues to be the predominant supplier of technologically advanced weapons systems. With the recent contracting of US domestic defence markets, there has been considerable Congressional pressure to shelter US defence contractors from overseas offsets demands. Thus, there has been considerable pressure to take into account various aspects of US-Australia defence trade in the design of Australian procurement mechanisms, such as offsets.

Since 1988, in response to the protectionist sentiments in the USA, a defence trade Memorandum of Agreement (MOA) has been discussed between the US and Australian Departments of Defence. The MOA would provide an umbrella waiver of the US Buy American Act for Australian producers in lieu of the present case-by-case approach (but not necessarily an automatic exclusion from other US protectionist measures). Seventeen US allies (mainly NATO) have similar agreements.[52] At present, Australia is unique among US allies in "having a MOA with the US Government which acknowledges that suppliers to

Australia through the Foreign Military Sales (FMS) system may be obligated to offsets".[53] Also, the USA has been encouraging Australia to consider the membership of the Government Procurement Code. Australia was not previously eligible for the Code membership due to the operation of the Commonwealth purchasing preference margin. With its adherence to the GATT principles, Australia may find it increasingly difficult to resist Code membership.[54]

Australia has no equivalent of the multilateral NATO Conference of National Armament Directors (CNAD) or the Independent European Program Group (IEPG), which facilitate intra European and US collaboration in defence production, R&D and procurement. Australia has MOUs in place with the USA on a case-by-case basis and bilateral umbrella MOUs on defence equipment procurement with the UK, New Zealand, Sweden and Norway. There MOUs tend to facilitate exchange of information on procurement and the scope for industry collaboration.[55] Often international pressures on Australian policies of support for Defence-oriented industry have more to do with the need for bureaucratic cultures to communicate than with security or economics.[56] For example, the US concept of "defence industrial base" and the "critical technologies list" — which have no counterpart in Australian defence planning — may impede Defence trade negotiations between the two countries. It is also worth noting that Australia does not attract, or seek, concessional arrangements in the form of aid which suppliers often have to provide to their poorer customers.

3.4   Broader Policy Goals and Offsets

It has been argued by us elsewhere that offsetting requirements are often part of normal contracting arrangements between businesses in that many commercial transactions involve the exchange of packages of goods and services whereby the purchase or sale of certain goods or services is contingent on the tied purchase/sale of some other products. In that sense, 'offsets' are an aspect of the normal transactional reprocity between willing buyers and sellers.[57]

All commercial transactors are free to adopt policies that prescribe the sort of contractual arrangements, including various offsetting arrangements, that they require from contractors. Government procurement agencies seeking to engage suppliers in such arrangements are doing nothing different from normal market operators. In the world of imperfect markets, complex transactions and asymmetrical information flows, it is possible that some such compensatory or offsetting requirements, including elements of barter countertrade, will enhance the welfare of the purchaser. This can only be assessed on a case-by-case basis.

Both commercial operators and governments are free to adopt mandatory 'offsets' policies whereby they refuse to transact with suppliers unwilling or unable to offer enhanced packages of goods or services supposedly at no extra cost to the purchaser. When such demands are so inflexible as to insist on an 'in kind' package enhancement rather than the equivalent or greater price discount — they are clearly inefficient. Operating such inflexible policies can only serve to handicap the buyer by restricting its ability to negotiate the most advantageous price-content-quality combination.

An important difference however between business organisations and governments is that few of the former would insist on applying mandatory offsets requirements that fly in the face of commercial self-interest. By contrast, there is evidence that governments have persisted with mandatory offsets obligations, for reasons which are essentially political.

In 1992, in their contribution to the review of the ADOP, the present authors argued that the preferred approach should be to adopt a stance consistent with a flexible and efficient procurement system in which government negotiators would be free to seek offsets if it were to the greatest advantage of Defence to have them, but otherwise to bargain for price discounts.[58] An obvious policy implication was that Defence should scrap the mandatory ADOP and instead instruct its procurement organisation to develop a procurement system that was customer-driven and oriented.

Since then, the mandatory Defence offsets Program has been relegated to a status in which it will be used only when it is of benefit to Defence (see above). We are certainly encouraged by this policy development. Although, various industrial vested pressure groups may see the move to flexible application of offsets requirements as detrimental to their parochial interests, it seems appropriate to conclude this paper with a quotation from one of the captains of the Australian defence industry:

"For me and for the great many of those in the industry, it is more appropriate to talk about the total package, which now goes under the heading of Australian Industry Involvement be that local content, designated work, or offsets. Quite frankly, very few of my colleagues bother to consider the esoteric differences between these. To them it is all work which is related to orders from the Defence Department to exacting standards and specifications demanding considerable technical and management skills and requiring considerable investment (in both financial and manpower terms)".[59]

Endnotes

1. Todd, A., **Defence Industries, A Global Perspective**, Routledge, London and New York, 1988, p. 226.

2. Ford, J., **Scitech Technology Directory, A Comprehensive Guide to Technology and Industry Development Assistance in Australia**, Scitech Publications Pty Ltd, Canberra 1990, p. 16.

3. DoD, **Defence Policy and Industry**, Report to the Minister for Defence, Department of Defence, Canberra, Nov. 1992.

4. White Paper, **The Defence of Australia 1987**, A Policy Information Paper, Department of Defence, AGPS, Canberra, 1987.

5. *Ibid.*, p. 76.

6. *Ibid.*, p. 76

7. Wood, D. and Carthigaser, T., **The History of Defence Offsets**, Defence Offsets Working Papers, Department of Defence, Canberra, May 1992.

8. *Ibid.*

9. Financial Review, 2 April 1970.

10. Stanier, R.M., The F/A-18 Hornet Industry Program, **Journal of the Royal United Services Institute of Australia**, August, 1990.

11. JCPA, **Implementation of the Offsets Program**, Joint Committee of Public Accounts, Report 270, The Parliament of the Commonwealth of Australia, AGPS, Canberra, 1987.

12. BIE, **Monitoring of the Offsets Program**, First Report, Bureau of Industry Economics, AGPS, Canberra, 1987.

13. DoD, **Doing Australian Defence Business**, Department of Defence, AGPS, Canberra, 1987.

14. Stanier, *op. cit.*

15. Guidelines, **Australian Defence Offsets Program, Guidelines for Participants**, Department of Defence, October 1989.

16. DoD, **Report on the Results of an Industry Survey Undertaken to Determine the Benefits flowing to Australian Industry as a Result of the Department of Defence's Australian Industry Involvement Program**, Department of Defence, July 1991.

17. Guidelines, *op. cit.*, p. 51.

18. Guidelines, *op. cit.*, p. 51.

19. DoD, 1991, *op. cit.*, p. 20.

20. Guidelines, *op. cit.*, p. 11.

21. Guidelines, *op. cit.*, p. 52.

22. DoD, 1991, *op. cit.*, p. 18.

23. Ford, *op. cit.*, p. 16.

24. Guidelines, *op. cit.*, p. 24.

25. Wood and Carthigaser, *op. cit.*

26. Price, R., **Defence Policy for Industry**, Canberra, 1992, p. 24.

27. BIE, *op. cit*; Purcell, P., **Assessing the Performance of the Defence Offsets Program — Part I**, Defence Offsets Working Papers, Department of Defence, Canberra, May 1992; Howe, P., **Assessing the Performance of the Defence Offsets Program — Part II**, Defence Offsets Working Papers, Department of Defence, Canberra, 1992; Dunne, R., **Statistical Analysis of Offsets Data, Appendix 1**, in Howe (1992).

28. BIE, *op. cit.*

29. Dunne, *op. cit.*

30. Purcell and Howe, *op. cit.*

31. BIE, *op. cit.*, Table 1, p. 39.

32. BIE, *op. cit.*, Table 3, p. 42.

33. BIE, *op. cit.*

34. Dunne, *op. cit.*

35. Purcell *op. cit.*

36. BIE, *op. cit.*, Table 2, p. 41.

37. Purcell *op. cit.*, Table 2, p. 4.

38. Purcell *op. cit.*, Table 1, p. 3.

39. Purcell op. cit., Table 4, p. 6.

40. Purcell *op. cit.*

41. Howe, *op. cit.*

42. Howe, *op. cit.*

43. Defence Industry Committee Report 1993, Department of Defence, Canberra.

44. Purcell, P., **Pressures for Change on the Defence Offsets Program**, Defence Offsets Working Papers, Department of Defence, Canberra, May 1992, p. 4.

45. *Ibid.*

46. Purcell, P., **Options for Change from Current Offset Arrangements**, Defence Offsets Working Papers, Department of Defence, Canberra, May 1992.

47. *Ibid.*

48. *Ibid.*

49. Purcell, **Assessing the Performance of the Defence Offsets Program — Part I**, *op. cit.*

50. *Ibid.*, p. 4.

51. Howe, *op. cit.*

52. Purcell, **Pressures for Change on the Defence Offsets Program**, *op. cit.*

53. *Ibid.*, p. 11.

54. *Ibid.*

55. Purcell, **Options for Change from Current Offset Arrangements**, *op. cit.*

56. *Ibid.*

57. Hall, P. and Markowski, S., 'On the Normality and Abnormality of Offsets Obligations', **Defence and Peace Economics**, Vol 5, 1994, pp. 173–188.

58. Hall, P. and Markowski, S., **The Anatomy of Defence Offsets Obligations**, Discussion Paper 1/92, Centre for Studies in Management and Logistics, University College, University of New South Wales, Australian Defence Force Academy, 1992.

59. Meibush, I., **A View from Industry**, Defence Offsets Working Papers, Department of Defence, Canberra, May 1992, p. 1.

Chapter 4

Offsets and Weapons Procurement: The Belgium Experience[1]

Wally Struys
Royal Military Academy, Brussels

4.1 The Economic Constraints Imposed by Belgium's Weapons Procurement

Before the crisis of the 1970s, the Belgian armament industry was relatively prosperous and offered close to 30,000 units of direct employment and more than 40,000 of indirect employment. However, employment levels fell dramatically in the 1980s, as is shown by Table 1.

Table 1: Employment in the Belgian Defence Industry

Year	Total Employment	Direct Employment
1980	42000	27000
1981	45000	28000
1982	37000	27000
1983	44000	27000
1984	39000	28000
1985	33000	25000
1986	28000	22000
1987	26000	18000
1988	23000	17000
1989	20000	15000
1990	17000	13000
1991	15000	11000

Source: Memento défense-désarmement 1992 — L'Europe et la sécurité internationale, Les Dossiers du Grip, No. 168–171, Avril-Juillet 1992, p. 259.

Direct employment refers to persons who:

- are active in the production of goods and services in companies that deliver specifically military final goods to the MoD,

- directly deliver to the MoD goods and services that differ only slightly from those offered on civilian markets; logically, sub-contractors and those who deliver supplies to sub-contractors could also be included in this category.

Indirect employment includes:

- persons active in the production of goods and services offered upstream from companies providing direct employment,
- employment generated by the purchases of those who have received revenues linked to defence expenditures.

4.1.1 Characteristics of the Belgian Defence Industry at the End of the 1970s

Like other European countries, Belgium has a fragmented defence market and a national defence base that is limited by its relatively small defence budget. Before the drastic cuts of the 1990s, the MoD's budget was approximately BEF 103 billion. Since the definitions of the national defence budgets diverge radically from country to country, comparisons are only possible when using a common interpretation. In order to underline the modest defence effort of a small country, we can use the NATO definition of defence spending to compare Belgium's budget with the defence expenditures of France, the UK and the USA: in 1990 Belgium spent BEF 155.21 billion, France spent BEF 1426.81 billion, the UK spent BEF 1336.29 billion and the USA spent BEF 10229.14 billion.

Unlike their counterparts in larger countries, defence firms in Belgium cannot survive on domestic weapons procurement alone. They specialise in light armament and ammunitions (see Table 2) and export mainly to Third World countries (see Table 3). Their degree of specialisation is so high that they are

Table 2: Belgium's Defence Turnover: Estimated Distribution by Sector

Sectors	Average Turnover 86–87 (in BEF billion)	%
Small arms and ammunition	20.2	50
Vehicles and mechanical engineering	8.2	20
Electronics	6.4	16
Aeronautics	4.2	10
Shipyards	1.5	4
Total	40.5	100

Source: Adam B, La production d'armements en Belgique, GRIP, Dossier "Notes et Documents", No. 139, Bruxelles, Novembre 1989, p. 19.

Table 3: Belgium's Defence Production and Exports

<table>
<tr><td colspan="4" align="center">Production and Export of Armaments in Belgium
(in BEF billion and in constant 1990 prices)</td></tr>
<tr><td>Year</td><td>Turnover</td><td>Total Export</td><td>Share of Export to the
Third World</td></tr>
<tr><td></td><td>(1)</td><td>(2)</td><td>(3)</td></tr>
<tr><td>1980</td><td>56.3</td><td>20.3</td><td>87%</td></tr>
<tr><td>1981</td><td>60.5</td><td>25.1</td><td>89%</td></tr>
<tr><td>1982</td><td>53.7</td><td>21.3</td><td>86%</td></tr>
<tr><td>1983</td><td>64.7</td><td>34.3</td><td>86%</td></tr>
<tr><td>1984</td><td>58.0</td><td>28.5</td><td>79%</td></tr>
<tr><td>1985</td><td>52.4</td><td>21.5</td><td>84%</td></tr>
<tr><td>1986</td><td>46.6</td><td>14.8</td><td>75%</td></tr>
<tr><td>1987</td><td>43.9</td><td>14.6</td><td>70%</td></tr>
<tr><td>1988</td><td>42.0</td><td>12.8</td><td>na</td></tr>
<tr><td>1989</td><td>37.2</td><td>10.3</td><td>na</td></tr>
<tr><td>1990</td><td>32.6</td><td>6.5</td><td>na</td></tr>
<tr><td>1991*</td><td>31.4</td><td>7.3</td><td>na</td></tr>
</table>

Note: *The 1991 figures are estimates.

Sources:
(1) and (2)   Memento défense-désarmement 1992 – L'Europe et la sécurité
internationale, Les Dossiers du GRIP, No. 168–171, Avril-Juillet 1992, p. 259.
(3)   Ministry of Foreign Affairs and GRIP. Table published in Adam, B. Zaks, A. et De
Vestel, P., Contexte et perspectives de restructuration de l'industrie de l'armement
en Wallonie, GRIP, Dossier "Notes et Documents", No. 161–162, Bruxelles,
Septembre–Octobre 1991, p. 9.

extremely vulnerable to fluctuations in military demand. For most of them, even the support of substantial exports is, however, too limited to make their defence activities profitable in a competitive market. As a result, the defence industry depends heavily on government contracts or on subsidies.

Belgium's defence industry is, for an important part, composed of companies that manufacture minor military products and firms that are heavily involved in producing or assembling parts, components and sub-systems into final military goods. The level of concentration is very high: in the 1980s, the four biggest firms accounted for more than 60% of the total defence turnover, and the top ten firms for more than 80%. Due to its modest size (see Tables 1 and 3), and to the time-lags between uncertain orders, the defence industry is very sensitive to cyclical fluctuations. Not only is the market for defence equipment bound to be uncertain, it is also more and more constrained by severe competition. Today, defence production is estimated at some 0.2 to 0.3% of GDP, versus 1% ten years ago.

The defence industry's relatively small size is responsible for obvious fundamental weaknesses such as limited production runs, diseconomies of scale, and a lack of social flexibility. The existence of only limited co-operation on an *ad hoc* basis (e.g. subcontracting for the production of parts or sub-systems in the framework of only one contract) has also contributed to the weakness of the defence industry.

Table 4 provides information on the size and significance of defence work for the most important defence companies prior to the major changes that

Table 4: Description of the Largest Belgian Defence Firms

	Employment (1987–1989)		Average Total Turnover (in BEF billion)	Estimated Share of Defence Work (in %)
	Total	**Defence**	**1986–1987**	**1986–1987**
Small Arms and Ammunition				
FN Group	6016	4456	17.9	60
PRB	1500	1500	4.4	90
MECAR	295	295	1.5	100
FZ	561	561	1.8	100
CMI	1932	386	7.3	20
Vehicles and Mechanical Engineering				
BMF	300	300	6.3	100
Aeronautics				
SABCA	1542	879	3.4	70
SONACA	1316	921	2.4	57
Shipyards				
Mercantile-Beliard	2201	440	5.4	20
Electronics				
ACEC	3778	567	11.7	15
MBLE	724	250	11.3	8

Source: See Table 2

occurred at the end of the 1980s and the beginning of the 1990s. All these firms were privately owned, with the exception of SONACA, a semi-public company, and CMI, a completely State-controlled firm. Until 1987, most of the defence industry was controlled by Belgian capital; two-thirds of all defence activities belonged to the largest holding company in the country, the Société Générale de Belgique (SGB). MECAR was a 100% subsidiary of Allied Research Corporation (USA), MBLE belonged entirely to Philips (Netherlands), and of SABCA's capital, 53% was held by Dassault Belgique Aviation, a subsidiary of Dassault (France), and 42.8% was held by Fokker (Netherlands).

A small country like Belgium cannot afford to maintain a defence industry capable of producing a complete range of weaponry. Entire programmes, covering the research, development, and production of defence goods, are prohibitively expensive for Belgium. The domestic market is too small, and the export opportunities are limited. As a result, indigenous development and production would be excessively costly. Moreover, the risks involved with R&D projects, taking into account the available resources, would also be excessive. Indigenous programmes are, therefore, not feasible.

However, the procurement of armaments from countries with a large defence base provides Belgium with access to sophisticated, relatively low-cost weapon systems. In the past few decades, most of the foreign acquisitions originated in the USA. When buying US weapons, one of two procedures can be chosen: Foreign Military Sales (FMS) which have to be negotiated with the Defense Security Assistance Agency (DSAA) or direct commercial procurement from US firms. Being a government-to-government transaction in which a foreign government transmits a letter of intent to buy a specified weapon system, a FMS is similar to a domestic US procurement inasmuch as the same regulations cover both. FMS is also useful for foreign governments that feel more comfortable with a process in which the DoD handles all of the administrative work.

The Belgian government, however, never seriously considered FMS purchases as a regular way of buying weapons, even if downright FMS procurement offers, at first sight, numerous interesting advantages: the risks are minimal, it is easier to write-off the investment, and the army could operate a sophisticated weapon system that Belgium could not afford to develop itself. The reason for the rejection of the FMS option is that the secondary effects of weapon procurement are extremely important for Belgian industry. Since the most important economic aspect of defence is found in the field of armaments' acquisition, Belgium's economic policy has always included the need to ensure some economic fall-out for the national economy, instead of entirely "exporting" it to the seller's country.

As a result, and taking into account that opportunities to participate in an integrated R&D and production programme are very rare, successive Belgian governments have, since the 1960s, chosen to deal directly with foreign suppliers. This enables domestic industry to participate in the production of weapon systems. In most cases, this participation has been based on integrated international production, without participation in the R&D phase.

In the beginning, some emphasis was laid on production under licence, which can be advantageous when generating exports to third countries. However, because of the limited production run for the domestic market, this approach often entailed considerable additional expense. Moreover, the rather well developed Belgian industry was frustrated by the fact that it had to produce according to foreign plans and engineering data only. The rising cost of equipment, and mounting competitive problems, led Belgium to broaden its demand for economic compensation, with demands for technology transfer, import substitution and co-development economic offset agreements.

Since the late 1960s, Belgian decision-makers have increasingly resorted to co-production on the basis of bilateral and multilateral agreements. In these cases, R&D is centralised, and the production is distributed among several participants in the programme. This formula is more profitable, since it can be combined with an offset policy, which implies that new orders can be placed with Belgian companies within the framework of the procurement contract.

As a consequence, Belgium has become a champion of procurement abroad with offsets.[2] This solution involves large international production projects based on a common need. The achievement of part of the activities is entrusted to one or more Belgian firms. Due to the scope of the project and the amount of sub-assemblies to be produced, these projects are very much appreciated by the industry. They create an opening in the international market and pave the way for later co-production.

Table 5 shows the recent major acquisition programmes of the MoD, with their distribution of offsets between direct and semi-direct on the one hand, and indirect on the other hand, as well as the regional distribution. Due to the fact that the offset policy is always subject to heavy criticism, no official figures could be provided by the authorities. The offset shares reported in Table 5 originate from the press. Since the 1970s, Belgium's offset requirements have been set at a minimum of 50%, but actual agreements often achieved between 70 and 100%. In recent years, even these higher figures have been surpassed, as shown in Table 5.

Table 5: Recent Major Acquisition Programmes and Associated Offsets

Year	Programme	Original value (in BEF billion)	Offset value (in %)	Offset distribution (in % of total offsets)		Regional distribution (in % of total offsets)		
				Direct and semi-direct	Indirect	Brussels	Flanders	Wallonia
1976	CMT	12.4	96	58	42	—	—	—
1980	AIFV	21.8	100	70	30	8	50	42
1983	M 109	6.5	90.6	100	—	3	65	32
1983	F-16 FOB	45.3	58.8	62.7	37.3	14.5	37.5	48
1985	Iltis Jeeps	2.1	300	6.5	93.5	7	52.4	40.6
1986	Volvo Trucks	4.3	500	21.6–32	68–78.4	0–5	80±3	20±2
1988	Mistral	2.9	100	75	25	7.82	52.75	39.43
1988	Agusta Helicopter	11.9	73	63	37	6–10	45–55	35–45
1989	Carapace Msl	5.3	80	66	34	6–10	53–63	30–40

Source: Belgian Press

4.1.2 The Recent Upheaval of the Belgian Defence Sector

It was already essential at the beginning of the 1980s to rationalise production and the allocation of resources in the field of armament production, but the sector had to wait until 1988 to undergo drastic changes. After most defence firms recorded losses in 1986 and 1987, it became clear in 1988 that the defence industry could not continue to function as it had done, given its structural handicaps. At the same time, Belgium witnessed the aborted take-over bid for the SGB by Carlo de Benedetti, followed by the acquisition of a majority shareholding in the capital of SGB by the French Group Suez. Subsequent to these events, important rationalisations started to take place in the defence sector.

Profound restructuring led to a spectacular sale of shares to foreign firms, mainly French, British, American and Dutch. Since 1989, more than 50% of the turnover of the "Belgian" defence industry has been under the direct or indirect control of French financial groups. FN-Moteurs, the aero-engine department of the FN Group, was sold to SNECMA (France) in June 1989, and changed its name to Techspace Aero in October 1992. At the time of writing, SNECMA holds 51% of the capital, the other shareholders being the Walloon Region (30%) and Pratt & Whitney (19%). FN re-organised its other activities around its "Defence and Security" department and its subsidiary Browning. The civilian production departments were eliminated and their activities gradually abandoned. In order to avoid winding up the business, FN Herstal was sold to Giat in December 1990. A new company was created: FNNH (Fabrique Nationale Nouvelle Herstal) took over all Defence and Security activities. Most (90%) of the capital of FNNH is owned by the French firm Giat with the remainder held by the Walloon Region.

PRB (Poudreries Réunies de Belgique) was Belgium's second largest armaments manufacturer and produced ammunition and propellant charges for guns, howitzers and mortars. It had five production facilities. It had a subsidiary, FZ (Forges de Zeebrugge), a manufacturer of missiles and ammunition. However, SGB, its major shareholder, neglected PRB's strategy and management. At the beginning of important financial difficulties in 1986, SGB pooled PRB with its other chemical activities in a new company, GECHEM. In the meantime, in December 1988, new capital was injected into the GECHEM Group, with SGB increasing its ownership share from 80% to 90%.

Unfortunately, the pooling of PRB with GECHEM turned out to be a disaster. The GECHEM Group decided, in November 1988, to sell off PRB which employed 1,900 persons after laying off 330 employees in 1987. In 1989, PRB was sold to the British Astra concern, which induced more dismissals, bringing down the number of employees to some 1,500 (from 2,500 in 1983). FZ was taken over by the French Thomson Brandt Armaments in the same year.

After examining PRB's debts and investment requirements, Astra proclaimed that it had been misled by PRB's management. As a result, SGB and Astra quarrelled continuously about the financial terms of the deal, and Astra eventually refused to finance any further investment in the company, which led, in 1990, to bankruptcy and the dismantling of PRB. Its assets were sold off piece by piece. The factory in Matagne was sold to MECAR, the facilities at Clermont were sold to the French firm SNPE (Société Nationale des Poudres et Explosifs), Kaulille was "demilitarised" and sold to a civilian firm, and Balen and Kaulille were dismantled.

ACEC (Ateliers de Construction Electriques de Charleroi) was near bankruptcy in 1988. In 1989, the company's activities were gradually dismantled and sold in four parts. The transportation and energy departments were acquired by the French Alsthom, a subsidiary of CGE. The defence division of ACEC, ACEC-SDT (Space, Defence, Telecommunications) merged with Alcatel-Bell, entirely belonging to the Dutch Alcatel NV, that was in turn controlled by the French firm CGE with 61.5% of the shares. At first, ACEC kept a minority share of 20% in the new Alcatel Bell-SDT company, which tried to focus its activities more on the civilian market, especially in the field of mobile telecommunications and space electronics. The other shareholders were Alcatel Bell Téléphone (55%) and the SRIW (Société Régionale d'Investissement de Wallonie — Walloon Regional Investment Company) (25%). Today, Alcatel Bell Téléphone owns 75% of the shares and the SRIW 25%.

MBLE was a 100% subsidiary of Philips. In January 1990, Thomson CSF (France) acquired close to 50% of Philips' defence activities. In the framework of this agreement, MBLE Défense (military telecommunications) was created with Thomson CSF becoming a 40% shareholder and Philips 60%.

OIP went bankrupt in December 1988 and was bought by Oldelft (Netherlands). A new firm, owned by Oldelft with 52% of the shares, OIP-INSTRUBEL, was created.

It is interesting to observe that SONACA has been one of the few Belgian companies which has successfully reduced its exposure to defence contracts. SONACA is now almost entirely State-owned (95% owned by the Walloon Region and 5% by the SRIW (Société Régionale d'Investissement de Wallonie — Walloon Regional Investment Company)). SONACA managed to increase its civilian production through its participation in the Airbus project.

4.2 Economic Compensations (Offsets) and the Belgian Economy[3]

4.2.1 Definition and Classification

The result of the above-mentioned policy is that offsets (called "economic compensations" in Belgium), permitting a high degree of local content, have become a prerequisite in Belgium's armament procurement policy. The only important exception was the procurement of M109 155 mm artillery guns, which were bought off-the-shelf. From the viewpoint of Belgian industry, offsets allow participation in the production of the purchased equipment by producing material or components at different stages of the production programme. They are in fact a modern kind of barter, but from the Belgian point of view, offsets are preferable to other forms of countertrade, because they can promote industrial and trade development on a long-term basis.

Within the framework of Belgian economic policy goals, offsets are thus to be considered as deals struck between the Belgian government and companies, that require an equipment supplier to buy goods from its client country or company at a value equal to a certain percentage of the primary sale's cost. As a result, the prime contractor commits himself to make purchases from Belgium sub-contractors rather than from those in the producing country.

In Belgium, there are three sorts of offsets:

- **Direct offsets** represent the national economy's shares in producing the equipment and in the supplies, work and services incorporated in the defence equipment that is the subject of the contract and is being produced only to meet the needs of the Belgian army. Direct offsets are directly related to the product delivered.

- **Semi-direct offsets** characterise the workload of the national economy in producing the equipment and in the supplies, work and services incorporated in identical equipment to the equipment specified in the contract, but being produced either for the originating country or for third countries. Semi-direct offsets are thus also directly related to the product delivered.
- **Indirect offsets** represent the products, supplies, work and services intended for the countries that awarded the contract, in any field of activity other than those which form the subject of the contract. Hence, indirect offsets embody the purchase of unrelated products or services.

4.2.2 Advantages of Offsets

The main objective of arms' procurement is, of course, the fulfilment of defence needs. This aim can, however, be combined with the pursuit of other economic policy goals. Belgium considers offset agreements politically and strategically advantageous for both governments and companies. For governments, offsets represent a means of ensuring economic development while exercising a certain degree of leverage over the contractor. Indeed, the aim is usually not to improve the political acceptability of the foreign source, or even to procure arms at cost-effective prices; these objectives are in fact secondary. After the satisfaction of military needs, the main goal is the achievement of important cyclical macro-economic advantages such as an improvement in employment levels, the economic growth of domestic defence and other industries, and improvements in the distribution of income and the balance of payments. In addition, the Belgian decision-makers repeatedly mention the following main features of offsets deals:

- the promotion of the growth and the development of high technology industries thanks to the transfer of advanced military technology;
- the compensation of trade imbalances created by large arms sales;
- the creation or preservation of foreign exchange;
- the achievement of competitive advantages;
- the access to new commercial opportunities thanks to the transfer of international marketing expertise and global reach of large companies;
- the promotion of investment in local industry and of local value-added programmes; and
- the creation of jobs at the local level.

Indirect offsets allow the Belgian economy to benefit from indirect and induced effects in all its sectors. They can be achieved through trade, development, work force training, and they can include ventures in high-technology manufacturing, environmental efforts, health care projects, telecommunications, or anything that brings value-added to the Belgian economy. The political, economic and even psychological importance of offsets in Belgium can be confirmed by the fact that whenever an important defence contract is signed, the media never fails to call it the "contrat du siècle", the deal of the century!

Since the investments are partially financed from abroad, their risks are low and their costs rather limited. Consequently, offsets have also been responsible for structural macro-economic advantages. Without offsets, Belgium would never have been able to sustain aircraft or engine manufacturers, and the acquisition of know-how in advanced modern technology would have remained a dream.

Belgium views offsets as a benefit to both parties in defence arms deals. Without offsets, the government would never have been able to afford expensive foreign weapon systems; offsets are considered as a way of doing business. This view has been supported by suppliers. In the past, the US industry repeatedly expressed its worries that amendments stiffening requirements for reporting offsets on defence exports would hamper efforts to export US defence goods in a competitive world market.

4.2.3   Disadvantages of Offsets

From the economist's point of view, direct and semi-direct offsets present significant handicaps as well. They are antithetical to free trade and they can alter the nature of sales transactions by including terms unrelated to price and performance of the product or services. Offsets can introduce market rigidities, cause growing state intervention, and create distortions in the world economy and trade.

Offsets are not only market-distorting, but also economically inefficient, especially in the long-run. Whereas southern NATO nations have used offsets extremely well as an industrial development tool, Belgium used them more as a means to maintain its defence industrial activities and to improve its technical quality. They are, however, short-term solutions of little use in the long-run. Offsets operate on a contract-by-contract basis, with sub-contracting benefits drying up once the foreign supplier has completed its offset obligations, because compensation contracts do not compel the principal contractor to maintain industrial ties with the subcontractors. Offsets are evidently more efficient in order to help an infant industry to establish new technological activities, to grow and to mature, than in a well established economy, subject to structural difficulties and to considerable competition.

Offsets have led to limited co-operation on an *ad hoc* basis, thereby weakening the Belgian defence industry. Priority was given to short-term protectionist behaviour of firms versus a long-term cost-efficiency rationale. It is hardly surprising that offsets gave rise to heavy lobbying, and consequently to an overprotection of national enterprises and to the existence of an overcapacity in the production of arms systems, taking into account the small size of Belgium's defence industry. Offset orders became essential for political and protectionist reasons and led to adverse effects in the long-run, because direct and semi-direct offsets do not encourage diversification. The firms that profit from the existence of offsets become dependent on them, eventually relying completely on them, and perpetuating their underdevelopment or dependence by masking the need for rationalising or to restructuring. As a result, offsets masked shortcomings and prevented management from taking appropriate measures. Direct and indirect offsets favoured the persistence of surplus or competing capabilities, non-profitable activities, piecemeal contracts and of firms lacking initiatives. Considering that Belgium never developed a coherent network of major defence firms and subcontractors, the defence production sectors were not restructured in time and the technological revolution did not give way to the expected qualitative results. Belgium's defence firms were largely offset dependent. Realising this after a few weeks in office, Mr Delcroix, the new Minister of Defence declared that he intended to abandon any offset policy in the future.[4]

But even on a contract-by-contract basis, the advantages are not ubiquitous, since offsets are not costless. More often than not, the decision to purchase equipment was made at a point when it was no longer possible to share in its research and development. In addition, production costs in Belgium tend to be higher than in big weapon producer countries, especially due to higher labour costs. Belgium is thus forced to pay an estimated 20 to 30% penalty for the purchased equipment. Moreover, the burden of this additional cost is carried by the MoD alone. However, offsets also pursue purely economic goals, which would justify funding by other departments (such as Economic Affairs, the Treasury, and/or Employment and Labour) as is general practice in the Netherlands. As a result, the offset policy diminished the purchasing power of already scarce defence resources.

As far as indirect offsets are concerned, the economic rewards seem to be the most interesting, because they can be spread through the entire economy. In reality, their drawback is in fact even greater than that associated with direct offsets. As offsets move into the civil sector, an increasing number of third parties become involved in economic compensation agreements, with the execution of offsets programmes increasingly being extended beyond the main contractors and sub-contractors. This is a convenient way for the main contractor to fulfil its obligations to the Belgian economy only in part, in quantitative as in qualitative terms, since it is extremely difficult to assess whether a foreign procurement is a consequence of the 'offset' contract: the same purchase could have been placed in the receiver's economy anyway! In one important case, the prime contractor demanded that purchases made prior to the expression of the need for a particular capability be accepted as an indirect offset. Belgium eventually partially accepted this claim, after much political and diplomatic debate, although such purchases had clearly not resulted from the offset agreement!

Contractors can also rely on several manoeuvres to dilute the impact of offsets on their profits, such as trading offset credits with other firms or overestimating the US$ value of the technology they are transferring.

Finally, it should be emphasised that offsets also represent a serious handicap for the selling country. Even if it is true that there is a long-standing industry position that the benefits of the sale of armament would be lost without offsets, government officials often add that offset arrangements erode the selling country's industrial base as technology and component production are transferred to foreign sources. Without the offsets associated with the sale of the European F-16's, for instance, the US defence subcontractors would have had the opportunity to compete for more of the subcontract work associated with this programme.

4.2.4 Control and Management of Offsets

The economic disadvantages associated with offsets can only be overcome through the careful management and control of offset-related activities. Both companies and politicians need to be reassured about the benefits of what is essentially a long-term commitment. In this respect, governments need to establish institutional and legislative frameworks for operating offsets agreements, and take into account all aspects of an economic compensation commitment, including the enforcement of offsets obligations, technological and intellectual property rights, and technology performance.

The final decision on Ministry of Defence purchases is made by the CMCES (Comité Ministériel de Coordination Economique et Sociale — Ministerial Committee for Economic and Social Co-ordination). This co-ordinates the acquisition process and makes its decision according to operational, financial and economic criteria. With regard to contract management, a section within the Ministry of Economic Affairs, called Defence and Industry, is responsible for the economic aspects of each contract. It specialises in the analysis of the economic and industrial aspects of defence purchases. Its objective is to promote the participation of Belgian industry both in the development and production of material corresponding to the MoD's needs and in co-operation programs between NATO member countries. In order to perform this duty, the Defence

and Industry Service keeps an inventory of the capacity of the defence industry
and participates in national and international working groups when economic
aspects of the equipment programs are concerned. It collects and conveys documentation and information to Belgian firms who wish to take part in defence
programs and promotes multinational co-operation in defence production.

The responsibility for controlling the implementation of offsets remains
with the Industrial Economy Section of the OBEA (Office Belge de l'Economie
et de l'Agriculture — Belgian Bureau of Economy and Agriculture). Created in
1967, the OBEA takes into account the following criteria:

- Effectiveness: are the orders actually placed?
- Novelty: do the purchases represent new or additional business for the
  Belgian firms?
- Belgian value added: what percentage of the value of these orders is manu-
  factured in Belgian plants?
- Technology: What technological improvement or renewal is brought about
  by this production?
- Employment: how many jobs are created or preserved and what is their spe-
  cific value?
- Regional distribution: what is the regional distribution in terms of produc-
  tion sites?

The OBEA reports to the Minister of Economic Affairs through Defence
and Industry; over the last 25 years, it has had to control over BEF 308 billion
worth of offsets precipitated by some 320 contracts.

4.3   Offset Policy and Federalisation

Although Belgium is a small country, for historical reasons its defence industry
is unevenly distributed across its three regions. The industrial revolution and the
subsequent economic development in the secondary sector largely took place in
the southern part of the country. The defence industry grew up in the same location. Table 6 clearly shows the discrepancy between the general distribution of
population and estimated employment in the defence-related industry in 1991.
The latter has always been largely located in Wallonia (70% of total direct manpower) and Brussels (8% of total direct manpower), with the remainder being in
smaller companies and sub-contractors in Flanders. For obvious geographic reasons, the shipbuilding sector is exclusively located in Flanders. As a result, each
region approaches the problem of economic compensation in a different way.

Table 6: Regional Distribution of Defence Production in Belgium

	Brussels	Wallonia	Flanders
Population	11%	33%	56%
Direct employment in the armament industry	8%	70%	22%

Source: See Table 2

Since Flanders lacks a military industry, the offsets that it seeks encourage future technological development. It is interested in spin-offs from defence purchases because they enable local companies to become more independent from military contracts. Furthermore, by insisting on high quality offsets, the Flemish industry obtains the basic technological knowledge to foster new high technology products. The Flemish defence firms generally consider direct and semi-direct offsets as more interesting from a technological point of view in the short-run, but as a poor solution in the long-run, since they rarely offer follow-up contracts. Indirect offsets generate more (non-military) future contracts.

Wallonia and Brussels have to deal with a completely different situation. Their companies operating in the defence industry are highly specialised in the production of military goods, and lay emphasis on direct and semi-direct offsets. They also try to stretch the contracts into the future by negotiating as many semi-direct offsets as possible. In recent years, Wallonia has become more interested in using R&D subsidies for civil programmes to fill the gap between military contracts or to compensate for lost military production.

Since the beginning of the 1970s, Flemish companies have begun lobbying in order to obtain more offsets and to penetrate the aerospace market. An industrial pressure group, the FLAG (Flemish Aerospace Group), succeeded in persuading the government not to take the existing production capacities into account and to spread the economic compensation associated with defence contracts across the three regions according to their population and their economic capacity. The offset associated with the second buy of 44 F-16s clearly shows the impact that this policy change has had, as well as the differences between the regions. The initial F-16 buy did not provide for any regionalisation of the offsets. As a result, the natural distribution of production activities resulted in Wallonia and Brussels receiving some 90% of the total offset. For the follow-on purchase, however, FLAG succeeded, thanks to heavy lobbying, in having restrictions imposed on the regional distribution of offsets (see Table 7).

Table 7: Total Offsets and Regional Distribution (in %) of the F-16 Follow-on-Buy

	Wallonia	Flanders	Brussels	Total Value
Direct and semi-direct offsets	48	0.2	14.5	62.7
Indirect offsets		37.3		37.3
Total	48	37.5	14.5	100

Source: MoD and Ministry of Economic Affairs.

In the 1980s, Belgium's constitutional changes towards a three-way federalisation of the state, implied an important shift in economic and industrial policy decision-making, away from national and towards regional authorities. Different interests and the absence of any political and financial co-ordination led to completely different industrial strategies.

After long years of laborious discussions, a political agreement was reached in 1985 on the distribution of future offsets: 54 to 56% would go to Flanders, 34 to 36% to Wallonia, and 9 to 11% to Brussels. The FLAG, however, immediately claimed a share of at least 65% for Flanders. Just as each firm tries to outbid its rival, so each region tried to do the same. As a result, the decision-making process, even for minor equipment, became very slow and all Belgian defence companies became shackled by the handicaps of fragmentation and regional division. In addition, the regional distribution of offsets generated some perverse incentives. Some companies decided to open additional production facilities in other regions in order to benefit from higher offset orders, which led to even more excess capacity. Another unwelcome response was that foreign firms began to make their proposals directly to Belgian firms and not to the MoD, hoping that local authorities, newly-endowed with cash under the country's regionalisation policy, would be far more willing to fund a project rather than the financially strapped military. Moreover, it is not always obvious whether an offset should be considered beneficial to Flanders, Wallonia or Brussels. The offset activities of SABCA in Haeren, near Brussels, are an example of the complexity of the matter. If the location of the head office determined the beneficiary of the offset, it would be imputed to Brussels. If the language spoken by the workers was the criterion, 73% would be credited to Flanders since 800 of the 1,100 workers are Flemish. Another distribution would be possible if the overall activities of SABCA, including those in Wallonia, were to be considered.

More recently, substantial reductions in demand, as well as the growing constraints on available resources, have led the politicians in Flanders and Brussels to abandon all important economic support for the defence-related industry. Only the Walloon region continues to support its defence industrial activities, though in a fairly moderate way.

4.4   Case Study: The F-16 Program

4.4.1   The Requirement

In 1973, the Government expressed the need to replace the Air Force's F-104G Starfighter combat aircraft from the early 1980s. Similar statements were made by the governments of Norway, Denmark and the Netherlands. The four countries decided to pool their purchases and buy the same aircraft in order to benefit from longer production runs and the better offset that would follow from their increased bargaining power. To present themselves as a buyer's cartel in front of the potential sellers, they formed a common steering committee.[5]

4.4.2   The Choice

Taking into account the needs of the four Air Forces, it was rapidly established that only three fighter aircraft came into consideration: Dassault's Mirage F1 M53 (France), Saab-Scania's Viggen (Sweden) and the winner of the American contest between General Dynamics' F-16 Fighting Falcon and the Northrop Cobra; the USA chose the F-16 in 1975.

For political and military reasons, the Viggen never had a real chance in Belgium. Since Sweden was a neutral country, the supply of aircraft and spare parts in periods of crisis would have been too hazardous. In fact, the government of Sweden never expected to sell its aircraft to Belgium and France. It only hoped that the consortium of the four buying countries would fall apart, in which case they were confident of being able to sell the Viggen to Norway and to Denmark.

Being a neutral country, Sweden could not comply with another European demand. The seller country was asked to commit itself to put a certain number of the same aircraft that the European consortium would buy at the disposal of European defence. France promised to engage as many aircraft as the largest number that would be bought by a single country, and the USA committed itself to 240 aircraft to be stationed in Europe.

After thorough testing and evaluation, it appeared to the Belgian MoD that the F-16 presented slightly better technical and military characteristics than the Mirage F-1, but probably not in a decisive way. The final decision would clearly depend on the economic analysis of the offsets proposed by the USA and France.

In May 1975, the three other countries decided in favour of the F-16. In Belgium, the Flemish pressure groups supported the American case, while the aerospace industry, which already had experience of co-operating with Dassault after a purchase of Mirage V fighter-bomber aircraft, was in favour of the French aircraft. This led to several delays, and to the other countries pressing the Belgians to follow their decision as soon as possible. In the end, after several visits by the Belgian Minister of Defence to Paris and Washington, the government opted for the F-16, mainly for two reasons: first, a possible decision not to follow the other three countries would have led to a rupture of the consortium and would have compelled Belgium to accept all of the disadvantages of a small scale deal; and second, the offsets offered by the USA were undoubtedly more attractive than the French proposal.

During negotiations, the French government argued that the consortium should purchase the Mirage in order to facilitate the development of a real European aerospace market. Impressed by this argument, three members of the consortium decided that a certain number of the proposed aircraft purchases were subject to confirmation by their respective governments prior to 31 May 1978: Belgium 14 F-16As; Denmark 10 F-16As and the Netherlands 16 F-16As and 2 F-16Bs. The value of these aircraft was meant to give birth to a common fund in order to finance joint R&D projects in Europe. Attempts were made to include the UK and Italy but these failed, and the three countries decided to take up their respective options and to buy all F-16s.

4.4.3 The Specifics of the Contract and its Offsets

In the MOU[6] (Memorandum of Understanding) between the US government and the four EPGs (European Participating Governments), the parties planned the following F-16 purchases:

- United States: 650 (of which 15% were two seats)
- Belgium: 116 (of which 12 were two seats)
- Denmark: 58 (of which 12 were two seats)
- The Netherlands: 102 (of which 12 were two seats)
- Norway: 72 (of which 12 were two seats)

The prices, based upon January 1975 US$, extended by the US government for the airframe, engine, duplicate tooling and industry management, were contractually established NTE (Not To Exceed) prices contained and defined in signed agreements between the US government and General Dynamics Corporation (GD) and United Technologies Corporation (UT). The FSD (Full Scale Development) share was firm and fixed by the US government. The radar and GFAE (Government Furnished Aerospace Equipment) prices were estimates added to the contractors' NTE prices. The foreseen unit price of the F-16 was US$6.091 million, with the following breakdown of the NTE price:

- Airframe: US$3.450 million
- Engine: US$1.445 million
- Radar: US$0.372 million
- GFAE: US$0.153 million
- FSD Share: US$0.470 million (including engine)
- Industry management: US$0.005 million
- Duplicate tooling: US$0.196 million

The EPGs and their industries were assured that they would be offered the opportunity to participate in and obtain maximum benefit from work performed during full scale development. This would facilitate the preparation of drawings and production tooling for the European industries to meet jointly established production schedules.

The US government provided data for and encouraged participation in future aircraft, engine, avionics and munitions updates or modification programs for the F-16 aircraft. The US also promised to utilise the EPGs' depot level maintenance and overhaul facilities, and industry maintenance facilities in these countries on a mutually agreed basis for USAF F-16 aircraft operated in Europe. Authorisation was also given to GD and UT to place contracts with EPG sub-contractors for the US requirements and for third country sales as was mutually agreed between GD, UT and their respective subcontractors.

The US government guaranteed European industrial participation by ensuring offsets for the initial EPG purchase, defined as 100% of the procurement value[7] of up to 348 aircraft, according to the following obligations imposed upon the contractors:

- 10% of the procurement value of USAF purchases of the F-16 aircraft totalling 650 aircraft (final assembly of the USAF F-16 aircraft was to be in the US).
- 40% of the procurement value of all EPG purchases of the F-16 aircraft (final assembly of the EPG aircraft and engine assembly was to be in Europe).
- 15% of the procurement value of all third country purchases of the F-16 aircraft. For any sales to third countries, the US government was to incorporate in the price of the aircraft the average 15% EPG co-production commitments (by procurement value). Non-participation of a European country in a particular third country sale would be compensated for by a larger percentage participation in other third country sales. The US government agreed to continue this 15% participation arrangement beyond the 100% offset commitment, provided reasonably competitive terms prevailed.

Based upon US Government and EPG purchases of 650 and 348 F-16 aircraft respectively, the US Government committed itself to a combined US industry and DoD offset on the F-16 program of 58% of the initial EPG F-16 procurement. Furthermore, assuming third country purchases of 500 F-16 aircraft (total purchase 1,500), the US Government was to provide a target offset of 80% of such initial EPG F-16 procurement. The US government commitment was primarily to be fulfilled with co-production within the F-16 program. However, if this was impossible for any reason, the difference up to the committed offset percentages was to be filled by other compensatory work of comparable technology. It should also be noted that the parts and components which the industries in the EPGs are specifically instructed by the US government or the US prime contractors to buy and to incorporate in European co-production items, were not counted as offsets.

In Copenhagen, the representatives of GD found more than 40 firms that could participate in the production of components and parts for the F-16, but most of these companies were too small. Their industrial structures were below "critical mass" standards and the required capital investments would largely have exceeded their financial capabilities. In Norway, the selection of the participating firms was easier. For these two countries, the MOU stipulated that since Denmark and Norway did not have a genuine aerospace industry, a possible problem in providing sufficient offsets should be compensated by any production work, provided it was at a comparable technological level as the F-16 program.

The US government agreed that insofar as Belgium and the Netherlands were concerned, the first priority for alternative compensation arrangements would be the aerospace industry. Two production lines were constructed: Fokker (the Netherlands) and SABCA (Belgium). In Belgium, the main participants to the F-16 contract and their US contractors are listed in Table 8.

Table 8: F-16 Direct and Semi-Direct Offsets: Items and Main Participants

Item	Belgian Sub-contractor	US Contractor
Aft fuselage and vertical fins	SONACA	General Dynamics
Wings	SABCA	General Dynamics
Final assembly	SONACA/SABCA	General Dynamics
Integrated servoactutor	SABCA	National Waterlift
F100 engine parts	FN	United Technologies
Radar computer	MBLE	Westinghouse
Operational flight trainer	SABENA	Singer Link
F110 engine parts	FN	General Electric
INS Lamina	MBLE	Singer Kearfott

Source: MoD and Ministry of Economic Affairs

4.4.4   Conclusion

As shown in Table 9, the commitment to a minimum offset level of 58% of the cost of the F-16 procurement to the EPGs as a whole was more than satisfied. The target offset of 80% (including third country purchases) was also reached. The distribution of the offset between the EPGs was however unequal, due to their divergent aerospace capabilities. Denmark and Norway, especially, had some difficulties to meet "reasonably competitive terms" as defined by the principles and procedures laid down in Annex A to the F-16 MOU.

Apparently, only Belgium obtained the promised offsets. It should however be stressed that the mentioned percentages refer to turnover figures; in terms of value added activities, the differences between the EPGs seem more reasonable. Nevertheless, Belgium certainly came out of this contract as the principal beneficiary, thanks to the fact that the US government ensured the implementation of the F-16 co-production participating plan, even when the resulting offset exceeded the US government offset commitments. Belgium obtained 35 to 40% of the promised 15% of the procurement value of all third country purchases of the F-16 aircraft. Since — at least theoretically — the third country sales have not come to an end yet, this percentage could rise further. The production sharing commitment established in the MOU remained even in effect for the Belgian follow-on F-16 aircraft purchase of 1984.

For Belgium, the only serious drawback was the final cost of the aircraft. This had over-run by about 30 to 35% and was almost entirely due to the offset. Despite the fact that all terms and conditions applicable to the NTE price, secured for the US government from its prime contractors GD and UT, were accorded to the EPG, the 'Not To Exceed' prices were exceeded. The US government stressed the fact that this was mainly due to significantly higher production costs in Europe than in the USA.

Table 9: Actual Offsets Associated with the F-16 Purchase

Participant	F-16 Offsets (as a % of the cost of aircraft purchased)	F-16 Offsets (third country purchases included)
EPG	58.8%	81.0%
Belgium	77.8%	103.5%
Denmark	53.3%	65.8%
The Netherlands	52.8%	76.1%
Norway	44.8%	67.2%

Source: MoD and Ministry of Economic Affairs

4.5   Case Study: The AIFV Procurement Program

4.5.1   The Requirement

On the eve of the 1980s, the main AIFV (Armoured Infantry Fighting Vehicles) used by Belgium were its 771 M-75 and 534 AMX-13, acquired as early as 1958. Their economic lifetime had already been stretched and the obsolescence of the M-75 was compounded in 1975 when its manufacturer terminated the production of spare parts. In addition, the maintenance costs of the AMX-13 were found to be excessive in relation to its utility. If the Belgian Army was to pursue its mission into the 1980s and beyond, it would need 1,189 new armoured vehicles.

It was assessed, according to NATO recommendations, that the new vehicle would have to meet the following protection, mobility, armament and transport capacity criteria:

- protection from conventional and non-conventional attacks,
- the mobility of a Leopard tank coupled with amphibian capacity,
- endowment with an anti-armoured vehicle gun,
- and the capacity to transport 10 equipped men with a load of about a ton.

4.5.2   The Choice

It was important to acquire only one vehicle for reasons of economies of scale in use and maintenance. It was also desirable to buy a vehicle already in service in other NATO countries, with limited functioning and training costs. Given these constraints, the choice was between the French AMX-10 (a 14-ton aluminium armoured vehicle with a 20 mm gun), the US M113 A1 (11 tons, aluminium-made, and already used by several armed forces), the US AIFV (a 13 ton steel and aluminium vehicle with an optional 25 mm gun) derived from the M113 and manufactured by FMC (Food Machinery Corporation), the French VAB 6 × 6 (13 ton, in steel) and the Swiss Piranha 6 × 6 (9.6 tons, in steel). The first three vehicles are full-tracked, the other two equipped with regular wheels. Before submitting their proposals to the government, the military had a long technical and tactical debate on the respective pros and cons of full-tracked and wheel vehicles, and eventually decided to go for the full-tracked solution. Consequently, they proposed a procurement mix of 514 AIFV and 675 M113 A1.

The Belgian government decided in 1979 to purchase 514 AIFV and 525 M113 A1, which did not concur with the planned total of 1,189. The decision to purchase only 525 M113 A1 instead of the 675 initially planned was motivated by the government's desire to reserve the production of 150 vehicles for the Belgian manufacturer ACEC (Aciéries et Constructions Electriques de

Charleroi). Since the Army did not mention ACEC as a potential contender when submitting its preliminary request to the Ministry of Defence, the participation of ACEC in this market surprised more than one observer. It was actually the Ministry of Economic Affairs that introduced ACEC to this market, knowing that the company had been developing an electrical transmission vehicle with the French manufacturer of the AMX-10. However, this project failed although ACEC maintained its ambition to develop a vehicle with electrical transmission and designed the "Cobra" in early 1977. Although the Cobra was not technically ready, the services of the Prime Minister in charge of industrial promotion requested in November 1978 that an order of 100 to 150 vehicles be set aside "in order to give the opportunity to a Belgian company to submit a tender". This was in contradiction with the military's desire for a homogeneous supply of vehicles and for fast delivery (ACEC was believed to need two years for the development of the Cobra) and did not contribute any additional employment to the economy. For the government, however, this seemed to be an interesting opportunity to let a Belgian company design and produce an entirely Belgian-made vehicle, provide a showcase for world markets, and generate technological spin-offs for the civilian industry. In spite of the negative advice of the military, the government awarded a BEF 1 billion "prototype development credit". The decision was made to reduce by 150 units its order of AIFV and M113 A1, leaving it thus at 1,039 vehicles. At the same time, the government took an option on another 150 M113 A1 until 31 December 1980.

The development of the Cobra turned out to be a technical failure and the production stage was never reached. The Army was eventually left 150 vehicles short of its stated needs because the deadline went by without the government realising its option on an additional 150 M113 A1.

4.5.3 The Specifics of the Contract and its Offsets

The initial contract value was BEF 22.1845 billion (in 1986 prices). Apparently, this choice represented the most expensive of the solutions proposed by the military, but it was very attractive in economic terms. Direct offsets to the Belgian industry were set at 70% of total costs (BEF 15.529 billion). Under certain restrictions, 50% of new investment in infrastructure and expenditure on heavy equipment and construction could be counted towards the offset. Direct offsets were to take into account only the first level subcontractors. Indirect offsets were set at 30% of total contract value (BEF 6.66 billion). To be eligible, such contracts had to generate new or additional business and were to be at the same technological level as the object of the deal. Indirect offsets were principally meant to cover production contracts given to BMF by FMC for third country clients. The basis for the computation of the economic offsets was not the

turnover, but the **added** value, i.e. the additional activity for the Belgian economy. The contract also stipulated that if direct offsets were higher than 70%, the
obligations regarding indirect offsets could be reduced accordingly.

In 1977, a new company had been formed, Belgian Mechanical Fabrication
(BMF), in anticipation of the offset associated with the AIFV program. Its shareholders were ASCO[8] (owning 55% of the capital), CMI[9] (37%) and the holding
Groupe Bruxelles-Lambert (8%). This company became FMC's licensee, with
its main plant in the industrial zone of Aubange, near Athus (southern
Luxembourg province, in the Walloon region). The shells of the vehicles were to
be manufactured in Aubange, providing employment during production phase
for slightly over 300 employees (150 productive and 50 administrative personnel). The engines and the transmission gear of the vehicles would be imported
from the USA, and the guns from Örlikon (Switzerland). The management of
the program would be located in the Liège region.

The contract also had a regional distribution requirement, with a margin of
±2%. The Flemish region was to receive 50% of both direct and indirect offsets,
the Walloon region 42% and Brussels 8%. Special provisions were made with
respect to the allocation of the other activities — and thus the related economic
offsets — to one region or another. The regional allocation of production equipment was conceived as follows:

- Equipment produced in Belgium: place of manufacture.
- Equipment produced abroad: if sold through a Belgian company, the headquarters of this company determines the regional location; if the seller is not
  a Belgian firm or if the equipment is purchased abroad, the regional location
  is determined by the place where the equipment is installed.
- The sub-contractors' regional distribution is determined by the place of
  production.
- The regional distribution of offsets is established on the basis of the regional
  location of the benefiting Belgian companies' production centres, except for
  orders of a final value greater than BEF 500 million for which the first level
  of sub-contractors was to be accounted for. BMF's benefits were to be allocated to the Brussels region where it has headquarters.

The AIFV program was also one of the first to present severe cumulative
financial penalties. The supplier agreed to a penalty equal to 10% of the amount
of the non-respected economic commitments as regards both direct and indirect
offsets, taken separately, and to a penalty equal to 5% of the negative spread
between the actual regional distribution and the agreed distribution in the contract. A deviation of 2% based on each region's quota was to be tolerated before
this financial penalty was implemented.

4.5.4 Conclusion

The contract was signed in 1980 and was supposed to end in 1988. It lasted in fact until 1990, because some direct offsets caused long political discussions on their acceptability. In the end, the government accepted 66.5% direct offsets[10] (thus 3.5% short of the agreed percentage) and BEF 9.5 billion indirect offsets, or 42.8% of the contract value, instead of the promised 30%! As a result, the foreseen penalties on the direct offsets had to be paid. As far as offsets are concerned, the AIFV program can be considered a success.

The MoD considered the cost of the program too high. According to the National Armament Director, the cost over-run of the program came close to 100%, essentially due to the existence of offsets! Moreover, from an economic perspective, the long-run effects are not be so positive either. One of the main reasons for awarding the contract to BMF was the opening of its plant in Aubange, which constituted a real industrial opportunity for this economically impoverished region. But this factory could not be rationalised from an economic point of view since the aluminium input had to be transported from the Antwerp region to Aubange for manufacturing, then back to Antwerp for assembly!

Moreover, after the construction of the 1,039 vehicles for the Belgian Army, the plant has been virtually empty, functioning only for maintenance, though the Americans promised, in addition to the offsets for the Belgian contract, that the Aubange plant would receive all M113 orders for the rest of the world, since FMC was to stop this production and switch to other activities. This promise was, however, never respected. The only order came in August 1989 from the Turkish FNSS (FMC-Nurol Savunma Sanayii A.S.), formed by an association of FMC and Nurol, a local firm. This contract allowed BMF to participate in the supply of components for 285 of the 1,700 AIFVs ordered by the Turkish government.

The question is, of course, whether the construction of the new plant was worth the effort for the production of only 1,039 Belgian AIFVs plus a rather symbolic additional order. In the context of regional employment policy, it can be noted that the plant is still operational. However, only minor contracts have been received and the total workforce has fallen from 300 to 60.

4.6 Appraisal of the Belgian Offset Policy: Asset or Burden for the Economy?

In the opinion of the present author, economic policy goals can be pursued by a defence purchase, on the condition that the primary aim (the acquisition of a weapon system that responds to military, operational and technical standards) is respected. However, this rationale does not imply that only short-term policies are to prevail. Notwithstanding the benefits that can be generated from *ad hoc* economic offset arrangements, a better approach from the buyer government's point of view is to integrate offset requirements and priorities into development policy.

In the Belgian case, economic offsets have, however, led to limited cooperation on a *ad hoc* basis, which has been responsible for the weaknesses of the defence industry. It is not a surprise that offsets gave rise to heavy lobbying, and consequently to the overprotection of national enterprises and to the existence of an overcapacity in the production of arms systems, even in a small country like Belgium. In the meantime, nothing was done to find a solution for the problems associated with structural disarmament. Belgium never developed a coherent network of major defence firms and subcontractors, the defence production sectors were not restructured soon enough, and the technological revolution did not give way to the expected qualitative results.

It is not extravagant to state that offsets were not only market distorting, but also economically inefficient. Whereas southern NATO nations have used offsets extremely well as an industrial development tool, Belgium used them more as a means to maintain its defence industrial activities and to improve its technical quality. Because the Belgian Government has almost always the required foreign firms from which it bought defence goods to place orders in Belgium as offsets, domestic firms have been overprotected and this has led to overcapacity. In the meantime, little has been done to find a solution to the actual and prospective fall in demand for defence goods. Indeed, there has never been an explicit and rational defence-related industrial policy in Belgium apart from frequent local and regional job-saving actions. Due to the lack of a coherent defence industrial policy, the armament industry therefore went into a crisis more than a decade ago.

The eagerness of the Belgian authorities to protect defence firms against all economic good sense triggered the adoption of belated measures leading to obsolete structures, bad qualitative results and perverse effects, e.g. when the main objective of defence procurement actually becomes the fulfilment of the needs of industrial and employment policy. In this respect, regional or sectoral protectionism plays an analogous role. As a result, costly and excessive production capacities were created or maintained. For example, the decision to buy 44 additional F-16s in 1984 came two years earlier than originally planned in order to assuage the Belgian aerospace industry which lacked other orders to fill the gap.

Belgium's successive governments have not yet been involved with any active conversion-type policy initiative either. They have left it to industry to adjust to market forces. Industrial groups decided to sell their defence activities.

Companies which failed to make profits were sold and several companies were on the verge of bankruptcy. Some were saved; others were merged, swallowed up by foreign firms, or eventually went to bankruptcy. When an important defence firm, PRB, went bankrupt in 1990 and the unions appealed to Wallonia's government for help, the reply was that this was out of the question, because there were no plans to convert the purely military production activities into more stable, civilian markets.

In conclusion, notwithstanding the attractive economic advantages, my assessment is that the economic balance of offsets is negative in the long-run.

4.7   The Future of Economic Offsets in Belgium

As a result of decreasing national defence budgets, the prime contractor base is shrinking drastically in the armaments' market. The future of economic offsets in Belgium is therefore intimately linked with the future of defence procurement. Moreover, another constraint that will undoubtedly affect defence procurement in the long-run is the progress of European integration in the Single Market framework. Its subsequent applications in different sectors[11] will eventually lead to the establishment of a common foreign and security policy and, maybe, to some kind of European armaments market. Just as the nature of NATO can no longer be reduced to a military mould, the role of the EU (European Union) will no longer be limited to the civilian economy. Even if this prospect still seems rather remote, somewhere on the long road to a unified economy, the EU will actively be concerned with the military aspects of the economic relationships within its territory and with foreign countries. Moreover, one of the consequences of détente is that the military component of western security policy yields more and more to political, economic and social considerations. The role of the EU in these areas can no longer be ignored.

This evolution remains, however, at an embryonic stage, and the results today are in no way commensurate with the progress being achieved by the Single Market. Yet, when the time comes for defence to fall under EU regulations, offsets will no longer be admitted as a business practice. Associated with this, the long-awaited suppression of Article 223 of the Rome Treaty — that allows any member state to take measures to protect the essential interests of its security in connection with the production of or trade in armament — will be considered an unavoidable measure in the framework of a common defence policy within the future Political Union.

If implemented, however, such a measure would raise important problems in the Belgian defence industry. When an industry manufactures complete final military goods (thus separately marketable), it should benefit from a common defence market, provided there are no national rules or specifications preventing it legally or artificially from competing. Yet, this is not the case of the Belgian defence industry, which is entirely made up of subcontractors for foreign companies. This industry suffers from a fundamental handicap: it does not reach the critical size to be reasonably competitive with massively state-supported competitors. Belgian firms could compete successfully in a common market on the grounds of the efficiency of their research, development and production activities. However, these are fields that are widely influenced by state intervention. Financial support of the defence industry in countries like France and the United Kingdom, or even in a small country like the Netherlands, is considerable compared with the Belgian case. The Belgian defence industry suffers from this situation and would presumably benefit from a European market and from European regulations establishing a level-playing field with regard to state support.

The decision, in 1992, not to suppress Article 223 of the Rome Treaty for the time being, augurs ill for a termination of protectionist behaviour. Indeed, in the past, the lack of state support in the defence industry was counterbalanced by offset orders. The suppression of Article 223 would imply the disappearance of offsets and would threaten the defence sector if no measures were taken to allow small countries' defence firms to redeploy in a new competitive European context.

In the meantime, defence offsets are still allowed. The current Belgian government, however, expressed its view that offsets are not the best way of sustaining the industry's access to sub-contracting and supply contracts. In May 1992, the new Minister of Defence declared that in the future, the armament acquisition process in Belgium would no longer be guided by offset policy, but by the postulate of purchasing the best material at the lowest price. He also declared his opposition to any economic or industrial approach to armament contracts, hence committing himself to purely political decision-making.

This statement, that could have resulted in a rejection of any offset policy and of project-specific offsets in favour of a long-term view of *juste retour* for weapon programs, will probably not survive harsh lobbying from the industrialists. In February 1993, the Minister backtracked to some extent when, in a declaration to the FLAG members, he commented that offsets must pursue prospective goals, and that they must offer a high technological added value to the economy and that claimed offsets must be substantiated by thorough verification. The abandonment of offsets seemed to have succumbed to the pressure from national industries and certain government sectors to increased international defence co-operation. With declining defence budgets there is less work for national defence industries; consequently, many companies want to secure government contracts.

When the Belgian government resumes its purchases of weapon systems, Belgium will probably continue to invite prime contractors to provide offsets until a Single Market for armament exists. The only difference might be that offsets will no longer be project specific, i.e. required and calculated for each order, but package-related, which means that offsets would be determined for a package of several projects together. This might, however, further weaken the purchasing power of Belgium's weapon acquisition budget, even in the short-run. The trend toward internationalisation of weapons systems might not survive the increased calls for protectionism that will likely follow the significant contraction of production brought on by the reduction in purchases by most countries. The prime contractors might have legislation enforced allowing foreign countries to retain offsets, but at a high price. By way of illustration, in the US, a recently proposed bill states that if the DoD enters into a contract with a foreign purchaser or a country that demands a favourable offset, the US Secretary of Defence must require that an arrangement be included in the pact benefiting US firms, especially subcontractors, injured by the offset policy of the foreign firm or country concerned. Should a foreign country or firm that demands favourable offsets purchase a weapon system from a US firm, the President of the United States is to be notified as to the amount of damage the offset will cause US firms. The President would then be required to recover that amount from the foreign government.

Offsets strengthened Belgian defence firms in the short-run, but made them vulnerable to structural changes. The improvement in East-West relations, the fall of the Berlin wall, and the collapse of communism hastened or exacerbated the crisis. Today, the Belgian defence industry is faced with an extremely limited choice. Theoretically, the future could offer three possible strategies: put an increased emphasis on foreign sales, allow national companies to merge or to be sold, or get out of the defence business. The first possibility is no longer a realistic option taking into account the increased competition from Third World countries, from industrialised partners, and from the former Warsaw Pact producers. The phase of mergers and buy-outs has already been largely completed. Since the end of the 1980s, the defence industry has demonstrated its determination to build an improved industrial base for European defence by increasing mergers, teaming and joint ventures. As a result, more than 80% of the "Belgian" defence industry already belongs to foreign investors. The current mergers, regroupings and take-overs by foreign firms will nevertheless, in most cases, not automatically lead to an international division of labour, taking into account the parallel efforts to rationalise, reduce production costs, curtail overall expenses and protect national production capacities. The only remaining option for other companies which cannot adjust to the new situation is therefore to disappear from the defence markets.

Endnotes

1. In Belgium, this topic is extremely sensitive in the political and economic realm. As a consequence, very few official data are published about the impact of offsets on the defence industry, the distribution of offsets (especially among the three regions in the recently federalised country), and the degree of fulfilment of the offset obligation. The author sourced the data that is not publicly available from his personal knowledge, from unofficial statements, from interviews and from inside information. Purely speculative statements or allegations have been discarded.

2. Van der Stichele, M., Commandes publiques et clauses économiques, in Bulletin de Documentation, Ministère des Finances, Bruxelles, Octobre 1983.

3. Struys, W., Aspects économiques de la production de systèmes d'arme dans l'Europe des Neuf, PhD. dissertation in Economics, Université Libre de Bruxelles, Bruxelles, 1977, p. 98–99 and 296–298, and Struys, W., Défense et Economie: Mythes et Réalités, in Sécurité et Stratégie No. 26, Bruxelles, Mai 1989, p. 110–112.

4. Mr Delcroix declared on May 22, 1992, to Belga, Belgium's press agency that "... the choice of [defence] material was all too often determined on economic grounds and that the previous governments used to attach more importance to the economic compensations than to the order itself. I intend to abandon the economic compensations policy; I advocate a political, rather than an industrial approach of purchase of armaments."

5. For the history of the program, see Bontinck, P., Ekonomische aspekten van het F-16 multinationaal produktieprogramma, Koninklijke Militaire School, Afstudeerwerk, Brussel, 1978.

6. Memorandum of Understanding between the government of the United States and the governments of Belgium, Denmark, the Netherlands and Norway relating to the procurement and the production of the F-16 aircraft, signed on 9 June 1975 by the Belgian Minister of Defence, Mr. Paul Vanden Boeynants.

7. The procurement value is defined as the dollar value of aircraft flyaway cost plus initial spares, support equipment, data, training equipment and the pro-rata charge for non-recurring costs. For Belgium, this cost was 878.9 million US$.

8. ASCO, created in 1954, is specialised in precision engineering and received its first defence contract in 1960 for NAMSA. ASCO manufactured a variety of armament and precision mechanical components for missiles and armoured vehicles.

9. CMI (Cockerill Mechanical Industries), is a subsidiary of the steel giant Cockerill-Sambre whose capital is predominantly owned by the Walloon Region (98.2% in 1989). In the defence sector, CMI manufactures a turret and a 90 mm gun for light armoured vehicles. In October 1987, when the order for the Belgian Army was completed, CMI became the only shareholder of BMF, justifying this operation by the fact that BMF's activities were complementary to those of CMI's Defence department.

10. If Economic Affairs had been strict, only 64% would have been accepted. As a result of the political discussions, the currency fluctuations of the US$ and the CHF were taken into account, as well as the bankruptcy of the Forges de Jemappe, a Belgian subcontractor. Note that the Belgian government refused to counterbalance the deficit of direct offsets by the surplus of indirect compensations.

11. For the effects of the Single Market, see Struys, W., The Internal Market for Defence: Implications for the Different Member States, Paper presented at the CEPS (Centre for European Policy Studies) Policy Seminar No. 44, "The Future of the European Defence Industry", Brussels, 5 June 1992, and Struys, W., The Grand Market and Arms Co-operation in the European Community: Problems and Prospects — Le Marché Unique et la Coopération en matière d'armements dans la Communauté Européenne: Problèmes et Perspectives, Paper presented at the "European Security and Defence Economy after 1992: New Challenges and Opportunities" Colloquium, Defence Study Centre (Belgium) and The Institute for Foreign Policy Analysis (USA), Palais d'Egmont, Brussels, 22 June 1990.

Chapter 5

In Search of a Strategy: The Evolution of Canadian Defence Industrial and Regional Benefits Policy

James Fergusson
Research Associate
Centre for Defence and Security Studies
University of Manitoba, Canada

5.1 Introduction

Arguably, the practice of seeking industrial offsets is most pronounced in the case of defence purchases. For the majority of nations, defence purchases generally represent the largest proportion of capital or industrial goods bought by governments. As a result, these procurement decisions have significant economic, political, and social implications. In addition, industrial offsets are also driven by national security considerations. States seek to maintain, in varying degrees, a viable defence industrial capacity as a means to avoid dependence on foreign sources which could have significant implications during times of war. Although the practice of obtaining industrial offsets is generally viewed negatively from a economic efficiency perspective, because it promotes the inefficient allocation of resources, undermines industrial competitiveness and productivity, and distorts trade, the combination of political, economic, social, and security considerations makes states willing to absorb these inefficiencies.

In the case of Canada, its defence industrial offsets policy and behaviour can be understood largely in terms of the constant interaction between economic and political considerations; considerations which, in the Canadian case, are embraced by the ideas of Industrial and Regional benefits. Moreover, security considerations, which have at least been an important factor for many states in defence-industrial policy deliberations, are notably absent in the Canadian case. Of course, National Defence identifies and sets the requirements for capital acquisitions, and it is the lead department. Nonetheless, the specific decisions with regard to capital purchases in terms of the ordering of priorities, product selection, and contract requirements are based in many cases on other considerations and the input of other departments and agencies within the government. The net result has not only meant the inefficient allocation of limited defence resources, but also inefficient and inconsistent offset decisions which attempt to seek some form of balance between economic and political requirements. In other words, Canadian defence offset policy has consistently reflected the competition and conflict between Industrial and Regional Benefits (IRBs).

In order to understand this competition and conflict, and the relative neglect of security considerations, the relatively unique Canadian political context as it relates to defence is paramount. This context provides the setting for examining the evolution of Canadian policy, and the attempt by the Canadian government in 1985 to reform its IRB policies. These reforms, it can be argued, played a significant role in the development of current offset policy in general, and the cancelled EH-101 Shipbourne Helicopter offset package in particular. Whether this package would have been successful can not be gauged, but it is evident that the decision will significantly affect the capabilities of Canada's Armed Forces and future capital decisions. Thus, the cancellation serves as a useful indicator of the underlying structural and political impediments to the development of a successful long term defence offset strategy.

Before undertaking this analysis, it is important to identify briefly the significant impediments to research in this area. By their nature, offsets policies and decisions reside in a politically charged atmosphere. Ranging from concerns about the political fallout in Canada of the regional distribution of offset contracts, the economic inefficiencies of such decisions, the relationship between government and business, inter-bureaucratic rivalry, to the violation of the spirit, if not intent of the defence industrial relationship with the United States, government and industry are reluctant to discuss openly Canadian offset policy. In fact, Canadian officials are loath to use the term offset to describe contractual Canadian content in off-shore purchases, and will clearly state that Canada does not have an offset policy. Instead, they are described as Industrial and Regional Benefits.

5.2   The Canadian Context

The dominance of domestic economic and political considerations in Canadian defence capital spending, to the relative neglect of security or strategic military factors, is fundamentally a function of the defence climate in Canada. Although it is somewhat a misnomer to argue that Canada has an **amilitary** society,[1] it is evident that the salience of defence issues in Canada is extremely low. Moreover, political isolationism, which is generally seen as a unique American phenomenon, was Canadian policy during the Interwar years and isolationism remained, as it did in the United States, a latent force in Canada throughout the Cold War. With the end of the Cold War, a return to isolationism is a distinct possibility, despite Canada's post-World War II internationalist focus. As many observers point out, Canada faces no clear military threat to its security. Furthermore, there exists an underlying, albeit reluctant, acceptance that the United States will defend Canada against any foreign threat. Dwarfed by the United States and its military capability, unconsciously an atmosphere of "free riding" has existed, reinforced by a belief that Canada's contribution to collective defence would always be marginal and symbolic, regardless of the effort. If anything, this belief, in relation to Canada's current geopolitical situation and the underlying fiscal and constitutional issues facing the nation, has been reinforced with the end of the Cold War.

Even during the Cold War, support for defence was low as evident in the linear decline in the size of Canada's Armed Forces and Canadian defence spending since the end of World War II.[2] For the political elite, defence considerations have been driven by a set of foreign and domestic policy considerations. In terms of foreign policy, defence was seen as the *price to be paid* to obtain influence and a seat at the table. This, in part, reflected beliefs about Canada's role in the international system which developed in the post war years during the so-called "Golden Age of Canadian Internationalism", and the dilemma of being a neighbour to the world's superpower. From the former, the Canadian psyche institutionalized a set of roles of a benign nation acting for the greater good and eschewing force as a national option. From the latter, Canadian elites sought to avoid the dependency of a bilateral relationship by subsuming the United States in multilateral institutions of which NATO and the United Nations were central. In both cases, defence and the role of the armed forces inherently drifted away from strategic-military considerations to foreign policy ones.

Domestically, defence on its own terms has had little, if any, political payoffs for elites. With the notable exception of the 1962 federal election,[3] defence issues have played no significant role. There is also no significant constituency in Canada which supports defence. Finally, the relative insignificance of defence issues in Canada is reflected in the status of the Minister of National Defence. It is a junior post, and although defence represents a significant area of government spending, the Minister rarely sits on the key Cabinet Planning and Priorities Committee.

The impact of this political reality is manifested in the complexity of the Canadian system. Although the Department of National Defence (DND) sets the primary capital requirements, specific procurement decisions involve several other departments. The Department of Industry, Science, and Technology (DIST) is tasked with the IRB element itself, and, in conjunction with regional agencies, with reviewing, evaluating and advising on industry proposals and final selection.[4] The Department of Foreign Affairs and International Trade

(DFAIT) is involved through its mandate on foreign relations and export policy. The Department of Supply and Services (DSS) is tasked with the issuing of tenders, contracts, and contract management. Treasury Board has the authority to approve all procurement expenditures. Above all of them is the Cabinet which is not reluctant to intervene in the process, if not circumvent it through "demand purchases". Cabinet, through the Committee on Foreign and Defence Policy, must recommend all major procurement.

These factors in combination set the context for Canadian defence policy, spending, and capital procurement. Although defence considerations set the basic criteria for force capital requirements, specific decisions with regards to the purchase of capital goods to meet these requirements have been driven by political-economic considerations. For the political elite in Canada, capital spending in defence is perceived as a major vehicle for promoting a variety of non-defence interests. It represents the largest single area of discretionary spending available to the federal government. As a result, capital spending is used to promote political interests and support a wide range of socio-economic interests in the areas of industrial and regional development. Politically, spending is used as a means to funnel federal dollars into key political regions and ridings. Industrially, capital spending is used to support the establishment of new industries, sustain existing industry, and enhance Canada's industrial competitiveness. Regionally, defence capital dollars are a means to re-direct federal monies to disadvantaged areas. In other words, defence capital spending may be conceived as the centrepiece of an "industrial strategy" and Canada's IRBs policy perhaps meets this conception, notwithstanding the various factors which run contrary to the efficient implementation of such a strategy.[5]

The appearance and evolution of Canadian defence offset policy is also a function of nature of Canada's defence industrial capacity. Unable to support a full-scale integrated defence industrial base because of the small size of the Canadian market and the inability to compete internationally in all areas of defence production against the larger spenders and consumers, Canada's defence industrial capacity evolved in the context of a unique relationship with the United States. Through the Defence Production Sharing Arrangements (DPSA), Canada agreed to purchase integrated weapons platforms from the United States in return for privileged access to the American defence market. Notwithstanding certain legislative, administrative, and psychological barriers, Canadian firms are treated as American firms in Department of Defense (DOD) procurement.[6] As a result of this relationship, Canada's defence industry evolved towards specialization in the second and third tier of defence production, and in the process, established a variety of relationships with American producers. Thus today, Canada's defence industry primarily consists of sub-system and component producers in a variety of high technology niches concentrated in the electronics and aerospace sectors.

While Canada has benefited greatly through its unique defence industrial relationship with the United States, Canada has faced a significant dilemma. Unable to support an independent full scale defence industry at a reasonable cost, Canada was forced to recognize that substantial amounts of capital spending would flow outside its border. In the 1963 follow on agreement of the DPSA, both parties pledged to maintain a rough balance in defence trade. However, since the end of the Vietnam War, Canada has faced an annual deficit in defence trade with the United States.[7] In fact, the first deficit in 1972, after five years of Canadian surpluses, was followed closely by a policy to seek offsets in defence purchases.[8] Whether this shift from a surplus to a deficit position had an independent impact on the Canadian decision to institute a defence offset policy is unknown. It is possible that in conjunction with the Defence Structure Review of 1975, which set in place the foundation for the major procurement projects of the next decade, Canada's defence industry had by the mid-1970s lost the capacity to undertake licensed production such as occurred in the 1960s. Regardless, the 1970s mark the beginning of the formulation of Canada's search to obtain industrial and regional benefits in purchases from foreign manufacturers.

The search for industrial and regional benefits in offshore purchases is part of the wider process of Canadian defence procurement. As the case with most nations, Canadian procurement policies are biased towards supporting domestic interests in all departments and agencies. However, Canada does not have any legislative requirement on par with the "Buy American" Act which dictates preferences for Canadian suppliers. Moreover, Canadian policy is to promote competition and receive the best value for dollars spent. Finally, GATT provisions with regards to Government Procurement, the Free Trade Agreement (FTA) and the North American Free Trade Agreement (NAFTA) have also served to limit Canadian preferences and focus the search for domestic benefits in defence.

The DSS, through existing practice and its responsibility for Canada's defence industrial base (DIB), has in place a set of policies and procedures designed to favour domestic sources. In addition, the exclusion of defence from the GATT, the FTA, and the NAFTA has had the effect of focusing Canada's IRBs in the area of defence. Essentially, Canadian policy on selection is based on three considerations: technical performance; socio-economic benefits; and support for the DIB. In terms of the relationship between them, socio-economic factors are the decisive criteria for source selection as long as the bid meets the minimum technical requirements. This applies to contracts above the C$2 million threshold, including Major Crown Projects (MCPs) which exceed the C$100 million threshold. In the process of seeking competitive bids, preference is given first to Canadian manufacturing firms, then Canadian firms acting as authorized agents of foreign firms, and, finally, foreign firms. In addition, a 10% premium is applied to the foreign content of the bids. In other words, although price competitiveness remains a central consideration, the Canadian content premium, which encompasses the wide range of domestic benefits to be accrued from procurement, alters the procurement environment in favour of Canadian firms and/or foreign firms willing to establish a production capacity in Canada or working relationships with Canadian firms. Finally, procurement is restricted to Canadian firms as long as at least two sources are available and one responds.

Of course, this latter condition rarely obtains for major capital or crown projects given the structure of Canada's DIB. Thus, competition for these projects, when it occurs, largely revolves around the ability of foreign firms to outbid competitors along the premium of Canadian content. Thus, given a range of technical equivalence in integrated weapons platforms, Canadian content becomes the fundamental criteria for choice. Moreover, the 10% Canadian content premium, ceteris paribus, can be considered a benchmark of the additional costs borne by DND in procurement; a cost which may compound the rigidities and increased costs of defence procurement in Canada as suppliers are unable to obtain needed goods from the most cost-effective sources due to offsets.

5.3   Stage One of Canada's Industrial and Regional Benefits

The first stage of Canada's IRB policy roughly covers the period 1975 to 1985, and concludes with the Nielsen Task Force Report on Government Procurement. During this period, Canadian policy can be best illustrated by three MCPs; the Leopard I Main Battle Tank (MBT), the P-3 Aurora Long Range Patrol Aircraft, and the CF-18 Hornet.[9] All three projects are common in the sense that they were proven designs in the production stage and in service. However, each project demonstrates distinct differences in both the motives for the purchases, the specific offset packages, and the benefits and costs of various approaches to offsets.

The purchase of the Leopard 1 MBT was motivated by the recognition of the obsolescence of Canada's existing MBT fleet of Centurions. At the time, the Leopard 1 was the newest MBT available, with both the American M-1 Abrams and the British Challenger in the design stage.[10] Regardless of this consideration, the decision cannot be divorced from wider political objectives of the Trudeau government to diversify Canadian trade away from dependence on the United States — the so-called Third Option.[11] The government sought a contractual link with the European Community which had, in turn, met with opposition from Canada's allies, particularly Germany, over Canada's unilateral decision to reduce its military commitment to Europe by 50% in 1969.[12] Thus, the Leopard purchase had a significant political motive underlying it.

According to Todd, the contract with Krauss-Maffei entailed a commitment to offset 40% of the contract value of C$236 million through industrial benefits over a period of ten years.[13] The meeting of the offset requirement was, however, left open-ended. As result, only one Canadian firm, Vestshell of Montreal, participated in the project directly. The preponderance of the offset work amounted to basic casting manufacturing, and the purchase of raw materials including plywood and rapeseed; the latter goods being accounted with the blessing of the Canadian government through contracts with the Netherlands. Also, the majority of the benefits (75%) were directed towards Quebec and Ontario. As a result, Todd concludes that the Leopard I offset package failed to deliver significant industrial benefits and technology transfer to Canada.

Roughly at the same time of the Leopard purchase, Canada decided to purchase the P-3 Long Range Patrol Aircraft (LRPA) from Lockheed, designated the Aurora (Orion in the United States). According to Tucker, the decision was the result of an extended process in which a variety of factors were at play.[14] These included American pressures to reduce their balance of payments deficit with Canada and support financially troubled Lockheed, DND desires to procure a new Anti-Submarine Warfare Platform compatible with the United States Navy and Canada's naval role in NATO, the Department of Industry, Trade, and Commerce goal to support the Canadian aerospace industry, and the governments aspiration to maximize industrial benefits and procure a platform for sovereignty protection. The final decision to procure the P-3 from Lockheed was a function of the priority assigned to the industrial benefits package, followed by the ASW role which reflected the return of NATO as the priority in Canadian defence policy.

The offset package attached to the Aurora purchase was limited because the platform was already in production. There was little opportunity to obtain direct offsets in this area. Nonetheless, the package amounted to 100% offsets to be met over a fifteen year period.[15] Direct offsets were located in the Anti-Submarine Warfare (ASW) suite deployed on the platform; a pattern that would be repeated through the inter-relationship between the Canadian Patrol Frigate (CPF) programme and the aborted EH-101 project. The specific breakdown of direct to indirect offsets, or regional distribution can not be confirmed. Nonetheless, according to one source, Lockheed committed to $C414 million in Canadian subcontracts out of a total of $C1.2 billion, which may represent a direct offset proportion of 35%.[16]

The final MCP of this stage is the CF-18 Hornet purchase. This decision with regard to the offset package is perhaps the best documented of all of

Canada's offset purchases and became the central case of both the Auditor-General's Report of 1984 on defence and the 1985 Nielsen Task Force Report on Government Procurement. In contrast to both the Leopard I and P-3 Aurora, which were the most modern proven platforms in service for their respective primary roles,[17] the competition to replace the CF-101 Voodoo, the CF-104 Starfighter, and the operationally committed CF-5 appeared to benefit from the abundance of new state of the art fighters on the market. However, the limit placed on funding for the project and the minimum buy level effectively removed half of the competitors from serious consideration, including the preferred fighter, the F-15, of the Air Force. Moreover, a further competitor was eliminated as too risky because it was still in the developmental stage and no one had agreed to purchase it. The net result left only two serious competitors, the General Dynamics F-16 and McDonnell Douglas F-18. Even then, widespread support for the F-18 among the military largely removed any "true" degree of competition. In other words, given fiscal restraints, unproven technology, and military preferences, there was only one possible option for the government — the F-18.

Nonetheless, the public competition which did emerge between General Dynamics and McDonnell Douglas was fought on offset packages; a pattern evident as well in the fight between Lockheed and Boeing over the LRPA MCP. According to Boyd, the inclusion of the GD F-16 on the short list, with the F-18 as the military preference after the removal of the F-15 on cost grounds, was an attempt to pressure MD into improving its offset package.[18] The process became public in light of the two federal elections of the period and influenced by the state of relations between Ottawa and Quebec. The final decision was made possible by showing the Quebec caucus of the Liberal government that the McDonnell Douglas package would provide greater benefits to Quebec than the General Dynamics one.

The offset package itself amounted to 100%, which entailed $C2.453 billion in indirect offsets and $C.453 million in direct industrial participation.[19] There were some substantial benefits accrued by Canada through the CF-18 offset package.[20] It resulted in the creation of a new GE engine blade and veins plant in Bromont with a world product mandate which continues to rank among the top of the GE group. In addition, the CF-18 purchase resulted in significant export contracts to other countries which subsequently purchased the F-18. Nonetheless, the process through which the package was formulated and the overall IRBs accrued by Canada were roundly criticised.

The first major critique of the CF-18 purchase was the 1984 Auditor-General's Report. Although the report is relatively sketchy, it noted that the project lacked clearly defined objectives, regional considerations were largely ignored in the negotiating phase, and there were problems with the offset approval proposal and reporting of benefit claims.[21] More damaging was the 1985 Nielsen Task Force Report. Specifically, the report argued that of the C\$2.45 billion offset package, 57% consisted of work which would have been done in Canada regardless of the contract, and further (unspecified) amounts of the sub-contractor work was not caused, although claimed, by the contract itself. Finally, the majority of benefits were build-to-print short term work which translated into little technology transfer and long-term benefits. Also, the Task Force estimated that for the Aurora and CF-18 purchases, Canada absorbed at least C\$125 million in additional costs associated with the offset package. Finally, although regional breakdowns are unavailable, according to the 1994–95 estimates, \$C63 million of the indirect industrial benefits was targeted for the setting up of the aforementioned GE plant (\$C60 million) and investing in UDT Industries in Quebec.[22] Otherwise, it would appear that the contractor was not contractually restricted on a regional basis; an inference consistent with the critiques of Canadian IRB policy in this period.

Overall, this brief survey of the three MCPs of this first stage illustrate a variety of important considerations. First of all, the three projects indicate a rejection of weapons platforms in the design or developmental stage. The state of the Canadian Armed Forces at the time, in conjunction with the political and fiscal constraints in Canadian defence policy and procurement, combined to dictate purchases of existing proven platforms. In so doing, however, opportunities to buy into the development phase and potentially reap technological and export benefits in the future were minimized. Rather, the purchase of existing proven platforms restricted the areas in which industrial benefits in general and direct benefits in particular could be realized. Moreover, the promise of technology transfer largely failed to materialize.

Second, the distinctions between the three projects imply the absence of any clear consistent set of offset policies relative to military requirements. Although in each case the military received an effective platform to replace its obsolete existing inventory, only the Aurora represented the preferred military choice, particularly in terms of Canada's military commitments. Moreover, this choice cannot be divorced from underlying economic considerations. Also, the decisions reflected a lack of consistency in Canadian defence policy itself. The Leopard I purchase, driven by wider political concerns with regard to Canada's relationship with Europe contradicted the policy emphasis to shift the role of the Canadian Army from a heavy armoured one to a mobile light reconnaissance one. Although there was a consensus in DND surrounding the requirements for a New Fighter, cost and industrial considerations significantly constrained the process. As Manson points out, military criterion were never "so overpowering as to dictate on their own merits, the selection of a given aircraft or to eliminate others".[23]

Third, it appears that the basic goal, with the exception of the Leopard I, was to seek 100% offset packages, dominated by indirect ones. This, as noted above, is partially a function of the purchase of existing platforms. In addition, it appears that the contractors were relatively unconstrained in the details of meeting their offset commitments; a point made in the Auditor-General's 1984 Report. That is, the critiques of the offset packages directed towards little technology transfer and the need to address regional concerns reflect this point. With regard to regional concerns, the concentration of the aerospace and electronics industries in Ontario and Quebec largely ensured that the bulk of offsets would be directed towards these regions. Treddinick points out that these two provinces account for 92% of the offset contracts for the Aurora and CF-18 in 1981.[24]

It can be argued that this stage in the evolution of Canadian IRB policy was a learning one. The confluence of a variety of factors including the recognition of obsolete state of Canada's equipment inventory with its military and political ramifications, the shift in defence policy back to NATO in the mid-1970s, the general state of the economy at the time and nature of Canadian defence industrial capacity, and the dominant Ottawa-Quebec political rivalry created pressures which affected the procurement process in general, and offset policy in particular. In effect, this stage can be labelled as a minimalist strategy. That is, a greater concern for simply ensuring that MCPs would not amount to the outflow of Canadian dollars offshore, but would have domestic economic and underlying political value. In so doing, however, the detailed requirements, particularly to ensure industrial benefits, obtain technology transfers, and enhance Canada's industrial competitiveness, of an effective offset policy were largely absent. Above all, the second stage, which can be traced to the Canadian Patrol Frigate (CPF) project, appears as a maximalist strategy in which procurement emphasized a shift to platforms in the development stage, assembler/production capacity, direct benefits and increased regional considerations. In other words, the safe, but low payoff, approach of stage one was replaced by a higher risk approach which promised greater industrial and regional benefits.

5.4　Stage Two

A central critique of the Task Force Report was the failure of existing IRB practice to enhance industrial competitiveness and export opportunities. According to the report, this failure is a function of the small size of Canadian purchases. Corporate incentives to provide significant industrial benefits are seen as a function of the relative importance of the purchase. For example, the purchase of 138 CF-18s can be seen as relatively important for MD because it was the first export contract for the platform and thus portended some advantage in subsequent international competitions.[25] However, its overall significance to the producer was marginal given its size and existing orders in the United States. In other words, there was little incentive to go beyond short-term sub-contracts to Canadian suppliers which likely had long established relationships with either the firm or the American market.

The failure of Canada's IRB policies also undermined the ability to obtain export opportunities. Canada's defence firms are largely dependent on exports and their success in the international marketplace is a function of their ability to create, penetrate, and/or exploit export niches. The Canadian defence market is important to these firms in a variety of ways. It provides a basis for exports through Research & Development support and the initial purchase of new products. Canadian contracts provide useful bridging between foreign contracts. Also, such contracts can establish working relationships with foreign firms. Regardless, Canadian firms are vitally dependent on exports, and the offset packages associated with the aforementioned projects had little payoff for establishing new markets for Canadian firms; a view strongly held by industry to this day.

Along with the additional critiques related to the absence of regional considerations and the failure to acquire life-cycle support contracts as a means to enhance long-term benefits, views echoed by the Auditor-General, the 1985 Task Force Report set the basis for the establishment of a new policy for IRBs.[26] Central to the new policy was the rejection of the previous goal of seeking 100% offsets in procurement in favour of a more flexible policy in which cost efficacy and operational requirements would be the major defining factors. IRBs were to be focused on acquiring long-term direct benefits related to the platform or system being bought. Although indirect benefits would not necessarily be rejected, they were to be significantly downgraded. The central goal was to use IRBs to ensure long term commercial viability, which implicitly meant export opportunities. Finally, the new policy also emphasized the use of offsets for regional development.

Table One provides the list of defence MCPs of roughly the last decade.[27] Reflecting the policy recommendations of the Task Force Report, only two contracts (Table Two) entail a 100% or more offset requirement: the two Light Armoured Vehicle purchases for the Militia (MILLAV) and Regular Army (LAV); and the Short Range Anti-Armour Weapon (SRAAW). In the case of the LAV, the platform itself is produced under license by General Motors Canada in Ontario, and the initial Militia purchase included 60% direct and 40% indirect offsets. The follow-on LAV purchase for the Regular Army included 100%

direct and 15% indirect offsets; an indication of some degree of technology or production transfer between the first and second purchase. More interestingly, both LAV purchases were demand buys emanating from Cabinet. The first was based on an unsolicited bid stemming from the end of the initial production run

Table 1: Major Crown Projects — 1982 to Present

CPF — Canadian Patrol Frigate consisting of an initial contract St Johns Shipbuilding in 1983 for six frigates, expanded in 1987 to twelve frigates.

TRUMP — Tribal Class Destroyer Update and Modernization with Litton Systems Canada as Prime Contractor in 1986 as a mid-life update to Canada's fleet of four destroyers.

LLAD — Low Level Air Defence project awarded Oerlikon-Buehrie in 1986 being implemented by Oerlikon Aerospace of Quebec.

SARP — Small Arms Replacement Project consisting of the C7 rifle, C8 carbine, C9 light machine gun, and C79 optical sights awarded to Diemaco of Ontario in 1984, with the exception of the C9 being produced by Fabrique-National of Belgium.

HLVW — Heavy Logistic Vehicle Wheeled Contract to UTDC of Ontario in 1988.

AMSA — Arctic Maritime Surveillance Aircraft, Arcturus, awarded to Lockheed for three aircraft in 1989.

MILLAV — Militia Light Armoured Vehicle contract awarded to General Motors of Canada (in Ontario) for 199 wheeled and 8 tracked armoured personnel carriers (APCs), and an additional contract awarded to FMC of California for 22 APCs in 1990.

CANTASS — Canadian Towed Array Sonar System awarded to Computing Devices Canada, Indal Technologies (Canada), Martin Marietta (US) and Litton Systems Canada authorized (stage III) in 1988.

CF-5 — Avionics Upgrade with Bristol Aerospace of Winnipeg signed in 1990 for 40 aircraft. In the last budget, the project has been cancelled.

CH-146 — Utility Tactical Transport Helicopter awarded to Bell Helicopter Textron of Montreal for 100 helicopters based on the Bell-412 in 1992.

LAV — Replacement for the Lynx awarded to General Motors Canada (Ontario) for 229 vehicles in 1992.

LSVW — Light Support Vehicle Wheeled project for a minimum 2751 trucks to replace the 5/4 ton truck in service awarded to Western Star Trucks of British Columbia in 1992.

EST — The Electronic Support and Training System to provide an effective airborne electronic warfare training awarded to Lockheed Canada in 1993.

SPAAW — Short Range Anti-Armour Weapon (heavy) as a cooperative undertaking with France awarded to Aerospatiale in 1993.

TTT — Tactical Transport Tanker contract to acquire five C-130 Hercules to Lockheed (US) in 1990.

TCCCS — Tactical Command, Control and Communications System for the Army awarded to Computing Devices Canada as the prime contractor in 1991.

Table 2: National Defence Major Crown Projects and Percentage of Industrial Benefits

Project	Cost (C$mill)	Industrial Benefit	Direct	Indirect
CPF	9050	48.7%	36.3%	12.4%
TRUMP	1804	48.7%	33.4%	15.2%
LLAD	1039	62%	unspecified	
SARP	355	85%	85%	—
HLVW	365	77%	47%	30%
AMSA	207	51%	8%	43%
MILLAV	156	100%	60%	40%
CANTASS	106	75.6	75.6%	—
CF-5	86	unspecified*		
TTT	323	43%	unspecified	
TCCCS	1899	64.8%	33.7%	31.1%
CH-146	1293	39.1%	21.9%	17.2%
LAV	883	115%	100%	15%
LSVW	279	64.4%	36.5%	27.9%
EST	202	52.9%	39.7%	13.2%
SRAAW	212	100%	70%	30%
AVG		68.5%	49.8%	25%

* The CF-5 project was awarded to Bristol Aerospace of Winnipeg, and thus one can infer that the contract entailed only direct benefits. No specific breakdown of benefits is provided.

for the United States Marines. The second purchase coincided with the purchase of the C-146 Griffon Helicopter from Bell with its production based in Quebec and indications that the General Motors production line was nearing an end with the completion of the Saudi Arabia purchase.[28] Finally, the initial purchase did not meet many of the military requirements for the Militia and the second purchase decision reflected a low priority within National Defence.[29]

It should also be noted that the CF-5 upgrade may also contain a large proportion of Canadian content with the awarding of the contract to Bristol Aerospace of Winnipeg, although specific figures are not available. Bristol Aerospace had participated in the original production of the F-5 under license from Northrup, and the decision to award the avionics upgrade to this firm largely reflected the politics surrounding the CF-18 maintenance contract which had been awarded to Canadair in Quebec.[30]

Overall, Canadian offsets averaged 68.5% for this period, with direct and indirect offsets averaging 49.8% and 25% respectively. Underlying this pattern was the increased emphasis on participation in the production and/or assembly stage of the various platforms. Specifically, ten of the sixteen MCPs involved Canadian participation in the production/assembly of the platform itself. In all these cases, direct benefits are larger than indirect ones. Even in the remaining cases with one exception, direct benefits are larger than indirect ones, which in turn may reflect investment in areas of Canadian industrial strength.[31]

The shift towards Canadian participation in the production phase of MCPs can be seen as a strategy to improve the prospects for exports. However, it remains to be seen as to whether the strategy will produce benefits. In many of the cases, the projects reside in areas where strong international competition exists, and there is no evidence that there was any commitment beyond Canada or North America.[32] Also, the premium associated with the projects raises questions of cost competitiveness. For example, the CPF represents a "state-of-the-art" naval vessel, but it is also one of, if not the most expensive frigate in the international market; a market area of high protectionism.[33] Despite indications of a potential export contract to Saudi Arabia, there have been no export contracts for the platform.[34] In addition, the ability of Canadian firms to export in general is hampered by existing Canadian export control policies and procedures.[35]

The failure to acquire foreign markets for these products has significant implications for the cost-effective spending of limited and shrinking defence dollars and future defence procurement. The additional costs associated with supporting the initial setup of a production capacity, relative to existing foreign production in which initial costs have already been absorbed and amortized, represents a significant premium for defence. Although part of the 1985 reforms included the shifting of costs associated with industrial benefits away from National Defence towards cost-sharing with the responsible government agencies, it still amounted to a premium for defence purchases and for government spending as a whole.[36]

Canadian participation in the production/assembly stage as the centrepiece of a strategy to ensure meaningful industrial benefits also had implications for future procurement. Unless an export market could be established for the new capacity, the firm became dependent on Canadian purchases; a dependency with economic and political implications. As implied above, the second LAV decision can be understood as a function of the previous decision and government concerns with regard to lost employment and the political balance of contracts between Ontario and Quebec. In the case of the CPF, part of its industrial benefits package included the creation of Paramax in Montreal to undertake the systems integration for the new frigate. Subsequently, Paramax would also become the prime contractor for the systems integration in the now aborted EH-101 project, discussed below. Related, the government now faces the issue of the future of Canada's naval shipbuilding base which was re-established with the CPF project.[37] The only planned future Canadian contract, already signed with Fenco as the prime contractor, is for the Maritime Coastal Defence Vessel. Although the contract entails a commitment to build the ships in a Canadian shipyard, it remains to be seen if this means St.Johns and/or the other company involved, MIL of Quebec. The failure to award this part of the contract to either or both will effectively have significant implications for their future; a future in one region, the Atlantic, which is economically depressed and has high levels of unemployment.

Finally, future procurement decisions are affected in another way. Decisions to use Canadian capacity leading to the procurement of a system which doesn't clearly meet military requirements affects associated procurement decisions. For example, the CH-146 decision has apparently affected decisions with regard to an air mobile howitzer. Just recently, Canada announced the purchase of the GIAT Light 105mm MKII ostensibly as the best gun of its class available, but more likely as the only gun which is light enough to be lifted by the CH-146.[38] At the same time, Canada has completed an arrangement in which the Netherlands is upgrading the current 105mm pack howitzer and purchasing the C-7 rifle from Diemaco. In other words, at a time of budget reductions and a defence review in which some are questioning the utility of maintaining the artillery, Canada is in the process of holding two separate 105mm howitzers, and upgrading its current holdings as a means, apparently, to support Canada's only small arms producer.

Another concern underlying industrial benefits policy during this period was the nature of competition. Although the information provided in the National Defence estimates may simply have failed to report a competitive bid process, only three of the identified MCPs mention the decision based on competition. An additional one, the TCCCS, reports a competitive bid restricted to Canadian firms. The Auditor-General also reports that the CPF and HLVW competitions were restricted to Canadian firms.[39] According to other sources, the MILLAV, LAV, and CF-5 were ministerial directed or demand purchases. The SARP purchase may also have lacked a competition given that Diemaco is the only small arms producer in Canada. Finally, the AMSA purchase is likely to have been without competition given the previous purchase of the Aurora and the logic of eliminating any significant additional related infrastructure.

It is not possible to estimate the extent to which the absence of competition or restricted Canadian competition translated into additional costs. In some cases, such as the HLVW, LLAD, and AMSA, they appear to have been the lowest bidder. Moreover, it is difficult to ascertain the degree to which the project definition stage in some cases largely eliminated competition on military grounds and related cost grounds, as in the case of the CF-18. Recall that both the Aurora and CF-18 decisions occurred in the context of competitions partially along the lines of offset packages. In the case of the MCPs of this period, many of the decisions occurred without competition. For example, both LAV purchases, the CF-5 upgrade, the CH-146 Griffon, the Arcturus, the CPF, and the HLWV either were demand buys or occurred in the absence of an international competition. The shift in emphasis towards long-term benefits was translated in a desire to ensure that the production/assembly stage would occur in Canada. Thus, existing production capacity or the willingness of a foreign firm to set up a production capacity in Canada became a central consideration, regardless of specific military priorities or requirements.[40]

Underlying this consideration is the process through which offset commitments are formulated. According to the Auditor-General, the onus on offset packages remained with the various companies. Yet, there is little evidence that the subsequent contracts were related to competition along the lines of offset packages, which had been experienced in the 1970s. On the contrary, the combination of restricted bidding to Canadian firms and demand bids in many cases ensured that offset package competition would not obtain; a situation which may have introduced further inefficiencies. Of course, this environment may also have created the conditions whereby companies recognized the requirements for successful bids; an environment of a relatively high level of Canadian direct content and participation in the production/assembly stage. Along with this requirement, there also existed the demand for regional distribution.

Table Three reports the regional distribution of contracts as available. The averages for the various regions are 30.9% for Quebec, 27.9% for Ontario, 18.7% for the West, and 10.8% for Atlantic Canada. Of course, these figures are only illustrative. The Ontario proportion is likely to be significantly higher, reflecting at a minimum that both the MILLAV and SARP projects were produced in Ontario. Only three projects report the West and Atlantic Canada receiving the largest share of industrial benefits; the TCCCS project which entailed a commitment to set up a production capacity in Alberta; the LSVW produced by a firm in British Columbia; and the aforementioned CPF.[41]

It appears evident that contract awards were significantly influenced by regional considerations. Whether this has translated into some form of codified distribution which bidding companies had to respond to is unclear. Nonetheless, companies formulating bids for MCPs were likely, ceteris paribus, to be more successful if their offset packages contained a regional distribution. Problematic, however, for any company is its ability to find Canadian firms, or willingness to create new capacity in the various regions outside of Central Canada. With the Canadian industry largely located in "Golden Triangle" of Greater Toronto,

Table 3: Regional Distribution as a Percentage of Total Industrial Benefits

MAP	Atlantic	Quebec	Ontario	West	Non-Allocated
CPF	35.9%	30.3%	15%	2.4%	16.3%
TRUMP	1.2%	38.2%	56.5%	4.1%	—
LLAD	11.8%	63.4%	24.2%	2.6%	—
SARP$_2$	—	20%	—	—	—
MILLAV$_3$	15%	—	—	15%	—
TCCCS	2.3%	3.6%	13.1%	73.9%	7.1%
LAV	10%	8%	65%	10%	73%4
LSVW	2.1%	3.8%	17.4%	33.3%	43.3%
SPAAW	8%	80%	4%	8%	—
AVG	10.8%	30.9%	27.9%	18.7%	

Notes:
1. Based on available data reflecting contractual commitments. MCPs reported in Table 1 and 2 lacking this information are excluded.
2. No specific breakdown is provided except a 'best effort' commitment to Quebec for Canadian subcontract work.
3. No figures are available for Quebec or Ontario, but it is reasonable to surmise that the bulk went to Ontario where the vehicle was produced. It is also noted that the value achieved in the Atlantic and West regions was 177.6% and 124.1% of the commitment.
4. To be divided between the Atlantic and West.

Montreal, and Ottawa, offshore firms are significantly constrained in the formulation of their bids. For Canada, this creates obstacles for its ability to obtain technology/production transfer with export viability. It is likely the case that existing regional capacity does not have the technical skills or ability to absorb new technology easily. As a result, offset sub-contractors may only be available to do relatively low technology build-to-print work.

Politically, demands for ensuring some form of equitable regional distribution of contracts either for each project or over a series of projects reflect the nature of the federal political system. Publicly, there has been the longstanding belief that the federal government has privileged Central Canada in general, and Quebec in particular in the awarding of contracts; a belief which resurfaced over the aforementioned CF-18 maintenance contract. This perceived preference towards Central Canada is attributed to its political weight within the federal system, and towards Quebec is generally credited to the longstanding issue of Quebec separatism. At the same time, the federal government must also respond to growing western alienation. The net result is a set of political incentives to respond to these various factors with defence contracts as the means to respond. Examining the timing of recent MCPs tentatively indicates this response. The West receives the TCCCS and LSVW projects in 1991 and 1992 respectively, Quebec receives the CH-146, and Ontario the LAV in 1992. Moreover, the timing of the latter two announcements nearly coincide. Above all, as indicated in the chart on the regional distribution of MCPs, this is reflected in the dominance of one region in the majority of cases. Thus, along with the drive to acquire and/or ensure greater direct industrial benefits through the creation or use of Canadian production capacity, this period of Canadian policy entailed a greater emphasis on ensuring the spreading of defence dollars across the regions.

5.5   The EH-101 Case

Although the EH-101 project, designed to replace the Sea King and Labrador platforms for naval and search and rescue operations (SAR), has been cancelled by the new government, it is a valuable case for examining the current approach to defence offsets. Perhaps most indicative is the decision to cancel itself; a clearly political decision which had little regard for both the operational and economic realities surrounding the decision itself. In particular, considerations regarding the need to procure a New Shipbourne Aircraft (NSA) had followed on the decisions to procure the Canadian Patrol Frigate (CPF) and upgrade the existing TRIBAL Class Destroyers (TRUMP Programme), formalized with the establishment of the NSA project office in 1986, followed by the creation of the New SAR office in 1988. Regardless of the "writing on the wall", opposition to the final decision to purchase the EH-101 did not appear until its initial announcement in July 1992, and subsequently re-emerged with a cabinet shuffle and leadership race in the ruling Conservative Party in the winter-spring of 1993.[42]

Reflecting the nature of defence debates in Canada, opposition to the EH-101 decision was relatively ill-informed, at times superfluous, and became a political football with little consideration of both the operational realities with regard to the aging Sea Kings and Labradors, the economic realities associated with the industrial and regional benefits, and costs of cancelling the project. According to current estimates, $C578 million has been expended on the project[43] The alternative life-extensions options for the Sea Kings and Labradors would range from a minimum estimate of C$960 million to a maximum of C$2.4 billion. Thus, at a cost ranging from C$1.5 to C$3 billion roughly, compared to the $4.4 billion cost of the EH-101 over the thirteen years of the programme, Canada will save from C$1 to $2 billion, while maintaining a fleet of aircraft unable to meet fully operational requirements with a life extension to roughly 2010 (rather than roughly 2030 for the EH-101).[44] At the same time, the EH-101 provided a single platform to undertake two distinct operational roles, thereby saving costs associated with maintaining two separate infrastructures. It remains to be seen if the final decision will result in one or two platforms. Nonetheless, it is clear that the present government is not likely to reconsider the EH-101 for either role, and given the governments view that the maritime ASW role is relatively obsolete with the end of the Cold War, it may translate into a decision to purchase a new SAR helicopter while holding the decision on the maritime replacement in abeyance. If this is the case, then it is likely that two separate platforms will be procured with the additional costs associated. In other words, the net result is likely to be more expensive than the original EH-101 decision in the long run.

Regardless of the political factors which led the new Liberal government to cancel immediately the EH-101 project, the offset package negotiated for the purchase is indicative of a variety of long-standing considerations from previous cases. First of all, the decision to purchase the EH-101 did not seem to include any attempt to structure the competition around offsets. Similar to the Leopard case, only one existing operational maritime helicopter, excluding either an upgrade to the Sea King or purchasing new Sea Kings, was available: the Seahawk. An offset package associated with such a purchase would likely have been similar to the Aurora and Arcturus purchases; an existing platform, in which Canadian industry would likely only provide the electronics and ASW suite.

However, such a purchase would likely have only limited payoffs for future export contracts, as appears to have been the case in the past. Moreover, the Navy rejected the Seahawk on grounds that it would not meet the unique operational requirements of Canada.[45] Also, the Seahawk lacked the range, capacity, and margin of safety defined as necessary for Canadian SAR requirements.[46] As a result, Canada was left with choosing between platforms either in the design, research and development stage or non-maritime forms. Thus, in contrast to the Leopard and CF-18 cases, Canada choose to procure a helicopter which was in the developmental stage. Although the decision contrasted with previous decisions to reject untried and untested platforms, it did differ in comparison to the CF-18 case. Whereas the Northrup F-19 had not been purchased by anyone, there was a commitment from the British Navy to purchase the EH-101 and expectation that Italy would also purchase the platform, especially given that the EH-101 was a joint venture between Augusta and Westland.

It is unclear, nonetheless, the extent to which industrial considerations and related export opportunities played a role in the decision to procure the EH-101. Buying into a system in the development stage does portend greater possibilities for technology transfer, innovation, and future contracts. According to the Department of National Defence, the contract, with offset guarantees of 113% entailed significant technology transfer. This transfer may have been a function of direct Canadian participation in the providing 10% of the platform itself, and Canadian participation in providing 83% of the electronics packages under the lead of Paramax as the prime contractor for this part of the contract. In the latter case, this may entail the transfer of technology from American parent firms to their Canadian subsidiaries.

Regarding future contracts and export opportunities, the final agreement with EH Industries provided a guarantee for future export related work. Canadian industry's contract to build 10% of the basic air frame, included not only the initial 50 platforms to be purchased by Canada, but all future platforms sold by the Augusta-Westland group, as long as Canadian firms remained competitive. According to government sources, future sales of the EH-101 were estimated in the 800 range. In addition, future export opportunities may have resided in two areas. First, future sales of the platform may have created opportunities for Paramax, and other Canadian firms participating in the electronics component to bid on future EH-101 sales to other purchasers, either as a group or individually. Of course, they would have faced competition from the companies providing the similar package directly to Augusta-Westland relative to the purchase of the platform by Great Britain and Italy. Second, the EH-101 decision was closely tied to the CPF. While export opportunities for the CPF are doubtful, the ability to offer an integrated "state-of-the-art" frigate and operational helicopter could have been attractive to many.

The EH-101 decision is indicative of two other phenomena of Canadian defence offset. The awarding of the electronics, systems integration component to Paramax as the prime contractor can be partially understood as a by-product of an earlier decision. A subsidiary of an American firm, Paramax was created in Montreal as part of the industrial benefits package associated with the CPF. It was created to develop and integrate the electronics, combat, communications, and machinery systems of the new CPF. Although the CPF project is not yet completed, one can speculate a degree of dependency on defence contracts. In other words, the EH-101, and likely future related contracts will see Paramax in a prominent role. This is not to argue that Paramax is not major, leading innovator. Rather, simply to point out that past offset packages can act to constrain options for future contracts.

Finally, the EH-101 reflected the final complaint of the Nielsen Task Force and Auditor-General's report; regional benefits. The contract package contained a specific breakdown of regional distribution: 30% Quebec, 30% Ontario, 25% Prairies, and 15% Atlantic Canada. This may reflect a codification of regional requirements in current and future offset agreements. At the same time, examining the specific companies identified regionally in the various press releases indicates an underlying strategy of support to existing companies — the strong. There was no indication that the contract included any relatively new firms, or promises to create ones as a part of the contract, notwithstanding the creation of EH Industries.

5.6 Conclusion

The evolution of Canada's policy towards defence industrial offsets, Industrial and Regional Benefits, reflects, not surprisingly a learning process. From the inital decision to formulate a specific policy or strategy in the mid-1970s to the now aborted EH-101 project, there has been an desire to structure Canadian offsets in an attempt to maximize benefits for Canada. Recognizing the shortcomings of indirect offsets, lack of technology transfer, short term build-to-print, and the lack of long term export opportunities can be seen to have culminated in a strategy exhibited by the EH-101 IRB package. The search for these benefits was not simply motivated by balance of trade and payment concerns. As evident in the search for industrial benefits, Canada also sought defence offsets as a means to enhance Canada's industrial capability through foreign investment and technology transfer. Requirements for successful bidding on Major Crown Pojects included a guarantee of offsets. In so doing, foreign companies were led to establish either subsidiaries in Canada or working relationships with Canadian firms. Thus, the high proportion of foreign and particularly American ownership of Canadian defence firms can be partially traced back to offset demands.

The evolution of Canadian IRB policy can be said to have come full circle. The apparently licensed production of pre-1970s period is followed by a period of a low risk minimalist strategy in the 1970s and finally a return to acquiring a Canadian role in production/assembly. Relatively common to all is the problem of exploiting industrial benefits as a means to provide a foundation for expanding industrial export opportunities and international competitiveness, notwithstanding the continued problem of export licenses. In the process, failure would have significant implications for subsequent decisions whereby future decisions became hostage to past decisions. The EH-101 project, perhaps, can be seen as the logical extension of this search for ensuring that Canadian firms would become internationally viable through initial participation in the development phase of the platform. Unfortunately, the intervention of political forces leading to its cancelation clearly indicates one of the major problems in formulating an effective strategy.

It is difficult to weigh the relative benefits and costs of Canadian policy over time. There is no doubt that it has enhanced the technological capacity and competitiveness of Canadian industry in many cases, Canada's balance of payments situation, and has provided employment across the country.[47] In addition, one can not ignore the political benefits, real or perceived, that may have been derived from Canadian IRB policy. However, the price paid in many cases has been borne by DND in terms of its ability to acquire the military capabilities necessary to meet its many roles and commitments. The fundamental question facing Canada is whether it can continue to use defence dollars to meet a wide range of economic and political demands at the price of Canada's military capability. There is no doubt that defence spending will continue to shrink in the foreseeable future, and despite the intent in DND to protect capital spending, there is no doubt that it will shrink as well.

This is not to argue that Canada must forego entirely its search for IRBs in defence spending. Rather it is to recognize that there are structural limits which Canada faces in terms of its defence industrial capacity in which IRBs should be concentrated on to ensure that existing strengths and advantages are exploited. In some cases, Canada's DIB through its unique access to the American market and longstanding business links to American firms is a natural candidate for participation in Canadian purchases from the United States and elsewhere. But, these firms are likely to participate regardless of any formal policy. Of course, there are problems on the horizon in the context of American defence industrial policy as it may affect the DPSA relationship and thus Canadian access to the American market, and corporate re-structuring in the United States. But, in terms of the former, existing IRBs policy is likely to be central to American desires to re-structure the relationship. Paradoxically, it should be noted that the successful search for a free trade relationship with the United States coincided with an anti-free trade policy in the defence area.

For Canada, as for many small defence markets, it faces the dilemma of supporting the strong within Canadian industry at the price of the weak in a regional economic and political sense. The dilemma, in effect, is between the industrial strengths of Central Canada by in large and the industrial weaknesses of the rest of Canada. On top of both, of course, are the various domestic political forces within the Canadian federal system. Concentrating on the strengths is a strategy to support firms which have existed successfully for significant period of time, are likely to have well established ties to other firms both in Canada, the United States, and elsewhere, and likely to have developed and exploited export niches. Offset support to these firms, it can be argued, is a means to strengthen their competitiveness through access to new products with potential future export opportunities. In addition, these firms are also likely to be able to absorb new technology, thereby promoting technology transfer and long term viability. However, as noted above, these firms are also likely to be the ones which would benefit from Canadian offshore defence procurement independent of offset requirements. Their long established technology niches and industrial relationships make them viable partners for foreign firms on economic efficiency grounds. Of course, there is no guarantee that foreign firms would voluntarily use Canadian firms. Nonetheless, an offset strategy to promote the strong is, in effect, a minimalist offset strategy.

The regional side of the equation, representing a desire to redirect government spending towards economically disadvantaged and depressed areas of the country, thus appears as a maximalist offset strategy. Such a strategy implies supporting the weak and establishing industrial capacity which will have a significant impact upon local economies. Offshore contractors are forced to move beyond Canadian firms with a long established track record and possibly existing ties with these contractors and establish new relationships with Canadian firms. In so doing, the strategy is a vehicle for expanding Canada's industrial and technological base. Firms not normally able to compete for such contracts will become beneficiaries of government funding, and potentially technology transfer. However, the problem of ensuring long term viability remains relative to existing domestic and international capacity. Without any fixed guarantee of participation in future contracts from the prime contractor, particulary problematic if the product is already in the full production stage elsewhere, these "new" defence firms become wholly dependent on future Canadian contracts.[48] Of course, an offset strategy to mix the benefits of the minimalist and maximalist perspectives is hinted at in the various critical reports. In this case, direct Canadian participation in production can be directed towards the strong, while relatively long-term maintenance and support could be directed towards the weak. Of course, this division of labour itself is problematic relative to the geographic distribution of capacity, and the associated costs in training and qualifying companies for participation in these contracts.[49] Moreover, any attempt to construct a rational offset strategy is in constant conflict with forces which bring into play a wide range of political considerations.

Overall, the formative years in the evolution of Canada's IRB offset practices revealed numerous shortcomings. Many of the shortcomings can be related to a learning process, and the Task Force Report provides a strong foundation for integrating the lessons of the past in terms of subsequent procurement. However, there remains an underlying tension in the very nature of IRBs. Requirements to use offsets for improving industrial competitiveness and export opportunities are in conflict with requirements to support regional development. Above this conflict are the political forces which operate on a different calculus; one that generally undermines the development of an effective offset policy.

Regardless, it is clear that the dilemmas facing Canada in developing a coherent IRB strategy are not likely to be resolved. The complexity of the system itself with its numerous government and non-government actors, and the external forces driving for a reduction in obstacles to some form of free trade in defence confronting domestic demands for the use of federal dollars for economic and political ends, both of which are likely to increase in degree in the future as other countries seek new defence markets and federal spending as a whole declines, are fundamental impediments to the development of a coherent IRB strategy. The victim, if there is one, is likely to be National Defence which will increasingly find itself unable to procure the military equipment it needs to meet its commitments; a situation somewhat affordable during the Cold War which will continue in reflection of the wider political and social context of Canadian attitudes towards defence.

For companies seeking to penetrate the Canadian market, they will continue to face requirements to formulate their bids in terms of providing industrial and regional benefits. Despite recent announcements of Canada seeking "the best value for money spent" in support of Canadian military requirements, business as usual will continue. Of course, Canada in light of defence cuts after the Cold War will have some degree of leverage in enticing foreign firms seeking new markets to provide these benefits. However, the premium Canada pays in so doing will have wider foreign policy implications in terms of its ability to meet its military commitments and thus acquire influence on the international stage and may likely be one of the many indications of Canada's drift back to isolationism.

Endnotes

1. Tucker argues that a non-military tradition is one of the dominant aspects of Canadian political culture, which has created a preference for diplomatic and pragmatic approaches to international politics. Robert Tucker. **Canadian Foreign Policy: Contemporary Issues and Themes**. Toronto: McGraw-Hill.1980. Middlemiss and Sokolosky provide an overview of the various explanations pertaining to the low salience of defence in Canada. D.W. Middlemiss and J.J. Sokolosky. **Canadian Defence: Decisions and Determinants**. Toronto: Harcourt, Brace, Jovanovich. 1989.

2. During the 1980s, Canadian defence spending did rise in absolute terms. However, in relation to the poor state of equipment after decades of neglect,

this increase did not amount to an expansion in Canada's military capability. In fact, Canadian spending as a proportion of GDP only marginally increased, as a proportion of Federal spending remained largely static, and equipment holdings in relation to the past shrank. See D. Middlemiss. "Canadian Defence Funding: Heading Towards Crisis". **Canadian Defence Quarterly.** 21:2. 1991.

3. Diefenbacker's indecision with regards to the acquisition of nuclear war-heads for the BOMARC missile, as part of deeper concerns about Canadian-American relations are seen as central to the outcome of the 1962 election. However, defence should be considered as the symptom of larger problems within the Conservative government. Outside of the conscription issues during both World Wars, the only other election which had a major defence component was the 1911 election in which the naval question played some role. Even here, it was overshadowed by the debate over free trade with the United States. Interestingly, many thought in the run up to the 1988 federal election that the issue of nuclear submarines would be a major issue. It was overshadowed by the debate on the Free Trade Agreement (FTA) with the United States. Finally, in the most recent election, many believed that the EH-101 decision would be significant, even though it had a marginal, if any impact on the crushing defeat of the government.

4. These agencies are the Atlantic Canada Opportunities Agency (ACOA), the Federal Office for Regional Development in Quebec, and Western Economic Diversification Canada.

5. While IRBs reflect elements of an industrial strategy, Byers points out that there is no systematic link between economic policy and industry in Canada as a whole and in the defence area specifically. R. Byers "Canadian Defence and Canadian Procurement: Implications for Economic Policy" in **Selected Problems in Formulating Foreign and Economic Policy**. D. Stairs and G. Winham, eds. Toronto: University of Toronto Press. 1985.

6. Privileged access is primarily the function of the waiver of the **Buy American** restrictions. Existing American legislative barriers include Small and Disadvantaged Businesses Set-Asides, the Berry Amendment (food and clothing for the military), the Burns-Tollefson Amendment (naval vessels), and the Bayh Amendment (Research and Development). Also, Canadian firms are unable to compete on certain projects for national security reasons.

7. For the period 1959-1986, Canada had a balance of defence trade deficit of C$2.437 billion. Robert Van Steenburg. "An Analysis of Canadian-American Defence Economic Cooperation" in **Canada's Defence**

Industrial Base. David Haglund. ed. Kingston: Ronald P. Frye. 1988. By all accounts, this deficit has continued. It should be noted, however, that large portions of defence related trade is not tracked between Canadian suppliers and American producers.

8. The Auditor-General reports that beginning in 1976, offsets became commonplace in Canadian policy. Auditor-General. **Report of the Auditor-General of Canada to the House of Commons 1992**. Ottawa: Supply and Services Canada. 1992. According to Todd, "Canada pioneered offset deals in the 1970s, ..." D. Todd. **Defence Industries: A Global Perspective**. New York: Routledge. 1988. It should be noted, depending on one's definition of offsets, that Canada prior to the 1970s undertook a variety of licensed production arrangements with American firms, as in the case of the F-104 Starfighter and F-5 Freedom Fighter.

9. The fourth MCP is the Canadian Patrol Frigate, which began in 1983. The original project entailed the purchase of 6 Frigates, shore facilities, and support from St. Johns Shipbuilding Limited. Subsequently, the contract was divided between St. Johns Shipbuilding of New Brunswick and MIL of Quebec, and in 1987, the contract was amended for an additional 6 Frigates. The overlap between the stages noted above, the appearance of the Auditor-Generals Report of 1984 which was critical of the CF-18 offset package, and the uniqueness of this project relative to the three mentioned above, it is discussed within the second stage.

10. The military's preference apparently was to procure existing American M-60s off-the-shelf.

11. The Third Option was initially introduced by Mitchell Sharp, then Minister for External Affairs in 1972. Basically, the original paper argued that Canada faced three options with regard to its international economic position: a status quo position which entailed dependency on the relationship with the United States; closer economic integration with the United States; and diversification towards expanded economic relationships with Europe, the Pacific Rim, and elsewhere. Mitchell Sharp. "Canada-U.S. Relations. Options for the Future". **International Perspectives**. Autumn. 1972.

12. Beyond the unilateral nature of the decision which violated the spirit of multilateralism in NATO, it is generally argued that opposition to the decision by Germany was not directly a function of the military importance of Canada's commitment to Europe and West German defence per se, but rather driven by a perceived inter-relationship between the Canadian and American commitment. A Canadian withdrawal, it was feared, would ignite

isolationist forces in the United States possibly leading to an American military withdrawal.

13. D. Todd. *op. cit.*, p. 231.

14. R. Tucker. *op. cit.*, pp. 155–162

15. Details are unavailable due to the confidential nature of the Request for Proposal (RFP).

16. Cited in R. Tucker. *op.cit.* p. 174.

17. In contrast to the Leopard I, there were several contenders besides the P-3 Orion and modified Boeing 707 LRPA. The others were quickly rejected for either failing to meet the requirements, too costly to maintain, or unproven. In comparison to the second stage, proposals to procure a Canadian produced platform were rejected.

18. F.L. Boyd. "The Politics of Canadian Defence Procurement: The New Fighter Aircraft Decision". in **Canada's Defence Industrial Base**. David Haglund.ed. Kingston: Ronald P. Frye. 1988. Boyd also points out that Canada missed several opportunities prior to the 1980 decision including participation in the Tornado Project, and proposals by Grumman to procure the F-14 and MD to procure the F-15. These missed opportunities were in part a function of funding considerations relative to the above mentioned Leopard I and Aurora purchases.

19. The figure of 100% is derived from confidential interviews and are inconsistent with the values reported above. The indirect/direct values are provided in National Defence. **1994–95 Estimates. Part III. Expenditure Plan**. Ottawa: Supply and Services Canada. 1994. Total forecast expenditures, non-recurring costs, as of March 31, 1994 are $C4.859 billion. On this basis, the indirect/direct proportions are 50% and 9% respectively. It is also noted that MD has provided industrial benefits valued at $C4.199 billion, representing 86% of forecast expenditures. Also, MD has transferred technology worth $C294 million on a commitment of $C291 million.

20. Among the elements of the offset package include fibre optics, composite materials, metals processing, and MD assistance to Canadian firms in licensing programs from American firms in the areas of wind energy, auto parts, health care products, and food processing. Office of Management and Budget. **Impact of Offsets on Defense-Related Exports**. 1986.

21. Auditor-General. **Report of the Auditor General of Canada to the House of Commons**. Ottawa: Supply and Services Canada. 1984. pp. 12: 30–32.

22. National Defence. **1994–95 Estimates. Part III. Expenditure Plan**. Ottawa: Supply and Services Canada. 1994.

23. Cited in Boyd. *op. cit.* p. 145.

24. J.M. Treddenick. "Regional Impacts of Defence Spending" in **Guns and Butter: Defence and the Canadian Economy**. B. MacDonald. ed. Toronto: Canadian Institute of Strategic Studies. Proceedings. 1984.

25. There are two elements to this perception: the requirement for the home nation to purchase the system; and the ability to obtain an initial export contract. The absence of both significantly explains the failure of the Northrup competitor to the F-16 and F-18 in particular. In the case of Canada, many individuals over time pointed out the significance of Canadian capital decisions for other nations. As a nation which rarely purchases new systems, its decisions are viewed as important indicators of the utility and value of the system by other nations.

26. Both the Task Force and Auditor-General's Reports argue that overhaul and maintenance, spare parts, and product support would provide not only significant contracts to Canadian firms, but also serve to a basis for increased export opportunities. In some cases, this may be correct. Such contracts may enable some firms to establish new export niches in the upgrade and life-extension component of defence production through the transfer of the requisite technology from the producer. However, life-cycle support is likely to have limited utility for establishing new export markets. It is the logical focus for most nations which import their major weapons platforms. Moreover, if the producer is willing to transfer the technology to Canada, it is likely either to be willing to transfer the technology to others as well or demand assurances that the technology will be restricted in application.

27. The list represents 16 of the 24 MCPs identified in the 1994-95 Estimates. Seven projects were excluded. They are the CF-18 and CF-18 AAM, North Warning System, Strategic Airlift Replacement, Militia Training Support centre, the New Shipbourne Aircraft/SAR Helicopter, the Maritime Coastal Defence Vessel and the Military Automated Air Traffic Control System. The CF-18 is discussed in the previous section and the NSA/SAR is discussed below. The North Warning System relates to a variety of considerations underlying traditional funding relationships in NORAD. The Strategic Airlift was a contract to purchase 5 used Airbus A310s consisting of three from Canadian International and one from International Markets and Blenhiem Aviation respectively. There were no industrial benefits associated with the purchases. The Militia Training support centre is a relatively

distinct project type and the Air Traffic Control Systems and Coastal Defence Vessel industrial benefits are under negotiation.

28. Ch-146 Griffon is based on the civilian Bell-412 Helicopter.

29. Auditor-General. **Report of the Auditor-General of Canada to the House of Commons 1992**. Ottawa: Supply and Services Canada. 1992.

30. The decision to award the CF-18 contract to Canadair met with substantial public opposition when it became known that Bristol had the best technical and price package. It was generally believed that the CF-5 contract was awarded to Bristol in Winnipeg as compensation for the loss of the CF-18 contract. It should also be noted that Bristol had received a contract at the same time from the USAF to upgrade elements of their F-5 fleet. Bristol and the Canadian government are currently involved in a legal dispute with Northrup over the rights to compete for foreign contracts to upgrade the F-5; a very lucrative market given the size of the F-5 fleet internationally. See B. Opall. "Northrup, Bristol to Settle Simmering F-5 Upgrade Dispute". **Defense News**. 9:11. Mar. 21–27. 1994.

31. The exception is the Arcturus Arctic and Maritime Surveillance Aircraft which involved the purchase of three CP-140s equipped for these roles; the same aircraft as the Aurora. Part of the package does include a commitment by Lockheed for Canadian participation in the F-22 project.

32. The production of the LLAD in Quebec included, it appears, a mandate for production in North America. Similarly, the LAV production line also has a North American mandate.

33. See Ian Anthony. **The Naval Arms Trade**. Oxford: Oxford University Press. 1989.

34. The current debt load of Saudi Arabia to the United States for military purchases significantly reduces the probability of an export contract. See P. Finnegan and B. Opall. "U.S. Grants Flexibility in Saudi Loan Repayments" **Defence News**. 9:21. May 30–June 5, 1994.

35. Essentially, the government seeks industrial benefits and technology transfer to enhance the international competitiveness of Canadian firms, but these firms then face significant obstacles in acquiring the necessary export permits to exploit opportunities stemming from IRBs; a point noted in the recent Auditor-General's report. Auditor-General. **Report of the Auditor-General of Canada to the House of Commons 1992**. Ottawa: Supply and Services Canada. 1992. p. 402.

36. In some cases, the awarding of the contract regardless was to the lowest bidder, such as in the case of the Low Level Air Defence system, and the Heavy Logistic Wheeled Vehicle (HLWV). In the former case, it represented the first export contract for the LLAD, developed by Oerlikon in Switzerland and assembled by Oerlikon Aerospace of Quebec, which may have been motivated by hopes of using the Canadian contract as a means to penetrate other markets, particularly the United States where the Sgt. York system was in the process of being cancelled. The HLWV contract, assembled by UDTC of Ontario, used components from Steyr of Austria. Interestingly, UDTC no longer produces heavy trucks.

37. The problem confronting Canada is almost identical to that confronting the United States shipbuilding industry. In the latter case, this industry is almost wholly dependent on U.S. Navy contracts and maintenance of this part of the defence industrial base is a major issue confronting the United States today. In Canada, defence spending accounts for 62.4% of employment in the shipbuilding and repair industry, and 100% of employment in shipbuilding in New Brunswick (i.e. the CPF). Major Serge Caron. **The Economic Impact of Canadian Defence Expenditures**. Occasional Paper 1–94. Kingston: Centre for National Security Studies. 1994.

38. "Canadian Gun Order is a first for NATO" Jane's Defence Weekly. July, 2, 1984. p. 16.

39. Auditor-General. **Report of the Auditor-General of Canada to the House of Commons 1992**. Ottawa: Supply and Services. 1992. p. 397.

40. This point has already been noted above in the case of both LAV purchases. The CH-146 purchase is designed to replace three previous helicopters: the Kiowa, Huey, and Chinook. While the CH-146 can perform the functions of the Kiowa and Huey, it lacks the any significant heavy lift capacity previously available with the Chinooks.

41. The government in the mid-to-late 80s had also decided to procure a Class 8 Icebreaker from Versatile of Vancouver, which could be seen as an attempt to balance the regional distribution of contracts. This decision however fell victim to budgetary limitations. It is possible that the MCDV may be awarded to Vancouver in lieu of the cancelation of this project. If so, the future of St. Johns Shipbuilding may become a major political issue.

42. Specifically, the leading candidate, who would subsequently win the leadership race, to replace Brian Mulroney, Kim Campbell, was moved into the Defence portfolio.

43. National Defence, **1994–95 Estimates: Part III Expenditure Plan**. Ottawa: Supply and Services Canada. 1994. p. 160. It is unclear whether this figure accounts for all remaining outlays and penalties associated with cancelation. Unofficial estimates put the final total near the C$1 billion range.

44. Part of the political debate surrounded the original cost estimate of C$4.4 billion which was the estimate base on current dollars and included infrastructure, maintenance, training, and support. Almost immediately after the announcement, the figure grew to C$5.8 billion and higher based upon future inflation rates.

45. According to Project members, the SEAHAWK could not operate independently from its naval platform; a requirement defined as vital for the New Shipbourne Aircraft. In particular, this entails the ability of the helicopter in its ASW role to act independently of the mother ship. In contrast, the SEAHAWK requires a direct linkage to its mother ship.

46. Additional range was viewed as vital to support SAR needs in the North Atlantic. Similarly, the EH-101 has three engines and is able to fly with one engine incapacitated. Finally, the EH-101 was also to be equipped with a de-icing capability; also viewed as vital for service in the North Atlantic.

47. There are no figures available on employment generated by defence IRBs. According to the most recent study on the economic impact of defence spending, only 0.6% of industrial jobs in Canada are a function of domestic purchases. Major Serge Caron. *op. cit.*

48. Industry also notes that regional requirements result in reduced productivity and increased over-capacity. In the long term, the net result is short term regional contracts with little possibility of long term success, unless the government is willing to continue to support specific firms in specific regions through future contracts.

49. Joint Industry/Government Working Group. **Major Crown and Complex Capital Projects: Procurement Issues and Recommendations**. 1992

Chapter 6

Offsets and French Arms Exports

*Jean-Paul Hébert Interdisciplinary Research
Center for Peace and Strategy Surveys, Paris*

Offsets can play an important role in securing arms sales and the French experience bears this out. However, offsets have not always been so crucial. Indeed, the importance of offsets really began when the North European NATO countries were looking to order replacement combat aircraft in the mid-1970s. Competition to secure this order was intense and, since then, offsets have grown in popularity with the precise package offered usually being tailored to the requirements of the purchaser. The analysis of offsets is hampered by the absence of precise contract details. However, the need for such an analysis is particularly strong as, in the 1990s, new forms of offset are developing as aggressive exporters, backed by their respective governments, seek sales in an ever shrinking defence market.

6.1   The 'Contract of the Century': The Birth of Offsets

In 1974, the replacement of the north European NATO countries' combat air fleets gave birth to offsets. Belgium, Denmark, Holland, Norway and the Federal Republic of Germany were operating the F-104 Lockheed Starfighter which was becoming obsolete, having had many accidents.[1]

The four smaller countries took the decision to select only one supplier for their combined order to minimise the purchase price. The competitors included the Viggen (Sweden), the F-16 from General Dynamics (US) and Dassault's Mirage F1-M53 (France). The combined total order was to be about 350 aircraft, not including German purchases. The large size of this order, combined with the trans-atlantic rivalry between the potential suppliers, meant that the competition would acquire complex political and economic elements.

Dassault, strongly backed by the French government, offered an attractive offset: 70% of the manufacturing to be locally contracted.[2] In addition, its price was guaranteed without any further currency adjustment and the maximum inflation rate was to be 7% per year, with any additional inflation being paid for by the French government.

The American package was no less attractive. General Dynamics, bidding with the F-16, estimated that their offset would generate jobs for up to 5000 staff in Europe. In addition, they agreed to a US$ payment of only 20% of the price, the balance being accepted in local currency.[3] General Dynamics also proposed to erect in Europe a plant for manufacturing the necessary high-technology materials to be used in the aircraft. Furthermore, the USAF proposed to base 200 of the 650 aircraft that they intended to purchase in Europe and to have them maintained by the four European countries.

There were also other offsets not directly linked to the contract proper. These included the promise to examine the possibility of improving European landing rights at US airports and to improve the access of European tankers to oil transportation contracts normally reserved for US shipowners. Other proposals were of a more political nature, and were aimed at turning offsets to the US' advantage. In 1974, the US Congress passed a bill to offset the cost of American soldiers in Europe against the profit from American arms sales to NATO. The implication was that if US arms sales to NATO fell then there was the possibility that American forces in Europe would be cut. This was not attractive to many Europeans.[4]

We shall not further elaborate on this competition[5] which finally led to the success of the F-16, but it is very interesting to note so many and varied proposals as distinctive evidence of the negotiators' creativity. Finally, this degree of rivalry was to become typical of future competitions and meant that this contract was the first in which offsets played such an important role.

6.2   Common Offsets Practice in French Arms Exports

A Corinthe grapes and green olives market leader? DASSAULT of course ... And MATRA is a great vegetable seller; and THOMSON is an oil products dealer ...[6]

These are some of the more unusual offsets associated with the export of French arms although many more could be listed, such as the French RVI trucks sold for Moroccan jeans.[7] However, in order to analyse the offsets associated with French exports, it is necessary to define what is meant by the term 'offset'. Barter (the exchange of goods for goods) is not usually considered as a form of offset,[8] whereas a real offset involves a responsibility shared between the two partners for manufacturing some of the products exported by the contracting seller.[9]

As far as arms contracts are concerned, we shall define offsets in a broad sense, as a system of processes agreed upon by the seller and aimed at:

- either an immediate reduction of the buyer's payment (bartering or simultaneous sales from the buyer)

- or a deferred reduction of his payments by further sales generating counter-payments (deferred counter sales, sub-contracting, employment generation and so on)
- or technology transfers, offsetting part or the whole of the initial contract cost

We shall also include, as a form of offset, any other kind of incentive offered to the buyer (and of which there are many types).

6.2.1 Offsets Leading to an Immediate Reduction in Cash Payment

Experts usually name this offset "financial offset".[10] It may be a simple barter, or a simultaneous set of counterpurchases, the exact process being disclosed only in the contract which is seldom publicly available. Bartering involves an exchange of products without cash payment. Counterpurchase involves two separate payments, in any order: the arms buyer's payment coming first, or second to the offset payment by the arms seller. The payment itself may be made through warranted accounts in France, or "trustees' accounts" opened with British, American or German banks.

These kinds of contracts are often used for French arms exports, of which 75% to 85% involve third world countries usually selling raw materials or oil. With developed countries, the offset usually consists of a counterpurchase of industrial products or services.

6.2.1.1 The Counterpurchase of Raw Materials

This is common practice in Indian arms purchases, and also for their large civil equipment buys. For example, in 1987, when India bought 20 ATR 42 aircraft from the French firm Aerospatiale, there was a requirement to counterpurchase raw materials for 50% of the contract value i.e. FrFr 400 million.[11]

The same kind of demand had previously been met by GEC-Alsthom. To sign a contract with Cachemire for the erection of a water dam, 20% of the contract value was demanded in counterpurchases i.e. FrFr 720 million.[12] Similarly, Malaysia tried to obtain the counterpurchase of raw materials for a contract involving the purchase of 12 Mirage 2000 fighter aircraft in 1989.[13] The most important offset involving the diversified counterpurchase of primary products happened when Greece bought 40 Mirage 2000 aircraft[14] worth US$2.1 billion. This deal will be described further below. On occasions some of the Gulf Countries ask for such non-oil raw material offsets. This was the case with the Saudi Arabian purchase of Mistral missiles in 1989.[15]

6.2.1.2   Oil Supplies

French armaments exports have also generated important oil offsets. The reason for this is that some of the traditional buyers of French weapons are countries most familiar with such offsets. The four countries producing oil and heavily involved with offsets are Saudi Arabia, Iraq, Iran, and Nigeria. Together, they provide 60% of all oil offsets.[16]

Iraq's debt to France for military supplies was increasing in the early 1980s due to the Iran-Iraq war. Part of the payment for this equipment was through direct oil deliveries and, over the period 1983-1985, Total-CFP and ELF Aquitaine lifted about 80000 barrels per day.[17]

According to press reports, the negotiations between France and Saudi Arabia concerning the sale of 40 to 50 Mirage 2000 aircraft, worth US$2.2 to US$2.7 billion, involved "specially good terms"[18] for oil supplies: Total-CFP and ELF-Aquitaine would have lifted about 70 million barrels of crude oil over a two or three year period.[19] A similar arrangement had already been executed when Saudi Arabia purchased 10 Boeing 747s under a barter scheme involving 34 million barrels over three months.[20]

More recently, Saudi Arabia has moved away from the provision of crude oil supplies as an offset but this was to make room for petro-chemical offsets, as was shown in their proposal in 1989 for the Mistral missiles negotiation.[21] In 1984, the French government signed a contract for the supply of 18 Mirage 2000 aircraft (priced at US$25 million each) to Abu Dhabi. This contract involved the supply of two million tonnes of crude oil as part payment[22] and, ultimately, Total-CFP agreed to take delivery of 15 million barrels of crude oil.[23]

6.2.1.3   The Counterpurchase of Industrial Products and Services

This form of offset is, of course, most frequently associated with arms exports to developed countries. Scandinavian countries have often enforced such clauses in their purchases from France. For example, in 1986 Finland bought the anti-tank weapon Apilas from the French firm Matra-Manurhin worth Fin. MK 290 but the counterpurchase involved an equivalent FrFr 400 million purchase of paper machines.[24] In 1992 Finland initiated a competition between American, Swedish and French industries for the supply of its new air force fleet. This competition was very important for Dassault who had received no export order since 1986. As a counterpurchase, the French offered to develop their seaport traffic and sea transportation with Finnish shipowners.

In 1987, Sweden bought 10 Super Puma helicopters (FrFr 400 million) with undisclosed "industrial offsets".[25] Three years later, Norway bought Mistral anti-tank weaponry for FrFr 350 million with a requirement to spend about 75% of this amount on Norwegian industrial products.[26]

For a long while now Belgium has required offsets when buying French arms, and on some occasions has sought industrial counterpurchases. As early as 1985, and before development had been completed, Belgium committed itself to the purchase of Mistral anti-tank weapons from Matra. This decision involved about 1000 missiles and 150 launchers worth FrFr 560 million[27] against a 100% offset, part of which was to be industrial orders placed with Belgian suppliers. The final contract in 1988 was somewhat smaller (714 missiles) but worth FrFr 588 million[28] with a detailed offset requirement that balanced various regional interests (analysed further below) and which included a 25% counterpurchase from Belgian suppliers.[29] Some less developed countries also seek industrial counterpurchases when purchasing defence equipment. For example, India typically makes such demands when buying arms.[30] Part of the offset associated with the Greek purchase of Mirage 2000 aircraft included the purchase Greek industrial products. However, there were difficulties finding Greek industrial products that met the quality standards demanded by French buyers.[31] Despite these difficulties, the four French corporations responsible for the offset (Dassault-Aviation, Thomson-CSF, SNECMA and Matra) have purchased Greek products and services worth FrFr 350 million, including industrial products, during the two years 1987–1988.

Services, including tourism, play an important role in the Greek offset and the four French contractors contributed about 10% of the offset total in tourist services. The total offset was 60% of the FrFr 7.934 billion contract value, about FrFr 4.8 billion.[32] A Franco-Greek tourism company was incorporated under the name of "Vacances Mondiales", and signed a contract with the four French corporations worth FrFr 550 million to purchase holiday sites, rooms, suites, bungalows and so on.[33] These were then sold to the French public. It is worth noting that these tourism offsets were easier to fulfil than those requiring the purchase of Greek industrial products.

A counterpurchase requirement need not necessarily involve the vendor purchasing goods itself. It might, instead, involve the vendor seeking third parties to buy the goods produced by the purchaser. This is the type of commitment that Dassault made in 1988 when agreeing a 10 year hire-purchase contract for five business aircraft (Falcon 900s) with Australia. The offset involved Dassault helping to find buyers for the Australian second-hand Mirage III aircraft, bought previously from Dassault.[34] This agreement worked very well, and the Mirage III were purchased by Pakistan.[35] The same trading know-how was also the subject of negotiations in 1991 with Finland: Dassault offered as offset to help to market the Valmet training aircraft.[36]

Sometimes, the offset products are dual use and this is often the case with civil aircraft. When Brazil decided to purchase 12 Super-Puma helicopters, despite aggressive American competition, the French commitment to consider buying Brasilia Embraer[37] civil aircraft was of no small importance.

6.2.2   Offsets Reducing the Purchaser's Foreign Currency Burden

The difference between these and the previously described offsets is that, although they are part of the contract, they are actually executed some time later. They result in a reduction of foreign currency payments or alternatively generate an extra currency contribution to the balance of payments. Two main types of this form of offset can be identified: deferred counter-contracts, often involving the reverse sale of armaments; and the purchase of local manufactures, generating employment in the domestic economy, and made according to the terms of the contract by the seller.

6.2.2.1   Deferred Counter-contract

This form of offset consists of a system of "cross arms contracts", although the actual transfers need not be simultaneous. These counter-contracts need not be restricted to military production, but where they do include civil products these are usually manufactured by a company mainly producing military goods. This is specially the case for aircraft manufacturers. An important point is that the offset may sometimes be a simple "declaration of intent", without a formal firm commitment to purchase. This was the case when, in 1987, France bought five short take-off CASA 212 aircraft from Spain, as part of an exchange package which was to also involve a Spanish purchase of 18 Super-Puma helicopters from the French firm, Aerospatiale. However, Spain finalised the details of its purchase before the French.[38] A similar offset occurred a year later when France bought eight C-235 cargo planes worth FrFr 50 million each, in the hope of selling French equipment to Spain and of encouraging the Spanish to join the Rafale fighter aircraft program.[39]

Reciprocal purchase deals were also successfully achieved between France and Brazil. In 1988, Brazil, despite substantial US pressure, took the decision to again purchase French helicopters as they did in 1985. Worth a total of US$248 million, 16 Ecureuils and 36 Dauphins were sold, partly because of the attractive financing package offered by the French, but mainly because French agreed to equip their air force with Brazilian Tucano training aircraft,[40] manufactured by Embraer. Apart from the revenue, an obvious benefit of this sale for the Brasilians was the confirmation it provided of the aircraft's quality standards. The French purchase effectively provided a label "used by the French air force" for the Tucano. The first two of the proposed 50 aircraft were ordered in 1991.[41]

The same type of cross-contract considerations were present during the negotiations for the French purchase of the US AWACS aircraft. As a *quid pro quo*, France wanted the US to favour the French communications system, named RITA.[42] For their part, the American side saw the offset as running in the reverse direction, and reminded the French of their earlier decision to re-engine their KC-135 aircraft with the Franco-American CFM-56 engine supplied by General Electric/SNECMA.[43]

6.2.2.2 *Local Manufacturing Provided by the Seller*

This involves the vendor agreeing to purchase from the buyer parts and components to go into the equipment that is the subject of the contract. This bring closer co-operation between the two countries' companies than would a straightforward counterpurchase requirement. In some cases, this form of offset may even involve technology transfers, with coproduction or licensing agreements. Publicly available information is often not detailed enough to appreciate the exact size of the local contribution. Sometimes, only the existence of a local manufacturing agreement is known rather than its magnitude. In other instances, maintenance agreements are signed, or components are known to be locally produced, or there is a local assembly line, particularly for aircraft contracts. This form of offset may even go as far as the complete manufacture of the product locally.

Unspecific Local-Contracting:
The local sub-contracting arrangements are sometimes very vague. In 1987, when Sweden purchased ten Super-Puma helicopters, worth FrFr 400 million, little more was mentioned than that "this order includes industrial and technical offset".[44] Similarly, in 1992, when Finland finally opted for the US McDonnell Douglas F-18 aircraft, it was only known that 100% of the value of the contract would be offset by the purchase of Finnish goods.[45] And when the Austrian government purchased several hundred Mistral missiles worth FrFr 730 millions, "more than 100% was offset within a wide range of transport, telecommunication, space and publishing industries" according to the Matra-Hachette declaration.[46]

Sometimes the existence of an offset is reported without any further detail. In 1989, Switzerland took the decision to purchase anti-tank mines HPD F2 from the French firm TRT. This granted offsets worth 74% of the contract value to several Swiss companies including TAVARO (Sion) and MFA (Altdorf).[47] Similarly, when buying a number of Franco-German Milan weapons worth FrFr

350 million from MBB, Spain sought that two-thirds of the value of this contract should be spent by MBB buying goods from the Spanish firm Santa Barbara.[48] One year later, Spain again opted for a contract involving several hundred Mistral missiles and 200 launching devices, with a total value of some FrFr 830 million. It was formally agreed that various Spanish companies, such as INISEL, Santa Barbara, OCSA and ENOSA, would co-operate in the production of the equipment.[49] Thomson-CSF won a competition in the Netherlands for the supply of 14 Crotale missile systems worth FrFr 850 million thanks to co-operation arranged with Fokker and HSA[50] for the manufacture of the missiles.[51] A year later, the same exporter obtained a Turkish order for 14 radar systems worth FrFr 900 million with an agreement for the involvement of Turkish Company Tefeken in the manufacture of the product.[52]

Co-production involves a more definite commitment, involving a fairly equal importance of each partner. It was expressly mentioned only in the Belgium contract for the purchase of Mistral weaponry in 1988.[53] The co-production arrangement was based on the production of 30,000 missiles, which as of 1994, had not been achieved, despite numerous orders. This clause may possibly generate arguments as a similar one did in 1993 between the US and Taiwan. At the beginning of the year, Taiwan stopped payments associated with the purchase of F-16 aircraft worth about US$6 billion because of a disagreement concerning the share of production that had been forthcoming to Taiwan. The contract stated that 10% of the employment due to this order would be awarded to Taiwan through technology transfer and local production.[54]

Maintenance Sub-Contracts:
These operations generate employment over several years. They involve high local technical standards, but are less of a commitment than coproduction contracts. Such an agreement was, for instance, signed between the French firm SNECMA and the Greek company HAI[55] when Greece bought F-1 Mirage aircraft. This agreement involved the local maintenance of the aircraft and the Atar 9K-50 engine which equipped the F-1 in that part of the world.[56] Similarly, when France purchased US C-130 Hercules cargo planes, the negotiations commenced for 10 to 12 aircraft[57] with offsets at 60% to 70%.[58] At the end of the day, the contract covered six Lockheed aircraft, with a 60% offset spread over eight years[59] with long maintenance contracts to Sogerma, a subsidiary of Aerospatiale, and to Dassault Aviation.[60]

Sub-Contractor Production of Components or Parts:
Components and parts are frequent elements of offsets in the aerospace industry because such items are typically not produced by the prime contractor but are, instead, bought in from subcontractors. When Greece split its order for combat

aircraft between 40 American F-16 fighters and 40 French Mirage 2000, the main purpose was indeed to maximise the volume of orders for components and parts placed with Greek industry.[61] However, this later raised problems. Against Greek criticism of the delay in providing these sub-contracts, the French alleged that Greek manufacturers were finding it difficult to meet the necessary quality standards and needed to improve the quality of their labour forces.[62]

Similar problems did not arise with the Belgium purchase of the Mistral missile which involved a 100% of offset,[63] part of which comprised components for the Mistral system.[64] Spanish industry is also familiar with undertaking sub-contractor work, co-production or licensed production, with French industry. This explains why the purchase of 18 Super-Puma helicopters resulted in Spanish firms manufacturing several components. The sub-contracts went to CASA, AISA,[65] Marconi Espanola, Inisel, Sener, Berner, Gutmar, Ceta and Evec.[66] This FrFr 950 million contract was later disclosed to reveal that of the 18 machines, six will be delivered by Aerospatiale and the remaining 12 locally assembled by CASA. Furthermore, CASA will assemble as an offset 50 further machines to be delivered to other customers, and will manufacture governing wings and transmissions for Super-Pumas, grounding devices for the Gazelle (another helicopter made by Aerospatiale) and, on Gazelles, will fit and maintain Malika turbines.[67] The last aspect of this offset is particularly important as it involves a close relationship between the Spanish firm CASA and the French Aerospatiale.

A similar agreement could have occurred between France and Canada, should the contract for the purchase of the Leclerc armed vehicle materialise. In the case of a Canadian purchase of the Leclerc, a number of important subcontracts for major elements of the vehicle were to be placed in Canada.[68]

Local Assembly Agreements:
These agreements may significantly facilitate a sale because they involve knowhow transfers. The Super-Puma assembled in Spain, as mentioned above, is a good example of this phenomenon. Such attractive proposals have recently been offered by Dassault-Aviation.[69] In 1986, the assembly of a second set of 20 Mirage fighter aircraft for Egypt was offered to the Arab Industrial Organisation[70] together with the assembly of some Super-Puma helicopters. Similarly Dassault, facing intense competition when seeking sales of its Mirage 2000-5 aircraft, has offered large offsets including the local assembly of the aircraft as well as the opportunity to manufacture components and spares.[71]

Agreement Leading to Full Licensed Production:
These are the most demanding agreements, technology wise, and they lead to the strongest links between firms in the seller and buyer countries. They obviously improve not only employment but also the level of technical know-how in the

purchaser's economy. And because of the substantial capital which has to be raised both for investment and labour training, this form of offset is typically of a long term nature. The buyer, having invested large amounts of capital, will look for further orders from the seller. The latter, of course, will not be enthusiastic about technology transfers as these have the potential to generate further competition. The seller will also seek to concentrate his interests on co-operation with one particular buyer.

A good example of this kind of link occurred between India and USSR. India sought Russian military supplies but faced a shortage of foreign currency with which to pay for them. Hence India's desire for the Russians to purchase Indian industrial products which, of course, the Russians were happy to accept. Particularly remarkable was the Indian manufacture of T-72 armoured vehicles near Madras, and the production of Mig 27 aircraft in Nasik (by the Hindustan Aeronautics Co).[72] Because of the reputation of Indian technology in the aircraft industry, in the early 1980s, Dassault attempted to sell 110 Mirage 2000 aircraft which were to be locally manufactured.[73]

Nevertheless, among French arms exports, local manufacturing remains an exception. One such contract was signed with Egypt, within the framework of a government policy to help to develop this country's military industry, as an offset for the purchase of Sinaï 23-2 anti-aircraft systems[74] designed by the French firm Thomson-CSF, TBA, Hispano Suiza, and ESD.[75] This system consists of an armed vehicle and a 23 mm gun with a SATCP weapon, the Sakr Eye, made by the Egyptian government military workshop and the Sakr Company.[76] A smaller contract was signed with the German Federal Republic in 1988 for the supply of French designed BAP 100 bombs for destruction of landing runways. These were to be manufactured by the Bundesamt für Wehrtechnik und Besachaffung.[77]

6.2.3 Technology Transfers

This is the third kind of industrial and economic transfer. These transfers are not restricted to offsets. There are simple agreements for transferring licences, or know-how, or establishing co-operative ventures, or the co-production of goods for sale to third parties. Examples include Franco-Swedish co-operation;[78] Franco-Russian negotiations on nuclear weapons' dismantling;[79] the erection by France of an armaments plant in Thailand;[80] and the sale by the French firm, Manurhin Equipment, of three workshops producing munitions to Taiwan.[81] However, technology transfers were also involved in a number of offset arrangements that have already been described above, such as local manufacture and assembly. It is also significant that some contracts include explicit technology transfers and there is evidence that such transfers have been a key factor during the negotiations, particularly where underdeveloped countries are involved. In 1986, when discussing the possibility of the sale of a second batch of Mirage aircraft to Egypt, Dassault offered to build a high-technology composite materials plant, for civil and military purpose.[82]

A similar offer was made in 1985 when GIAT,[83] competing for the contract to supply 155mm guns to India,[84] offered to transfer the very up-to-date technology of its 155mm AUF1 through a licensing agreement.[85] Developed countries are also interested in such technology transfers. When considering the purchase of French aircraft in 1991, Finland ascertained that "Dassault had no objection to complete technology transfers, without restrictions even on the most advanced systems".[86]

Some of the contracts that have been actually signed involve developed countries. When ordering 988 Thomson Brandt artillery launchers and 60 mortars in 1988, Switzerland received, as offset, the licence to manufacture these mortars in Swiss government workshops.[87] And Austria, when buying Mistral weapons in 1993, obtained "a large co-operation and investment program" which is now in progress.[88]

However, less developed countries remain by far the main ones to push for such kinds of offset. Greece had already benefited from an important transfer of technology in 1983[89] concerning the maintenance and refurbishing of Mirage F-1 engines. This was enlarged some years later with the sale of Mirage 2000 aircraft. During 1987–1988, the four major French companies concerned[90] provided a total industrial investment worth FrFr 628 million.[91]

Egypt, as noted above, has obtained the technology to make locally the missile bought as part of its purchase of the Sinaï 23-2 anti-aircraft system as well as the right to export such products.[92]

Gulf countries, important customers for French armaments, have required technology transfer offsets with many of their purchases. In 1989, Saudi Arabia initiated negotiations for an offset agreement similar to that signed with both the US[93] and the UK. The Saudis require that part of the amount paid to France for armament supplies be invested into industry and high technology projects in their country.[94] Their aim is not to reduce their currency payment, but to help create factories as a contribution to Saudi Arabia's development. Particularly favoured would be Franco-Saudi joint ventures. These investments should be significant, the aim being that about one-third of the value of the defence contract be reinvested locally.[95] Offsets of this form and magnitude were requested during the negotiations for the sale of the Mistral missiles and anti-aircraft frigates[96] and led to a contract for the supply of 3 anti-aircraft ships one year later, worth FrFr 18 billion. The 35% offset concerned mainly civil and military high technology joint ventures not in the oil industry.[97]

Similarly, the Leclerc tank contract with Abu Dhabi involved a 60% offset "in order, through industry and technology transfers, and also new ventures, to contribute to the Emirates other civil and military projects".[98] In order to manage these offsets, GIAT Industries established a permanent office in Abu Dhabi in charge of generating joint ventures with technology transfers, worth a total of FrFr 2 billion within 10 years. This office, named "French Offset Partners", has already considered 250 non-oil industry projects.[99]

6.3   Other Clauses Being Equivalent to Offsets

The above description has focused on what are usually considered to be the standard forms of offsets. However, many procurement decisions might be influenced by other factors which can also be termed offsets. This category would include favourable financial terms, gift/countergift, and even political decisions. The truth is that, in a buyer's market, the buyer is strong just because he may potentially purchase and it is this strength that is the very source of offsets. Because the seller wants the sales contract, he will meet the buyer's conditions or at least some of them. This has, therefore, nothing to do with discounts, premiums or bonuses designed to enhance the product's marketing. These negotiations lead to a specific contract which will vary from one deal to another. These conditions will not identical in each sale, nor will there emerge a reference case which serves as the basis for all future deals. Here we are far away from conventional market competition and, for this reason, we now outline some of the forms that these more unconventional offsets might take.

6.3.1   Attractive Finance Packaging

Below we discuss a large variety of financial arrangements which might be attractive to the customer including payment terms, credits or gifts, and price reductions.

6.3.1.1   Payment Conditions

These are usually far more liberal than those found in more conventional lines of business. When selling to India, the USSR accepted deferred payments over 10 or even 20 years, with an interest rate of 2% and the possibility of paying in roubles.[100] Using the same factors (long deferred payment and low interest rates) Thomson-CSF won the Turkish order for mobile radar, against particularly strong American competition from General Electric. The total amount, FrFr 900 million, was "payable over even a longer period and at a lower interest-rate" according to sources.[101] In 1985, Brasil opted for Aerospatiale Super-Puma helicopters. Interest rates and the availability of deferred payments played an important role in securing the contract.[102] Nevertheless, the competing US firms protested on the basis that the "finance conditions as offered by Sikorski were just as equally attractive".[103]

6.3.1.2   Credits

It is not unusual for arms sales contracts to include a clause stating that the seller will grant, one way or another, a credit covering part of the purchase amount. This occurred with the Brasilian purchase of Super-Pumas. No details were obtainable in Paris, but the *Financial Times* announced the establishment of a French credit amounting to 185% of the contract value![104] And three years later, when Brasil took the decision to place a further order for French helicopters,[105] this contract was partly covered by credits provided by French banks.

India, thanks to their aggressive negotiators, obtained low interest rate credits when buying helicopters from France and the UK. With regard to their order for French equipment, FrFr 400 million were granted at a rate of 2.5% over 28 years.[106] In this instance, the finance package proved decisive in winning the competition. The UK had started negotiations with a credit covering two-thirds of the order (at that time for 27 helicopters).[107] But at the end of the day, the 21 Westland W.30, worth FrFr 650 million, had been offered with a 100% credit.[108] France had "offered as a free gift" 8 out of the 27 helicopters.[109] This kind of clause also occurred in the sale of 155mm calibre guns from the Swedish firm Bofors to India. Giat, the French firm, lost the contract because of "specially favourable Swedish credit terms and government subsidies". More precisely, a gift of FrFr 300 million was budgeted for by the Swedish administration in 1986 together with the provision of a further FrFr 400 million at a very low interest rate.[110]

It is rather difficult to precisely identify price reductions because they are rarely disclosed and also because in armaments sales the exact price of the contract can be difficult to determine. Nevertheless, in 1987 the French firm Thomson-CSF obtained the Turkish radar contract because it cut the price by half from its initial offer.[111] Orders from India are also often subject to important price reductions, from 10% to 30%.[112] It seems likely that the 40 Mirage 2000 aircraft sold to India in 1985 "have been actually priced at 75% of their initial rate".[113]

These finance clauses are more or less attractive. For instance, Gulf oil producing countries do not rate them as of major importance. The offsets agreed by France and Saudi Arabia in 1990 in the anti-aircraft ships contract is evidence of this: 35% of the total contract value of FrFr 18 billion is to be invested in joint ventures with a capital contribution of both countries (25% each in bank loans and capital sharing, the balance of 50% being provided by the Saudi government through a 15 year loan at a preferential interest rate).[114]

6.3.2 "Deception Counterpart" and Gift/Countergift

There may sometimes be only an informal link between different arms contracts. This is usually reported in the media as "deception counterpart" when an unsuccessful supplier on a big contract is awarded by the customer a less important contract to minimise the possible harmful effect on their relationship. As an example, the Swiss ordered 60mm mortar ammunitions worth FrFr 100 million from TBA[115] when the F-16 was finally ordered instead of Mirage 2000.[116] The same thing seemed to happen when Singapore ordered Dutch patrol aircraft instead of Mirage/Aerospatiale aircraft. Singapore ordered French Exocet missiles to equip these planes.[117] When, in 1988, Belgium signed a contract for the supply of Italian helicopters worth FrFr 1.8 billion rather than the French rival model, Belgium alleged that an "advance offset" had been the Mistral missiles order placed with France a few months earlier.[118]

Offsets can also be retaliatory. In 1992 France opted for the Swedish caterpillar personnel carrier, the Haegglund BV-206, in preference to the Finnish Sisu. It has been alleged that this decision was a consequence of the Finnish refusal to equip their combat airfleet with French Mirage 2000.[119] The French decision to purchase eight Spanish cargo planes (the CN-235) has been noted as a friendly gesture, not formally linked to the French Rafale program. However, the undisclosed hope was that Spain would make a reciprocal countergift[120] in the form of favouring the French program for a new combat aircraft.[121] However, calling this an "offset" is rather an over-statement because nothing was actually formalised in terms of an exchange of contracts or of cross-orders. Certain gifts have been more clearly linked with specific contracts. For instance, following the sale of Mirage 2000 aircraft, Greece complained about the poor performances of the aircraft's radar and the slow progress made with offsets. The case was solved in 1992 through the provision of a "discreet offset" involving the supply of a free (second hand) Falcon 900 business jet by Dassault Aviation.[122]

Different parties will take different views as to which transaction is offsetting the one under discussion. The French purchase of the AWACS system was delayed as the French sought US purchases of its equipment. The US mentioned their choice of the Franco-American CFM-56 engine to power their KC-135 aircraft. However, France considered that this purchase was made prior to the commencement of negotiations for the AWACS and could not be considered as an offset towards the new contract. The offset aimed at by France was an order for the French RITA system.[123] Later, the US argued that their purchase of the French BAP anti-runway bombs should also offset the AWACS sale but France persisted, still seeking an order for the RITA system.[124] Finally, the US ordered the RITA system, but not as formal offset for the AWACS purchase![125] The AWACS offset amounted to 130% of the contract, 80% through the purchase of CFM-56 engines and 50% in orders to the French aircraft industry over eight years. Assembly was to be by UTA, and refuelling beams were to be manufactured by Sogerma. Boeing also offered Thomson-CSF and the British firm Plessey the opportunity to bid jointly for the provision of a defence system for Ireland. Boeing suggested that French companies participate in the modernisation of American CH47-D helicopters and act as sub-contractors for the forward edge of the Boeing 747.[126] On top of all this, Boeing opened an office in Paris to negotiate with 150 potential French suppliers.[127] Despite the final agreement, it is still difficult to understand what offset what. Did the US offset the purchase of AWACS, or did France offset the sale of CFM-56 engines?[128] This kind of case illustrates the political side of offset agreements, an aspect which may become pre-eminent.

6.3.3 Political Offsets

These take many kinds and are usually difficult to identify. Nevertheless, a certain number of situations have occurred where offsets have been sought on political rather than economic grounds. The French desire to bring Spain into the Rafale program, led to the purchase of some Spanish Air Cargo CN-235 planes. This decision was clearly of political origin. Of course, there were also economic advantages (i.e. reducing unit R&D costs) but the main objective of this choice was political, as it sought to reduce the size of the consortium devoted to the production of the Rafale's competitor, the EFA2000 (European Fighter Aircraft).

More precisely, some political offsets are sometimes linked to arms contracts, or to their preliminary negotiations. As an example, the first Swiss evaluation of the American and French fighter aircraft in 1988 was largely overshadowed by the American promise to increase Swissair landing rights in the US.[129] Similarly, France promised to push ahead with the Finnish application for membership of the EU if the Finns purchased the Mirage aircraft rather than its American rival.[130]

The reverse link may also happen, that is where the arms contract is an offset rewarding a political decision. For example, in 1984 France started negotiations concerning possible armament sales to Libya in order to obtain their withdrawal from Tchad.[131] In some cases the political aim could even be to secure a change in domestic policy. When, in the last quarter of 1992, Turkey opted for an American helicopter rather than the Franco-German Eurocopter Cougar, it assisted the re-election campaign of US President George Bush who could claim responsibility for all the jobs that such an export contract would secure.[132] Similarly, the regional distribution of the offsets associated with the Belgian purchase of the Mistral missile (53% to Flanders, 39% to Walloon and 8% to Brussels) reflects domestic political considerations.[133] Finally, the armament sale may involve offsets to the benefit of third parties who feel aggrieved by the contract. When France sold a number of frigates to Taiwan, Peking, which had unsuccessfully used political pressure to prevent the sale, asked France to provide financial offsets, which were in effect cheap credits.[134]

It is of course no surprise to find political offsets linked to armament sales. These contracts often involve major political decisions, and consequently offsets cannot be restricted to industry matters.

6.4   Offsets Have Become a Basic Element of Armaments Sales Contracts

Not all of the various forms of offset occur with every export sale. The precise nature of the offset will depend on the intensity of the competition for the sale and various purchaser characteristics such as the level of its expertise in aerospace, its degree of industrialisation, its regional policies, and so on. Although offsets vary from one contract to another, this reciprocity has, for the last 15 years, been an essential element in winning any arms exports. It is still true that other elements (such as the equipment's performance, the delivery date, the price and financing arrangements) are of major importance. However, the significant trend is now towards common and disclosed conditions of armament contracts.[135]

It is an acknowledged fact that in most cases offsets can prove decisive in winning a contract. In the competition between France and Italy, to supply Belgium with attack helicopters, counter bidding was intense. The Italians offered offsets worth 73% of the contract while the French firm Aerospatiale went up to 117% offset but only on their own value-added.[136] The Belgian choice favouring Agusta was explained by "a slightly larger volume of offsets offered by Agusta".[137] Similarly, Matra obtained the Austrian order for anti-aircraft missiles against Swedish (Bofors) competition, thanks to a more substantial offset package, despite the lower price of the Swedish RBS-70 compared with the French Mistral.[138] In 1988, Brasil explained their choice of the French Aerospatiale helicopter in preference to the American Sikorsky by the better offsets offered by the Europeans.[139] The decision of India to share its order for helicopters in 1984 between the UK (the initial favourite) and France, was influenced by the French offset proposal, particularly as the initial British offer only included a financial contribution.[140] Of course, other examples could be cited where offsets alone were not sufficient to win a contract If this was not true, Dassault would not have lost the Finnish order for fighter aircraft, and Eurocopter would not have lost the Turkish helicopter order. Although not sufficient, offsets are necessary to win most arms export contracts.

Offsets are now openly discussed and formally shaped. It has been noted above that Boeing opened an office in Paris to manage the offsets linked to the AWACS contract[141] and GIAT-Industries did likewise in Abu Dhabi.[142] To improve the management of its Greek offset programme, Dassault Aviation appointed someone to work full-time on the project.[143] New national offset organisations have developed in France, and these are not solely dedicated to military contracts. The oldest organisation is AGECO (Trading Offsets Association) which is a non-profit group offering three main services to members: general information, including access to a data bank; assistance with writing contracts that include an offset; and help finding partners who might be willing to trade products acquired under an offset.[144]

The banking industry has also developed its own structures in this field: BFCE[145] is associated with the international trading company SECOPA; Banque de Paris et des Pays-Bas works with the international trading company SCOA; Crédit Lyonnais, in association with an American industrial group, has created GREFICOMEX; and several international trading companies are partly dedicated to offsets. Moreover, some large industrial corporations have developed their own offset networks: Peugeot incorporated FRECOM in 1982; Renault owns SORIMEX; and Thomson receives services from a subsidiary, named SOCOFINANCE.[146]

This network system assists the fulfilment of ever-increasing offset demands. For example, Finland went to the point of requesting "prior offsets" in 1992. This required that all potential bidders for the fighter aircraft contract had to fulfil an offset worth 10% of their own bid, irrespective of who ultimately won the contract. This can be regarded as an "entrance fee" which is payable to secure entry to the buyer's list. Defence is a buyer's market and competition is intense for the very few major contracts. The increasing use of offsets over the last 20 years bears witness to this.

For a number of years, the offsets granted by French firms were relatively limited as exporters concentrated on a small number of Gulf states that had very limited industrial infrastructures. Consequently, offsets were far from being the decisive factor that they might otherwise have been, had the purchaser been a developed country or a country attempting to expand its defence industrial base (eg India). More recently, French exporters have been looking to south-east Asia, where countries are much more interested in technology transfers and the development of their indigenous capabilities. Hence offsets play a much more significant role in the competitions to supply arms to these countries. Indeed, the view has been expressed that:

The requirement for an offset with all arms exports will soon be unavoidable. In this context of widespread and ever-increasing offset demands, there will be a need to improve communications between the defence industry (which has traditionally been rather isolated) and other large sectors of industrial activity. Particularly for large contracts, the latter might be able to assist arms exporters with their offset programmes such that both sectors benefit from the resulting co-operation.[147]

On the import side, offsets typically play a much less important role than that associated with French arms exports. French defence imports increased markedly over the period 1988–91 (partly due to the AWACS programme), but by 1993 had returned to the level seen in the 1970s (about FrFr 4 billion). Although the negotiations for the AWACS offset were rather protracted, the French government is likely to make similar offset demands if it considers buying US-designed equipment in the future. However, the French tend to prefer collaborative European development programmes to off-the-shelf purchases of US equipment and thus there is unlikely to be any marked upsurge in arms imports and associated offsets. The relative infrequency with which France requests offsets has meant that no well defined official policy has emerged, nor is there likely to be any great need for such a development. Negotiations will proceed on a case-by-case basis rather than within any pre-specified framework.

Endnotes

1. The version supplied to the Federal Republic under their own specifications had about 200 accidents out of 600 aircraft, killing 98 pilots. Hence the aircraft acquired the nickname of the 'widow maker'. See Menant G. in 'Paris-Match' No. 1331, 30.11.1974.

2. Worth about 3000 staff employed over a 10 year period. See Gerdan E. "Dossier A comme Arms" edited by Alain Moreau, p. 175–186.

3. Although this did not materialise, it would have been an important new feature in the aircraft business which is always quoted in US$.

4. "We are small, and as such we badly need protection from the powerful USA" quoted from a Norwegian government spokesman in Le Monde, 22.09.1993.

5. We shall not detail many of the other peripheral offsets that are alleged to have occurred, such as "under the table payments, intelligence tips, press leaks, etc": see Gerdan E., *op cit.*

6. Lenglet F. "Offsetting aircraft against grapes" Science et vie Economique No. 57 Jan.1990 p. 60–66.

7. J.P. Hebert "Les ventes d'armes" Syros Ed.Paris1988 p. 92.

8. Sauvin T. "La compensation internationale" Thesis Univ. Paris X 1991.

9. Sauvin T. "La compensation,nouveau moyen d'intervention de l'Etat dans les Pays industrialisés" Cahiers d'Economie mondiale T.5 No. 1 1992 p. 40.

10. Sauvin T. Thèse citée p. 25.

11. Le Monde, 10.03.1987.

12. Ibidem.

13. Le Monde, 27.02.1989.

14. Greece had taken the decision to share its order between the French Mirage 2000 and the American F-16. Le Monde, 16.11.1984.

15. Order of 600 Mistral missiles, each worth FrFr 1 million and the loading device as well. Le Monde, 13.06.1989.

16. Sauvin T. Thèse citée p. 206.

17. Le Monde, 18.02.1985.

18. Le Monde, 19.03.1985.

19. Le Monde, 2.03.1985.

20. Ibidem.

21. Le Monde, 13.06.1989.

22. Le Monde, 18.01.1985.

23. Le Monde, 2.03.1985.

24. Le Monde, 13.06.1986.

25. Le Monde, 27.05.1987.

26. Le Monde, 2 and 3.09.1990.

27. Le Monde, 22.06.1985.

28. Le Monde, 09.06.1988.

29. The global offset remained at 100% as originally demanded.

30. Le Nouvel Economiste, 19.03.1984.

31. Le Monde, 19.03.1988.

32. Le Monde, 25.02.1989.

33. Le Monde, 01.04.1988.

34. Le Monde, 20.12.1988.

35. Le Monde, 27.04.1990.

36. Le Monde, 13–14.10.1991.

37. Le Monde, 03–04.03.1985.

38. Le Monde, 22.10.1987.

39. Le Monde, 20.10.1988.

40. Le Monde, 28.06.1988.

41. Le Monde, 04.10.1991.

42. It is surprising that the French newspapers, when reporting the US decision in favour of RITA, did not stress this point.

43. Le Monde, 27.03.1985.

44. Le Monde, 27.05.1987.

45. Le Monde, 08.05.1992.

46. Les Echos, 27.01.1993.

47. Le Monde, 05.01.1989.

48. Le Monde, 11 and 12.02.1990.

49. Le Monde, 18.12.1991.

50. Later bought back by Thomson-CSF.

51. Le Monde, 12.04.1989.

52. Le Monde, 18.01.1990.

53. Le Monde, 09.11.1988.

54. Les Echos, 22.03.1993.

55. Hellenic Aerospace Industry.

56. Le Monde, 09.02.1983.

57. FrFr 120 million each, spares included.

58. Le Monde, 03.10.1987

59. Le Monde, 06 and 07.12.1987.

60. At this time Avions Marcel Dassault-Breguet Aviation AMD-BA.

61. Le Monde, 16.11.1984.

62. Le Monde, 19.03.1988.

63. Le Monde, 22.06.1985.

64. Le Monde, 19.06.1985.

65. Aeronautica Industrial SA.

66. Le Monde, 06 and 07.04.1986.

67. Le Monde, 21.11.1987.

68. Le Monde, 21.06.1989.

69. Who had formerly signed such a contract covering the co-production of Mirage III aircraft for Belgium.

70. Le Monde, 12.12.1986.

71. Le Monde, 03.03.1992.

72. Le Nouvel Economiste, 19.03.1984.

73. Ibidem.

74. Le Monde, 15.01.1988.

75. TBA = Thomson Brandt Armament; ESD = Electronique Serge Dassault formerly Electronique Marcel Dassault, now Dassault Electronique.

76. Le Monde, 01.09.1988.

77. Les Echos, 24.02.1988

78. Le Monde, 14 and 15.06.1992

79. Le Monde, 16.04.1992.

80. Le Monde, 24.03.1990.

81. Les Echos, 17.02.1993 and Le Monde, 18.02.1993

82. Le Monde, 12.12.1986.

83. Now GIAT-Industries.

84. Finally won by the Swedish firm Bofors.

85. Le Monde, 17 and 28.02.1985.

86. Le Monde, 13 and 14.10.1991.

87. Les Echos, 24.02.1988.

88. Les Echos, 27.01.1993.

89. Le Monde, 09.02.1983.

90. Dassault-Aviation, Thomson-CSF, SNECMA, Matra.

91. Le Monde, 25.02.1989.

92. Le Monde, 15.01.1988.

93. Program 'Peace Shield' — La Tribune de l'Expansion — 28.03.1989.

94. Le Monde, 29.03.1989.

95. Le Monde, 31.05.1989.

96. Le Monde, 27.05.1988.

97. Le Monde, 06.06.1990.

98. Les Echos, 15.02.1993 and Le Monde, 16.02.1993.

99. Le Monde, 18.02.1993.

100. Le Monde, 27 and 28.01.1985.

101. Le Monde, 18.01.1990.

102. Le Monde, 03 and 04.03.1985.

103. Le Monde, 08.02.1985.

104. Cf. Hebert J-P, Les ventes d'armes, Editions Syros, Paris, 1988, 186 pages (p. 92).

105. 16 Ecureuils and 36 Dauphins worth US$248 million.

106. Le Monde, 27.03.1986.

107. Le Monde, 26.12.1985.

108. Le Monde, 27.03.1986.

109. Le Monde, 27.03.1986.

110. Le Monde, 27.03.1986.

111. Le Monde, 08.05.1987.

112. Le Monde, 27 and 28.01.1985.

113. Le Monde, 24.01.1985 cf. Hebert JP (*op.cit*) p. 35.

114. Le Monde, 06.06.1990.

115. Thomson Brandt Armament.

116. Le Monde, 04.02.1988.

117. Le Monde, 06.04.1991.

118. Le Monde, 17.12.1988.

119. Le Monde, 14 and 15.06.1992.

120. On gifts and countergifts, see Batifoulier P., Cordonnier A. and Zenou Y. "L'emprunt de la théorie économique à la tradition sociologique: le cas du don contre-don" Revue Economique, Vol. 43, No. 5, Sept. 1992, Paris.

121. Le Monde, 20.10.1988.

122. Aircraft worth US$20 million. Le Monde, 06 and 07.1992.

123. Le Monde, 12.11.1984.

124. Le Monde, 27.03.1985.

125. France's first option was to purchase three aircraft worth US$550 million, Le Monde, 20.03.1987. France then decided to buy a fourth aircraft for US$116 million, Le Monde, 05.11.1987.

126. Le Monde, 16.05.1988.

127. Le Monde, 20.03.1987.

128. Hébert J-P, Stratégie française et industrie d'armement, FEDN, Paris, 1991, 396 pages (p. 289).

129. Le Monde, 09.03.1988.

130. Le Monde, 03.03.1992.

131. Le Monde, 21.11.1984.

132. Les Echos, 06 and 07.11.1992. The same sources thought that the end of the American presidential election might bring changes to this contract.

133. Le Monde, 09.11.1988.

134. Le Monde, 14.09.1991.

135. The existence of an offset should be taken into account when making statements that armament sales make a substantial net contribution to the foreign exchange balance. This is clearly erroneous, particularly where there is a 100% offset.

136. Le Monde, 27 and 28.11.1988.

137. Le Monde, 10.12.1988.

138. Libération, 29.03.1993.

139. Le Monde, 28.06.1988.

140. Le Nouvel Economiste. 19.03.1984.

141. Le Monde, 20.03.1987.

142. Le Monde, 18.02.1993.

143. Le Monde, 23.03.1988.

144. For further details, see Sauvin (*th.cit*) p. 74 sq.

145. Banque Française du Commerce Extérieur.

146. This 19.9% subsidiary of Thomson is an international trading company dealing in foodstuffs and metals. It has been involved in the Pechiney-Triangle case of disclosing confidential information in Stock Exchange transactions.

147. Berthault D. "Pour une politique d'exportation clairement définic, maîtrisée et audacieuse", L'Armement (NS), No. 43, Juillet-Août 1994, pp. 31–35.

Chapter 7

Offset Benefits in Greek Defence Procurement Policy: Developments and Some Empirical Evidence

Nicholas Antonakis[1]
University of Athens and Ministry of Industry,
Energy and Technology, Athens, Greece

7.1 Introduction

Until recently, NATO members have been characterised by a relative independence in the provision of armament systems. The basic arguments which are used to support this nationalistic procurement policy relate to the effectiveness of the domestic defence industry (a) to increase the operational independence of the armed forces (thus increasing the level of national security and the independence of foreign policy), (b) to produce new high technologies, which are difficult for the industries of opposing countries to copy, (c) to create job opportunities and to increase gross national income, and (d) to improve the balance of payments. However, in recent years the governments of the mainly European members of NATO have begun to recognise that an independent defence procurement policy involves significant costs. These are attributable to the duplication of R&D work as well as to the non-exploitation of economies of scale, learning economies, and the gains from the free international trade of armament systems.[2]

The cost of non-specialisation in production and the absence of free international trade in armament systems, combined with the continuously increasing cost of these systems[3] and the desire of NATO governments to decrease defence expenditures, has raised the interest of Western allies in the application of a NATO weapons standardisation policy. This policy, however, is inconsistent with the operation of political markets in member-countries, and particularly with the aims of producer interest groups (weapons firms), the Ministries of Defence and the Services. These problems have led the governments to adopt alternative policies for the procurement of armament systems which deviate from the "best case" model of standardisation (which would result in lower costs relative to the independent procurement policy). Co-production, work-sharing and licensed production refer to the domestic production of foreign-designed arms systems, either totally or partially. With these procurement policies significant R&D costs are saved, balance of payments problems can be avoided, work is provided for skilled labour, domestic defence capacity is maintained, and there are possible benefits from access to new production technology. Since these production methods compensate, to a certain degree, for the cost of provision of defence equipment to an economy, they are often included together with a package of other compensations (investment projects, transfer of technology, exports, tourism development etc.) in so-called Offset Benefits Agreements, which usually accompany every large contract for the procurement of armament systems from a foreign country.

The purpose of this paper is to examine Greek offset benefits policy. This policy is a relatively new development in Greece which has a less developed defence industry (LDDI) than some of the other NATO members. Section 2 outlines a brief history of the offset benefits policy in Greece. Section 3 describes the Offset Benefits Agreements which have accompanied the procurement of armament systems in Greece. Section 4 criticises the application of the offset benefits policy. The conclusion is reached in Section 5 that offsets might prove beneficial for the development of the Greek defence industry, provided that the appropriate policy measures create a defence industrial base capable of assimilating future offset benefits programmes. Throughout this paper, the term "Offset Benefits" (hereafter O/B) is used in the sense which is given in the Greek legislation. In other words, this term is meant to indicate an economic transaction which is a consequence of a public procurement and is intended to provide the purchaser with some additional benefits. These transactions may refer either to the object of supply, *per se* (direct compensation), or to another object (indirect compensation). Throughout the following, both forms of compensation are examined.

7.2   Offset Benefits Policy in Greek Defence Procurement

The Turkish invasion of Cyprus in 1974 and the continuing disputes over the boundaries of Greek territorial waters and airspace limits, created the need for a domestic defence capability to minimise Greece's foreign dependence and vulnerability in wartime. Thus, from 1975, efforts were made to create a defence industrial base in Greece, aimed at securing a minimum of national participation in defence procurement. At present, the Greek defence industry consists of six large sized publicly-owned corporations, which are the major defence contractors in the country, and thirty-eight small to medium-sized privately-owned corporations, aimed at securing a minimum share of sub-contracting in total defence business. The following Table presents the six public sector corporations and the four largest private sector firms of the Greek defence industry, with some indication of their major products and size.

MAJOR DEFENCE CONTRACTORS IN GREECE

Company	Industrial Activity	Total Assets	Net Fixed Assets (million drachmas)	Sales	Personnel
'A' Public Sector					
1. Hellenic Arms Industry SA	Manufacture of rifles, shotguns, mortars, ammunition, nitrocellulose (for the production of paints and varnishes). Engineering and manufacture of external stores and ground support equipment of fighting aircraft. Construction of 'Artemls-30' anti-aircraft system.	55472	12832	1771	1859
2. Greek Powder & Cartridge Co Inc	Manufacture of ammunition, explosives, 'Ygnis' boilers, sliding door systems, conveyor belts, hangars, roofs and other metal structures.	35151	9979	4324	1850
3. Hellenic Shipyards Co SA	Shipbuilding, ship repairs and conversions. Ship and marine engines repair. Construction and installation of steel constructions on ships. Metal constructions. Construction of train wagons.	30363	21941	10871	2345
4. Eleusis Shipwards SA	Shipbuilding, ship repairs and conversions. Metal constructions.	30363	21941	10871	2345
5. Hellenic Aerospace Industry Ltd	Construction of aircraft parts, electronic products and weapon systems, assembly, repair, maintenance, modification and training service for the full range of aviational equipment.	199919	176386	13887	3500

MAJOR DEFENCE CONTRACTORS IN GREECE — continued

Company	Industrial Activity	Total Assets	Net Fixed Assets (million drachmas)	Sales	Personnel
'A' Public Sector					
6. Hellenic Vehicle Industry 'Elvo' SA	Manufacture of trucks, military trucks, diesel engines, truck engines, buses, special purpose and armoured vehicles and various accessories.	15454	1918	9796	850

MAJOR DEFENCE CONTRACTORS IN GREECE

Company	Industrial Activity	Total Assets	Net Fixed Assets (million drachmas)	Sales	Personnel
'B' Private Sector					
1. Elviemek SA	Manufacture of explosives, ferrous sulphate and other chemical raw materials for explosives, ammunition.	2028	1147	1670	145
2. Vidomet SA	Nuts, bolts and miscellaneous metal stampings.	1233	497	298	82
3. Spider N Petsios & Sons Metal Ind SA	Metal components for the martian industry. Garbage barrels for garbage trucks. Store equipment (shelves etc).	1460	573	742	250
4. Kioleides NIK SA	Manufacture of vehicle bodies and chassis of all kinds, and train wagons.	1393	497	823	150

Notes: All data refer to 1990. Information on enterprises was compiled from:
a. Questionnaires prepared especially for this purpose
b. private interviews, and
c. the Government Gazette

Source:
a. ICAP Hellas SA[4]
b. Antonakis[5]

Defence firms in Greece are mainly concentrated in the hardware and transportation equipment sectors of the economy. In 1990, those two sectors accounted for 98.23% of total assets, 98.77% of net fixed assets and 94.54% of personnel of the defence market in Greece. As is shown in the Table, the basic production capabilities of the Greek defence industry include the construction of mobile weapons, mortars, anti-aircraft weapons, ammunition and explosives, parts and equipment of armament systems, armoured vehicles, as well as shipbuilding, ship repairs and conversions, and assembly, repair and maintenance of aircraft materials. Almost all corporations in the Greek defence industry produce not only defence materials for the armed forces of Greece or other countries but also channel a significant (though unknown from official data) share of their production to other sectors of the economy.[6]

The production capabilities of the Greek defence industry imply a particular structure for the provision of defence materials: the import of heavy materials, and the domestic construction and maintenance of certain structural parts of these materials in Greece, combined with the provision of light materials from domestic sources. It is obvious, therefore, that the O/B practice may contribute to the development of the country's defence industry and the improvement of its international competitiveness. The desire of Greek governments to increase the ability of the country's defence industry to exploit O/B, and in particular those associated with co-production in the procurement of defence materials, is evident in the following quotations which illustrate the official policy of the Greek Ministry of National Defence: "The co-production of defence materials is one of the most beneficial forms of O/B, which are agreed in large defence procurement contracts, as a large part of the procurement expenditures remains in our country. Consequently, the pursuit of co-production, either totally or in part, is carefully examined in each large procurement of the armed forces. Also, within the framework of bilateral agreements, one of the main articles is the co-production of defence materials. As a base, all goods which could be produced in the defence industry without demanding large expenditures for expansion, changes or adjustments of infrastructure are considered as efficient co-production projects. With this concept, production or manufacture of ammunition, explosives, guns, military vehicles, aviational equipment, electronic materials, naval construction works etc. are considered as efficient co-production projects".[7] With this statement, however, the Greek government does not claim that all co-produced goods cost no more than an off-the-shelf purchase without offsets. On the contrary, it is believed that this option results in higher costs generated from shorter production runs and the loss of scale and learning economies, duplicate tooling and the costs of transferring technology. To these, license fees should be added, which could be some 10% of sales.

Until 1985, there did not exist a formal O/B policy towards defence procurement. Some contracts were associated with certain agreements for the provision of defence materials in exchange for Greek agricultural products, within the context of a "clearing" arrangement. However, the need for a domestic defence capability to minimise foreign dependence and vulnerability in wartime, made it clear that the O/B practice, especially in the form of co-production, should constitute an essential part of any large procurement of defence materials. Thus, the practice of O/B in Greece started basically in 1985 with the decision of the government for partial renewal of the country's air-force fleet, with the procurement of 40 Mirage-2000 (fighter/striker) from France and 40 F-16C (fighter) from the USA. For this purchase, the government formulated various directives, which would also apply to the subsequent purchase of other defence and civil goods. These directives specified the necessary organisational and administrative structures for the materialisation of the Offset Benefits Agreements and the conditions for acceptance of offset transactions and guarantees.[8]

According to the terms of these directives, the O/B which a foreign firm is obliged to transfer to the Greek government, within the framework of defence procurement valued at more than 250 million drachmas, are divided into three categories: Category I, which includes the construction in Greece of sections of the work undertaken by the foreign firms, either for use in the main work, or for export and use in similar armament systems. The foreign firm is obliged to pay in foreign exchange the value of the sections constructed in Greece. Category II, which includes other products of the Greek defence industry which the foreign firm undertakes to purchase, and Category III, which includes other Greek industrial or agricultural products for export as well as the enticement of foreign tourists to Greece, following the initiative of the foreign firm. In the various categories it is possible for the O/B, instead of being limited only to purchases of Greek products, to take the form of imported technology into Greece, licensed production, educational programmes and investments. In the compensation calculations for the various types of O/B, for the promotion of the lowest bidder, the expenditures on goods included in Categories I and II are weighted with a base factor equal to 2 or 3, while those included in Category III are weighted with a base factor equal to 18. This means that an amount spent by a foreign firm in goods of any category, is divided by the corresponding base factor to count towards the firm's offset obligation. Also noteworthy is the fact that the governing directives foresee: the deposit from the supplier of a good performance guarantee covering 10% of the value of O/B; an expressed obligation for the replacement of transactions which have not materialised, for whatever reason, with other equally valued transactions in the same category; as well as other obligations which prompt the supplier for the materialisation of his offset obligation.

As regards the organisational structure for the materialisation of O/B, with the above mentioned governing directives, O/B Offices were legislated at the Ministries of National Defence, National Economy, Commerce and Industry, Energy and Technology. For defence procurement, the Office at the Ministry of National Defence is considered the most significant, since, according to the provisions of the PD 284/89, it is responsible for the evaluation of O/B offers. This Office deals with the materialisation of O/B Agreements in Categories I and II associated with the procurement of armament systems whose foreign exchange cost exceeds 100 million drachmas. A similar role is performed by the O/B Office at the Ministry of National Economy regarding O/B Agreements in Category III.

Having described the legislative framework and the organisational structure regarding O/B Agreements in Greek defence procurement, we analyse in the next section the basic O/B Agreements which accompanied the procurement contracts for (a) 40 Mirage-2000 aircraft from France, (b) 40 F-16C aircraft from the USA, (c) 4 Meko-200 frigates from Germany, and (d) the upgrading of the "Kanaris" directional firing system from the USA. The information given below has been taken from basic references[9] and from interviews of senior officers at the Ministries of National Defence and National Economy, as well as the major defence contractors in Greece, who are responsible for the materialisation of O/B Agreements.

7.3 Offset Benefit Agreements in Basic Defence Procurement in Greece

7.3.1 The O/B Agreement for the Mirage-2000 Aircraft

The O/B Agreement which accompanied the purchase contract for 40 Mirage-2000 aircraft from France, was signed in July 1985, between the Greek government and the companies Dassault, Snecma, Thomson and Matra. According to the Agreement, the companies are obliged to fulfil, within 15 years, O/B equal to 60% of the purchase price of the aircraft, i.e. approx. 7.1 billion French francs. To these, an additional O/B worth equal to 20% of the purchase price of the aircraft must be added, which constitutes an obligation on the part of the French government. Within the framework of this Agreement, the transactions which are considered acceptable are co-production and investment projects, transfer of technology, the promotion of exports as well as the development of tourism. For the good performance of the Agreement, a system of credit has been foreseen, determining the values of programmes and defining a system of penal clauses in the case of partial or total inability to complete the programmes. To the same end, the two-parties agreed:

a.   The signing of an Agreement between ITCO (Greek company with activities in the promotion of Greek exports) and FHP (subsidiary of Dassault, responsible for defence programmes),
b.   The propulsion of educational programmes in tourism which would be materialised by the French company Sfere, and
c.   The founding, modernisation and expansion of an export oriented company, Agroinvest.

7.3.2   The O/B Agreement for the F-16C Aircraft

The O/B Agreement which accompanied the purchase contract for 40 F-16C aircraft from the USA, was signed in January 1988 and is different from the Mirage-2000 contract. Following negotiations which took place throughout 1987, the two sides came to an agreement for the foundation of the Greek Investment Development Company S.A., with participants being the Greek Public and the American companies General Dynamics, General Electric and Westinghouse. This company, with capital stock which will gradually reach $50 million by 1996, and with a life of 15 years, will undertake activities which will guarantee immediate benefits to the Greek economy. Specifically, the company:

a.   Will undertake investment projects, mainly for the production of high technology goods,
b.   Will ease and insure the transfer of technology to Greek companies under favourable terms, and
c.   Will ease and promote Greek exports — mainly industrial — towards new foreign markets.

The company's activities will also include the founding of new corporations, the participation in existing corporations and the provision of services in technological and commercial areas. The Greek Public participates with 5% of the company's capital stock and with two members of the eight-member board of directors, who are appointed by the Minister of National Economy. Nevertheless, the corporation charter requires unanimity on the decision making process regarding approval of the entrepreneurial plans. Finally, this Agreement foresaw the co-production of structural parts for the F-16C (485 air-pipes and 253 tail-sections) from the Hellenic Aerospace Industry, valued at up to $84 million, the co-production of F-110 engine parts from the same company, valued at up to $15 million, as well as the construction of engine ground-equipment from the Hellenic Arms Industry, valued at up to $5 million. Thus, the total value of the offset obligation associated with the purchase contract for the F-16C aircraft is approximately $151.5 million. It is noticeable that for the completion of the above co-production programmes with the Hellenic

Aerospace Industry, the construction of a new building is required, covering a total of 23,000 sq.m., along with the procurement of advanced mechanical equipment and the hiring of 675 people.

7.3.3 The O/B Agreement for the Meko-200 frigates

In February 1989, the Greek government and the German company Blohm & Voss (Thyssen Rheinstahl Technik Group) signed the O/B Agreement which accompanied the purchase contract for 4 Meko-200 frigates, on behalf of the Greek Navy. According to the purchase contract, the first of the four frigates would be constructed for DM933 million at the shipyards of Blohm & Voss in Hamburg, while the following three would be constructed at the Hellenic Shipyards in Skaramanga, based on German designs and technology.

The initial Blohm & Voss offer foresaw O/B at a rate of 72% of the contract value shared out as 39% for Categories I and II and 61% for Category III. Subsequent negotiations, however, between the Greek Ministry of National Defence and the German company, led to a significant improvement in the terms of the offer, with an increase of the percentage of O/B for Categories I and II (from 39% to 45%) and a reduction of the percentage for Category III (from 61% to 55%). In addition, the ability to transfer transactions from Category III to Categories I and II was accepted, if problems in the materialisation of transactions in Category III existed. For the good performance of the O/B, a letter of guarantee was issued, valued at 10% of the level of transactions of Category III and 4% of the level of transactions of Categories I and II.

In the above O/B, some compensations must be added, worth equal to DM52.5 million, which will be given to the Greek Public in the form of grants. These include (i) royalties for the construction of the three frigates at the Hellenic Shipyards, (ii) the Naval Programming Center, where the software processing will take place, (iii) the seaboard acceptance tests in Greece, and (iv) the air-radars from Hollandse Signal Apparaten, which will be installed on the frigates.

According to the estimates of senior officers at the Greek Ministry of National Economy, the Meko-200 co-production programme will provide the Hellenic Shipyards with the opportunity to expand and to be placed among the few construction units in the West which will survive through the development of technology for specialised structures. Within the framework of this programme, 200 technicians have gone to Germany and are being trained in specific marine technology while, similarly, a group of technicians has examined the needs for renewal of the shipyard equipment, in agreement with Blohm & Voss. The investments which will be required for the materialisation of the programme are expected to reach the level of 3 billion drachmas. The cost of labour is estimated to be 30–40 billion drachmas, while approximately $200 million will be raised from the difference in wages in the two countries. The 500 additional workers who will be hired will come from the problematic cor- porations which will be privatised or closed, while a part of their wages will be funded by the EU.

In addition to the above, an attempt has been made to include in the O/B of this programme, the construction (at the Hellenic Shipyards) of 4 German merchant ships, at 35 thousand tons dwt each. Finally, with the opportunity of the co-production programme for the frigates, a special bilateral Agreement was signed between the Greek and the (then) West German government, accord- ing to which the latter undertook to deliver to Greece 75 Leopard-1 tanks and 28 F-104 aircraft.

7.3.4   The O/B Agreement for the Upgrading of the "Kanaris" Directional Firing System

In January 1988 the Greek government and the American company Unisys, signed a contract for the upgrading of the directional firing system "Kanaris", so that this may be used as a directional firing system for Harpoon guided missiles, which are launched from submerged submarines. The total contract value of this programme is $15 million while the O/B which will result are estimated to reach the level of $25.5 million, i.e. to exceed the contract value of the programme by 70%, and will be provided mainly in the form of transfered technology and know-how, falling under Category I weighted with a base factor equal to 3.

7.4   Critique of the Policy of Offset Benefits in Greece

From the description in the previous section of the basic terms of O/B Agreements which accompanied four large defence procurement contracts in Greece, it appears that the O/B practice may significantly contribute to the development of the Greek defence industry and increase its international com- petitiveness. The O/B Agreements of the last decade foresaw the promotion of significant co-production programmes and industrial exports as well as the cre- ation of job opportunities in Greece (the direct employment effect of the O/B Agreements described above is expected to be equal to 1,175 additional work- ers, i.e. approximately 7% of total defence industrial employment in Greece). However, the materialisation of O/B programmes, which is still in progress, pre- sents significant problems and delays, which should mainly be attributed to the following factors:

a. As referred to in the second section, the development of the defence indus-try in Greece was based on a small number of large-sized publicly-owned corporations, which were supported by a mixture of small to medium-sized private sub-contractors. However, the public corporations which are bureau-cratically inflexible, compete with the private sector companies, claiming programmes which, by their nature and size, should be referred to the smaller corporations. As a result, the latter have not developed new tech-nologies and are still characterised by short production runs and high pro-duction costs. It follows, therefore, that the private corporations have not exhibited the capability for the timely and correct absorbtion of the O/B programmes.

b. In Greece an absolute lack of coordination between pertinent public entities and the interested corporations exists, for the undertaking of O/B pro-grammes. The significant delays observed in the materialisation of these programmes must be attributed as much to the necessity for scrutinisation of the Greek defence industry by foreign firms, as to the need for the assimila-tion of O/B goals by the Greek corporations.

c. According to the Federation of Greek Industrial Corporations, the O/B Agreements described above did not include penal clauses where the obliga-tion was not fulfilled, and contractors were able to meet their obligations via increased tourism and exports rather than through technology transfers.

d. The French companies which signed the O/B Agreements for the Mirage-2000 aircraft, enforced lower prices and ordered relatively small numbers of the sections constructed in Greece, mainly due to the low sales of this air-craft internationally. In addition, Greek corporations have found it difficult to estimate the value of the transferred technology.

e. The possibility for the successful absorbtion of the programmes, within the framework of the O/B Agreements, is significantly limited by the opera-tional problems in the small to medium-sized corporations in Greece, and particularly by the high funding costs which impede development (in Greece, this cost exceeds 30%),[10] and the lack of necessary infrastructure, specialised personnel, quality control systems and correct programming.

The above problems, which have presented themselves in the materialisa-tion of the O/B Agreements, suggest various industrial policy measures to help the Greek defence industrial base better exploit the O/B which will follow from future defence procurement contracts. These measures should aim at:

a. The symmetrical growth of public and private corporations of the Greek defence industry. The public corporations should only undertake those programmes whose complexity, technology and investment requirements create prohibitive conditions for the participation of small to medium-sized corporations.

b.   The submission by the Greek side of specific needs for the transfer of technology and of special programmes for the development of defence corporations.

c.   The promotion of investments for the production of high-technology defence materials and the adoption of quality-control systems in defence corporations, and

d.   The obligation of foreign firms to submit specific proposals which will be included in the O/B Agreements and safeguarded with the threat of substantial penal clauses should these proposals not be fulfilled.

7.5   Conclusion

The production capabilities of the Greek defence industry and the particular structure they imply for the design of defence procurement, indicate that the O/B practice may significantly contribute to the development of the country's defence industry. From the description, in the preceding sections, of the policy developments and the terms of the O/B Agreements which accompanied the large defence procurement contracts of the last decade, it becomes evident that the O/B practice might contribute to the promotion of co-production programmes and exports as well as the creation of job opportunities in the Greek defence industry. However, the materialisation of O/B programmes, which are still in progress, presents significant problems and delays, which should be mainly attributed to the disproportionate growth of public and private corporations of the Greek defence industry, the lack of coordination between the public administration and the corporations undertaking O/B programmes, and the unclearly formulated terms of the O/B Agreements.

The lack of information on O/B Agreements, which is due to both the insufficient organisation of the statistical services and the secrecy usually surrounding the terms of defence procurement contracts, render particularly difficult the evaluation of the impacts of O/B on the Greek economy. The promotion of significant co-production programmes and the creation of job opportunities in Greece foreseen by the O/B Agreements of the last decade may have been undermined by the materialisation problems mentioned above, but this should not be regarded as indicative of the failure of O/B to achieve their goals.

Overall, we are led to the conclusion that the O/B practice might constitute a stimulating mechanism for the development of the Greek defence industry, provided that the appropriate policy measures create a defence industrial base capable of assimilating the benefits from future O/B programmes.

Endnotes

1. I am grateful to Stephen Martin for helpful comments and suggestions on an earlier draft of this paper. I remain solely responsible for remaining errors and opinions expressed.

2. Under the ideal situation where scale economies and gains from trade are fully exploited, standardisation in weapons procurement could result in unit cost savings of 20–30% (Hartley, K., **"NATO Arms Co-operation: A Study in Economics and Politics"**, Allen and Unwin, 1983).

3. Gansler, J.S., **"The Defence Industry"**, Cambridge, Mass: MIT Press, 1980.

4. ICAP HELLAS S.A., **"Financial Directory of Greek Companies"**, Athens, 1992.

5. Antonakis, N., **"The Political Economy of Defence in Post-war Greece"**, Unpublished Doctoral Dissertation, University of Athens, 1994, (in Greek).

6. Antonakis, N., **"The Defence Industry in Greece"**, *EPILOGI*, October, 1992, pp. 31–41, (in Greek), and *ibid*.

7. Remarks from an interview with the Director of the Defence Industry Service of the Ministry of National Defence at the international exhibition of defence materials, DEFENDORY, which took place in Pireaus, in October 1988.

8. Although these governing directives cover the entire spectrum of public procurement, it appears that in practice they have only been applied in the procurement of defence materials. Generally, O/B Agreements for civil procurement have not been reported in the Greek literature, except perhaps those which accompanied the contract for the Airbus aircraft of Olympic Airways in 1980. Then the Hellenic Aerospace Industry undertook the construction of the framework for the aircraft doors, which was a programme of advanced technology for that period.

9. The recent history of O/B in Greece, as well as the secrecy which usually surrounds the terms of defence procurement contracts, render particularly difficult the collection of data on O/B Agreements. For this reason, there do

not exist studies in the Greek literature on the subject of O/B. In addition, there are few papers of mainly journalistic approach, which have appeared in the country's daily and periodical press, and in which an initial attempt has been made for the evaluation of the basic O/B Agreements which accompanied some large defence procurement contracts. See, for example, Vardakos, J., **"Offset Benefits and National Economy", in "DEFENCE '88"**, *Hellenews-EXPRESS*, October, 1988, p. 10, (in Greek), and Vassiliadis, G., "National Strategy for Defence", in "**Defence and Economy**", *EPILOGI*, October, 1990, pp. 22–32, (in Greek).

10. The 1993 general average bank lending rates were approximately 29% for working capital and 27% for long-term loans (Bank of Greece, "**Monthly Statistical Bulletin**", Jan.–Feb, 1993). The cost of capital in Greece is estimated as the sum of either of those rates with the commission rate (0.5–2%, depending on the level of loan and the terms of lending), VAT (1–2%) and remaining expenses (0.5–1.5%).

Chapter 8

Defense Industrialisation Through Offsets: The Case of Japan[1]

Michael W. Chinworth
The Analytic Sciences Corporation (TASC),
Arlington, Virginia, USA
and
Ron Matthews
School of Defence Management, Cranfield Institute of
Science & Technology, Cranfield, UK

8.1 Introduction

Technology transfer, particularly offsets, has been the driving force behind the development of post-war Japan's defense industry. Yet Japan's lineage of foreign military technology absorption has more distant roots, dating back to the establishment of domestic naval and ordnance industries during the latter part of the nineteenth century. This suggests that emulation of 'best-practice' Western techniques has been the goal of Japanese defense industrialisation. But this is only partly true: Japan's fetish of technologically 'catching-up' with Western countries represents simply the preamble to the longer term goal of surpassing them.

Moving from aphorism to actuality, it is difficult not to be impressed by the success that Japan has enjoyed in pursuing its technological ambitions. In the defense-industrial field, Japan by the 1990s has built up a substantial, diversified military-industrial complex. Currently, there are around 2,000 contractors registered with the Japan Defense Agency (JDA). Of these, the 10 biggest account for about 65 per cent of domestic defense production value.[2] In addition, over 90 per cent of Japan's military procurement requirements is serviced by local defense manufacturers.[3] The value of this defense business is not insubstantial, given that Japan's defense expenditure is frequently cited to be the world's third biggest.

Japan's defense production capacity has been built up through technology offsets, notably licensed production of US military systems. But before examining how direct offsets have acted as the supply conduit for specialist defense products and processes, it is worthwhile pausing momentarily to consider the assertion that Japan lacks either a 'defense-industrial base' or an 'arms indus-try'.[4] This seemingly strange observation, clearly at variance with reality, is jus-tified by reference to conventional appreciation of the term, defense industrial base. The commonly held view is that a defense industrial base emphasises three key attributes, all of which are absent in the Japanese case. These attributes reflect the lack of significant dependence on:

a.   the production of arms or other related products;
b.   large government-financed or – supported R&D programs as the primary incentive for corporate involvement in defense production;
c.   arms exports (to increase economies of scale and thus reduce costs).

Although it is possible to quibble over the relevance and rigour of this proposition (it, for example, begs the question how 'significant dependence' is in practice to be measured, and why should any or all of these conditions necessar-ily define defense-industrial capacity), there is no contesting the uniqueness of Japan's defense-industrial approach.

There are several novel features of this 'model'. To begin, there is a consti-tution which explicitly bans war (the famous Article Nine), but which affords political interpretation to allow for 'defensive defense'. Article 51 of the UN Charter (providing countries with the sovereign right of self-defense) was called upon by early post-war Japanese Administration as partial justification for the creation of (self-) defense forces. There are practical, definitional problems here, however, not least of which is that the exercise of distinguishing between offen-sive and defensive weapon systems is often a meaningless task. Also, in addition to the constitutional difficulties facing Japan in the maintenance of a minimal defense potential, there are various policy positions that have been adopted by successive Japanese governments which: ban the manufacture, use and transit through Japan of nuclear weapons (three non-nuclear principles); and strictly restrict arms exports (three arms export principles) to countries that are Communist, subject to UN sanctions and are involved or likely to be involved in conflicts. The guidelines restricting arms exports were enunciated in 1967 when Japan was just beginning to indigenously produce warships and main battle tanks (Type 61). In 1976, Japan's arms export constraints were considerably hardened to cover all countries, over and beyond those restricted by the three principles. In 1983 the export restrictions were loosened slightly to allow defense technology transfers to the US.

At the same time, export of military-related production machinery, such as sophisticated machine tools, was also banned, as was Japanese participation in foreign-based arms production ventures. Furthermore, until recently, Japan's armed forces were not allowed to operate on foreign soil, even for UN peace-keeping operations. Japan endeavours to restrict defense expenditure to one per cent of GNP, spending a relatively small amount, around 2.5 per cent of the defense budget on defense-related R&D. Finally, the value of defense production accounts for only 0.5 per cent of total industrial output; a relatively insignificant amount when compared to the major arms producing nations.

The novel features of Japan's 'model' will be discussed later in this chapter where it will be observed that the characteristics of Japan's defense industrial base do appear out-of-kilter with those of western defense industries. Yet the Japanese approach to defense production is looking increasingly apposite to the circumstances of the 1990s, where the traditional characteristics of defense industrial capacity are something of an anachronism. In the contemporary strategic context, the subtleties of Japan's defense production strategy are becoming tellingly relevant to a world transformed by: the absence of a cold war psychosis; the halving of global arms exports since 1987; a reoriented emphasis on military systems displaying the characteristics of flexibility and mobility; and a penchant displayed by international governments and electorates for, if not 'peace dividends' (increased spending on schools and hospitals), then reductions in the social opportunity costs of high defense spending (restraining growth in government deficits).

Japan's defense-industrial strategy spliced into the country's broader techno-nationalistic approach, the developmental reliance on offsets and the US-Japan defense technology relationship are the focal issues of this chapter. Section II assesses the role of technology transfer and strategic industries in securing Japan's military-civil objective of technological self-sufficiency. Section III profiles official offset policies in the development of Japan's postwar defense industry, and the important message emerging from this discourse is that political, economic and strategic pressures will likely in the short run justify continued rises in Japanese defense spending and further involvement in defense offset programs. While Section IV examines the general aspects of absorption and diffusion of foreign defense technology into Japan's defense sector, the subsequent two sections (V and VI) address the relative costs and benefits of defense offsets to both Japan and the US. The remaining sections (VII and VIII) deal with the relative cost of Japan's defense indigenisation programs and the dilemmas of international programs, including the frictions generated by offsets and Japan's perpetual search for technological advancement. The chapter concludes with a prognosis for the years ahead, and the contribution that offsets will make in the future development of Japan's defense industry. The development of strategic alliances, with perhaps European technology partners, may diminish Japan's dependence on the transfer of defense technology from the US. A gradualist redirection away from over-dependence on the US towards diversification in defense technology sourcing/sharing may thus signal Japan progressively charting a more nationalistic, self-reliant, defense industrial course.

8.2   Japan's Defense-Industrial Strategy

To comprehend Japan's defense industrial strategy, and the role defense offsets play within this, it is helpful firstly to understand the uniquely Japanese rationale underpinning 'security'. As a concept, security is broadly defined. Metaphorically, it is the hub of a wheel, with the reinforcing spokes comprising various economic, political, diplomatic, international and technological dimensions. Industrial and technological strength are viewed by the Japanese as key considerations in attaining security. The perceived close relationship between technology and defense has been a constant theme in modern Japanese development. From the start, influential Japanese taught that the advancement of independent knowledge and scientific competence were as necessary as military power to achieve security.[5] The modern translation of this philosophy is the notion of 'comprehensive security'. But although not incorporated formally into policy, it mirrors well Japan's philosophical approach towards security. Technology is power, providing the key to self-determination and autonomy.

Japan's defense industrial strategy is consistent with the logic of the country's broad model of technological development. This can be conceptualised by reference to the schema in Figure 1. As a constituent part of its industrial culture, Japan has sought control over its technological destiny. However, this requires local abilities to research, innovate, design and manufacture modern state-of-art technologies. Foreign direct investment in Japan has thus been eschewed by the authorities, preferring instead licensed production whenever possible.

Figure 1: Japan's Technonationalism Model

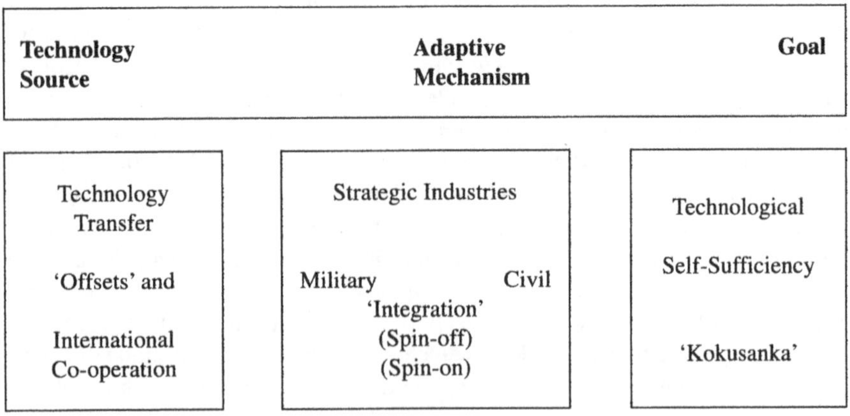

Technology Source	Adaptive Mechanism	Goal
Technology Transfer 'Offsets' and International Co-operation	Strategic Industries Military Civil 'Integration' (Spin-off) (Spin-on)	Technological Self-Sufficiency 'Kokusanka'

8.2.1   Kokusanka

Symbolising Japan's striving for technological self-sufficiency (and thus economic and military security) is the concept of *'kokusanka'*. Two American observers, Friedman and Samuels, offer the following observations on the concept, and how it influences Japanese thinking on technonationalism:

From Meiji to the present, private and public procurement decisions have been guided by the three unwritten principles of *kokusanka*: 1) domestic supply; 2) if domestic supply is not possible, licenses should be secured using domestic manufacture and equipment; and 3) equipment should have broader application than specific to the project for which purchased.[6]

As a policy-approach, *kokusanka* was established in 1970 by the JDA Director General, Yasuhiro Nakasone. A 'Basic Policy Towards Defense Production' policy statement emphasised the need for defense production indigenisation, stating that:

From the standpoint of autonomous defense, it is desirable for Japan to be defended with equipment developed and produced by Japan alone. From this point on the development and production of military equipment will be limited to Japanese industries as a matter of principle.[7]

Since the espousal of this policy position, there has been increasing domestic pressure for Japan to become self-reliant in arms production. A number of factors were responsible for this industrial orientation. There were firstly, security issues. The enunciation of Nixon's Guam doctrine around 1970 produced in Japan psychological after-shocks of seismic proportions. Importantly, there was a questioning of Washington's commitment to Japanese security. The sudden sense of isolation was heightened by President Nixon's unexpected visit to Peking, and his subsequent announcement, without prior consultation with Tokyo, that the world had moved from a bipolar to a multipolar economic and security system. The multipolar framework included China, traditionally an enemy of the Japanese. The Japanese security relationship with the US was also built around the argument that Japan was the bulwark against Communist expansionism of China and the Soviet Union.

There were also destabilising US-Japan issues in the economic sphere. The 1971 dollar devaluation, accompanied by the imposition of a 10 per cent import surcharge, negatively impacted on Japanese trade with the US and seriously undermined Japan's confidence in the US economy. The dollar crisis accentuated a growing unease in what was perceived as the relative decline of US economic power. This unease into the 1980s, especially in respect to America's continued military capability and commitment to defend Japan (and also its interests in Asia) which the Japanese felt were being enfeebled by US social and economic malaise, including debilitating foreign and federal deficits. Not only were the Japanese funding the US spending gap but, to the angst of American public opinion, were also, through direct investment, winning an increasing share of local manufacturing output. Later much publicised comments on the demise and emasculation of American industry by Shintaro Ishihara and also Mr Sakurauchi, Speaker of the Lower House of Japan's Diet, in response to US 'Japan-bashing' further inflamed the susceptibilities of the US public and its politicians.[8]

Justification for *kokusanka* was also strengthened by frictions beginning to surface in US-Japan defense collaborative arrangements. There was a growing concern that only indigenisation would suppress the accelerating costs of reliability and maintainability of foreign weapons systems that Japan was incurring at the latter end of their life-cycle. In addition, there was disquiet at what were perceived as American attempts to impede the flow of comparatively more sophisticated defense technologies into Japan. The US 'black-boxing' of F-15 related technologies, for example, not only caused a relatively low local 'high tech.' content for the fighter (as a percentage of total aircraft value, the technology transfers were lower than the prior F-4 program, yet transfers for the F-15 may have been qualitatively superior) but, more significantly, a Japanese appreciation that the US were afraid of Japan's technological capabilities, and that reliance on the US for defense technology would thus form a structural barrier to the growth of all Japan's high-technology industries.[9]

In the 1990s, Japan's interpretation of *kokusanka* now has a greater emphasis on commercialism. In support of this, Friedman and Samuels state:

The Defense Production Committee of Keidanren has justified kokusanka, which it has championed, in at least five ways: 1) Japan's unique policy of 'defensive defense' requires different equipment than that manufactured in Europe and North America; 2) the 'special spirit and body size' of Japanese military personnel, as well as Japan's special 'land, water and seas'; 3) licensing breeds dependence of the licensor on the licensee, ..[sic].. making upgrading difficult; 4) licensors are less willing to transfer technology to Japan, now that Japan's technological level has improved; and 5) co-development with other nations can succeed only if Japan has something of its own to offer. The significance of this and numerous other similar arguments is its almost total lack of any credible military rationales for autonomous weapons development.[10]

This final point is important. Japan's self-imposed policy of restricting arms exports robs domestic industry of scale. Combine this with the fact that off-the-shelf procurement of defense items from the US would be substantially cheaper (see evidence cited later in this chapter), then an additional defense-industrial rationale apparently exists, beyond either of those pertaining to economic or military considerations. While economic and military factors clearly do have roles to fulfil, using the defense industry as a technology 'driver' in securing indigenous civil technological development appears a plausible third rationale for local defense capacity. In consonance with other aspects of Japan's development strategy, there is a recognition that technological self-sufficiency is a long term goal.

8.2.2   Strategic Industries

Japan's mechanism for facilitating transition from technological serfdom to independence is via the promotion of 'strategic' industries through indicative and strategic planning. Emanating from policy discussion in 1970, the Japanese have fostered the development of what may be described as critical technology industries. There is not a tight definition of what constitutes a 'strategic' industry, but it is obvious it harbours the potential for generating: high value added production; rapid output growth; knowledge-intensive innovations; and horizontal and vertical industrial linkages with the wider economy.

There is a debate over whether US defense offsets have acted as a catalyst for developing Japan's strategic high-tech. industries. This debate has now crystallised into whether Japan is an ally or economic rival of the US. The fear is that rising bilateral technonationalism is creating fuzziness in the political bonding of the two countries.[11]

Undoubtedly, military spin-offs from US defense offsets have played a helpful role in the promotion of Japan's civil industries. Certain examples of spin-off stand out, not least the 'Bullet' train's brakes which are held to derive from local production of the F-86 aircraft, as well as other examples cited later in this chapter. Other less celebrated military spin-offs clearly do occur, including skills generation, process precision techniques and organisational efficiencies stimulated through defense offset work. The aerospace sector is a case in point, here. Around 75 per cent of Japan's aerospace production value is accounted for by military production.[12] However, because the aerospace industry is characterised by a high degree of industrial concentration, this means that incipient civil aerospace production is undertaken by the military aerospace manufacturers using the same premises, workers and even production machinery. Technological cross-threading such as this not only ensures synergy, but complements learning acquired through civil aerospace offsets. Although it is impossible to quantify the importance of such military spin-offs in aerospace establishments, such as, for instance, the Mitsubishi Heavy Industries plant where F-15 fighters are produced employing the same skilled operatives and process machinery as Boeing civil jets, it is clear a high level of integration is involved. The fruits of this civil-military production arrangement have been two-fold. Firstly, the growth in indigenisation. Note here, that Japan has made impressive strides towards self-sufficiency in component parts for aircraft; domestic manufacturers now supply almost 100 per cent of the polished skin for aircraft and approximately 80 per cent of the country's requirement for titanium forgings is met locally.

Secondly, the deepening aerospace skill base has facilitated not only increased offset work, but also an ability to engage in more sophisticated production activities. In the defense area, Japanese firms are responsible for frontier development of co-curing composites on the FSX aircraft wing structures; indeed, 80 per cent of the aircraft, including electronics, will be indigenous. On the civil side, Japanese aerospace companies have achieved progressive expansion of work responsibilities through successive collaborative projects. In this respect, the case of Boeing is instructive:

While there are 14 Japanese primary subcontractors to Boeing on the 747 and 737, there are 19 on the 757, and 24 on the 767. Seventy per cent of Boeing's foreign procurement for the 767 were from Japanese firms, and the Japanese value-added in each Boeing 767 reached, in some estimates, 30–50 per cent by 1991.[13]

Defense production investment through offsets has fostered several forms of beneficial spin-off, including industrial synergy and project management and systems integration expertise (especially under the FSX program). There is also the possibility that profits and overhead absorption under military programs have enabled Japan's defense firms to bid competitively on commercial contracts. Note in this regard, Mitsubishi's direct design and subcontracting links in Boeing's 777 project. However, the assertion that military offsets have sponsored Japan's civil technological development is overdone. The argument ignores the considerable physical and human capital resources Japan has accumulated through civil technology transfer and generations of substantial local educational investment. A more credible viewpoint is that defense offsets have furnished a military capability for Japan to produce and later develop comparable and enhanced weapons systems.

It is important to emphasise, however, that in contrast to the conventional understanding of the term, defense industrial capacity, Japan's defense sector has not been developed in technological isolation from other industries, rather it has been deliberately infused into the country's civil manufacturing base. Of course, this enables skills, techniques and organisational efficiency to be transferred via the traditional military-to-civil spin-off route. Significantly, however, it additionally provides an enabling mechanism for Japan's strategic civil, and also 'dual-use', industries to sponsor the technological advancement of defense products and processes. In this manner, innovations can be 'spun-on' from strategic industries to the defense sector.

Japan's strategic 'dual-use' industries, operating in the civil-military penumbra, have a wealth creating bias. They embrace, for instance, the aerospace, telecommunications, electronics, computer, ceramic-packaging, automobile-bearing and machinery industries. These key industries are targeted and guided by the 'visible' economic hand of the planning authorities, including MITI, and funded and nurtured to realise long term 'dynamic' global comparative advantage.[14] As a consequence, these industries have enjoyed remarkable growth performance. Japan's 23 per cent of machine tool trade is the world's biggest. Kyocera is the world's largest producer of ceramic packaging. More bearings are now produced by Japan than any other country, including the US. The Japanese car manufacturers come close to dominating world production. Japan has the world's 10 biggest microelectronic chip producers. Even its aerospace sector, the cinderella of the international aerospace business, achieved the world's fastest turnover growth (8.5 per cent) over the 1980–91 period.[15]

The strategic industries' product sophistication is illustrated by a 1989 US Department of Defense Report, which stated that Japan leads the US in certain critical technologies that possess dual-use application.[16] For example, microelectronic circuitry, gallium arsenide and other compound semiconductors and robotics, being not only the growth poles for civil economic development, but also the critical technology inputs for enhancement of the military's capability in mobility, communications and systems integration.

Civil-military technology sharing is a manifestation of a wider cooperative trait, representing a further distinguishing characteristic of Japan's defense-industrial model. While governments of western defense industries grapple with the trade-off between competition (choice and market forces) and concentration (scale), Japan has seemingly resolved the dilemma by treating these two factors as complementary rather than mutually independent. Competition occurs at the initial stage of bidding for development contracts, but thereafter, work is shared between the primary contractor — the winning bidder, and its sub-contractors — the losing bidders to the contract. Notably, the relationship is one of sharing technologies, efficiencies and innovative designs; a truly integrative, cooperative approach. In a typical case, 65 per cent of a Japanese prime contractor's work is subcontracted. Of total subcontracts, 20 per cent goes to other primes; 45 per cent is directed to domestic specialist parts suppliers; 17 per cent is accounted for by work let to 'back shops' or manufacturers with close links to the primes; and 18 per cent is spent on imports.[17]

This work sharing, cooperative aspect, has in part been cultivated because of the oligopolistic structure of the defense industry. 'Competition amongst the few' has in turn encouraged a high degree of technological cross fertilisation, whereby different though related civil-military collaborations with leading foreign defense manufacturers have led to a substantial build-up of technical expertise in a small number of industrial 'champions'.

Finally, it is important to make reference to Japan's unique defense R&D approach. The relatively low defense R&D spend, at 2.5 per cent of the defense budget, belies the important role this R&D funding plays in advancing defense production. There are two aspects of Japan's defense-related R&D requiring comment. Firstly, overall R&D expenditure is now roughly equivalent to that of the US.[18] But while around 50 per cent of US R&D spending is devoted to the military sector, approximately 80–95 per cent of Japanese spending — both public and private — is dedicated to commercial applications.[19] Emphasis on commercially oriented R&D not only maximises the socio-economic return to Japan, but the approach also facilitates viable spin-ons to the defense industrial base. A good example of this process is the manner in which the private sector has sponsored the development of the FSX fighter support aircraft's advanced phased-array radar. The Japan Defense Agency did not directly pay for any of the development of the underlying gallium arsenide chip technology, which was undertaken by a number of Japanese companies, including Mitsubishi Electric Co (MELCO) and Sumitomo Industries.[20]

A second facet of Japan's defense R&D model has regard to the role of the public sector Technical Research and Development Institute (TRDI). The TRDI has only modest funds available to support defense R&D, but this misreads its purpose. Its primary aim is not to act as a funding agency, but rather as a facilitator of potential defense-related technologies. The TRDI contracts provide seed finance for promising technologies already under development in the private sector. The requirement that at least 50 per cent of the funding must come from the private sector partner enables TRDI to extend its financial support to hundreds of fledgling projects in the private sector.[21] Of course, as is the case with western defense contractual arrangements, in the event the project goes to full-scale production then the company's R&D investment will be recovered in product price.

However, the practice of overhead recovery needs to be qualified, depending on the nature of the contract, whether it is competitive or non-competitive. For instance, in the UK, companies with non-competitive contracts (where R&D costs are unpredictable) will enjoy government funding set against development milestones. In the US, the defense contractual system is characterised by an even more generous degree of government financial support. Not only is the R&D element 100 per cent borne by the US government in respect of defense contractors under contract, but when 'competitive' R&D is conducted for the purposes of a new program (for example, the F-22 project) defense contractors can often recover parts of their investment *even if they lose the competition*. Currently, the US Department of Defense is considering reforming this system in favour of the Japanese approach which requires manufacturers to share the risk by investing in R&D and prototype development.

Defense R&D funds allocated to the TRDI have risen from below 1 per cent in the mid-1970s to 2.6 per cent in 1994 fiscal year (FSX prototypes account for 70–80 per cent of this budget). Reflecting Japan's focus on the development of state-of-art defense technologies, there have been calls recently for a doubling of defense R&D funding to 5 per cent of the defense budget. As Japan's defense R&D funds directly and indirectly promote local defense capability, it is likely that increased R&D funding if it were to materialise would reinforce the intermediate indigenisation-through-offsets effort, contributing towards greater longer term defense self-sufficiency.

8.2.3   Offsets

Defense offsets, the concern of this chapter, provide the technology source. Offsets have been a common feature of the technological development of modern Japan. Whereas in the late nineteenth and early twentieth centuries the technologies transferred were mostly from the then 'great' industrial power, Britain, in the post second world war period, technologies have flowed from the contemporary great industrial power, the US. A tenet of offset arrangements, however, is that they involve reciprocity. This used to be straightforward. Japan would procure defense items from the US, and as a *quid pro quo* the Japanese would be allowed to license produce the defense item. Offset arrangements are decidedly more complex today, now that Japan's defense-related industries are almost at technological par with their US counterparts.

American defense offsets to Japan have recently become a controversial issue because the relative costs and benefits of offsets to Japan and the US have changed now that the Communist threat has all but disappeared. Washington expresses particular concern over critical technologies haemorrhaging to Japanese defense establishments. The Americans argue that these outward flows provide the potential for future Japanese competition, the further erosion of the US' defense industrial base, and a threat to the economic viability of America's strategic industries. Tokyo, on the other hand, accuses the US of technological imperialism, because of its refusal to transfer frontier defense technologies in offset packages.

Politico-economic friction aside, defense offsets have earned US contractors substantial revenues since the 1960s, and on the Japanese side, have made a significant contribution to the indigenisation of Japanese defense production. The aerospace sector, designated a *kiban gijitsu* (key technology) by MITI, has made substantial progress in this respect: the F-1 fighter incorporated a Japanese fire control design; the T-4 — an intermediate jet trainer — was the first post-war aircraft for which the fuselage and engine have been developed in Japan; over

80 per cent of the equipment and materials used in the Japanese P3-C (Orion) are being acquired domestically; and the FSX fighter aircraft will have locally developed and produced software source codes as part of a suite of locally produced electronics equipment. Other aerospace developments include participation in the development and coproduction of the V2500 turbofan engine and local development of a next generation of assault helicopter.[22] Moreover, mostly all Japan's air defense missiles are now indigenously produced. But, of course, much of Japan's domestic defense production is undertaken under license.

In the naval area, all Japanese combat vessels are domestically manufactured. For example, Mitsubishi Heavy Industries (MHI) and Kawasaki Heavy Industries are producing one *Harushio* class submarine annually. Decommissioning of naval craft occurs much earlier in Japan, making Japan's navy one of the youngest — in terms of hull life — in the world.

Finally, the Japanese have made considerable progress in developing local production capabilities in land equipment. Japan Steel Works produces artillery pieces under license from numerous foreign defense contractors, including Royal Ordnance and Oerlikon-Buhrle. Japan has also reached near self-sufficiency in producing the full range of infantry weapons. There is a division of labour here, with Minebea, the bearings manufacturer, specialising in pistols and machine guns, Howa Machinery, in rifles, and Sumitomo Heavy Industries in light machine guns. Komatsu, the manufacturer of civil heavy earthmoving equipment, produces armoured bulldozers. Mitsubishi Motors, Hino, Isuzu, Toyota and Nissan provide self-sufficiency in 'B' vehicle production. These dual-use vehicles are also controversial exports. For instance, Toyota 4 × 4 vehicles have been linked to the 1980s Libya/Chad and Spanish Sahara conflicts. Indigenisation-through-offsets has also characterised the production of main battle tanks (MBT). Until recently, the mainstay of Japan's tank force was the Type-74. This 38 tonne MBT was produced by MHI, with the tank's 105 mm gun manufactured under license from Royal Ordnance. The Type-74's major subsystems are of Japanese design and production. Currently, JSW is the prime contractor for the 50 tonne Type-90 MBT. JSW is producing this tank's 120 mm smooth bore gun under license from the German company, Rheinmetall. Among several advanced features, the Type-90 tank employs composite armour using fillers developed by Kyoto Ceramic, with assistance from the TRDI.

8.3 Postwar Offset Developments

Throughout the postwar era, the Japanese government has favoured importation of foreign technology to help stimulate local industry. Indeed, this pattern of technology flows was established well before 1945, reflecting Japan's approach toward economic development as a whole.

The postwar defense industry, after being decimated by war and disassembled by the Occupation authorities, was soon reconstructed. With the establishment of a legitimate defense force in 1954, government once again looked toward foreign technology as a matter of policy to assist this rebuilding. Government policy statements to this effect have been clear and direct.

Japan's drive for defense industrial self-sufficiency can be explained by other factors as well. It is important to establish the government's rationale for maintaining a certain level of defense capability despite its longstanding security relationship with the United States. The first official Defense White Paper in the postwar era, published in 1970, spells out the justification:

[A] nation must not harbor vague expectations toward its partner or fall into dependence upon it, seeking to be saved by the partner. Such expectations and dependence will involve the danger of not only implanting a sense of irresponsibility toward national defense among the people, but also of degenerating the national spirit ... It is necessary to establish an autonomous defense system with the aim of defending our own country by ourselves and to develop the means of effective mutual cooperation within national consensus.[23]

Thus, two rationales were evident in JDA's early thinking: first, a nation could not be expected to maintain its side of the security bargain with the United States without having its own defense capabilities. Second, failure to do so would lead to lax attitudes in defense, and thus undercut the security relationship.

8.3.1 Official positions regarding offsets

Subsequent position papers have spelled out the strategic, economic, political and technological rationale for a domestic defense industry. Although the tone of official statements has varied slightly over the years, the general thrust of government policies has remained consistent. Japan has made clear its desire to develop a domestic arms industry, relying on foreign technology only as needed. The second White Paper continued the themes of the first in this regard:

Through indigenous research and development, it is possible to develop defense equipment fully suitable to the nation's terrain and situation, and such equipment can be easily maintained and supplemented. Second, developmental capability for defense technology will expand and improve, exerting a beneficial effect on industry. As a result, self-supporting maintenance and control of defense equipment becomes possible, and potential defense power can be cultivated.[24]

Having outlined the philosophy behind defense industrial production, the Defense Agency went on to describe the role of foreign producers:

Defense equipment which requires highly advanced technology for development, and cannot be realized with domestic technology or would necessitate enormous development costs, has been domestically produced through foreign license agreements. This has not only accomplished the acquisition of manufacturing technology, but also eased maintenance and resupply.

When equipment cannot be developed with domestic technology, or if production volume is limited so that licensed domestic production is too costly, procurement is made through importation.[25]

This policy established Japan's priorities: domestic development, licensed production, importation. The last clearly is the final option, and given consideration only when very limited volumes and/or exceedingly costly high tech items are involved. In most cases, the Japanese government has insisted that for major weapons systems, domestic options are less expensive. One of the significant points to note with the 1976 statement is that it was made as Japan was moving to consider the purchase of advanced fighters and missile systems (F-15 and later Patriot SAMs), so one can assume that the posture was articulated in this fashion in part to strengthen the government's negotiating leverage.

With major procurement decisions out of the way in several areas in the mid- to late-1980s (F-15 fighters, E-2C anti-sub aircraft, etc.), Japan could turn increasingly toward domestic development with the aim of fielding more systems that were 'home grown'. The pattern fits its tendency for import substitution evident in other commercial fields. In this case, Japan had by the early 1980s moved from an aid dependent importer of US systems to a producer of US systems with increasingly high offset levels. As it began to supplement this work with independent R&D, it could posture itself so that it could pose a challenge to traditional suppliers. In the short term, this increased its bargaining leverage with the US when dealing with offset and technology licensing issues. In the long run, it supplemented plans to develop autonomous capabilities.

JDA outlined the perceived need for increasingly independent R&D as follows:

The remarkable progress of science and technology in the industrialized countries has brought about major changes in military strategies and tactics. Consequently, the modernization of equipment has come to occupy an important position in the effort to maintain military power.

Advanced military technology also has a far-reaching ripple effect on civilian demand. For this reason, military research and development programs in various countries are being promoted also in hopes of generating such a spill-over effect.

Regarding defense-related technology in Japan, initial research was designed primarily to improve the equipment supplied by the United States. The country [Japan] was also preoccupied initially with the introduction and assimilation of technology from other countries. However, the level of Japanese defense technology has now reached the point where the country is capable of developing its own equipment ... which we believe are no worse than comparable technology in other major countries.[26]

The rationale for continuing these activities is evident: Japan was growing concerned after its F-15 experience about losing access to advanced technologies:

Of late, major nations have tended to become extremely cautious about exporting their up-to-date technology, although they are eager to export equipment in the form of finished products. Under such circumstances, it will be necessary for this country to establish a better R&D system in order to manufacture new types of equipment independently.[27]

In general, the three priorities noted above (domestic development and procurement, licensed production and importation) remained unchanged, although the shift clearly was toward greater reliance on domestic capabilities. In this context, offset programs had to be re-examined in the light of Japanese autonomous defense development capabilities. For the most part, however, the United States remained more concerned with providing equipment as part of Japan's larger commitments to its self-defense rather than the economic consequences. It was only with the FSX debate that the priority in the US shifted to economic factors (or at least assumed equal status with security considerations in offset policies).

The 1980 White Paper also noted US standardization efforts within NATO, and urged cooperation with those efforts. However, it also noted that Japan was unique, implying that while it might cooperate with US/Europe common R&D programs, it would not necessarily commit to common equipment development from those programs.

As defense spending/procurement increases reached a peak in the late 1980s, the Defense Agency pushed harder towards more complete domestic development, outlining its rationale for increasingly independent capabilities in the following manner:

... it is particularly important to continue efforts to maintain and improve the technological standards related to military equipment required for national defense in years to come. Japan is the second largest economic power in the Free World and has a high level of industrial technology capable of independently carrying out research and development projects in the field of high technology. The Defense Agency is conducting research and development by taking advantage of technological expertise accumulated in the private sector ... It has been increasingly necessary for the country to direct more positive efforts to research and development on equipment.[28]

Heavy reliance on the private sector was reinforced by a reorganization in July 1987 that eliminated minor research programs that could be pursued more effectively by private sector research facilities. In addition, the TRDI's role was defined to include research that lacks an immediately identifiable demand in commercial sectors. This could be an important development for TRDI's institutional role, perhaps representing a judgment by JDA that fielding advanced weapons systems will require selective development of specialised technologies with primarily military applications.

At the same time, however, a flexible approach was emphasised to maximise the utilisation of commercial technology in military systems — all with the
ultimate aim of making Japan equal or superior to other countries in terms of its
defense technology base.[29] This outlook is summarized in the 1993 White Paper:

The Defense Agency will positively utilise the private sector's technology on the basis of its excellent technology in the field of microelectronics and new materials including ceramics and composite
materials. Particularly in the area of basic research the Defense Agency will rely heavily on the
technology pooled in the private sector. Furthermore, the Defense Agency, carrying out a technological research project to integrate private technology into future high-technology equipment, will
build it up as a system that will meet the unique operational requirements of this country.
Accordingly, the Defense Agency will achieve effective improvement of superior equipment capable
of competing with technological standards of foreign countries.[30]

With the emergence of the FSX program, the JDA devoted greater attention
towards the rationale and benefits to Japan of cooperative R&D. Joint research
and development is considered to be important from the standpoint of not only
developing effective equipment through incorporating advanced Japanese and
US technologies but also promoting defense cooperation between the two
countries.[31]

Thus, the Japanese government shifted its posture on total autonomy in
defense equipment, recognizing bilateral cooperation as an interim measure in
reaching long term goals of developing a self-sustaining defense research, development and production capability. It also reflected a realisation that Japan could
not, in fact, embark independently on projects as ambitious as replicating an
F-16 fighter.

Nonetheless, long term objectives have not been abandoned, as indicated in
a subsequent White Paper:

Research and development on next-generation support fighter aircraft, various guided missiles and
other equipment and material will be promoted. Efforts will be made to enhance research and development, and to conduct research contributing to basic advanced technology in relevant fields.[32]

That is where JDA currently stands: something in limbo, caught in an uncertain threat environment, with a comprehensive review of security policies still
under way, and political changes in the short and long term that could later alter
the government's attitude on defense programs. The JDA remains committed to
independent capabilities, but recognizes the political necessity of remaining tied
with US R&D and production. This necessity is underscored by Japan's own
cutbacks on procurement. Thus, as an interim measure, Japan probably will
remain allied with the US for the foreseeable future, in terms of both formal
security relations and its procurement decisions, at least until the budgetary situation clears up in Japan.

The present stance on the domestic defense industry has moderated somewhat since the high growth periods of the early to mid-1980s, but still retains a focus on domestic development wherever possible. At one level, justification remains — as far as JDA is concerned — for the maintenance of at least the present level of forces and defense production capacity despite signs of relaxations in tensions in the world as a whole and in the Asia/Pacific region in particular as a prudent posture that will help assure that the positive signs evident in the region will continue. The JDA feels that even though the security situation in the area may be relaxing, a minimal defense capability remains desirable.[33] The JDA has become more circumspect in its support for domestic industry, noting vaguely that the 1976 National Defense Program Outline (NDPO) states that 'the posture of each service must be basically maintained with due consideration to qualitative improvements aimed at parity with the technical standards of other nations.'[34] This suggests that domestic industry and the Self-Defense Forces must maintain certain capabilities, but it does not explicitly state what types of capabilities, or where they are to come from, thus reflecting the present unsteady and uncertain state of defense production in Japan.

8.3.2 Threat Perceptions and the Need for Local Defense Capabilities: Justification for Offset Arrangements with the United States

There has been an intricate logic linking threat perceptions in Japan with the need for defense spending and a justification for local production and thus offsets from the United States. The perceived threat of the former Soviet Union — felt more strongly in the United States than perhaps in Japan — served as the justification for expanding Japanese defense spending from the late 1970s through the early 1990s. The JDA has argued for higher spending throughout its existence despite several distinct phases Japan's relations with the Soviet Union. The 1976 National Defense Program Outline, for example, was developed under the assumption that the United States and the Soviet Union would continue in a state of *detente* for the foreseeable future. Nevertheless, higher funding was justified consistently since then, first in order to meet the goals of the 1976 Outline, then under the justification of an increasingly hostile Soviet Union. While ties have not turned around completely, the JDA continues to request higher spending, now in order to maintain the gains made over the past decade in fulfilling a plan that originally was developed with a less hostile state of global affairs in mind.[35]

An expansion of Japanese roles and missions, beginning in the late 1970s and continuing throughout the 1980s, further justified higher emphasis on defense spending in general, and autonomous defense production in particular. For example, the Carter Administration formalised defense guidelines with

Japan in November 1978. These called for greater coordination between US and Japanese commands, joint planning for the defense of Japan in case of external attack, stepped-up joint military exercises, and mutual logistical support.[36] Former Prime Minister Zenko Suzuki agreed in May 1981 to assume responsibility for defending the sealanes approaching Japan to a distance of 1,000 nautical miles. (This zone encompasses the waters between Japan and the Philippines, swinging east from the Philippines to Guam.)[37] US and Japanese officials subsequently completed a joint sealane defense plan for the waters around Japan in December 1986. While this plan remains classified, it is worth noting that US officials had proposed in 1981 sea control missions for Japanese naval and air forces as well as the capability to close off three critical straits around the country (Tsushima, Tsugaru and Soya) to potential aggressors.[38] One of the difficulties facing policymakers today is that these commitments remain a part of established Japanese defense policies despite the changes in global and regional circumstances, contributing to pressures to continuing increasing defense spending at a time when most nations are reducing their budgets. Japan's recent acquiescence to United Nations peacekeeping roles reflects this situation.

Collectively, these commitments create a justification for continued defense spending and local defense production. Local production, in turn, warrants offset arrangements from the United States to compensate in part for Japan's willingness to assume greater defense burdens. (And it should be noted that the depth of conviction in Japan regarding the threat posed by the former Soviet Union has been a matter of longstanding debate.)

Restraints exist on Japan's defense spending that, in turn, hamper its ability to expand local production despite offset agreements. The country's total defense spending has been limited by policy and/or practice since 1976 to an amount equal to 1 per cent of the country's gross national product. Economic growth has enabled the defense budget to reach a significant level, but manpower requirements consume nearly half of the Japan Defense Agency's total spending (41.8 per cent of fiscal 1993's budget, for example, although this is a measurable decline from 45.1 of just eight years earlier), reducing the amount available for procurement.[39]

8.3.3   The Defense Plans

Japanese defense procurement has been orderly and predictable throughout the postwar period, only recently coming under the kind of intense scrutiny that defense budgets faced prior to the phased-in buildup periods. The buildup periods in the 1960s and most of the 1970s focused primarily on establishing some semblance of a genuine military force in the wake of US troop withdrawals and, in the mid-1960s, the suspension of military aid. These procurement programs took place over the 1958–61, 1962–66, 1967–71, and 1971–75 Japanese fiscal year periods.[40]

8.4   The Defense Industry and Foreign Technology

No country has received more licenses of military systems from the United States in the world than Japan. Between 1960 and 1988, the US licensed 28 major weapons systems to Japan; the second largest recipient over the same period was Italy, with 22 major system licenses. Taiwan and South Korea combined had 22 over the same period of time.[41] Recent licensed production programs include the following which are illustrated in Table 1:

Table 1: Selected Japanese Defense Programs Under License Production

---

Aircraft (fixed wing):
F-86
F-104 Starfighter (Lockheed)
F-4 Phantom (McDonnell-Douglas)
F-15 Eagle (McDonnell-Douglas)
F-16 Falcon (General Dynamics; base aircraft for FSX development programme)
P-3C Orion (Lockheed)

Aircraft (rotary wing):
KV-107/2A (Boeing)
CH-47D Chinook (Sikorsky)
UH-60J (Sikorsky)
UK-1H Huey (Bell)
AH-1 Cobra (Bell)

Missiles:
Nike Ajax surface-to-air missile (McDonnell-Douglas)
Nike Hercules surface-to-air missile (McDonnell-Douglas)
MIM-23 Hawk surface-to-air missile (Raytheon)
MIM-104 Patriot surface-to-air missile (Raytheon)
AIM-7F Sparrow air-to-air missile (Raytheon)
AIM-9L Sidewinder air-to-air missile (Raytheon)
BGM-71C I-TOW anti-tank missile
Multiple launch rocket system (MLRS — LTV/FMC)

Others:
M-110A2 203-mm self-propelled howitzer

Foreign inputs into Japanese industry are nothing new. Foreign technology inputs were critical in the development of Japan's defense industry almost up to the outbreak of World War II. The US Strategic Bombing Survey, for example, noted after the war's conclusion that:

the Japanese aircraft industry owed more to the US than it did to its own government. ... United States fighter and bomber pilots fought against aircraft whose origins could be traced back to United States drafting boards. Many Japanese engines and propellers came from American designs which had been sold under license in prewar years. Many top Japanese aeronautical engineers could claim degrees from Massachusetts Institute of Technology, Stanford and California Tech. Their best production men had served apprenticeships with Curtis, Douglas, Boeing, or Lockheed. Here and there, war-time German influence was evident, especially in the jet- and rocket-powered types that never became operational, but it can be fairly stated that the Japanese fought the war with aircraft on which the strongest influences in design were American.[42]

The period following the Korean conflict was fundamental in establishing attitudes within Japan involving the value of imported technology and techniques in general and defense related methods in particular. Much of the postwar period is characterized by an attitude that military technology and production methods represent the leading edge of advanced technologies, suitable for both infusions into the general economy and stimulating the economy through a 'pull-effect.' The visible influence of US military orders in Japan during the Korean conflict and immediately afterwards had a great impact on this attitude (although it must also be said that the depressed state of the Japanese economy at that time made any infusion of orders, technology and production techniques welcome).

US stimuli came through several sources with equally diverse technology transfer implications. Direct orders for military forces in Japan came in such areas as uniforms for GIs (thus providing a boost to the local textiles industry), aircraft spare parts production, engines — mostly spare parts — for trucks and military Jeeps, complete trucks (10,000 were procured in the Korean conflict period), ship repairs, ammunition, licensed radio production (from RCA through the US military, leading to the establishment of that industry in Japan), materials (especially steel) and other areas (see Table 2 for total procurements in the early postwar period). In addition to the stimulative impact of these orders, Japanese industry gained direct training and experience in production/industrial engineering, production control, quality controls, inventory controls, standardisation of production of advanced products, and other fields. Japanese companies tended to be favoured with the most advanced techniques at that time, due to the US military's emphasis on meeting its own standards.[43] At the peak of the Korean conflict, US forces in Japan directly employed over 270,000 Japanese citizens, over half of them in technical fields. While it would be an overstatement to credit these foreign inputs for the complete revival of the Japanese economy, they certainly were a factor.

Table 2: Special Procurements By US Forces During the Korean Conflict

Contracts of $10,000 or more	
Year	Value ($)
1950	328,922,000
1951	331,520,000
1952	476,426,000
1953	158,614,000
Total:	1,295,482,000
Total US Military Procurement in Japan	
Contracts of $10,000 or more	
Year	Value ($)
1956	256,871,000
1957	316,789,000
1958	200,453,000
1959	198,894,000
1960	171,534,000
1961	165,651,000
1962	222,441,000
1963	151,644,000
1964	144,971,000
1965	151,982,000
1966	206,450,000

Source: US Department of Defense; Daniel L Spencer, 'Military Transfer: International Techno-Economic Transfers via Military By-Products and Initiative Based on Cases from Japan and Other Pacific Countries', Defense Technical Information Center, Defense Logistics Agency, AD6606537, March 1967, pp. 52, 56.

These procurements represented on average, 75 per cent of total US military procurements in the Asia/Pacific region during the Korean conflict.[44] Military aid, support for US and Japanese military forces, and other financial sources provided additional economic stimuli to Japan during this period, underscoring the belief in industry circles that defense production could be profitable and a positive benefit to the economy.

The Vietnam war proved equally profitable in some respects for Japan, although by this time the relative impact on the Japanese economy was far smaller due to its rapid growth in the 1960s. Nevertheless, adding in such expenditures as expenses by US GIs during 'rest and recreation' (R&R) leaves in Japan, take estimates of the net inflow to the Japanese economy during this period to as high as $2 billion.

8.4.1   War as a Profit Making Activity

As early as the Korean War, US defense planners saw the utility of Japan serving as a forward line of defense in Asia, providing both a base for US forces in the region and a source of logistical support. With no domestic airlines or official military forces of its own, Japan resuscitated its domestic aircraft industry in 1952 by manufacturing spare parts for US military aircraft based in Japan — a full two years before the establishment of either the Self-Defense Forces or the Japan Defense Agency. Total aircraft production in Japan rose from ¥23 million in 1952 to ¥2,091 million the following year. During the period between 1952 and 1954, demand by the US armed forces in Japan constituted between 60 and 80 per cent of total aircraft production. The Japan Defense Agency gradually supplanted the US presence and by 1958 over 80 per cent of total aircraft production was directed to JDA needs.[45] The Pentagon also stressed the military advantages of US and Japanese forces using US-designed weapons in common, a theme that continues to this day.[46]

All these factors contributed to perceptions within industry circles that military production could be beneficial to the Japanese economy and individual businesses. This has not been a universally held view, of course, but has contributed to periodic pressures by industry and some government officials to import military technologies and expand defense production in Japan. As long as Japan remained under the US security umbrella, it was in a position to profit from these programs. These and other considerations provided incentives to Japan for importing US military technology through licensed production programs.

When the Pentagon has denied technology transfers to Japan, more often than not it came in the name of denying potential loss of the technologies into unfriendly hands rather than out of economic concerns. It appeared to be most concerned over threats that such technology could fall into the hands of the former Soviet Union or other unfriendly powers.[47] The Defense Department rejected the request of the Japan Defense Agency that Japanese firms have access to all software in co-producing the Patriot missile, including the guidance and target identification components.[48] Similarly, the Defense Department withheld data on electronic systems, radar equipment, and compounds used in the body of the F-15. In those instances, economic factors did enter into play, but the primary concern remained the loss of technology into Soviet hands.[49] Subsequent reviews of the F-15 and other MOUs often have resulted in the Defense Department releasing some materials technology and other previously withheld items.[50]

8.4.2 The Defense Industry and Diffusion of Technology Through Offset Programs

The number of major players in the Japanese defense market is limited, although, as mentioned in this chapter's introduction — over two thousand firms are registered with JDA as suppliers to the agency and the Self-Defense Forces.[51] This includes suppliers of more mundane items — shoes, clothing, etc. — and also higher technology firms that produce more advanced weapon systems. Mitsubishi Heavy Industries is by far the most important contractor, accounting for one-fourth to one-third of all defense production over the last several years (taken as a whole, the Mitsubishi group accounts for an even higher percentage). The top 10 contractors account for about 65 per cent of total outlays.

At the 'teeth end', Japan's defense contractors have gained from the government's technology, offset and diffusion policies. An important feature of the Japanese approach is that imported know-how has been channelled to specific contractors. The missile industry, for example, has benefitted from this form of industrial targeting. In missile production, a small nucleus of Japanese companies have combined foreign and domestic resources to develop both new and improved versions of existing missile systems. The ASM-1 anti-ship missile, which was developed as a replacement to the US-supplied Harpoon, emerged from this strategy.

The Defense Agency is using the technology from this missile in the current development of the SSM-1 surface to ship missile.[52] Military missile research, design, and production is proliferating into surface-to-air missiles, air-to-air missiles, anti-tank missiles, and even Cruise missiles.[53] Missiles thus represent a leading edge of Japan's effort to produce wholly domestic models of advanced weapons, as well as future research and development thrusts — perhaps even despite the current downturn in defense funding.

Most Japanese defense contractors are multifaceted companies, which produce mainly civilian goods. Defense production has fluctuated but as previously mentioned accounts for only a tiny proportion of Japan's total industrial output and defense related sales, representing small percentages of total sales for most companies.[54] For example, only 15 to 25 per cent of Mitsubishi Heavy Industries' total sales have been in military equipment over the past decade, even though it consistently has ranked as Japan's number one contractor over the same period.[55] Many companies continue to diversify and de-emphasise defense sales as the short-term prospects in the defense market darken (in contrast to the 1980s, when firms diversified in order to emphasise defense related sales).[56] On the one hand, this had led to concerns that licensed technology finds it way into commercial products. On the other, it means that few major contractors are solely dependent on defense related sales for their survival.

Defense sales have dominated certain sectors. For example, over 80 per cent of the value of Japanese aircraft production goes to the Self-Defense Forces. Defense sales also play an important role in electronics. Just over four per cent of total shipbuilding is in the defense sector, an insignificant figure in terms of its overall impact on the industry but important because of its stability and reliability during lean years. 'Dual use' technologies that 'spin on' from the commercial sector are becoming increasingly important in defense production strategies, as they are to the overall development of the Japanese economy.

The dominance of military sales has been cited by many outside analysts as evidence of Japan's larger plans to build its aircraft industry through offsets and licensed production programs. Past attempts to develop commercial aircraft have been largely unsuccessful, leaving Japan's industry dominated by the production of military aircraft.[57] In the 1980s the government and industry emphasised co-production and co-development with foreign firms, both on the military and civilian sides. Military production has given Japanese firms opportunities to develop airframes, avionics and jet engines. Electronics companies in particular have participated in aircraft production to gain an additional outlet for electronics technologies used mainly in civilian products. On the other side, Japanese technology specifically developed for military aircraft, like radar systems and airframe materials, could have potential applications to commercial aircraft as well as more advanced military aircraft like the FSX fighter.[58]

8.5   Specific Programs: Industry/Government Motives; Benefits to Japan

Offsets have been most noticeable in the aircraft industry, an area of high priority for Japanese government and industry since the Occupation authorities banished Japanese producers at the end of World War II. Partly as a matter of pride and partly as a matter of economic stimulus, both industry and government leaders viewed this sector as key to the future of Japan and a number of related industries. Military production at times has been viewed as one avenue to achieving the dream of bringing Japan back into the ranks of producers of world class aircraft.

There has been a lengthy debate concerning the long term intentions of industry and government regarding the use of military programs to stimulate the domestic aircraft industry. One view (Samuels and Whipple)[59] sees the emphasis on military production as a shift from earlier failures to launch independent commercial ventures, with military aircraft seen as technological stimulants that will pull domestic aircraft production along with related critical support industries. This view sees consistency in long term Japanese efforts, with government essentially a committed party to the development of a domestic aircraft industry almost at all costs.

Other analysts (e.g. Green)[60] see conflict throughout the postwar period, with industry and government seeking comparable goals, but often at odds with one another concerning the most effective means of achieving them. While the shades of difference in this view are not dramatically different from the earlier school of thought, the tactical differences between and within government and industry circles have often affected the choice of specific systems over the period.

Hall and Johnson[61] provided the classic analysis of the Japanese aircraft industry and the US role in developing it. Hall and Johnson illustrated the systematic approach of Japanese companies to absorb and disseminate technology from major US aircraft manufacturers throughout the fledgling Japanese industry. Certain characteristics of this long term technology 'pooling' process are worth noting. First, a select handful of Japanese companies were involved, each focusing on different elements of the industry or specialties within the aircraft. For example, Ishikawajima-Harima Heavy industries has been the 'designated producer' of engines in the industry, with Kawasaki assuming a secondary role. Mitsubishi Heavy Industries was from the outset the primary aircraft producer/ systems integrator. Other companies focused on tail sections, avionics, wings, etc. Moreover, firms tended to cluster by aircraft type, with Mitsubishi focusing on fixed wing and Kawasaki and Fuji serving as the primary producers of rotary winged aircraft.

The second feature is that most US firms worked in isolation of one another *and* their Japanese collaborators. Few US firms had the integrated approach and perspective that characterised the Japanese approach during this period. Most worked in isolation, concerned primarily with their own short term profit perspectives, secure in the knowledge that the incremental information or assistance provided Japanese firms, in and of itself, would be insufficient to transform the Japanese firm into a major competitor. (Collective knowledge and experience was another matter.)

The third, and perhaps most important element, was that the US government for a long time had encouraged these transfers, and individual companies at the prime contractor level were well aware of the significance of their assistance to Japanese firms. The US government felt throughout most of the postwar period that Japan represented a special case in terms of military production and the assistance it should receive in producing military systems. While not blind to the potential competitive implications of these transfers, government officials for the most part have sided with transfers under the assumption that it was necessary to encourage transfer of production technology to Japan for a number of reasons. These included: the fact that as a more pacifist nation, such offsets were required to encourage purchase and deployment of advanced weapons systems; the desirability of having firms in this forward deployed area familiar with US systems in the event of a conflict; and, the attractiveness of offsets to Japan as a means to assure long term political and military alliance with the United States.

While economic factors were not ignored, for the most part Japan was not viewed as a competitor or potential competitor through these and other programs for several reasons. First, production volumes were too small to achieve economies of scale and thus the efficiencies that came with it. Second, Japan by policy restricted its arms exports, a restriction that has grown stricter throughout the postwar period. This minimises the likelihood that the US would face its own equipment in the international marketplace or, worse, in the hands of a potential adversary. Third, even though Japanese companies have moved up the scale in terms of research, development and production capabilities, they have yet to master the art of systems integration sufficiently to challenge established weapons producers (although this is one of the most important objectives of the current FSX program).

This is not to say that Japanese firms have not tried. Indeed, just the opposite is true, with some successes noticeable in a number of areas. Japanese firms have attempted to assimilate foreign technology, modify it appropriately, and repackage it as an indigenous product. In many cases, the imported technologies, components and systems have provided the standard by which industry could judge its own progress and set its own objectives. Knowledge of US systems has assisted in the development of a number of domestic alternatives, although their effectiveness compared with their imported predecessors is debatable. In some instances, individual components and subsystems have been developed systematically, replacing their imported counterparts until the imported system resembles its original only in superficial appearance. This has transpired in the case of F-4 Phantom fighters, whose internal electronics have been replaced by indigenous components almost entirely. From the outside, the aircraft still resembles the aircraft license-produced from the US McDonnell-Douglas Corp., but on the inside, it now has become a virtually made-in-Japan aircraft. In other cases, whole substitutes have been developed, reflecting near comparable performance characteristics and objectives, but produced entirely by domestic firms.[62]

8.6   Benefits to the US: Short Term Profits

If offsets have been so disadvantageous to US industry and government, why do they remain in effect? Commercial considerations have been paramount in the decisions of US *companies* to enter into co-production. Profits have been lucrative. Representative is the experience of the Raytheon Co., the designer of the Patriot missile, which stands to realise at least $776 million from its co-production deal, mostly clear profit since the US government funded the development of the missile.[63] Like other co-production programs, the Patriot program in Japan is likely to generate additional opportunities for system upgrades and thus additional income for Raytheon.

License fees and the lucrative upgrade business have rivalled or surpassed the profits companies could make through off-the-shelf sales without posing any problems associated with expanding production for comparatively small orders. In addition, US firms have been dissuaded from holding out for direct sales by their assessment of several factors: the Japanese government's commitment to progressive co-production of American weapons rather than purchase; the parallel policies of NATO governments favouring co-production; the occasional possibility of Japanese co-production deals with European competitors; and Japan's growing capabilities to produce similar, if less technologically sophisticated, systems without foreign participation.

8.6.1 Short Term Costs and Long Term Interests of Offsets to Japanese Industry and Government

The importance of the defense buildup strategy to Japanese industry — and government — is demonstrated by the willingness to pay a significant premium for local production. The Office of Management and Budget estimated in 1986 that Japan will spend approximately 55 to 80 per cent more by producing the Patriot system locally than it would have by buying the same number of units directly from Raytheon.[64] Cost differences in the US and Japanese produced F-15s have been placed at similar levels (although these may be suspect, given the life cycle costs associated with the program to Japanese buyers). The JDA looks to domestic production to increase its military prowess, provide a hedge against the decline of its principal ally and assure an autonomous military technology base. Industry sees domestic sales opportunities, export potential and bargaining leverage with foreign firms. Greater capabilities spurred industry and government ambitions for heavier reliance on indigenous development of new systems to realise these objectives. And as other missile development programs have demonstrated, neither government nor industry is likely to give up on a program once it has established bureaucratic momentum — witness the TAN-SAM program. The momentum and the leverage to continue offset concessions from the US have stalled over the last two years, leaving future strategies and objectives in doubt.

8.7 The Issue of Costs

On the surface, these programs have come at a cost. Most overseas estimates have concluded that the limited production of foreign systems in Japan has come at a penalty of at least 50 per cent in most systems, sometimes well beyond double the costs if they had been imported. The Nike-Ajax produced domestically, for example, would have cost 1.4 times the off-the-shelf purchase price had it been produced locally. More recently, US estimates have placed the cost of producing licensed versions of the US F-15 and F-16 (in the form of the FSX fighter support aircraft) at twice the US price. Once locked into a program, Japanese buyers, while not necessarily at the mercy of the US vendor, nevertheless have little room for negotiation and leverage. The ultimate costs of F-15s purchased from McDonnell-Douglas in fact approached the 2:1 ratio that the company claimed would result if the aircraft were license produced.

Japanese sources dispute these figures, sometimes with American evidence to support their claims. Hall and Johnson, for example, concluded that if economies of scale, finance and other factors were taken into account, Mitsubishi Heavy Industries probably could have manufactured the F-104 at a 10 to 25 per cent *saving* due to the company's relative efficiency vis-a-vis the US manufacturer (a theme articulated numerous times in commercial markets) and fewer manhours due to the effective absorption of Lockheed's learning from the program.[65] Japanese sources claim that from the standpoint of life cycle costs, licensed produced aircraft are no more expensive than their US counterparts (which also spend far more time on the ground than their Japanese counterparts in maintenance and repairs). When adding in costs associated with licensing the system, Japanese sources claim that local development and production may in fact be far less expensive.

8.8 Developing Competitors: The Dilemmas of Cooperative Programs

Critics of cooperative programs between the United States and Japan insist that they help stimulate the development of competitors through transferring US technology to highly competent and committed Japanese firms that use such technology for development of indigenous weapons. Proponents of such programs, however, have insisted that at least a degree of technology transfers are needed to close a sale. Without such offsets, they insist, Japan would take one of three alternative courses: 1) wait it out until US firms are more forthcoming with transfers; 2) go to alternative suppliers (when feasible), particularly European firms, which are known for their more generous conditions of sales;

or, 3) develop domestic development programs — perhaps with the assistance of other countries — until a satisfactory system is developed.

The progression of US defense technology development to Japanese offset and finally the evolvement of Japanese indigenous systems is illustrated in Figure 2. This details the improvement pattern of Japanese technological

Figure 2: Japan's Offset Domestic Technology Development Cycles

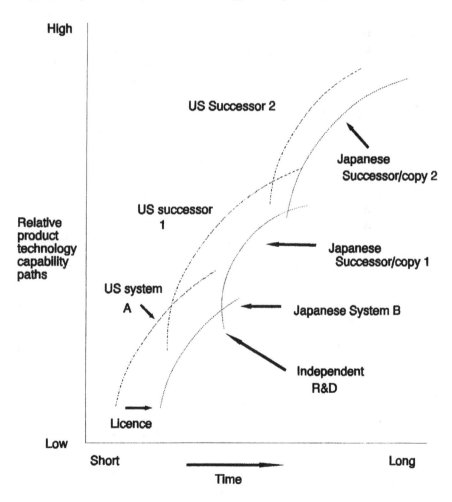

capability through licensing and 'mirror-image' R&D programs. Japan's technology emulation efforts close the gap with the US/West in general, but by that time a US successor system has been developed, obliging the Japanese to play catch-up again. This process continues as long as Japan's defense budgets, and particularly, those of procurement and development, expand. Up until the 1990s, Japan's technology gap with the West was becoming wider. The trend is now uncertain and may even reverse, given that the contemporary public finance scenario is one of shrinking budgets, major programs ending and replacement decisions being delayed.

The dilemmas of coproduction and other programs involving a substantial degree of technology transfers are illustrated in Raytheon's experience with Japan in the Sidewinder air-to-air missile. Japan sought Raytheon's Sidewinder AIM-9B in the 1970s at a time when domestic development of a similar guidance system was a high priority. When it became evident that the Sidewinder guidance package was not available for release to Japan, the JDA embarked on a development program that resulted in the AAM-1, a Sidewinder replacement that was to be utilised on domestic F-1 fighter support aircraft. The AAM-1 was in line to become JDA's favoured air-to-air missile, replacing the US Sidewinder entirely. But according to one analysis of the Japanese defense industry, the domestic guidance development was temporarily suspended once the US indicated to the Japanese government that the more advanced Sidewinder AIM-9L would be available for local production in Japan. This option appealed to the JDA because it would give greater access to the Sidewinder guidance and would thus assist the long term goal of developing domestic counterparts. MHI completed an agreement with Raytheon to license produce the Sidewinder in Japan in 1980, and the JDA shifted its infrared guidance efforts from AAM-1 production to further research in the TRDI.[66]

MHI experience in Sidewinder manufacturing has now found its way into these development efforts. However, if the US government and Raytheon had not agreed to make the more advanced AIM-9L available for local production, it is also safe to assume that the United States could easily have been closed out of the market for infra red guided air-to-air missiles altogether since both Japanese industry and government appeared satisfied with the progress of its AAM-1 program until a clearly superior alternative was available.

The scenario is one that has been repeated in other sectors as well. A US firm develops a system, licenses part of it out to a Japanese producer, and ultimately ends up partially or totally dependent on the Japanese producer, who by this time has become the more efficient and less expensive producer of the component or complete system. Even though licensing technology might have helped retard domestic industry development in some cases, it also appears to be contributing to competitive pressures in the long run. If this situation is wide-spread and continues unabated, then it does indeed cast a negative light on coop-erative defense programs because they would be contributing to the strengths of a competitor at the expense of US industry. Furthermore, as more efficient and less expensive producers abroad offer components to US firms, it will be increasingly difficult for the United States to continue pressure on the Japanese government to refuse exporting military components, especially if US suppliers do not exist or are incapable of meeting demand for the component in question. The next logical step in this chain would be US encouragement that Japan make an exception in its arms export rules for the United States only, but that would go far in setting the precedent necessary to allow a more active presence by Japan in international arms markets.[67]

It is more likely that government and industry have been interested in mili-tary offsets for their benefits in *military* production. Throughout the 1980s, the Japanese government was in the process of developing a full line of advanced precision guided munitions, not simply a single missile system. The underlying strategy was to enhance domestic industrial capabilities and reduce dependency on the United States for future weapons programs. It is in these areas that the military specifications satisfied by offset concessions are likely to be immedi-ately applicable.

The same conclusion can be drawn for transferring F-16 technology to Japanese industry for the FSX program. Some critics of the FSX project believed that F-16 technology would make its way to Japanese commercial air-craft development and production programs. Once again, there may be diver-sions of technology from FSX to non-military efforts, if only because of the commonality of production facilities, workers and managers. However, Japanese firms, MHI in particular, already have numerous opportunities with US com-mercial aircraft producers that allow considerable transfers of technology directly to potential competitors. As one study noted, 'Boeing has pursued a course that will materially and directly transfer technological capability to the Japanese civilian aerospace industry.'[68] Therefore, if the FSX project aids the domestic commercial aircraft industry in Japan, it will only supplement far more extensive programs already underway and likely to continue for years to come. F-16 transfers *are* directly applicable to industry's ability to design, manufacture and integrate another military aircraft, however.

This is not to deny Japan's interest in military technology transfers for their potential commercial benefits. But the wide variety of reasons for this interest in other military technology as described in the case studies bears repeating. For example, from a government policy standpoint, an additional thrust is on generating domestic sources of advanced technology in military systems and for finding additional outlets for technological advances generated in the commercial sector — the 'spin-on' theory of defense production.[69] By utilising new or existing commercial technologies for other applications, military production can thus become a means of recouping research and development expenditures as well as a means of reducing unit costs in civilian sectors, but this depends on buoyant defense budgets — an unpredictable factor in the 1990s.

Regarding flowback of Japanese technologies to the US from Japan, it should be noted that the US government has been highly sceptical of Japan's willingness to release its own advanced technologies to the US.[70] Recent developments notwithstanding (such as the flowback of Japanese improvements on P-3C technologies to the US), it is safe to say that such scepticism remains strong.

Japanese analysts have noted many of the fundamental problems perceived in US-Japan technology transfers.[71] As a nation that depended heavily on technological inputs for growth and development, Japan historically and increasingly in the modern day has viewed technology as the key to the country's economic future, assets not to be distributed freely. Throughout the postwar period, on the other hand, the United States viewed technology transfers in a different light, more often than not in the context of its own military superiority *vis-a-vis* the former Soviet Union and as a commodity that was to be shared with its allies in the name of united deterrence of that perceived threat.

Hall and Johnson demonstrated that, at least for one major program and period of time, Japan was able to absorb foreign technology cost effectively, producing major systems at a lower cost than would have been possible through off-the-shelf purchases while enjoying the benefits to the economy as a whole derived from extensive technology transfers. Similar benefits were derived from participation in other programs, such as the Patriot surface to air missile program, F-15 and others (although the economics involved in those programs are less definitively determined than by Hall and Johnson for the F-104 program). Japan may be unique in this regard for several reasons. As noted earlier, the country was able to benefit in part from these transfers due to a pre-existing workforce with high skill and education levels, as well as mobility, flexibility and lower wage levels. US technology transfers have been steady and ramped up over the decades, moving to increasingly more advanced levels of production. Japan has benefitted from a virtually unrestrained flow of technology, in the sense that it has been steady and consistent over a nearly fifty year period, far more so than other Asian nations and many European ones. The United States consistently has treated Japan as an exceptional case from a policy standpoint, offering it production and technology offsets for advanced systems that it would not offer to other allies. For example, Japan remains the *only* country in the world to produce the F-15 outside of the United States, a remarkable exception that is likely to remain unchanged for the history of the program. If Japan has been able to benefit from military offsets, it certainly has been due in part to the consistency and scale of such transfers.

8.9 The Future

The cost-effectiveness of offsets has come under scrutiny in Japanese budget drafting circles as part of a broader re-evaluation of military spending in the country. A number of factors have combined to make military production — and therefore offsets that accompany such production — less attractive than it was in the 1970–1990 period. These factors include far higher capital costs in Japan (compared with periods of negative real interest rates during Japan's 'bubble' period of economic growth); low profitability of most major heavy industrial companies; the greater transparency of military contracts in Japan (making it far more difficult to disguise overruns, under-the-table payments, etc.)

Part of the increased cost from defense programs can be attributed to the process through which the defense buildup has been funded. The JDA does not make progress payments like the US system for procurement and major R&D programs. Instead, marginal down payments are made, with the bulk of payments completed near or upon delivery of a system. This has enabled the JDA to have its cake and eat it, too, in that it could fund a substantial military buildup while maintaining total spending under 1 per cent of GNP, a political necessity in the postwar environment. One reason defense contractors could do this was because real interest rates and other capital costs were so low during the postwar period. Thus, companies and the JDA could afford the costs associated with delayed payments because they were marginal.

Under current conditions, money costs make this delayed payments scheme far more expensive and thus less attractive to both industry and government. This may be one (additional) reason that the Ministry of Finance is less than enthusiastic about funding more procurement and R&D programs (the ministry has a philosophical bias against defense spending in general).

Arthur Alexander predicted the ultimate decline of Japanese defense spending because of these and other economic, technological and experience factors.[72] Alexander concluded that defense acquisition and R&D expenditures were likely to cool off in the 1990s and that if the government was determined to pursue greater autonomy in defense production, it would face unexpected (and, by implication, unacceptable) cost increases. He also concluded that while Japanese industry has been adept at adapting US systems and developing 'indigenous' counterparts, Japan would remain dependent on the US for advanced systems for years to come. Of course, this also implies that Japan will continue to look towards the US for offsets in cooperative defense programs (and that the United States will maintain its own pattern of developing advanced systems, subsequently making the technology available to its allies).

Alexander has some strong points and arguments, although they must be balanced against the dynamics of the procurement and policy process in Japan. Countervailing pressures remain that will force continued consideration of importation and indigenous development of advanced weapon and military systems for the foreseeable future. Among them are:

- Industry's continued interest in cost-effective importation of advanced technologies *per se* (the Samuels argument, although not quite as extreme)
- US pressures to assume greater burdens in defense
- Uncertainties surrounding the threat environment in the Asia/Pacific region
- The need to update and expand certain capabilities in response to new roles and missions (particularly UN peacekeeping)
- The right wing, which, while not the force that it once was, nevertheless is an ever present thorn in the side that continues to press for a strong Japan
- Potential political changes, resulting in a leadership more amenable to defense spending.

So, there are factors that favour continued, limited production of defense systems. In the short run, the situation will revert to that characterising the mid-1970s: occasional coproduction of certain systems, with no new, dramatic crises comparable to the FSX. The MLRS agreement reflects that trend, and it will likely remain that way for the coming procurement cycle. A further consideration is whether Japan will be able to diversify sources for new equipment in the future, minimising its dependence on the United States. US businessmen in Tokyo like to complain of having their hands tied in comparison with their European counterparts, and point alarmingly to the sale of three BAe aircraft to the Maritime Self-Defense Forces as evidence that the US is losing its foothold in Japan. This is debatable, for several reasons. The first is the necessity to maintain the security treaty, thus justifying (primarily) US purchases. The second is that most major programs are completed. Fielded systems means maintenance and upgrades, services that are likely to be provided by *domestic* firms, not US companies (or European ones, for that matter). Third, the high tech, 'sexy' systems Japan seeks remain in the US. Even if EF2000 literally took off, Japan would be more interested in the F-22 because it represents the best technology in the field. Thus Japan is more likely to be interested in funding a limited R&D

program in comparable technologies to give government negotiators leverage in gaining access to the F-22 somewhere down the road.

What is interesting is that there remains circles that continue to promote concepts such as small aircraft carriers, next generation aircraft programs (comparable to the US F-22 program), and other costly, very advanced commitments (MHI and the JDA continue to promote the idea of codeveloping a Hawk replacement, for example, and the government remains interested in advanced ballistic missile defense concepts). Some of these ideas are being circulated on behalf of the JDA by industry, clearly with industry's profit motives evident as well. Proponents of an expanded defense research, development, production and deployment capability remain within the country. The next few years should indicate whether they will continue to make these rumblings 'underground' for the next decade or so, or whether they will emerge as the mainstream in defense spending trends over the same period.

What is certain is that technology offsets will continue to play an important role in developing Japan's defense industrial base. The technology development strategy will continue to be the successful incrementalist approach followed to date, irrespective of whether defense technology absorption is driven by: ideology/ philosophy; the continued process of 'catching up' with the West; efforts to foster indigenous industrialisation; the need to overcome permanent/sporadic technological deficiencies of the Japanese economy; or, as a short term benefit to Japan, to offsetthe political headaches associated with the US alliance. In conclusion, then, it can be stated with conviction that Japan's long-standing offset philosophy, supported by contemporary policy initiatives, has fostered a strong, technologically advanced and increasingly self-reliant defense-industrial base. In many respects, Japan's postwar 'model' of defense industrialisation is unique.

There is little doubt that, for instance, government promotion of dual-use strategic industries, R&D policy and, most importantly, the culturally intangible factor that drives Japan to seek technological dominance, have all contributed to the gradual but inexorable achievement of its defense industrial ambitions. Although Japan's defense budget in the final years of this decade will continue to be squeezed, defense production capability will not diminish; rather the opposite will occur, sponsored by the technological synergies (particularly in the electronics industries) of civil-military convergence. The defense environment in Japan, as elsewhere, has changed tremendously, but its commitment to domestic defense production has not abated. There will continue to be a Japanese defense industry in its own unconventional manner, and once major programs are completed (especially the FSX) the 'offset-development-diffusion' technology cycle easily could resume, post-2000.

Endnotes

1. Appreciation is expressed to Gregg Rubinstein, Arthur Alexander, Julia Burn and Mike Wright for comments on earlier drafts. Thanks are also due to Luisha Gulliver for assistance with the production of Figure 2.

2. US Congress, Office of Technology Assessment, **Arming Our Allies: Cooperation and Competition in Defense Technology** OTA-ISC-449 (Washington DC: US Government Printing Office, May 1990), p. 104.

3. See, R. Drifte, **Arms Production in Japan: The Military Applications of Civil Technology,** (Boulder, Col.: Westview Press, 1986).

4. Ibid., p. 3, and see also, 'Japanese Defense Industrialisation', (ed.) by A. Edgar and D. Haglund in R. Matthews and K. Matsuyama, **Japan's Military Renaissance?**, Macmillan (1993) pp. 138–9.

5. D.B. Friedman and R.J. Samuels, **How To Succeed Without Really Flying: The Japanese Aircraft Industry and Japan's Technology Ideology,** The MIT Japan Program, Center for International Studies, MIT (1992) p. 7.

6. Ibid., p. 8.

7. Cited in, M.J. Green, **Kokusanka: FSX and Japan's Search For Autonomous Defense Production,** The MIT Japan Program, Center for International Studies, MIT (1992) p. 25.

8. See, Shintaro Ishihara's controversial statements in his book, **The Japan That Can Say No,** Simon & Schuster (1991). Mr Sakurauchi spoke in January 1992 of a global economic race, noting disparagingly that the US acted as Japan's subcontractor.

9. M.J. Green, *op.cit.*, pp. 34 and 41.

10. D.B. Friedman and R.J. Samuels, *op.cit.*, p. 8.

11. On this point, see J. Richard Walsh, 'Technonationalism in US-Japanese Security Relations: The FSX Controversy', **Armed Forces & Society,** vol. 19, no. 3 (Spring 1993) pp. 377–91.

12. Interview with Takashi Nishioka, Head of Mitsubishi's Aerospace Business, **Jane's Defence Weekly,** (April 24, 1993), p. 32.

13. D.B. Friedman and R.J. Samuels, *op.cit.*, p. 23.

14. For a discussion of this point, see Arthur Alexander, **Of Tanks and Toyotas: An Assessment of Japan's Defense Industry,** RAND N-3542-AF (1993) p. 21.

15. 'How Britain's Aircraft Industry Has Come Close To Stalling Speed', **The Times** (July 22, 1993).

16. See US Department of Defense, **Critical Technologies Plan,** Committee on Armed Services, US Congress (March 15, 1990).

17. D.B. Friedman and R.J. Samuels, *op.cit.*, p. 39, fn. 105.

18. As a proportion of national output (2.9 per cent) Japan's R&D spending is now the highest in the world. See 'Public Paucity in the Land of Plenty', **Financial Times** (September 3, 1991).

19. M.W. Chinworth, **Inside Japan's Defense,** Brassey's (US) Inc. (1992) p. 39. It should be noted that most license fees (which include payments paid by Japanese subcontractors to US subcontractors or subsystem/component licensed production, as well as R&D recovery charges that were levied by the US government until recently) to Japan are included in procurement contracts, not as part of the R&D budget, since they have been incurred in coproduction or licensed production programs. Any fees associated with technology transferred to a research or development program would be included as part of the R&D program's expenses, but most of these expenses have been marginal until the advent of the FSX program. Prior to this, the costs had been limited usually to those associated with transfer of a data exchange package or comparable set of documents/samples. Fees for various aspects of the F-16 that have been charged by General Dynamics/Lockheed as part of the FSX joint development program come under the research budget for Japan, since this budget funds the entire program. Some suspicions have been raised that other parts of the budget have absorbed similar costs in the past as well, and may do so again in the future, depending on the nature of the program. For example, it is speculated that the computer upgrade program for base defense (the so-called BADGE system) was covered entirely under facilities budgets, not under procurement contracts. If that were the case, any royalty or license fees paid by Japanese contractors/government to foreign companies under that program for technology would have also fallen under the facilities budget.

20. Ibid., p. 44.

21. Ibid., pp. 35–37.

22. K. Ebata and P. Beaver, 'Japan To Build Own Design Helicopter — OH-X Project', **Jane's Defence Weekly** (September 7, 1991) p. 407.

23. Japan Defense Agency, **Defense of Japan 1970** (Tokyo: Japan Defense Agency, October 1970), p. 33. The first defense white paper was largely the work of the then JDA Director General and later Prime Minister Yasuhiro Nakasone.

24. Japan Defense Agency, **Defense of Japan 1976** (Tokyo: Japan Defense Agency, 1976), p. 125.

25. Japan Defense Agency, **Defense of Japan 1976** (Tokyo: Japan Defense Agency, 1976), p. 126.

26. Japan Defense Agency, **Defense of Japan 1980** (Tokyo: Japan Defense Agency, 1980), p. 183.

27. Japan Defense Agency, **Defense of Japan 1980** (Tokyo: Japan Defense Agency, 1980), p. 187.

28. Japan Defense Agency, **Defense of Japan 1988** (Tokyo: Japan Times, 1988), p. 135, 136.

29. Japan Defense Agency, **Defense of Japan 1987** (Tokyo: Japan Times Co., Ltd., 1987), p. 140.

30. Japan Defense Agency, **Defense of Japan 1988** (Tokyo: Japan Times Co., Ltd., 1988), p. 136.

31. Japan Defense Agency, **Defense of Japan 1989** (Tokyo: Japan Times Co., Ltd., 1989), p. 184.

32. Japan Defense Agency, **Defense of Japan 1991** (Tokyo: Japan Times Co., Ltd., 1991), p. 89.

33. Japan Defense Agency, **Defense of Japan 1992** (Tokyo: Japan Defense Agency, 1992), p. 97.

34. Japan Defense Agency, **Defense of Japan 1992** (Tokyo: Japan Defense Agency, 1992), p. 83.

35. The 1976 National Defense Plan Outline details the basic force structure and policy goals behind Japanese defense budgets. It assumed a continued state of detente between the United States and the Soviet Union as one of its fundamental tenants. Even though tensions between the two countries accel-

erated then reduced between 1976 and the present, defense planners in Japan argue that reductions in present forces should not be made since its force levels are just now achieving the levels proposed in 1976, when detente was a given. Instead, planners feel that present forces should at least be supported at their present size and level of capability.

36. US Congress, Senate Committee on Armed Services, "United States-Japan Security Relationship — The Key to East Asian Security and Stability." Report of the Pacific Study Group, 96th Congress, 1st session. (Washington DC, US Government Printing Office, 1979), pp. 22–27.

37. Asahi Shimbun (Tokyo), March 28, 1981; the London **Times**, March 31, 1981. See also the statement by Assistant Secretary of Defense Francis West before the House Subcommittee on Asian and Pacific Affairs, March 1, 1982.

38. Ibid., West's statement, March 1, 1982.

39. Japan Defense Agency, **Defense of Japan 1993** (Tokyo: Japan Times Co. Ltd.), p. 283.

40. Japan Defense Agency, **Defense of Japan 1979** (Tokyo: Japan Defense Agency, October 1979), pp. 36–37.

41. US Congress, Office of Technology Assessment, **Global Arms Trade: Commerce in Advanced Military Technology and Weapons**, OTA-ISA-460, (Washington DC: US Government Printing Office, June 1991), p. 8.

42. US Strategic Bombing Survey, **The Japanese Aircraft Industry**, Washington DC, 1947, p. 4; quoted in W.W. Lockwood, **The Economic Development of Japan** (Princeton, NJ: Princeton University Press, 1954), p. 331.

43. Daniel L. Spencer, "Military Transfer: International Techno-Economic Transfers via Military By-Products and Initiative Based on Cases From Japan and Other Pacific Countries," Defense Technical Information Center, Defense Logistics Agency, AD6606537, March 1967, pp. 32–35.

44. Daniel L. Spencer, op.cit., p. 54.

45. Society of Japanese Aerospace Companies, Inc., **Aerospace Industry in Japan, 1987–88**, pp. 3–13.

46. US General Accounting Office, **US Military Co-production Programs Assist Japan in Developing its Civil Aircraft Industry**, p. 1.

47. Michael W. Chinworth, "Industry and Government in Japanese Defense Procurement: The Case of the Patriot Missile System," MIT-Japan Science and Technology Program Working Paper 88–04, p. 21.

48. Chinworth, "Patriot Missile System", pp. 24–25.

49. Reinhard Drifte, "Japan's Growing Arms Industry," Geneva, P.S.I.S. Occasional Papers Number 1/85, 1985, pp. 75–76.

50. US General Accounting Office, "US Military Co-production Programs Assist Japan in Developing its Civil Aircraft Industry," p. 7.

51. Japan Defense Agency, Chotatsu Jisshi Hombu no Gaikyo (Overview of the Central Procurement Office), July 24, 1989, p. 9. There are 2,287 contractors registered with the CPO, of which 1,401 — slightly over 61 per cent — are classified as small and medium sized businesses.

52. Japan Defense Agency, **Defense of Japan 1988** (Tokyo: Japan Times Co., 1988), pp. 138–139.

53. "Japan Uses SSM-1 Expertise to Develop Cruise Missile," **Aviation Week**, March 21, 1988, p. 59.

54. **Boei Nenkan 1989**, p. 480. This figure might understate defense's contribution to the overall economy because of the degree of dual use technologies and products utilised for JDA purposes, particularly in the electronics sector.

55. **Japan Company Handbook** (Tokyo: Toyo Keizai Shimposha, 1988), p. 726; Jieitai Sobi Nenkan (Tokyo: Asagumo Shimbunsha, 1989), p. 524, 526.

56. **Nikkei News Bulletin**, December 30, 1988, "Fujitsu to Boost Defense-Related Business." For additional information about the Japanese defense industry, see Michael W. Chinworth, "Japan's Defense Industry," **JEI Reports**, No. 1A, January 9, 1987 (Pt I) and No. 7A, February 20, 1987 (Pt II).

57. Richard J. Samuels and Benjamin Whipple, "Defense Production and Industrial Development: The Case of Japanese Aircraft," MIT-Japan Science and Technology Program Working Paper 88–09, pp. 3–4. In addition to collaboration on military aircraft, Japanese firms have entered into joint ventures with the Boeing Co. for the Boeing 7J7 and the V-2500 international aircraft engine consortium led by Rolls-Royce and Pratt and Whitney. Nevertheless, the commercial aircraft industry remains relatively small compared to US and Western European counterparts.

58. This was a hotly disputed issue. For a range of views, see Richard F. Grimmett and Larry A. Niksch, "FSX Fighter Agreement With Japan," CRS Issue Brief, updated August 22, 1989; John D. Moteff, "FSX Technology: Its Relative Utility to the United States and Japanese Aerospace Industries," CRS Report for Congress, April 12, 1989; "US-Japan FSX Codevelopment Program," prepared testimony of Frank C. Conahan, Assistant Comptroller General, National Security and International Affairs Division, General Accounting Office, before the Committee on Science, Space and Technology, May 11, 1989; Michael W. Chinworth, "Strategic Technology Management in Japan: Commercial-Military Comparisons," **ONR Scientific Bulletin**, April–June, 1989, pp. 41–58.

59. See, Samuels and Whipple, *op.cit.*

60. See, M.J. Green, 'Kokusanka: FSX and Japan's Search For Autonomous Defense Production', **MIT-Japan Science and Technology Program Working Paper 90–09**, May 1990.

61. See, G.R. Hall and R.E. Johnson, "Aircraft Co-Production and Procurement Strategy," RAND Report R-450-PR, May 1967.

62. For details of upgrade programs, refer to various annual issues of Japan Defense Agency **Defense of Japan**, (Tokyo, Japan Times Co., Ltd.) and **Jieitai Sobi Nenkan** (Tokyo: Asagumo Shimbunsha).

63. US Department of the Army; Office of Management and Budget, "Second Annual Report on the Impact of Offsets in Defense-Related Exports, December 1986, pp. 11–29.

64. OMB, December 1986, pp. 11–29.

65. Hall and Johnson, *op.cit.* The authors concluded that "in fact, no premium was paid. The Japanese obtained the planes at a lower cost than they would have paid in the United States" (p. 157). Among the reasons cited for this situation were Japan's (at the time) lower labour rates. This advantage has long since evaporated.

66. Koichiro Yoshihara, **Nihon no Heiki Sangyo** (Tokyo: Shakai Shisosha, 1988) pp. 124–125; 130–131.

67. The Office of Technology Assessment examined the proliferation of weapons producers due to technology transfers in its report **Global Arms Trade**, OTA-ISA-460, (Washington, DC: US Government Printing Office, June 1991).

68. **Arming Our Allies**, p. 82. For a more extensive discussion of the pitfalls and successes in civil-military integration, see **Arming Our Allies**, pp. 77–83; Jacques S. Gansler, **Affording Defense** (Cambridge, MA: MIT Press, 1989), pp. 273–282, 312–313.

69. **Nihon no Sentaku (Japan's Choices)** (Tokyo: Ministry of International Trade and Industry, 1988), Chapter 3; **Defense of Japan 1976**, pp. 95, 125–126; **Defense of Japan 1988**, pp. 136–138; **Nihon no Sentaku**, pp. 112–116.

70. Comments by General Accounting Office on OMB, December 1986 report, contained in OMB, December 1986, Appendix C, p. C-3.

71. See, for example, Naruhiko Ueda, "Gijutsu Kokuboron," **Kokubo**, July 1990, Vol. 39, No. 7, pp. 56–60.

72. See, Arthur Alexander, *op.cit.*

Chapter 9

Saudi Arabia and Offsets[1]

Abdulla M. Al-Ghrair
School of Defence Management, Cranfield Institute of
Science & Technology, Cranfield, UK
and
Nick Hooper
Centre for Defence Economics, University of York, UK

9.1   Introduction

The dictionary definition of offset is to balance one thing against another, or to compensate. During the Cold War offset became more or less synonymous with a defence or defence-related countertrade; the balancing of an international defence purchase by the supplier buying goods from the customer's economy.

This Chapter deals with such offsets in Saudi Arabia. The geographical, historical and economic background to the offset programmes is outlined, followed by a description of Saudi Arabian offset policy in the context of the development of the Kingdom. The Al Yamamah offset programme is used as a case study. The joint ventures established with a number of foreign companies under offset provisions are described. Finally, the overall impact of offset deals on the national economy is discussed.

9.2   The Kingdom of Saudi Arabia

The Kingdom of Saudi Arabia covers some 2,240,000 square kilometres of the Arabian Peninsula, on the southwestern edge of Asia. It has a coastline 1,760 kilometres in length on the Red Sea, and 560 kilometres on the Arabian Gulf.

The history of Saudi Arabia began many centuries before the prophets, but historical records date back to the time of the prophet Ibrahim (Abraham). However, the modern Kingdom was conceived and carved out in stages during the 20th century, beginning with the late King Abdulaziz ibn Abdulrahman Al-Saud in 1902. The name of Saudi Arabia was attributed to it in the year 1932.

Saudi Arabia is an independent monarchy, governed by the King, Deputy Premiers and a Council of Ministers. King Fahd ibn Abdulaziz, the Custodian of the Two Holy Mosques, succeeded King Khalid ibn Abdulaziz in 1982. He is assisted by HRH Crown Prince Abdullah ibn Abdulaziz, the Deputy Premier and

Commander of the National Guard, HRH Prince Sultan ibn Abdulaziz, the second Deputy Premier, Minister of Defence and Aviation and Inspector General, and by the ministers appointed to the Council of Ministers. This Council is responsible for endorsing state budgets, drawing up economic development plans, and managing defence and foreign affairs.

The Kingdom is divided into 13 administrative regions, each headed by a Governor appointed by the King. All legislation, agreements with other nations and concessions for oil and mineral exploitation are subject to government approval and declaration in the Royal Decrees. Many government bodies have been set up to carry out special programmes, either as autonomous bodies or affiliated to different ministries.

9.3   Development of the Kingdom Since 1970

Since 1970, the Kingdom has carried out five interdependent five-year development plans. The plans have set out systematically to transform the economy of Saudi Arabia and reduce its dependence on crude oil. While each Plan has included a balanced series of measures carrying forward all aspects of economic development, each has also had a focus on a particular aspect of development.

The First Plan (1390–1395 AH; 1970–1975) concentrated on programmes for social and economic development, with total expenditure of SR 32.8 bn. Developments in the oil market in the 1970s significantly increased the resources available, with the result that the Second Plan (1395–1400 AH; 1975–1980) was far more dramatic than originally envisaged, amounting to some SR 500 bn. The Second Plan continued the basic social and economic reforms, concentrating on the industrial sector's contribution to gross domestic production. The Third Plan (1400–1405 AH; 1980–1985), amounting to some SR 800 bn, shifted the focus from building infrastructure to increasing production, especially in the agricultural sector.

Although much had been achieved, the transformation of the economy had not been completed when a downturn in the oil market led to a significant reduction in resources. As a result, the Fourth Plan (1405–1410 AH; 1985–1990) totalled only some SR 100 bn. Initiatives in the Fourth Plan were aimed at private sector agricultural, industrial and commercial development. There was also emphasis on economic and social integration with the member states of the Gulf Cooperation Council (Bahrain, Kuwait, Oman, Qatar, Saudi Arabia, and the United Arab Emirates).

The current (Fifth) Plan (1410–1415 AH; 1990–1995) is aimed at reducing dependence on crude oil production as the main source of national income.

Industry and agriculture received top priority, with emphasis on the diversification of the production base and the development of manpower to provide a high quality and efficient workforce for the national economy.

When the Council of Ministers endorsed the overall aims of the Fifth Development Plan special emphasis was placed on the following aims:

- constantly developing the Kingdom's self-defence capabilities, while deepening the loyalty and affiliation of citizens
- identifying and implementing all means of increasing the state's revenues, provided there are no unwanted social or economic effects
- upgrading the performance, efficiency and cost effectiveness of Government institutions, without lowering the standard of service rendered to citizens
- increasing the part played by the private sector in the domestic economy through encouraging domestic capital investment inside the Kingdom and setting rules and regulations for financing development plans and programmes by private companies under the supervision of the State
- balancing regional development to meet the needs of the population while ensuring full benefit from the available facilities and services, by selecting centres for growth and development
- encouraging more people to enter the private sector
- replacing non-Saudi manpower with suitably trained and skilled Saudi manpower.

While current rates of growth expressed in real terms have slowed considerably, GDP in current prices grew nearly 50% between 1989 and 1993. Inflation over this period averaged 1.8% (consumer price index). Non-oil private sector activity accounts for some 25% of total GDP, achieving 3.4% growth in 1993 (down from 4.0% in 1992).[3] Table 1 presents some further macro-economic statistics for the Saudi economy in 1993.

Table 1: Selected macro-economics statistics for the Saudi economy in 1993[2]

Total GDP	$120.75 bn
Real GDP growth 1992–1993	0.7%
Oil share of GDP	23.5%
Non-oil private sector share of GDP	24.5%
Exports	$40.7 bn
Imports	$30.5 bn
Trade balance	$10.2 bn

Source: Statistical Summary (various years), Saudi Arabian Monetary Authority, Riyadh.

9.4   Joint Ventures in Saudi Arabian Development

A key factor in the development of the Saudi economy has been technology transfer through a variety of institutional arrangements, principally the joint venture. In each case the key objective has been to obtain the primary benefit of the venture while at the same time enhancing the Kingdom's national capabilities and capacity.

The development of the oil industry, which has provided the means and impetus for the economic development of the Kingdom, is the most far-reaching example. From the earliest days, Aramco (now Saudi Aramco) has been much more than an American conglomerate extracting oil in return for Royalty payments. Partly from necessity and partly because of the relationship which developed between the company and the Kingdom, Aramco effectively took on the role of a development agency. As Moliver and Abbondante point out, 'manufacturing in the Kingdom got its start from Aramco. The oil company was forced to establish various industries to support its workers, since there was essentially no manufacturing sector in Saudi Arabia at the time'.[4]

The contribution made by Aramco extended far beyond ensuring support for its workers. Indeed, the easiest way to meet the needs of the workforce, particularly in the early days, would have been to rely on imports. But Aramco built ports, roads and communities. It was asked by the Government to set up the school system (ABGS, Aramco built Government schools), and the electricity system it established in the Eastern Province became the model for the national system (SCECO, Saudi Consolidated Electricity Company). A policy of 'Saudiisation' ensured that nationals were trained to take over from expatriates, culminating in the appointment of a Saudi chairman, Ali Naimi, in 1989. Technology transfer perhaps reached its peak when Aramco itself was transferred to Saudi ownership in 1980.[5]

The role of Aramco in the development of Saudi Arabia is reflected in the special relationship which developed between the Kingdom and the USA. The US became a major supplier of advice, expertise and qualified manpower in the exploitation of oil and the development of the infrastructure and industry. As the West purchased the oil, the Kingdom purchased the West's skills and expertise, resulting in a mutually beneficial partnership.[6]

The development of a downstream petro-chemical industry was firmly based on the joint-venture concept. Two industrial cities were established under a Royal Commission, at Jubail on the Arabian Gulf and Yanbu on the Red Sea. SABIC, the Saudi Basic Industries Corporation, became the joint venture partner of major international petrochemical companies to establish a series of petrochemical plants which have successfully entered world markets. Other ventures include an iron and steel plant at Jubail (HADEED) and an expansion of the Jeddah steel rolling mill to meet domestic needs. These ventures provided a further avenue for the transfer of managerial, professional and technological skills necessary in a modern industrialised economy.[7]

The role of joint ventures in the construction and manufacturing sectors was recognised when joint ventures were given equal treatment with wholly Saudi-owned enterprises in exemption from the requirement to subcontract 30% of the value of their work to Saudi companies.[8] Studies by Aramco showed that in 1983, 30% (by turnover) of construction activity in the Kingdom was carried out by joint ventures, including some of the largest, most complex projects.[9]

At the end of 1992, there were 336 licenced industrial joint ventures in the Kingdom (although not all might be operational). Of these, over 40% are in fabricated metal products, machinery and equipment. The chemicals, petroleum, and plastics products sector has 21% of the joint ventures, with a further 15% in construction materials, ceramics and glass. The US is the most common foreign partner, with 66 joint ventures, followed by the UK (32), Germany (29) and Switzerland (25). France follows (13) and Japan with 5.

Like all markets, Saudi Arabia has its own characteristics, and entry can be difficult for companies originating in a different culture. The use of law based on the Shariah means that many western business practices cannot be directly applied to the Saudi market. Joint ventures enable foreign businesses to rely on their local partner and avoid the steep learning curve facing those new to the Saudi market. However, the partner has to be chosen with great care as the future of the venture rests on the working relationship between the partners.

A further reason for the growth of joint ventures is the range of facilities available to such enterprises. These include interest-free loans of up to half the capital cost from the Saudi Industrial Development Fund (SIDF), a ten-year tax holiday, freedom to repatriate capital and profits, low cost utilities, exemption from duty on essential imports and tariff protection for the products at a level of up to 12%.

In the case of the US, collaboration has progressed beyond individual joint ventures to the point where there is a close commonality of interest in the economic sphere. This in part reflects the history of the development of the oil industry and in part the roles of Saudi Arabia as oil supplier and the US as oil consumer. However, it also reflects the common recognition of collaboration as a beneficial approach to economic activity. The relationship is formalised in the Saudi-US Joint Economic Commission.

9.5   The Saudi-US Joint Economic Commission

The Saudi Arabian-United States Joint Commission on Economic Cooperation was established in June 1974 to promote programmes of cooperation between the two countries in the fields of industrialization, trade, manpower training, agriculture, science and technology. On February 13 1975, the two governments signed a Technical Cooperation Agreement providing a framework within which the Joint Commission began operations. Since that time, the Commission has become an active government-to-government mechanism by which the expertise present in various parts of the United States and Saudi Arabian governments and their respective private sectors can be bought together, to the following ends:

- helping Saudi Arabia achieve its development goals by providing technical expertise in key areas
- strengthening economic and political ties between the two nations
- encouraging better understanding between the American and Saudi Arabian peoples.

The Technical Cooperation Agreement has been extended in five-year increments and is currently valid through to the year 2000.

Since the Joint Commission began operations in 1975, the two governments have signed 36 project agreements. Currently, there are 21 projects in progress, with 15 projects and sub-projects having been completed.

9.6   Administration and Management of the Commission

The Commission is chaired jointly by the US Secretary of the Treasury and the Saudi Arabian Minister of Finance and National Economy. Saudi Arabian Ministries, in conjunction with their counterpart US action agencies, are responsible for the implementation of Joint Commission Projects. Ministerial-level Joint Commission meetings are held alternately in Saudi Arabia and the US/ Delegations attending the meetings include senior officials of the two governments having an active role in the programmes. With the exception of one project on solar energy, all are funded entirely by the Saudi Arabian government. The US Department of the Treasury is responsible for disbursing the funds, according to bilateral agreements. Four of the 21 current projects are managed or supported by private US firms or institutions, under contract to the US Department of the Treasury, Department of Energy and US Customs. King

Abdulaziz University, King Faisal University and King Saud University are involved in projects, along with Saudi Arabian ministries and agencies.

There are clear parallels between the role of joint ventures and intergovernmental collaboration and the development of offset policy. Offsets associated with military purchase can be seen as an extension of the process of technology transfer initiated through joint venture and collaboration.

9.7   The Saudi Arabian Offset Programme

The Saudi Arabian government (SAG) has recognised the new global economic environment and the utility of offsets. Within Saudi Arabia, offset programmes are not seen in the same way as conventional forms of countertrade. Offsets are programmes of private sector projects created by the Kingdom of Saudi Arabia, the UK and French governments, and US companies, leading to partnerships between Saudi companies and UK, US and French firms. The individual projects within these programmes are long-term business partnerships. The Kingdom's goal is to achieve successful business ventures that will mutually serve the interest of all investors. The projects are the choices of investors, as long as they meet the offset requirements. The SAG's effort is directed towards assisting and bringing together foreign and Saudi investors. Once this is achieved, the SAG allows them to pursue their own ventures.

9.8   Technology Transfer

Technology transfer occurs where a seller grants permission for the buyer to use the seller's high technology processes within the businesses created under the offset programme, and helps the buyer acquire the technical skills necessary to make use of that permission. As such, technology transfer is not a type of offset, but is an essential part of almost all offset arrangements.

These technical processes are the result of research and development. They are comparable to patents if they are a seller company's proprietary property, or to national defence secrets if the processes are the property of a seller nation. Usually permission is granted only for use during the specific life of an offset agreement. Both seller company and the nation that developed the technology have financial reasons to restrict the use of the process, since they invested in the development.

The Saudi objective of encouraging the transfer of technology was high on the offset agenda, and appears at face value to be very attractive and most desirable. However, there are many factors which make the achievement of this objective very difficult.

Where offset arrangements involve transferring production of the military equipment, offset defence purchases may be very expensive because of technology transfer by the seller. At the extreme, the seller will calculate all the possible direct and indirect costs of the technology, and then increase the prices of the defence part of the sale proportionally. Since the seller has invested large amounts of money in the research, they consider it their right to recoup these costs from the transfer. However, governments typically recoup their R&D costs by a levy on direct exports, thus reducing the apparent premium on offset deals. In some cases, such as the Al Yamamah (British Aerospace) contract, offsets are not directly related to the defence sales. There may however, be some increase in price due to the administrative and other costs associated with the offset programme.

The Saudi Arabian government has identified the transfer of technology as a prime motive for the offset programme. Transfer takes place through research and development as well as manufacturing and production. Indeed, research and development ensures the transfer of the capability for technological development, as well as the ability to make use of existing technologies. Offsets can also help a country make the best use of its resources, develop products appropriate for international markets and hence help exports, and support or establish service industries and the economic infrastructure.

For the foreign partner company, offsets can offer a way of buying into a market. Companies can gain access to an otherwise closed or difficult market by offering benefits for the local economy. Joint ventures established under offset regimes can offer continued access to the economy after the primary deal has ended. This compares with the experience of UK companies wishing to sell defence equipment into the US market, traditionally reserved for US companies. Local manufacturing facilities are essential, and may originate from opportunities to sell equipment under offset programmes.

There are other advantages to companies from offset arrangements. Government support and commitment can speed up consideration and approval of projects, and help may be offered in identifying priority sectors and potential ventures. Typically, an offset programme ensures that consideration is given at the highest level to any problems which arise.

Companies generally do not like to part with technology, as its dispersion may have implications for their own future viability. Sharing technology with another nation, even through an offset deal, is not attractive since the effect is to create competition for themselves. In some instances, companies will only offer technology which they know is about to be replaced by new developments. For military technology, the transfer could also mean giving away a military advantage which was provided by the monopoly of technology. In such cases, even though the company may be willing to share the technology, their government may not.

From the point of view of the buying nation, the technology transfer sounds very attractive, but the use of the technology requires a highly skilled workforce, which can learn and make effective use of the opportunity. There is tremendous competition in high technology. Every nation is trying to maintain its advantage by continuous and vigorous research and development. Today's latest technology is obsolete by tomorrow. The items produced by current technology may not sell tomorrow if another nation has made an advance in that field. Thus acquiring high technology is of limited value without the ability to carry out research and development. It makes the buying nation, at best, a branch factory of the company that permitted the transfer.

The offset experience of other nations suggests that high technology capabilities are still under the control of developed nations. They are not willing to just give away technology to developing nations.

Development of high technology capabilities in defence-related industries is not expected to be economically feasible following the end of the Cold War and the emergence of the so-called New World Order for promoting peace. The world market is flooded with military hardware and developed nations are facing difficulties in making new sales. The global defence industry is shrinking in output and capacity. Under these conditions, there is little opportunity for developing nations to sell defence products which are produced under licence with borrowed technology.

The manufacture and assembly of components, subsystems and major assemblies under licence, as is done in Turkey and Egypt, is difficult for Saudi Arabia, for the following reasons:

- the equipment proportion of the contracts, which would give rise to opportunities for manufacture and assemble, is typically quite small
- as Saudi Arabia's population is small and there is a shortage of skilled workers, there is no pressing requirement to establish factories with the sole aim of providing skilled jobs such as those in defence work
- at a time when the defence industries of developed nations are converting to the production of non-military items, any military production set up in Saudi Arabia should be for dual-use items.
- the Kingdom should concentrate mainly on the production of non-military items that have a wide market, with the possibility to change to military items if needed in the future. The government is the sole customer for

military equipment, while non-military items have unrestricted markets with many customers.
- the sale of all defence-related equipment produced under licence is controlled in one way or another by the nation of origin of the technology
- an offset should be directed towards establishing industry for which there is a big demand, or to produce goods that are consumed in both the military and civil sectors, such as memory chips, communication equipment etc.
- the over-riding problem with the transfer of technology through offsets is that the receiving nation will always lag behind the latest technological developments. If an industrial nation like the US has difficulty maintaining its lead in some technologies, then the developing nations have little chance of keeping pace with developments.

This suggests the important conclusion that offset programmes should emphasise the establishment of research and development centres, working closely with universities such as the King Abdul Aziz City for Science and Technology.

9.9   Saudi Arabian Offset Programme Objectives

Offset programmes in the Kingdom of Saudi Arabia, as in other nations, are initiated along with the purchase of defence products and services. The offset part of the contract is an agreement by the foreign sellers to joint investment in the Kingdom, on a 50–50 basis with Saudi investors. However, the objectives of the Kingdom's offset programmes are somewhat different from those elsewhere. The aim is to achieve sound economic diversification, rather than to sustain or create defence industrial capabilities. Thus investment is encouraged in the fields of advanced technology that have long-term business potential.

The Saudi Arabian offset programme can be seen as an extension of the long-term civil programme of technology transfer to contracts in military sector. Offsets can and are making a valuable contribution to the creation of a diversified economy, but there is a real and overriding problem in that trained Saudis are not available in the required numbers and with the appropriate skills seeking employment of the type offered by the offset projects. Government departments and the private sector are also competing for the available trained Saudis.

The first military offset programme of the Kingdom was part of the Peace Shield purchase of defence equipment. The offset policy was first developed for this programme and subsequently applied to the UK Al Yamamah agreement. The subsequent agreement with the French government was a framework agreement to provide offsets against future contracts. As a matter of policy, all the agreements were written in a way which made it easier for investors. This led to changes in the Guidelines, which became more flexible than when first set out in 1983.

As well as the transfer of technology through research, development, manufacturing or production, the objectives of offset policy include efficient use of Saudi Arabia's natural resources, establishing industries with export potential, and creating service industries to enhance, develop, support or maintain the infrastructure of the Kingdom.

The 1983 General Guidelines included a list of 'Candidate materials, products, processes and systems' appropriate to the offset programme. This list was not intended to be exhaustive, but aimed at providing examples of appropriate technology. The items on the list were state of the art commercially viable products, rather than research and development.

The objective of transferring high technology into the Kingdom has been clarified. Some early offset proposals were based on attractive high technology which has proved difficult or impossible to transfer. The Offset Committee has increasingly emphasised that the 'transfer' element is more important than the 'high' aspect of technology. The Committee prefers a successful transfer of medium technology to the hope for high technology. Medium technology is more susceptible to transfer and more appropriate to the other objectives of offset policy.

9.10   The Saudi Economic Offset Committee

The Saudi Arabian Government constituted the Saudi Economic Offset Committee (EOC) in 1983 as the primary authority to administer the offset programme. The EOC is composed of high level representatives from the Ministry of Finance and National Economy, the Ministry of Planning, the Ministry of Commerce, and Ministry of Industry and Electricity. The Director General of the Saudi Industrial Development Fund (SIDF) and the Managing Director of Saudi Arabian Basic Industries Corporation (SABIC) are also members The Committee is chaired by the Assistant to the Minister of Defence and Aviation. Lehman Brother Kuhn Loeb, a US international banking firm, was contracted in 1983 to provide advisory staff to the committee. This role has now been taken over by the Carlyle Group.

9.11   EOC Responsibilities

The EOC provides oversight of offset matters within the Ministries, and coordination between Ministries. The responsibilities of the Committee are:

- to determine the requirements of the Saudi Economic Offset Programme
- to approve proposals and packages
- to monitor the progress of the programme
- to facilitate implementation and enhancement of the programme
- to approve offset credits as earned by a contractor.

There have been three major influences on the development of the offset programme: the Peace Shield, Al Yamamah and Saudi-French defence contracts. These programmes have a potential total offset investment of $25 bn over a 25 year period.

9.12   Peace Shield

The $3.8 bn Peace Shield I programme was for the installation of a ground-based air defence capability. According to reports in the *Middle East Economic Digest*, the attitude of potential suppliers changed during the bidding process.[10] During initial discussions between the Kingdom and prospective bidders, 'companies were generally incredulous when told the Saudis would be seeking an offset programme with a high technology transfer content. In the end, the companies came round to the idea, not only that the offset scheme was manageable — but that they could come up with worthwhile proposals'.

The formal request for proposals for Peace Shield was sent to bidders on 26 April 1984. Responses, including offset proposals, were due by 7 November 1984, with the aim of reaching agreement on offset proposals in December 1984. In the event, General Electric was chosen to supply 17 radar stations. Three US industry groups headed by Boeing, Litton and Hughes, placed bids for other Peace Shield support systems. The offset proposals from the three groups were forwarded to the Kingdom with signed memoranda of agreement in December 1984. In February 1985 a contact was awarded to Boeing, which included a 35% offset expectation for the value of the technical equipment.

The EOC's procedures for review, approval and evaluation required detailed documentation from the contractor. A number of pre-signing actions were necessary and were undertaken by all companies bidding for the contracts. The contractor's offset commitment legally began when the supply contract for the sale of defence equipment to the Kingdom was signed.

Once an offset joint venture was implemented, it would receive no more assistance than any other business. However, it would be monitored by the Committee to ensure compliance with the agreement on technology transfer, the training of Saudi personnel and adherence to the financial and investment plans.

The Saudi Arabian participants are 'companies organised in Saudi Arabia, whose equity capital has been raised fully or in part through public subscription'. Every company must be pre-qualified by the Offset Committee to participate in offset joint ventures.

The bidders on defence contracts come from world-wide industry. In the Peace Shield bid, the prime contract bidders (Boeing, Litton and Hughes) were American, but with some non-American sub-contractors. For subsequent offset contract proposals, the American group would be better described as an international group. Together, the Saudi Group and International Group form the Contractor Group.

Within the Contractor Group, various partnerships and offset projects are arranged. When Boeing was selected as the prime contractor for Peace Shield defence products and services, the obligation for offset joint ventures by Litton and Hughes ceased. However, they were invited, but not obliged, to continue the projects they had proposed. A holding company, Boeing Industrial Technology Group (BITG), was set up with overall project management responsibility for the offset programme. The initial partners were the Boeing Company (49%), Westinghouse (18%), Saudi Amoudi (13%), ITT (11%) and SOMC/Basil (9%). BITG was capitalised at $75 million.

The Boeing offset programme was later described by *Aviation Week and Space Technology* (January 1992) as 'elaborate', with Boeing arranging development of a $600 mn high technology industry in the Kingdom. Currently, the Peace Shield air defence installation is 'at least two years behind schedule' and USAF '... officials partially terminated Boeing's ... contract recently'. The termination was due to allegations of delay in providing computer software for the command and control function.

The offset programme is a separate agreement between Boeing and the Saudi government that will not be 'impacted substantially' by the termination. Boeing, as a member of a series of joint venture companies, was '... expected to develop modern industry in the Kingdom, with emphasis on technology transfer and export potential'. A Boeing spokesman did not expect the Peace Shield termination actions to influence the four offset companies already in operation (Advanced Electronic Company, Aircraft Accessories and Components Company, Al Salam Aircraft Company, and International Systems Engineering), but creation of new offset companies would stop. The four Peace Shield offset companies are 'financed by the Saudi Government, Saudi banks, Boeing and Boeing's Saudi partners'. The fifth Peace Shield Offset Company is the Middle East Propulsion

Company (MEPC) which is almost ready to begin operations. This was formed under a separate offset agreement with General Electric. The partners are General Electric, Pratt & Whitney, Rolls-Royce, together with Saudi companies.

In July 1992, Hughes Aircraft Company took over the Peace Shield installation procurement, valued at $837 mn, and brought in additional offset project proposals worth $200 mn. These new Peace Shield II proposals include direct offset joint ventures in software and systems engineering, and repair of electronic equipment from radars and satellites. Indirect offsets from Hughes parent company, General Motors, concern local assembly of automobile parts and manufacture of petrochemical products used in European automobile manufacturing.

The Boeing and General Electric offset initiative has resulted in five operating companies set up to support the Peace Shield operations. The market prospects beyond Peace Shield support, and the impact on the wider development of the Saudi Economy, are open to question. Technically, the offset obligations may have been met in full or part, but there remains a question as to whether they meet the intent of the programme. The Hughes proposals, along with the Al Sawary and Al Yamamah described below, would appear to offer much more prospect of meeting both the contractual obligation and the wider expectations behind the desire for offset programmes.

The US company AT&T is now involved in an offset programme associated with a contract for the telephone extension project valued at some $4 bn (SR 15 bn), with their local agent Abdullah Said Bugshan and Brothers Co. AT&T will establish local engineering and manufacturing partnerships in the Kingdom, of which three have been discussed so far: Advanced Electronics Co, Riyadh, to produce electronic circuits for AT&T switch and transmission systems; International Systems Engineering, Riyadh, to provide network management and software expertise to the Ministry of PTT; and with the Saudi Cable Co to engineer, manufacture, assemble and treat copper and fibre optical cable. AT&T plan to invest a total of $4 mn over a three year period.[11] It remains to be seen what impact this programme will have on the development of the Saudi economy.

The AT&T offset programme differs in that it is related to a civil rather than a military primary contract. This has raised the issue of offset programmes as non-tariff barriers to trade. According to the Middle East Monitor, the US government view offset requirements as non-tariff barriers, but raise no objection to offsets related to military sales. It does, however, have strong objections to offsets on commercial civil contracts.[12] If offsets are regarded as non-tariff barriers they would be in contradiction of the GATT rules aimed at ensuring competition and free trade. The Saudi offset policy, at least as far as it applies to civil contracts, could be in direct conflict with the recent application by Saudi Arabia to join GATT.

9.13   Al Sawary II

Al Sawary II, agreed in 1990, involves procurement of French built frigates for the Saudi naval forces, at a cost of $3 bn. It is similar to Peace Shield in that it has an investment obligation of 35% of the procurement technical costs over ten years. A total of 37 projects for French offset participation have been proposed, including glass, precious metals, smart cards and agroindustry, with a total capital value of SR1.8 bn.[13] The French participation will be managed by Thomson-CSF, which already has an active business presence in the Kingdom, including the modernisation of the Shahine air defence system. France is the sixth largest exporter to the Kingdom.

9.14   A Case Study of the Al Yamamah I and II Offset Programme

The Al Yamamah agreement was a major defence contract between the Kingdom of Saudi Arabia and the UK. It included the purchase of military aircraft with associated training and support, civil aircraft, helicopters, naval ships and construction projects. British Aerospace is the prime contractor. Estimates of the total value are four to six times larger than Peace Shield, at around $7.6 bn. The contract has so far (July 1994) been worth some £14 bn to the UK economy, with annual revenue currently running at some £2 bn. Over 4000 British Aerospace staff are employed in the Kingdom.[14]

The Al Yamamah contract itself can be viewed as a countertrade deal, in that part of the payment was agreed in terms of 500,000 bpd of Saudi crude oil, to be sold at market prices with the proceeds credited to an escrow account in London, from which British Aerospace and other contractors would be paid by the British Government.[15] Press reports suggested that the figure was increased to 600,000 to cover Al Yamamah II.[16] In addition, the Saudi government has made payments into the account to meet peaks of expenditure.[17]

The defence sales element of Al Yamamah I was signed in September 1985, and Al Yamamah II was signed in November 1988. The first (defence) contract for Al Yamamah I included a commitment by the UK government to use its best endeavours to encourage offset investment. This became an offset programme when a memorandum of agreement was signed by the two governments in July 1988. While there are some similarities to the Peace Shield agreement, Al Yamamah does not have a contractual obligation to offsets, but there is an investment target of £1 bn ($1.5 bn), or 25% of the technical sales cost over ten years. Unlike the Peace Shield offset programme, joint ventures under the

Al Yamamah offset are not restricted to high technology industries and most are not defence-related.

There is not over-emphasis on the transfer of high technology. Rather than seeking state of the art technology, the Saudi government are keen to acquire proven, commercially applied technology which can immediately be put into production to benefit the economy. Any UK company is invited to invest, not just those involved with the defence element of Al Yamamah. In Phase II, the UK companies were again to use 'best endeavours' to generate £1 bn of UK investment in the Kingdom. This approach mirrors the general UK attitude to offsets, which are seen by the UK government as commercial agreements facilitated by association with defence projects.

Under the agreement, British Aerospace receives offset credits for the capital value of investments accepted under the offset programme. These credits are for the total foreign contributions to the capital value of the project (cash, in kind and debt) and are not restricted to the value of the British Aerospace investment. For certain technologies there may be a multiplier applied to the value of investment, which for a highly sought technology such as silicon chips could result in a credit of up to five times the total value of the investment. On the other hand, technology licensing may result in less credit than the value of the project.

In addition to credits for joint ventures, British Aerospace can receive credits for facilitating the export of products from Saudi Arabia. This is not restricted to products from joint ventures set up under the offset programme, but may apply to exports from any Saudi manufacturer. British Aerospace's role can end at the point of contractual negotiations for the export sale. The Saudi supplier remains responsible for the deal. These credits are typically on a one-for-one basis, ie the full value of the export deal is credited to the offset programme. This encourages British Aerospace to seek matches between the products manufactured in Saudi Arabia and those used by the companies which supply British Aerospace. This mirrors the Aramco efforts through the Houston office of the Aramco Local Industrial Development Department to encourage US companies to use Saudi products.

A typical joint venture financial package might involve 50% funding by the Saudi Industrial development Fund (SIDF) at preferential rates (currently 5% initial charge plus 1% a year administration fee on the outstanding balance, but no interest payment). A further 25% of the capital would come from commercial loans, leaving 25% contributed in equity by the partners. Half of the partner's equity may be from the Saudi partner, with the remaining half (12.5% of the total) supplied by the overseas joint venture partners. This may be the technology supplier, or may be shared with British Aerospace. The Saudi partner may thus contribute 12.5% of the equity in return for half of the company and of the profits, with the foreign technology partner and British Aerospace each contributing 6.25% of the equity in return for a quarter of the company and of the profits.

The majority of offsets under Al Yamamah are expected to be indirect, such as pharmaceuticals (Glaxo and Saudi Import Co), vegetable oil manufacturing, petroleum, food processing (eg sugar refining: Tate & Lyle and Savola), health care and environmental equipment. Direct offset proposals have included a missile engineering factory (British Aerospace and Dowty) to repair and modify the Kingdom's Sidewinder, Alarm, Skyflash and Sea Eagle Missiles, with prospects of markets in other Middle East countries. Rolls-Royce joined the Middle East Propulsion Company, set up under the Peace Shield Offset Programme and which now encompasses all the world's primary jet engine companies. By April 1992, investment under the UK offset programmes totalled SR2.3 bn ($614 mn).

Since both Peace Shield and Al Yamamah offsets supported Saudi Arabian air force contracts, there were mixing and cross-contractual arrangements. In the Al Yamamah proposal, Rolls-Royce entered the MEPC company established under Peace Shield offsets. The electronic capability created by Peace Shield offsets in AEC would support the electronic components of Al Yamamah defence products. AEC production would also include US equipment systems purchased for the Kingdom's armed forces with UK sub-systems. When Dowty sold its shares in AACC after the takeover of Dowty by the TI Group, British Aerospace acquired a 30% share of AACC. A large amount of accounting effort would be needed to identify which programme should receive the offset credit for exports from these companies.

There are a number of potential advantages of using the offset route to new ventures, rather than acting independently. The range of incentives available for joint ventures under Saudi regulations is also available under the Offset Programme. In addition, British Aerospace and its associates are able to offer a range of business support services to help newcomers considering entering the Saudi market. These include project and investment appraisal, introduction to potential partners, and technical and marketing support. Offset companies gain fast-track access through the planning and approval systems. Finally, British Aerospace is prepared to invest in the offset ventures, whether or not they involve British Aerospace technology, and whether or not they involve British companies or markets in which British Aerospace currently operates.[18]

This list of support activity, while important to encourage others to help British Aerospace meet its offset obligations, also reflects the approach taken to the offset programme by the company. Although the terms of the agreement are for "best endeavours", British Aerospace is clearly taking a long-term view of the potential from offsets. This in part reflects the commercial realities in that future business opportunities for the company in the Kingdom are likely to be influenced by, if not depend upon, the Kingdom's assessment of the offset programme. At the same time, these commercial realities apply also to Boeing, which did not seem to approach the offset issue in the same way.

The need to part with technology, often seen as vital to the competitive position of a company, is not generally a barrier to participation in the offset programme. Saudi Arabia is keen to acquire fully developed and commercially proven technology which can be immediately applied. For most companies, replacements for such technology are already under development. If a market opportunity exists, inevitably some company will move into that market. Establishing a joint venture provides a share of the market and the basis for a long-term presence which many companies see as preferable to the risk of losing the whole market to a competitor.

Initial progress on the Al Yamamah offset programme was certainly slow. This reflected in part the delay in reaching agreement (the offset package was finally agreed some two and a half years after the deal). It also reflects the time it took British Aerospace to realise both the obligations and the opportunities involved in the offset programme. Continuing restructuring and reorganisation within British Aerospace, coupled with declining defence markets eventually focused attention on the importance not just of the Al Yamamah deal but also on the potential offered by the offset programme.

9.15   The Peace Shield Offset Companies

Four companies have been established by the Boeing Industrial Technology Group (BITG). These are now effectively operating as independent companies. A fifth company, the Middle East Propulsion Company, was established by General Electric.

9.15.1   Advanced Electronic Company

AEC is a joint venture between: National Industry Company, Saudi Arabian Airlines (Saudia), Boeing Industrial Technology Group (BITG), National Commercial bank, and Gulf Investment Corporation. There were two objectives behind the establishment of AEC. The first was to provide the Kingdom with the most advanced military and commercial electronics equipment available in the world, at competitive prices. The second was to maximise the synergistic benefits from bringing the latest technology and manufacturing expertise to the Kingdom.

The Advanced Electronic Company (AEC) will initially assemble Jaguar tactical radios for the Saudi Abrams tanks and Bradley armoured vehicles, from parts kits. The kits are supplied by the UK Racal Electronics Group, and are the first Saudi electronics industry production to support indigenous defence requirements. Assembly is expected to reach 200 units a year. In the future it will manufacture the electronic components, together with 20,000 printed circuit boards for other equipment for the Abrams tanks.

AEC must be able to produce a wide variety of electronic products in small quantities. In the developed world, such small quantities would not be practical or economical. The proposed solution is a generic production line with the flexibility to be reconfigured from one type of electronic product to another. This would keep the line in continuous operation and provide income to justify the start-up and operating expenses. AEC's major income generator was not to be production, but the integration of electronic components.

In communications, AEC manufactures and integrates its own designs for use in the Kingdom's armoured vehicles, along with base and hand-held radios. In integration, AEC has completed a definition study for a fully automated air traffic control system for the Kingdom. In the Logistics field, growth has included a recent contract with the Kingdom's Post, Telephone and Telegraph for repair of printed circuit boards, along with maintenance services for Saudi AWACS radar and avionics. Technology transfer has been assisted by placing Saudi personnel on the engineering teams of joint venture partners for on the job training. This exposes the Saudi's to a wider range of projects than would be possible within the Kingdom.

The experience of AEC has been typical of the offset companies. According to *Middle East Business Weekly*, a central issue of the venture's slow development has been the sheer complexity of the project. Development was slow both in putting together the business arrangement and in establishing industrial capability. Under the offset proposal, AEC was to begin to generate gross income in 1986 and to have positive net earnings by 1990. The market was expected initially to be limited to the Kingdom's defence and security forces, and then to expand to the Gulf Cooperation Council countries. Forecasts made in 1985 were for 2000 employees and annual sales of around $388 mn in 1995.

AEC has grown rapidly since its inception in 1988. Sales in 1991 were above SR174 m ($46.5 m), with a total workforce of 240. In August 1994 the company moved into permanent facilities in the industrial park at the King Khalid International Airport at Riyadh. AEC has now received ISO9002 quality certification. Its 1994 sales were SR242 m ($65 m). Total manpower as of

July 1995 is 310, of whom 58% are Saudi. The largest company contract is SR900 m ($240 m) from AT&T to manufacture equipment for the new Saudi telephone system (TEP6). The contract will run for seven years. AEC also has contracts with the Kuwaiti government to repair their Ericsson telephone switching circuit boards and with McDonnell Douglas to manufacture F-15 electronic parts.

9.15.2 Aircraft Accessories and Components Company

Aircraft Accessories and Components Company (AACC) was established to maintain, repair and overhaul aircraft components such as flight controls, pneumatics, fuel and hydraulic systems. Initial technology was provided by the UK Dowty Group, with other equity shareholders being Saudi Arabian Airlines (Saudia), Boeing Industrial Technology Group (BITG), Saudi Advanced Industries Company (SAIC), and Arabian Aircraft Services Company (Arabasco).

The Dowty Group subsequently withdrew from the venture and its shares were acquired by British Aerospace, giving it a 30% stake. AACC has been in operation since October 1990, and reported total revenues of SR17 m ($4.5 m) for the period February 1991 through September 1992. Employees are thought to total 50, with plans to expand to 100 within twelve months. In 1995 the contract with the RSAF was renewed for three years, with total revenue of SR75 m ($20 m). The company is restructuring its ownership and revising its business plans to accommodate further expansion. The company has become the first of its kind in the Kingdom to achieve ISO9002 quality certification.[19]

AACC has a three-year contract with the Royal Saudi Air Force (RSAF) to repair and overhaul C-130 propellers, which is being undertaken in the Kingdom for the first time. Two new contracts have also been initialed: a SR50 m ($13 m) agreement with BAe to overhaul Tornado accessories and an agreement with McDonnell Douglas to overhaul F-15 hydraulics.

9.15.3 Al Salam Aircraft Company

Al Salam Aircraft Company (ASAC) is a repair, overhaul and modification centre for commercial and military aircraft. There is no similar facility in the Kingdom, and only a few in the Middle East. Incorporated in 1988 as a joint venture, it is a equally owned by BITG and Saudi partners and located on the industrial park at King Khalid International Airport in Riyadh.

The initial equity was provided by National Industry Company, Saudi Arabian Airlines (Saudia), Boeing Industrial Technology Group, Saudi Advanced Industries Company (SAIC) and Gulf Investment Corporation. Reported revenue for the period June 1989 to May 1992 was SR 208.6 m ($55.7 m). Forecasts are for a workforce of 850 and $100 m annual sales in ten years. Latest plans for the period 1993–1996 show an average loss of SR61.3 m ($16.4 m) a year.

ASAC began as a subcontractor to Boeing to maintain aircraft sub-systems. Preliminary plans saw 66% of the work being on RSAF F-15, Tornado, C-130, KE-3A and E-3A aircraft. When Saudia joined the venture in 1987, it added its fleet of 80 commercial aircraft to the customer base. However, the failure to win the C-130 and helicopter maintenance contracts was a significant lost opportunity.

This venture needs extensive facilities for hangars and maintenance shops, together with specialised equipment for maintenance work. As a result, construction, pre-operating and interest costs are high, and difficulty has been experienced in securing additional loans to allow production to start. ASAC started operations in July 1993 from its permanent facility at King Khalid International Airport. The company has overhauled Saudia 737 and Airbus aircraft, and anticipates a contract to overhaul 747 aircraft in 1996. The company also has a contract to maintain the ARAMCO fleet of about 40 aircraft.

9.15.4 International Systems Engineering

International Systems Engineering (ISE) provides planning and integration support for computer software and hardware incorporated in the products of other offset companies. It is thus an exception to the manufacturing requirement imposed on most offsets. ISE will offer a wide range of computer-related systems, development of high-technology software and training for Saudi nationals.

The technology is supplied by the Boeing Industrial Technology Group (BITG) and BDM International. The other equity holder is United Systems Engineering Company, a consortium of six Saudi software companies. Reported revenues for the period June 1989 to May 1992 were SR10 m ($2.7 m). 1993 sales were SR8.6 m ($2.3 m), and 1994 sales grew to SR16 m ($4.3 m). The July manpower is 48, of which 70% were Saudi, including 58% of the technical staff. Current contracts include: Peace Sentinel, SR16 m ($4.3 m) through May 1998; King Fahad Airport, SR41 m ($11 m) through December 1997; TEP6 telephone expansion, SR4 m ($1 m) through September 1995; and miscellaneous International Airport projects valued at SR29 m ($8 m) through January 1998. Forecasts are for sales of $90 m and a workforce of 260 in ten years.

9.15.5 Middle East Propulsion Company

Middle East Propulsion Company (MEPC) is a joint venture capitalized at $70 m, which is involved in several offset programmes. The initial shareholders were National Industrial Company, Saudi Arabian Airlines (Saudia), Saudi

Advanced Industries Company, Gulf Investment Corporation, Pratt & Whitney and General Electric. This represented the Peace Shield offset commitment. When Rolls-Royce joined under the Al Yamamah offset programme, the 50% equity held by Pratt & Whitney and General Electric was subdivided equally with Rolls-Royce. General Electric and Pratt & Whitney have been involved in previous joint efforts to supply Saudi Arabia with engines for military and civil aircraft.

MEPC was set up to establish and operate a civil and military aircraft jet engine repair and overhaul facility at the King Khalid International Airport industrial park, primarily to serve the needs of Saudi Arabia's civil and military aircraft. The Government provided undeveloped land for the project and was to provide infrastructure, for occupancy by 1988. However, the construction contract for fencing and earthmoving was not awarded until August 1989. The project is reported to have been set up in March 1992.

9.16   Al Yamamah Economic Offset Programme

One joint venture is already operating under the Al Yamamah Offset Programme and a further two are in the course of implementation. Other projects are awaiting approval or are under consideration, and some have been cancelled or withdrawn. The three ventures being implemented have a total capitalization of nearly £200m, or one fifth of the objective of £1 bn. The British Offset Office in London coordinates the investment effort with British companies.

9.16.1   Saudi Development and Training Company

The first joint venture under the offset programme to commence operation is equal partnership between British Aerospace and Y B A Kanoo. Based in Dammam, the Saudi Development and Training Company provides development and training packages and personnel profiling services specifically tailored to the needs of clients. The venture has started operations and currently has contracts with ARAMCO, SABIC, BAe, and several banks.

9.16.2   Glaxo Saudi Arabia

Glaxo products have been distributed in Saudi Arabia by the Saudi Import Company (SIC) since 1957. A joint venture was formed in 1983, and by 1994 held 6% of the market with sales of some £20m. Glaxo contributed 49% and SIC 51% of the joint venture's SR98m capital. Under the offset programme a factory is being built in Jeddah to manufacture tablets, creams, ointments, liquids and antibiotics, including Zantac, Zafran, respiratory and dermatological products. The first production run is scheduled for October 1995. Certification by the Ministry of Health is underway. Further, there are plans to develop new products in the Kingdom. This would result in true technology transfer, including the R&D capability.

9.16.3   Tate & Lyle

The third venture being implemented is a sugar refinery which is due to commence operation in early 1996. Located in Jeddah, it is a joint venture between Tate & Lyle and Savola, a Saudi food company. Tate and Lyle will hold 15% of the equity. The plant will produce 500,000 tons of refined sugar a year for the Saudi and export markets. Refinery construction began in January 1995.

9.16.4   Other Al Yamamah Ventures

British Aerospace has invested in the Peace Shield company AACC and Rolls-Royce in MEPC (see above). Approval has been given for a joint venture between Y B A Kanoo and Al Zamil of Saudi Arabia, Culligan Italiana (the European arm of the US Culligan Group), and British Aerospace to manufacture domestic and industrial scale water treatment equipment. This plant is under construction and is expected to be operational in 1995, using technology supplied by Culligan. The Offset Committee has also approved a venture to manufacture reinforced stone, but the Italian partner Tecnomaiera has withdrawn following bankruptcy.

A project to establish a missile engineering facility is awaiting approval by the Offset Committee. This was proposed as a joint venture between British Aerospace, Dowty and Hughes of the US to modify, upgrade, test, repair and manufacture under licence. The position of Dowty in this venture must now be uncertain following their take-over by the TI Group.

Plans to manufacture protein for fish food from natural gas have been stalled until international agreement is reached on the release of bio-protein into the food chain. The project is a joint venture between British Aerospace and Dansk Bioprotein, who propose to build a pilot plant in Norway to demonstrate the technology before proceeding with the construction of a plant to supply some 40,000 to 50,000 tons a year.

Other proposals include a materials handling system venture with Vanderlande Industries and motor vehicle assembly and manufacture. There have also been plans for a mineral wool plant, and a facility to recycle lubricating oil. After an assessment of the market, Scarab are proposing to licence the production of their street sweeping equipment to gain experience before embarking on production in the Kingdom.

After a hesitant early start, the Al Yamamah Offset Programme appears to be making good progress. Projects with a capital value amounting to one fifth of the objectives of £1 bn are being implemented, and others are awaiting approval or under consideration. British Aerospace are demonstrating their commitment to the intent as well as the letter of the agreement through the range and depth of their contribution. The projects are fully researched and their commercial viability assessed before they are submitted, and British Aerospace is further demonstrating its commitment by investing in most of the ventures. Most of the projects have a true technology transfer element which will increase their contribution to the development of the economy of Saudi Arabia.

9.17   Offsets in the Economy of Saudi Arabia

The task which faced Saudi Arabia at the beginning of the 1970s was to develop an industrialised economy. The offset programmes associated with military procurement contracts should be seen as part of this process of industrialisation and development, and in particular as a contribution to reducing dependence on oil. Offsets continue a well-established process of technology acquisition through collaboration and joint ventures.

As with any large-scale exercise, there were successes and disappointments. A number of high-technology ventures have been established which may not have been without the impetus and encouragement given by the need to meet offset obligations. This is particularly likely in the case of the US Peace Shield programme, where high technology ventures may have implied too much risk for commercial investment left to the market. The UK offset joint ventures are more problematical, not having the same high technology content and being a more natural extension of activities already undertaken in the Kingdom. They represent a natural progression of local capability which the market might be expected to identify and meet, although perhaps offsets brought forward their fulfilment. But all of this can be no more than speculation. We will never know what would have happened without the offset programmes.

The experience of Saudi Arabia offers examples of what can be achieved through offset programmes, and also why they may not fulfil their promise. The Peace Shield Offset Programme administered by the Boeing Industrial Technology Group and General Electric appears to have met the letter of its obligations by setting up five joint ventures. These are all high technology, defence linked companies. British Aerospace, while slower to start, appear to be aiming at the intent rather than the letter of their obligations. Rather than defence-linked activity, British Aerospace are seeking ventures with a long-term future, in which British Aerospace has an equity stake. It remains to be seen which will be the most viable approach in commercial terms.

Technology transfer needs an environment in which it can succeed. The systems which allow technology to be absorbed must be developed before transfer can take place. As Saudi Arabia chose a market based system, this means the development of a market economy in which businessmen see and pursue opportunities to profit from the technology available. The success of offset programmes in Saudi Arabia will inevitably depend in part on the extent to which this prerequisite has been or can be met.

The future of offset programmes could be threatened by the assessment of offset as a non-tariff barrier to trade, which would conflict with membership of GATT. This is a wider issue than the Saudi offset programme. At the least, the GCC countries will have to decide whether the export opportunities offered by GATT membership will more than outweigh the loss of offset benefits. At the other extreme, international agreement will have to be reached on whether the US government's interpretation of offset agreements under the GATT rules is accepted. In its strictest form, the view that offset is a non-tariff barrier to trade would preclude all GATT members from running offset programmes.

There have been press reports that offset requirements were dropped from Saudi US deals after Peace Shield because '... the offset requirement has slowed the already laborious procurement process'.[20] This suggests that while the technology and economic systems seem to have been created to allow advantage to be taken of technology transfer, bureaucratic and administrative systems are less able to do so. It is to be hoped that the objective of the Fifth Plan to 'upgrade the performance, efficiency and cost effectiveness of Government institutions' will ensure that there are no unnecessary barriers to technology transfer through future offset programmes.

Endnotes

1. The authors would like to acknowledge the assistance of British Aerospace Defence Ltd and the Secretariat of the Saudi Economic Offset Committee in the preparation of this chapter. The interpretation and opinions expressed are those of the authors, as is the responsibility for any errors or omissions which remain.

2. The Saudi Riyal has been fixed at SR3.745:$ since June 1986.

3. Calculated from **Statistical Summary**, Saudi Arabian Monetary Authority, Riyadh, various years.

4. Moliver D.M., Abbondante P.J., **The economy of Saudi Arabia**, Praeger, New York, 1980, p. 60.

5. Al-Farsy F., **Modernity and tradition: the Saudi equation**, Kegan Paul International, London, 1990, p. 102.

6. *Ibid.*, p. 287.

7. *Ibid.*, p. 177.

8. An amendment to Resolution 124 of 29 5 1403, contained in circular 3/1743 of 24 11 1404; MEED, **Saudi Arabia: Joint ventures exempt from 30 per cent rule**, *Middle East Economic Digest*, 21 December 1985, p. 102.

9. Aramco, **Trends of the construction industry in Saudi Arabia**, LIDD, Dhahran, 1984.

10. MEED, **Saudi Arabia: Joint ventures exempt from 30 per cent rule**, *Middle East Economic Digest*, February 1985.

11. *Arab News*, 14 August 1994.

12. MEM, **Offset problems to GATT entry**, *Middle East Monitor*, September 1994.

13. $480 mn: *Arab News*, June 1990.

14. Bird S., paper to the *CBI Conference on Saudi Arabia*, London, 15 July 1994, unpublished.

15. BZW, Barclays de Zoote Wedd report of 14 April 1992.

16. *Financial Times*, 9 September 1994, p. 18.

17. *Times*, 23 December 1992, p. 12.

18. **Investment in the Kingdom of Saudi Arabia**, BAe, 1994.

19. *Arab News*, 13 August 1993.

20. Marlowe L., **Saudi Arabia**, *Financial Times Supplement*, December 12 1990, p. 11.

Chapter 10

The Teeth of the Little Tigers: Offsets, Defense Production and Economic Development in South Korea and Taiwan[1]

Dean Cheng, Asian Analyst, Center for International Studies,
Massachusetts Institute of Technology
and
Michael W. Chinworth, Senior Analyst, Asian Technology,
The Analytic Sciences Corporation (TASC)

10.1   Introduction

With the end of the Cold War, popular support in most Western countries (especially Europe and the United States) for large military-industrial complexes capable of sustaining a global war effort has receded. As a result, Western defense industries have entered into an extended period of contraction and rationalization, as they support reduced military forces, produce fewer systems overall, and suspend development of new programs. This inevitably will lead to declines in defense industrial capacities in most Western nations, even as various capitals seek to assure sufficient military capabilities to deal with future challenges.

The political and military situation in East Asia, however, is considerably different from that in the West. Asia is likely to remain concerned with defense production and purchases. The end of the Cold War, far from resolving local conflicts, has removed one of the dampening factors on real and perceived ethnic, territorial, historical and even ideological conflicts in the region.[2] Many of these nations view indigenous weapons production capabilities as essential to guaranteeing their territorial integrity, particularly as the United States withdraws militarily from the region.

Beyond the security dimension, however, many Asian states value arms industries as a means of raising the sophistication of their military establishments, and of their economies as a whole. This is particularly true of newly-industrialized countries that have sought to graduate from heavy-industry centered economies into ones focused on higher aspects of technology; arenas related to military power, but with significant technological and financial benefits in their own right. The defense-industrial base is therefore viewed as a means of injecting advanced technologies and their attendant research processes

245

into an economy, accelerating economic growth. This combination of externally driven threat considerations and internally driven desires for greater economic development, especially into higher technology fields, is likely to make arms industries a continued growth area in many Asian economies.

The United States and other advanced powers have played a critical role in the development of local defense industries, and are likely to remain central in future developments.[3] Local producers have demanded offsets in order to secure more advanced technologies for both military and economic purposes, as well as to gain access to markets for local products that might otherwise not be possible.

Western industry, in turn, generally has acquiesced in this strategy for both economic and political reasons. Economically, offsets have often been the *sine qua non* for landing a contract. This often has resulted in competition among Western corporations to provide increasingly generous offset deals; in some European programs exceeding 100 per cent of the value of the original sale (although the average for South Korea and Taiwan is closer to 48 per cent). Politically, arms sales packages (including not only offsets, but provision of training, maintenance, etc.) have served to strengthen diplomatic and military ties. This has been especially true for transfers from the United States, with Washington's concerns during the Cold War with global containment and regional stability. The political and economic consequences of those offsets — greater R&D and production capabilities in future potential competitors over the long-run — have been acceptable risks in pursuit of this larger politico-military strategy.

The end of the Cold War has upset many of these previous calculations regarding offset packages. Western nations in general, and the United States in particular, increasingly are concerned about the implications for economic competitiveness of earlier defense offset and technology transfer policies. At the same time, however, competition among Western arms producers in Asian markets is likely to increase as their respective domestic markets shrink. This will result in added pressures to sell and license arms technology to Asian buyers, with fewer strings attached, particularly if the former continue to restrain licensing to other countries for economic and security reasons.

Two prominent examples in Asia of these trends are the Republic of Korea (ROK) and the Republic of China (ROC).[4] There are a number of similarities between the two states. Both South Korea and Taiwan are halves of divided states which continue to face significant threats from their alter-egos, insofar as their opposite numbers have never renounced the use of force in pursuit of reunification. Nor is the threat chimerical, as both the Democratic People's Republic of Korea (DPRK) and the People's Republic of China (PRC) maintain substantial military establishments directed specifically towards the ROK and the ROC respectively; both have also displayed a willingness to use these forces in the pursuit of political objectives.

As a result, the ROK and ROC have developed their military capabilities; this has included heavy investments in their defense industrial capacities in order to ensure an adequate level of defense. Given initial disparities during the 1950s, both the ROK and the ROC chose to pursue policies of matching communist quantity with capitalist quality. Thus, both Seoul and Taipei have placed a premium on possessing leading-edge weapons systems emphasizing advanced technologies to counter substantially larger Communist military establishments.

These technologies, though, have now become the essential sinews of modern economies, including Taipei and Seoul's; thus, the two states perceive a natural synergy between the modern military-industrial complexes necessary to support their respective militaries, and the development of high-tech economies generally. Both Seoul and Taipei have developed plans to reduce reliance on heavy industries (e.g., steel, oil refining, automobiles) and emphasize more high-technology sectors such as aerospace and advanced electronics to assure their own growth — in essence moving up the economic "food chain." As one Korean industry specialist noted, "Asian countries, with their strong economies and bright prospects, are beginning to think that if they are driving things, maybe they should have a piece of the business."[5]

Up to now, technology transfers from the United States — the primary source of both complete systems and component technology — have played a key role in the economic development of both states, as the US sought to support its Asian allies against perceived security threats. While the United States remains interested in buttressing the security of both Seoul and Taipei, it is also much more sensitive to the potential competitive implications of these transfers in both commercial and military industrial sectors. The "lessons" of past cooperative measures with Japan remain vivid. In many US circles, these programs are perceived as having contributed to the growth of a competitor at the expense of American industry. Consequently, relatively generous transfers cannot be presumed in future cooperative military programs with the United States. As both Taiwan and Korea remain committed to their goals of both expanding military industrial capacity and enhancing commercial capabilities through military technology transfers, the two countries may be compelled to look increasingly to other sources of military technology transfers even while maintaining their traditional security ties to the United States. This is a feasible strategy in light of the abundance of new alternatives resulting from changes in global defense industries brought about by the end of the Cold War.

This shift, meanwhile, occurs in the context of potentially dramatic changes in the security and political outlook for both South Korea and Taiwan.

Diplomatic breakthroughs, key leadership transitions, and internal political movements all could take place virtually at any moment in the coming decade, affecting perceptions within either or both countries for the need to pursue military offsets from foreign producers. For example, the ultimate passing of Kim Il Sung from the Korean scene is almost certain to affect the situation on the peninsula.[6] Similarly, reconciliation between the People's Republic of China and Taiwan could take place in rapid order if the political climate radically changes. In the absence of such transformations, however, the countries are pursuing policies to encourage continued production offsets and technology licensing to encourage domestic economic growth, stimulate local defense industries, and secure certain political and diplomatic objectives (although with differences in each theme evident).

This chapter examines the development and possible future prospects of the South Korean and Taiwanese defense industries, with a particular emphasis on the role of technology transfers and military production offsets in building, sustaining and expanding Taiwanese and Korean capabilities. First, it will provide an overview of the defense industrial capabilities of both countries, with a focus on the role of technology transfers, offset agreements and other forms of military cooperation in their development. After establishing this baseline, it will examine anticipated needs and desires in South Korea and Taiwan for the coming decade, with attention on the role of international contributions and participation in these programs. Finally, possible political/diplomatic ramifications of these trends will be examined.

10.2   Republic of Korea

With the end of the Cold War and the Sino-Soviet rapprochement, the Korean peninsula is now the most heavily militarized border in the world. Both the ROK and the DPRK maintain standing militaries of over one-half million each (over a million in the case of the North). Unlike the NATO and Warsaw Pact armies along the old Inter-German border, the forces on both sides have seen action in the course of the Cold War. Not only did the North invade the South in 1950, but Pyongyang has continued to mount armed probes of the Demilitarized Zone, most recently in May 1992. Nor have tensions declined with the end of the Cold War: the furor over North Korea's nuclear program illustrates the continued state of disquiet on the peninsula, as well as its implications for regional and global order.

To offset the North's numerical superiority, Seoul has emphasized close cooperation at all levels with the United States, while pursuing a technologically-oriented defense directed ultimately toward a more autonomous capability. Both of these efforts have gained impetus since the North has acquired such relatively advanced weaponry as third- and fourth-generation fighter aircraft, ballistic missiles and possible nuclear technology. As the likelihood of substantial American military draw-downs has grown (both under the American East Asian Strategic Initiative as well as the accession of Bill Clinton to the White House), the emphasis has further shifted in favor of an improved, indigenous defense capacity.[7]

10.2.1 Development of the Defense Industrial Sector

As late as 1969 — immediately prior to the announcement of the Nixon Doctrine and the subsequent draw-down of U.S. forces from the region — the ROK had no military industry to speak of.[8] With the decline in the credibility of the American commitment after the promulgation of the Nixon Doctrine, however, the South Korean government began to push for the development of an indigenous defense industrial capacity by establishing the Agency for Defense Development (ADD) in 1970. This was followed by the establishment of the Special Law for the Promotion of Defense Production and Procurement in 1973, which sought to foster a defense industry through such incentives as military draft exemption for engineers and skilled workers, special cost accounting for defense contracts, and long-term low interest loans.[9] The impetus for expanding the local military-industrial base was further increased after the Vietnam denouement and the Carter administration's promise (eventually rescinded) to withdraw all American forces.[10] A special defense tax was approved in 1975 to raise the necessary capital for domestic defense industrial development. In 1978, then-President Park Chung Hee's government enacted the Aerospace Industry Development Act, which was intended to assist and fund the domestic aerospace industry. (That act was replaced by the Aerospace Industry Development Acceleration Act of 1987).[11]

The 1989 Development and Promotion Law for Korean Aerospace Technology established a committee consisting of representative of the Ministries of Trade and Industry, Finance, and National Defense as well as the Economic Planning Board to promote South Korean aerospace development.[12] This was followed by a Special Law for the Defense Industry, aimed at encouraging technology transfer to the fledgling defense industries. Mechanisms enabling technological cooperation and defense production cooperation between Korea and the US also were established as part of the American security relationship with the ROK, including the Technology Cooperation Committee under the ROK-US Security Consultative Meeting, based upon the Data Exchange Agreement signed in 1963, as well as the Scientist and Engineer Exchange Agreement of 1975.

In addition to legislation, Seoul has provided modest funding aimed at improving the military-industrial base. In the 1971-1990 period, the ROK invested \$1.2 billion in defense research and development. More recently, the ROK has emphasized the improvement of the Korean arms industry's efficiency and competitiveness. In particular, Seoul has committed itself to easing governmental controls over domestic arms makers. Towards this end, the National Defense Ministry will augment funding to private sector initiatives in research and development.[13]

Even with these efforts, the Korean arms industry still faces substantial hurdles in its efforts to increase its level of sophistication and general capability. In the aerospace arena, for example, there has been a continuing shortage of financial resources despite government investment, a lack of qualified personnel, and an inefficient material acquisition system, all rooted in a relatively low base of experience.[14] Hong Jai Hak, president of the Korea Aerospace Research Institute, suggested, for example, that the shortage of trained R&D personnel in the ROK will hinder any rapid assimilation and absorption of related technologies.[15] For instance, by 1994, the aerospace industry alone will require a base of 2,200 science and engineering college graduates and an additional 1,200 specialists with advanced degrees. The Korean educational system has thus far produced only about 160 experts, and local universities are expected to add only 200 scientists and engineers annually.[16] As a result, the ROK military-industrial complex has been limited in its ability to expand.[17]

Another problem hampering greater development of the Korean defense industry has been chronic under-utilization of the available base. Despite the continued threat posed by the North, Seoul has chosen to commit fewer and fewer resources to defense procurement, as Northern economic crises cripple their apparent ability to wage (and sustain) a war on the peninsula. As a result, the Korean defense industry has seen decreasing government procurements and lower military demand overall (even as it provides a higher percentage of total government procurements). Defense production facilities were operating at an average rate of only 59.9 per cent of capacity between 1984 and 1988, a situation that has not improved.[18] One of the major challenges for Korea's defense industry, therefore, is achieving sufficient economies of scale and lower unit costs of equipment through higher production volumes. Central to this strategy is promotion of arms exports (much of the excess capacity of South Korean plants reflects unfulfilled export production plans).

Seoul has undertaken several measures in order to alleviate these problems. The ROK plans to invest 5 per cent of the defense budget in R&D to help mitigate the effects of these shortages.[19] In addition, it has focused more on expanding arms exports (although most of it has been in small arms sales). By the late

1980s, however, Korean arms exports totalled only $265.6 million annually, a sharp decline from peak sales of nearly $1.2 billion in 1982, and may have been as low as $100 million by the end of the decade.[20] The government is currently counting on orders from Arab states in the wake of the Gulf War to increase that amount substantially.[21]

10.2.2 Current State of the Industry

Seoul's efforts at developing an indigenous arms industry have resulted in some 83 defense corporations.[22] These include 11 in infantry weapons, nine in ammunition, ten in mobility equipment and logistics, 12 in communications, six in warship and naval systems, three in aircraft and helicopters, and 32 in other related areas.[23] Domestic industry has provided about 61 per cent of total government procurement since 1974, amounting to $16.2 billion and involving about 260 items of military equipment. Much of that equipment is licensed from Western firms.[24] Defense now represents an average of about 11 per cent of revenue for companies involved in the military sector, employing about 45,000 people directly (compared with 2.7 million in the United States in 1993).[25] Activities are relatively diversified: aerospace has received special attention, but there is considerable effort directed toward improving production capabilities in land systems, naval systems, electronics and other sectors.

Aerospace technology — Aerospace has seen the most focused development program of all Korean defense industrial sectors. The ROK has had a long-term aerospace industry development plan since the late 1970s, with an initial focus on licensed production of foreign systems, including the F-86, F-104 and F-4, and Seoul hopes to become a major player in the global aircraft industry by 2000. Despite these efforts, however, there is still no wholly indigenous aircraft industry, due to low production volumes. Nonetheless, these programs were sufficient to produce the current base of 17 companies, including six involved primarily in aircraft projects, eight in airframe, engine, avionics, airframe accessories and parts production and the remaining three focusing on aircraft maintenance. There are still, however, less than 100 local aerospace-related subcontractors, and a total of only 3,000 workers employed directly by the aircraft industry in Korea.[26] Daewoo, Samsung and Korean Air dominate the industry.[27] Total investments as of 1990 appear to amount to only $560 million, of which half is committed to industrial infrastructure.[28] Seoul hopes to become a major player in the global aircraft industry by 2000.

It is in light of this developmental history that the ROK has pursued the Korean Fighter Program (KFP), with an emphasis on technology transfer. The KFP program will involve an initial off-the-shelf purchase of 12 F-16s, followed by 36 aircraft assembled from kits in the ROK and 72 aircraft produced by Samsung. The total value of the package has been estimated at upwards of $3.0 billion.[29] Its significance can be seen when compared to the value of total offsets from the United States to South Korea between 1980 and 1987 of $457.8 million (see Table 1 below for detailed breakdowns). The KFP is seen as a means of expanding local production, broadening the experience pool of domestic work-force and industry beyond simple "metal-bending;" and moving into domestic design and development. It represented the core of the Aerospace Industry Development Plan (AIDP).[30] The importance of technology transfer may be seen in the decision of the ROK to switch from McDonnell Douglas' F/A-18 to the then-General Dynamics, now Martin-Lockheed F-16 as the basis for the Korean Fighter Program. Officials stated that the key reason for the switch was "greater access to technology offered by General Dynamics."[31] The program will include virtually all manufacturing data for the air-frame, as well as offset provisions that will facilitate future South Korean aircraft design, development, and production. The ROK is expected to be involved in the production of the KFP's engines as well. Samsung is expected to begin co-production soon for the P&W F100-PW-229 IPE engine, which will equip the KFP.[32]

The ROK hopes that upon completion of the KFP project (which was to have begun in October, 1994), Korean aerospace firms will have acquired about 80 per cent of the technologies needed for manufacturing F-16s.[33] Indeed, GD

Table 1: Value of Total US Firms' Offset Obligations to the Republic of Korea, 1980–87 (millions of dollars)

SIC Code	Description	Amount $
3721	Aircraft	143.6
3489	Ordnance/accessories	94.2
3812	Search/navigation equipment	35.7
3631	Household cooking equipment	30.6
3511	Turbines	14.8
8611	Business associations	13.7
3728	Aircraft parts	12.9
3559	Speciality industry machinery	12.0
9999	Nonclassifiable	65.6
	Other	34.7
Total		**$457.8**

Source: Office of Management and Budget, Offsets in Military Exports (Washington, D.C.: US Government Printing Office, April 16, 1990), p. 167.

committed itself to assisting Korean production of an indigenous fighter, and was one of the companies pushing for an Aerospace Industry Development Program as a "forerunner to the ROK's indigenous aerospace production projects," involving the creation of a commercial and military aircraft manufacturing base in the ROK.[34] As Kim Yong-Ho, corporate director for GD in Korea pointed out, "there are essentially three areas: manufacturing, management and design and development. KFP can provide advances to each of those three areas, but at quite different degrees in each level."[35]

US government and industry officials acquiesced in this program based on their belief that the ROK will be unable to achieve self-sufficiency in any of the areas of the KFP program involving technology transfers. To ensure this, the US vetoed any transfer of cutting edge technologies, such as complete access to all advanced materials/composites technologies, especially for the "hot" sections of the engine (i.e., the combustion chambers).[36] The United States also denied access to much of the sensitive software technology, especially computer software development related to the radar, the radar-warning receiver, and codes for the on-board computer (the government will permit access to maintenance software).[37] US policymakers also rejected a Korean proposal that the three main Korean aerospace corporations provide an initial 15 per cent of aircraft parts in the second phase, and eventually 50 per cent of all parts in the third phase.

Partly in response to these restrictions, the ROK has continued to express an interest in the Panavia Tornado ECR (Electronic Combat/Reconnaissance) variant, as a possible Wild Weasel.[38] This is in part due to the need for a large, modern aircraft to engage in electronic warfare, but also in order to gain access to the attendant production and weapons technology. In addition, the ROK Air Force has ordered a number of BAe Hawk-100s — light attack/trainer aircraft. (British Aerospace had obtained offset pre-qualification by subcontracting work on Hawk wing sets to Daewoo.)[39] Where the United States views nascent Korean aerospace capabilities with mixed emotions, many European firms apparently see opportunities for aircraft maintenance, parts production and aircraft assembly.[40]

Apart from projects with foreign firms, Seoul is pursuing a number of indigenous programs. One of the most important, but also longest-term, is the indigenous fighter aircraft, currently known as the FXX. The KFP is believed to be the starting point of the FXX, but little is publicly known of the project at the present time.[41] Indeed, it may be premature to discuss a next-generation program so far in advance of the KFP. Meanwhile, Korean industry has begun to explore the possibility of an indigenous trainer for basic training and flight screening to replace their current flight-line of T-41s, in order to expand their expertise before entering into the risky (and highly expensive) FXX project. There also is interest in developing an indigenous primary trainer (the KTX), possibly involving not only local design and production of the airframe, but also the turboprop engine. Reports indicate continued research into a KTX-2, which would be an advanced jet trainer to replace the T-33 and T-37. As a part of the F-16 offset, General Dynamics was believed to be assisting both ADD and Samsung on the KTX-2.[42] South Korean officials hope that the country will be able to undertake such projects independently by 2000 — a very ambitious time line in light of the time required in developing and manufacturing complicated, large scale systems.

In addition to aircraft, the ROK aerospace effort has involved research in space technology. The ROK in 1978 became the seventh nation to produce a surface-to-surface missiles, and currently produces its own short-range artillery rockets.[43] The ROK is now pursuing development of a mobile surface-to-air missile (SAM) system — the Pegasus program involving the mating of the Thomson-CSF Crotale NG surface-to-air missile system to the Korean Infantry Fighting Vehicle (KIFV) chassis. Thomson is expected to transfer significant technology to Lucky Goldstar, which is charged with developing the missile and seeker systems.[44] This follows the introduction of the Short Brothers Javelin and Matra Mistral short-range air defense missile systems The latter deal, valued at $184.5 million, was the result of a Matra offer of technology transfer in other areas to the ADD and Lucky Goldstar (its local partner). General Dynamics, which had offered the Stinger missile, had been unable to offer sufficiently advanced technology to the ROK due to DOD opposition.[45]

With shifts in global military markets and budgets, the ROK has also begun to show greater interest in gaining access to civil aircraft technology. In the course of McDonnell-Douglas' wooing of Asian aerospace concerns for its aborted MD-12 in late 1991, all three major Korean aerospace corporations dropped their fierce infighting and indicated they would be willing to jointly build the plane's nose or tail section.[46] Meanwhile, Korean Air has become a major sub-contractor on the A330/A340 program.

Overall, Korean aerospace companies, however, remain relatively small scale and limited in expertise. Samsung and KAL, for example, did not begin aerospace production work until 1977. Combined military and civilian aerospace production of the three big Korean companies and about 20 smaller subcontractors reached only $267 million in 1992.[47] While domestic industry has probably been able to move more rapidly along the learning curve as a result of these and other programs, they have not yet been able to leap-frog to a level that enables them to compete directly with major Western producers.

Nor are prospects very good for significant growth in the near-term, as global economic conditions and local inefficiencies force profit margins to decline or even disappear entirely. KAL's aerospace division, for example, has reported operating losses every year since 1986, while Daewoo Heavy Industry's aerospace division has consistently lost money since it was founded in 1984. Samsung has said that the aerospace portion of its business, too, is in the red.[48] The large idle capacity at all three Korean companies due to over-investment in the 1980s has exacerbated this situation.[49] These losses have moderated the willingness of high level management to continue massive investments into these areas. Nonetheless, Korean aerospace companies will likely try to take advantage of offset requirements to gain access to more advanced technologies, both in design and production. The ROK also may attempt to purchase overseas aerospace corporations or subsidiaries to gain a stronger foothold in these industries. In the meantime, the KFP assumes the role of holding the budding industry together until other opportunities develop.

Land systems — Despite all the attention paid to the KFP program, battlefield small arms continue to be the defense industry's "bread and butter," according to industry observers.[50] The bulk of the ROK's defense industry, which marked its first steps with licensed production of sidearms (the Colt M-16, in 1973) is still geared towards small arms, ammunition and military vehicles. This segment of the industry has gradually expanded to include AFVs.

Production currently centers on the Type 88 or K-1 MBT (formerly known as the ROK Indigenous Tank, or ROKIT), and the Korean Infantry Fighting Vehicle (KIFV), as well as self-propelled guns. The Type 88 is the centerpiece of the ROK armored formations, supplemented by a variety of M-48 series vehicles directly purchased from the United States. Produced by Hyundai beginning in 1985, with substantial assistance from the GD Land Systems Division, it may be the most effective tank on the peninsula.[51] It also provided sufficient technological spinoffs to bolster Hyundai's production of heavy duty trucks, underscoring to those in industry the validity of the concept of military production serving as a stimulus to commercial industry.[52]

The KIFV is a variant on the FMC Armored Infantry Fighting Vehicle (AIFV), which has also been purchased by the Netherlands. Designed by the Special Products Division of Daewoo Heavy Industries, Ltd to operate with the Type 88, the KIFV includes a domestically produced version of the German MAN D-2848M V-8 turbocharged diesel powerpack, coupled to a locally produced UK Self Changing Gears transmission.[53] The KIFV is supplemented by the Fiat-OTO Melara 6614 wheeled APC, license built by the Asia Motor Company.[54]

Other heavy vehicles include the M109A2 self-propelled 155mm howitzer. The M109 is of one of the oldest and arguably most successful Korea-US co-production arrangements, beginning in 1984. It involves cooperation between Samsung Shipbuilding and Heavy Industry and BMY Combat Systems, and production will total some 500 units.[55] Like the KFP program, however, the most crucial components continue to be imported from BMY.

Naval Systems — The ROK Navy, which has historically been the poor relation of the Korean military, has been enjoying a resurgence due to the block obsolescence of many of its surface combatants (which were mostly ex-USN destroyers of WWII vintage) and Japan's naval expansion. Korea's new destroyers, currently known as the KDX, will have a number of new electronics systems. At this writing, it is expected that the vessels' command and fire control systems (CFCS) will be provided by a consortium headed by Atlas Elektronik of Germany, and including Oerlikon Contraves of Switzerland, Siemens Plessey Radar of the UK, and the American firm of FMC. The South Korean participants are Samsung and Goldstar.[56] Samsung Shipbuilding & Heavy Industry will automatically have a major share of any production agreements, especially in the electronics systems, given the very stiff local content requirement.

The ROK has also begun to build a submarine fleet, comprised of six Type 209 submarines, under a licensed production contract from Howaldtswerke Deutsche Werft AG (HDW) of Germany. Five of the submarines will be constructed at Daewoo's Okpo shipyard, with Krupp Atlas Elektronik supplying both the sonar and integrated command systems.[57] The ROK Navy probably will seek an additional six to seven boats of a larger ocean-going type.[58]

To equip these boats, the ROK has sought to produce an indigenous heavy-weight torpedo to allow them to engage in both anti-submarine and anti-surface warfare. Reports indicate, however, that this effort, currently led by Goldstar and the Agency for Defense Development, has run into trouble, due in part to inexperience in Korea in the development of such weapons. "Usually offset arrangements connected to foreign procurements are used to bring in technology transfer and coproduction packages," notes one source. That appears not to have been the case with the torpedo program, however.[59]

Support Systems — One of the most important deficiencies in the ROK military and Korean technology is command, control, communications and intelligence (C3I). This weakness has been a primary obstacle to accelerated transfer of Operational Control (OpCon) from the United States to the ROK, since the Korean Army currently lacks the necessary sophistication to observe and fight on the modern battlefield. One effort to improve that situation involves the cooperation of Lucky Goldstar with Matra in the development of the KOREASAT telecommunications satellites.[60]

10.2.3   Role of Foreign Offsets

As can be seen from this brief description of past, current and anticipated programs, foreign suppliers of systems and technology have played a critical role in the growth and development of the Korean defense industry. At present, more than 80 per cent of the ROK's deployed arsenal continues to be American-made, although in recent years, the US share of equipment procured by the South Korean government has dropped from 90 per cent to just over 50 per cent.[61] Furthermore, according to some estimates, at least 80 per cent of all foreign technology in current Korean weapons systems still originates from the United States, the remainder spread among France, the UK, Italy, the FRG and Switzerland.[62] Similarly, the "two-way street" in defense acquisitions is lopsidedly in favor of the United States. In 1989, for example, Korea purchased $577 million in American defense items, while the US purchased only $91 million in Korean equipment, mostly comprised of spare parts and componentry.[63]

Korean officials are fully cognizant of the past American role in the development of their defense industrial base, not only through the provision of defense equipment, but also through US technical data packages (TDP) provided throughout the 1970s (TDP purchases dropped precipitously after 1982 and ceased in 1986 altogether).[64] Policymakers view these transfers in the context of broader economic development plans, with military technology representing leading edge capabilities that will drive commercial development as well.[65] The Korean Ministry of National Defense recognizes this linkage explicitly, as well as the use of offsets to further the country's economic growth and development objectives:

In procuring materials from defense industries, items to be purchased through open tenders will be extended to include those that will satisfy not only military needs but also the needs of domestic industry, and which will encourage technological development.

In the case of foreign purchases of military equipment, materials and services, since July 1982 the ministry has been utilizing military offset programs to ask foreign contractors to provide certain benefits in return [for sales or fees] such as technology transfers, licensed part production or buybacks. [In] this way, foreign purchases can be made in an economical and efficient way, and still contribute to the development of domestic industries.[66]

It is therefore not surprising that South Korea remains committed to close military industrial ties with the United States, but is interested simultaneously in broadening its contacts with other nations (as reflected in the growing European share of Korea's overseas purchases) in order to further its economic and political objectives. The Korean government addresses those issues frankly:

There is no doubt that necessary military weapons and equipment should be developed and produced locally for the development of the nation's defense industry. However, as the weapon systems become more sophisticated ..., local defense industries reach their limits. Purchasing of the expensive weapons from abroad becomes inevitable.

Beginning in 1983, therefore, the ROK government implemented the "offset" system, designed to develop the local defense industry with expensive technology imported from advanced nations, and to help it export parts and components to the technology exporting nations. In fact, the system has helped improve the financial status of the local defense industries, enhanced the logistics support capability of the ROK military, and contributed to overall national security.

The offset system was originally devised as a defense burden-sharing scheme between the United States and NATO member countries after the end of Word War II. Today, the system has been adopted by many countries around the world. The ROK will continue its efforts to utilize the system to further its national interest.[67]

At the same time, disappointment has been expressed that production of end items has not resulted in the economic/industrial stimulus originally anticipated. Most Korean arms industries remain able to handle only low-tech component production, and are deficient in such areas as industrial infrastructure, composite and advanced material fabrication, and systems integration and advanced electronics.[68] The state of third country export sales reflects these condition.[69]

Economic offsets have not always produced the desired results from Korea's perspective. Between 40 to 50 per cent of total acquisition costs of such production still flows back to US producers, strengthening the position of American companies in the Korean market at the expense of local firms.[70] The current situation therefore is perceived as giving the US a strangle-hold on Korean technology development. Technology transfers have been sufficient to help build only a modest domestic defense industry, and key, advanced technologies — the "good stuff" — are withheld, thwarting further development. Indeed, the American "provide aid and enjoy control" rule, begun with the pressure on the Korean Army to purchase Colt weapons, is a continued irritant in military-industrial cooperation between the two powers.[71] In the case of the Korean Fighter Plane, this was especially galling, as the United States imposed a 30 per cent cap on the value of the offset packages that American corporations could offer the ROK.[72]

The government's preferred solution to this situation is to push for even greater technology transfers from multiple sources — ranging from the United States and Western Europe to Israel — and increased local production of US and other foreign equipment in Korea through expanded cooperative programs, including various offset schemes. "International cooperation," notes one observer, "greatly affects [the ROK's] self-sustaining capacity for defense and makes a substantial contribution to the economic growth of the country."[73] In the Korean view, those transfers must greatly exceed current levels to achieve their desired results.

To promote this objective while maintaining some semblance of international cooperation between Seoul and Washington, the ROK has promulgated a five-prong approach toward military production with regards to the United States. This plan includes calls for:

- industry-to-industry cooperation, especially through the generous licensing of US systems to Korea
- cooperative mobilization
- greater production shares for Korean industry, including not only Korean production of a majority of parts but also buy-backs by the US government
- joint research and development, focusing on overall system development, component design, and transfer of basic research; and
- cooperative marketing in third-country markets, including sales rights for Korean firms.[74]

This last aspect is especially important, as Korean officials argue that only through exports to third countries can sufficient economies of scale be achieved.[75]

If Korean officials desire closer economic links between the two states, however, their American counterparts have evinced far less interest. In the first place, Korea appears to already be at the outer limit of its technological grasp.[76] Indeed, according to one estimate, about 46 per cent of domestic procurement contracts continue to depend on overseas imports of components and parts.[77] As one analyst notes, "Korean defense companies simply cannot digest such advanced systems as in the Korean Fighter because the technology gap is too wide."[78]

Moreover, as noted earlier, neither American government nor business has any desire to spur Korean competitiveness at the expense of US high technology industries.[79] Concerns about cooperating with the ROK have been exacerbated by the fact that Korea has been on an intellectual property rights watch list since May 1989, due to Seoul's poor enforcement of patents and widespread counterfeiting.[80] Such fears have been further strengthened as Korea has made an explicit linkage between military production and economic development, particularly in high technology and advanced industrial sectors. ROK government officials, especially defense planners, openly view the two as intimately related, with the defense industries a primary means of injecting increased technological sophistication into the economy as a whole. At the same time, a technologically-advanced economy helps maintain the military-industrial base, providing an indigenous capacity capable of providing better support for the services. In addition, Washington is less inclined to support generous technology transfers, licensing and production agreements to preserve production at home during a period of contraction in the domestic arms industry.

In response to American concerns, Koreans are quick to emphasize that Seoul is not another Tokyo, a theme that was particularly in evidence during the Korean Fighter Plane debate, although that did not lessen opposition in Washington. Proponents of expanded defense production in Seoul argue that ROK companies can play a role in the American defense industry through subcontracts on US projects.[81] Many of the Korean proposals are rooted in the country's relatively lower cost labor, which would additionally assist the United States by reducing unit costs, thus saving money for all concerned over the long run. Many Korean defense companies, moreover, continue to believe in teaming with the United States for both political and economic reasons. Greater interdependence, they feel, guarantees continued extension of the US security umbrella, even though much of the incentive behind greater domestic production is due to a decline of Korean confidence in that guarantee. Indeed, some analysts believe that the US will always enjoy an inside track so long as it remains intimately connected with the ROK's defense.

As American wariness has continued, though, Koreans have become increasingly attracted to European suppliers, who have shown a greater willingness to transfer technology to the ROK. As long as the Korean defense manufacturing sector views international cooperation and joint ventures as key to acquisition of advanced technology (as well as to decrease American leverage), the ROK's interest in alternative partners is likely to remain strong.[82]

On the whole, then, offsets have only had a limited effect, in economic terms, for both the ROK and its foreign partners (in terms of creating new competitors, not necessarily in terms of profitability of such relationships, or of their political benefits). The potential advantages to American and European companies of partnerships, and the likelihood of supplying the US market with spare parts production or more advanced development capabilities, remain unclear. At the same time, although the Koreans have demanded particular parts or components, they have shown limited ability to benefit from the transfer of technology *per se*. Indeed, the main economic benefits of technology transfer may lie more in the transfer of general manufacturing know-how rather than specific componentry fabrication techniques.

10.3   Republic of China

Taiwan's experience in indigenous defense production and foreign partnerships offers both similarities and contrasts with South Korea. While external security considerations are similar (i.e., a hostile state possessing military forces that are substantially larger), the Taiwanese approach towards resolving them has been very different due in no small part to the different diplomatic standings of Seoul and Taipei.

The primary focus of the Kuomintang (KMT, or Nationalist government) has been securing the island bastion, as well as scattered outposts, from depredations by the communist regime in Beijing. As an island nation, Taiwan has faced somewhat different problems from its peninsular counterpart. On the one hand, the difficulties of amphibious warfare has precluded, since the 1960s, much call for a significant American military presence on the island itself (in contrast with the commitment made to Korea). Instead, the KMT regime has enjoyed a somewhat more discreet shield in the form of the Seventh Fleet, which first entered the Taiwan Straits in 1950 during the Korean War, and has since been at least an implicit peacekeeping force separating the two regimes.

With the American shift from Taipei to Beijing during the 1970s, however, culminating in American recognition of the PRC as the "official" China in 1979, the ROC could no longer assure itself of automatic American support in the event of a PRC invasion. More importantly, the possibility of a Communist blockade of the island has always been something of a grey area with regards to an American response. As a result, the ROC's defense strategy has emphasized retaining control of the air and sea space in the immediate vicinity of Taiwan itself. There has also been a growing allocation of resources aimed at ensuring that Taiwan could secure its sea-lanes of communications, with special emphasis on developing a robust ASW capability against China's large (if obsolescent) submarine fleet.

These efforts have become harder as Taiwan's precise diplomatic status remains in doubt. (Taiwan lost its ally in Asia when the Republic of Korea established formal diplomatic relations with the PRC in 1992, severing its ties with Taiwan in the process.) As a major power, the PRC consistently has demanded that political relations with Beijing must come at the expense of severed relations with Taipei. The lack of diplomatic recognition, coupled with potential Chinese retaliation for arms sales to Taiwan, has meant that unlike their Korean counterparts, the Nationalist military's access to complete foreign weapon systems has been much more limited and uncertain. As a result, the ROC has been compelled to develop an indigenous arms industry with much more urgency than the ROK.

Changes in global markets, on the other hand, have made Taiwan more attractive to Western sellers despite the political risks formerly associated with expanded sales. Although justified on security grounds, for example, the US sale of F-16s to Taiwan (reversing a political/military policy of more than a decade) was decided at least in part on economic grounds. With the US Air Force scaling down its orders of the aircraft, risking irritation with Beijing seemed like a small price to pay to preserving thousands of US jobs, even if only for a few months or a year, in the face of a continuing defense build down at home. France's renewed interest in Taiwan's arms market reflects similar thinking and attitudes.[83]

This shift in Western attitudes should provide Taiwan with greater options and alternatives with regard to weapons purchases and offsets in the short term, although structural limitations still constrain industry's ability to move rapidly into autonomous production of high tech, advanced systems.

10.3.1   Development of the Defense Industrial Sector

Like the ROK, Taiwan did not begin development of its military-industrial sector until relatively recently. With the American commitment to Beijing not to provide Taiwan with qualitatively superior weapons (including the Harpoon anti-ship missile), the ROC found itself with no choice but to develop a military-industrial sector. Compounding the problem of initial start-up costs has been the fact that Taiwan, unlike the ROK, has a strict policy banning arms exports.[84] This has obvious implications for achieving economies of scale, and has influenced Taiwan's mix of military and commercial projects with overseas partners.

Moreover, unlike either the ROK or Japan, Taiwan does not possess large-scale industrial conglomerates such as the *chaebol* in Korea or the *keiretsu* in Japan. Instead, the Taiwanese economy is dominated by thousands of small companies. While this has not necessarily affected the development of some industrial sectors (including computers), such a fragmented composition has influenced those areas involving large capital requirements.

As a result, much of Taiwan's defense industrial research has been conducted at government-run institutes, such as the Chungshan Institute of Technology and Science. Established in 1968, the CSITS now employs over 6300 scientific and technological personnel, and over 8500 technicians.[85] The four research institutes and six R&D and manufacturing centers of the Institute are charged with conducting "research, development and design for national defense science and technology."[86]

10.3.2   Current State of Defense Industry

Taiwan remains diplomatically isolated, limiting its access to military sales and credits from abroad. This has not prevented various corporations from continuing sales of dual-use technology to Taiwan. Nonetheless, Taipei still must look primarily to its domestic industry to supply the bulk of equipment for its armed forces. Like Korea, Taiwan has placed emphasis on the aerospace sector for security and economic development. The government's strategy of importing foreign aerospace technology has been more flexible and multi-dimensional, exploring high tech commercial options in addition to the tried and true pattern of military offsets. Naval programs are ambitious, while the attention to ground systems is limited compared with South Korea (for obvious reasons).

Aerospace — One of the highest priorities of the ROC military has been preserving control of the airspace around Taiwan. With the mounting obsolescence of the mainstays of the ROC Air Force (ROCAF) — the F-104 and the F-5 — and Washington's refusal to provide the FX/F-20 follow-on to the F-5, CSITS and the Aero-Industry Development Center (AIDC) began research in the early 1980s aimed at developing an indigenous fighter. The result was the Ching-Kuo Indigenous Defense Fighter (IDF). The centerpiece of an effort to establish a first-class aircraft production capability, the IDF has such advanced features as wing flaperons, a sidestick controller, head-up display (HUD), and wholly moving tailplanes. (It involves relatively little use of composites, however). In the course of its design, significant effort was also devoted to the development of the powerplant, the F125/TFE1042. This engine is jointly produced by Garrett Engine division and the AIDC. Garrett produces and ships the hot section assembly to Taiwan — including the turbine, combustor and compressor — where they are mated with the fan, afterburner and cases, manufactured by Aero Engine Factory.[87] General Electric has expressed interest in designing an alternative, more powerful engine for the IDF.[88] British Aerospace was also involved in component development.[89]

Despite the strides shown by the ROC military-industrial complex embodied within the IDF (which remains the first indigenously produced Asian fighter outside the PLA Air Force), the Ching-Kuo is, at best, an aircraft with limited performance capabilities. This is hardly surprising, given the Taiwanese aerospace industry's circumscribed experience (total Taiwanese aerospace output in 1989 was only $630 million, mainly involving low-technology items such as valves and fasteners). As a result, the IDF will replace only the F-104s currently in the ROCAF inventory. The new backbone of the Taiwanese flight-line will instead be the F-16, following former President Bush's decision to allow the sale of 150 F-16A/Bs to Taipei. The experience gained thus far, however, will probably be bolstered by anticipated technology transfers from France in the wake of the sale of 60 Mirage 2000-5's (with an option on 40 more.)[90] This will include programming software and data encryption algorithms for the ICMS-2000 integrated countermeasures system.[91]

Taiwanese research in missile programs has been more successful. Although it started later than most other Asian states, the Taiwanese now produce a significant array of home-grown tactical missiles, mainly in the air-to-air and anti-ship categories. These include the Tien Chien (Sky Sword) series of air-to-air missiles and the Hsiung Feng anti-ship missiles. In this regard, Taiwan has benefited from generous technology transfers from other countries, including Israel.[92] This is most visible in the development of the Hsiung Feng anti-ship missiles, which are clearly derived from the IAI Gabriel.

A potentially major stride forward for the Taiwanese aerospace industry, with significant American involvement, is the development and production of the Tien Kung (Sky Bow) surface-to-air missiles system, a Patriot derivative subsumed within the Modified Air Defense System (MADS) and replacing antiquated Nike air defense systems. Under the terms of the $1.1 billion deal,

Raytheon will provide the missile forebody, ground support equipment, training, maintenance, technical support, while Taiwan will provide an indigenously developed aftbody.[93] Additional local improvements will allow the air defense network to interact with existing HAWK surface-to-air missile batteries.

Land systems — Most of the ROC Army's conventional weapons are direct purchases from the United States, including the M109 self-propelled gun. However, Taiwan has deployed a number of M48H "Brave Tiger" main battle tanks (MBTs), which were developed by Taiwan's Armored Fighting Vehicle Development Center, in cooperation with General Dynamics' Land Systems Division.[94] The Brave Tiger is essentially a modified M48 turret, equipped with a state-of-the-art fire control system (including a dual-axis-stabilized gun sight with a thermal-imaging capability akin to that on the M-1 Abrams) mounted atop an M60A3 chassis.

Naval systems — Coastal defenses, particularly if the PRC makes good on its threat to further develop a "blue-water" navy through acquisition of an aircraft carrier, remain a prudent posture in light of Taiwan's security position. The current Taiwanese defense build-up includes a major modernization and expansion of the navy. This includes 12 Oliver Hazard Perry-class frigates under the Kwang Hwa-1 program — all to be built in Taiwan (probably at China Shipbuilding Co.) through a technology transfer agreement with the United States. This will include the acquisition of "the most-sought-after knowhow for the construction of large warships (especially in the field of welding) through a complete technology transfer package."[95] It is not yet clear if the United States will also provide the ROC with its most advanced towed array sonar technology with which to equip the ships.

There currently are reports that the second batch of vessels in the Kwang Hwa-1 program may be altered to fulfil an air defense role. This might incorporate a modified SPY-1 radar system, akin to that installed aboard the Arleigh Burke-class AEGIS destroyers of the USN.[96] The ships are being fitted out with the GE/RCA ADAR-2N phased array radar, the same system used by the ROC Army's Chang Bai air defense system.

In addition, under the Kwang Hwa-2 program, Taiwan is acquiring some 16 Lafayette-class frigates, worth $4.8 billion. The first two to four ships will be constructed in French yards, while the remainder will be built in Kaohsiung shipyards with French assistance.[97] That may extend to weapons integration and personnel training. The command-and-control electronics and sensor package of the Kwang Hwa-2, meanwhile, is understood to be completely in the hands of Thomson-CSF.[98]

Taiwan is also engaged in discussions with the Netherlands for licensed production of diesel submarines, along the lines of the agreement for the Kwang

Hwa series of frigates.[99] The general terms would involve shipping components and technology from Dutch shipwrights to Taiwan for local construction of subs.[100] Multiple factors enter into the sale, but the most relevant here are the potential for production offsets and technology transfers (both of submarines and accompanying weapons systems).[101] In light of declining markets in other countries, Taiwan's negotiating leverage has been enhanced.[102]

Meanwhile, Taiwan remains interested in improving its overall shipbuilding capabilities, with the obvious attendant benefits for military surge production. Despite its overall proficiency at construction of such ships as very-large crude carriers (VLCC's, also known as super-tankers), Taiwanese industry estimates that construction of larger naval combatants could not be accomplished without substantial assistance from foreign ship-builders. An aircraft carrier, for example, would require some 14 years for Taiwan, even with substantial foreign help.[103]

10.3.3 Role of Offsets

As with the ROK, foreign offsets have played a significant role in the development of the ROC's military-industrial complex. In particular, Taiwan has shown interest in acquiring additional experience in systems integration. Thus, Raytheon determined in February 1992 that, with the construction of a missile facility capable of integrating Patriot and indigenous missile components, Taiwan had moved to develop its own integrated air defense system. Raytheon thereupon agreed to license portions of its system to Taiwan, while providing Taiwan with significant technology transfer and the opportunity to test its integration skills through the incorporation of domestically developed components with the Patriot system.[104]

At the same time, Taiwan has also used domestic offsets in order to gain military technology. In particular, Taiwan has dangled the prospect of participation in its multi-billion dollar national development plan to improve the country's civil infrastructure as an incentive for access to modern weapons technology. This approach has been particularly evident in Taipei's policy towards Paris, which has been offered major new contracts in exchange for trouble-free weapons sales.[105]

Meanwhile, like the ROK, the ROC's development strategy, particularly with regards to offsets, is aimed not only at fostering its military capabilities, but also at improving its commercial competitiveness. Thus, with both MADS and a 1989 joint effort with Hughes Aircraft Co. to upgrade the Ten-One air defense system, the Taiwanese sought to enhance the inter-operability of civilian air traffic controllers with military systems.[106] Similarly, the F-16 deal has been questioned in relation to Taiwan's access to technology. Indeed, members of the

KMT, noting that the program would cost at least $4 billion, have already called for conclusion of a technology transfer agreement and co-production of the aircraft.[107] Ting Shou-Chung, a member of the Yuan (Taiwan's parliament), for example, has insisted that "this whole deal has to meet two criteria. One is to meet our defense needs. The second is to build up our aerospace industry."[108] Taiwan had previously announced that it wants aerospace revenue by 2000 to amount to $6 billion, 80 per cent exported.[109]

Unlike the ROK, however, the Taiwanese effort to secure military technology *per se* has been removed from its efforts aimed at acquiring the basis of a more robust (and technologically sophisticated) economy. This is due, in no small part, to Taipei's diplomatic isolation. When the subject of co-production of the F-16 was raised, General Dynamics balked, both due to the past transfer of technology to Taiwan under the IDF program, and because co-production would be inefficient in terms of saving American jobs. Faced with a choice of holding out for a better offsets and technology deal, or promptly acquiring F-16s, Taiwan chose to forego (albeit unwillingly) significant production shares in the F-16 deal in order to secure the aircraft. Taiwan, unlike South Korea, has not always had the option of shopping for the best deal.

This has not prevented, of course, Taiwan, from seeking offsets and coproduction agreements from the civil as well as military side. One of the most hotly debated aerospace topics of 1991–1992 was Taiwan Aerospace Corporation's attempt to acquire a major equity position in McDonnell-Douglas' commercial aircraft business. Faced with chronic losses, McDonnell-Douglas had sought new partners to help current production and finance a new generation of commercial airliners to compete with Boeing and Airbus. TAC, a quasi-government corporation consisting of 11 shareholders representing some of the largest Taiwanese companies, including steel, autos and shipping giants, stepped to the fore, despite a total absence of aerospace experience. The group offered to purchase a 40 per cent equity share for $2 billion, in return for technical training and a testing/certification system for a components industry. That, in turn, would have increased the sales of the current 130 Taiwanese vendors for IDF components (mainly machinings, forgings and castings).[110] As important, better testing and certification would have significantly improved the quality of Taiwanese products, which has proven to be a limiting factor in Taiwan's ability to exploit the current millions of dollars of offsets already incurred. Only by improving them to world-class levels of quality is it likely that Taiwanese components will be willingly incorporated into the products of major multinationals.

The deal ultimately collapsed in May 1992, due mainly to opposition within Taiwan.[111] Members of the Yuan questioned whether the technology gained would in fact be worth $2 billion. Doubts also existed concerning the amount of technology to be actually transferred. At the same time, elements within the United States also questioned the desirability of such a deal. Although McDonnell-Douglas viewed the transfer as akin to the creation of an Asian version of Airbus Industrie, necessary in an age of hyper-expensive aircraft development costs, it was feared that aerospace would suffer the same fate as automobiles or consumer electronics if technology were transferred to Asian competitors.[112] Such concerns were exacerbated by reports that at least one of the Taiwanese investors had ties to a Japanese trading company.[113] The US government officially expressed concern that advanced military technologies would be compromised through the arrangement (even though DOD has strict regulations segregating military and commercial facilities and governing access to military installations by foreign nationals).[114]

In the wake of the failed agreement with McDonnell-Douglas, the Taiwan Aerospace Corporation has moved to join with British Aerospace PLC to construct jointly the four-engine RJ line of passenger jets and develop the four-engine BAe 146 (which has not generally been a commercial success). In addition, they may jointly develop further a two-engine short-range regional passenger airliner version of the BAe 146. This will involve an initial investment of some $230-$250 million by TAC (of a total investment of $500 million), for which TAC would gain responsibility for 50 per cent of British Aerospace's regional-aircraft production including central fuselage sections, the aircraft's vertical fin, horizontal stabilizer and doors.[115] Taipei has indicated that it expects Taiwan Aerospace, Air Asia Co., an aircraft repair company, and Condor Industry Corp., a maker of valves and auto parts, to be major beneficiaries. Several other companies that currently supply items such as fasteners to foreign auto makers and electronics companies also are expected to be positioned to move into aerospace.[116]

Meanwhile, Taiwanese engineers will participate in research and development. According to British Aerospace, there "will be no charge or limits" on attendant technology transfers.[117] British Aerospace, in return, would not only receive a major infusion of capital, but would reduce the cost of the BAe 146 and RJ parts by at least 20 per cent.[118] It is unclear, however, whether Taiwan can, in fact, fulfil British Aerospace's expectations. At present, Taiwan has no more than a handful of parts suppliers of international standard. The expected savings, therefore, may be no more than wishful thinking.[119] Nonetheless, Taiwan Aerospace Corp. hopes it eventually will be able to construct the entire aircraft fuselage.

Shipbuilding technology transfers through earlier US-Taiwan agreements have been more successful from Taiwan's viewpoint. A tentative understanding with the Dutch RDM shipyard in February 1992 for Taiwanese submarine construction would have involved technology transfer, training and spare parts, but was aborted when Beijing vigorously protested the deal. In the crowded field of shipbuilding, however, there remain additional potential partners. In the case of submarines, for example, Taiwan can benefit from the desire for sales expressed not only by the Netherlands, but also France and Germany.[120]

10.4   Assessments and Policy Implications: Defense Industries in Taiwan and Korea

Offsets have played a significant role in the development, as well as the increasing sophistication, of both the South Korean and Taiwanese defense industries, albeit to differing degrees in their respective contexts. US policymakers have justified offsets for their common role of binding both states to the United States in particular and the West in general; their impact on the general economy has been more problematic. This section will assess the political role of offsets to date and in the future; their contributions to the growth of defense industries in both countries; their role in overall growth for both economics; and, the policy implications of current trends.

10.4.1   Political Role of Offsets

From the perspective of the West, the raison d'etre of economic offsets has rested not on their economic benefits for the recipient — which usually has been only a secondary consideration — but on the perceived political benefits for the provider. In particular, the United States utilized the transfer of technology as a means of placating both Seoul and Taipei in the course of the Cold War, and especially after the US began to disengage from Asia in the mid-1970s. Washington sought to signal both states that it viewed them as sufficiently important to regional stability that it was willing to provide them with technology. It is no accident that both the Korean and Taiwanese defense industries really took root only in the wake of the Nixon Doctrine.

With the end of the Cold War, the need to preserve political ties through technology transfer has declined. The US has now proven far less amenable to the transfer of technology on security, political or diplomatic grounds, even though the threat posed by the DPRK and the PRC remain. Ironically, with the end of the Cold War, the political tool of technology transfer, which previously involved the flows of advanced technology to the ROK and ROC from the United States and the West, is now being applied by these one-time recipients to such one-time ideological opponents as Russia and China. As the previously clear-cut dividing lines dissolve, both South Korea and Taiwan are utilizing access to relatively advanced technologies to gain political capital from the former communist giants.

This trend is particularly evident in the case of South Korea. With the end of the Cold War, and the achievement of industrial power status, South Korea appears intent upon making itself a full-fledged player upon the regional stage, rather than remaining simply the focus of great power rivalries and concern. Seoul apparently believes that sales of arms and related technologies, as well as the establishment of a reputation as a major source of technological innovation, will be important elements in its efforts to improve not only its overall security situation, but also in gaining influence and leverage throughout Asia. Towards that end, achievement of a world-class technological base has not only economic, but political and diplomatic ramifications. If Korea is to survive as an economic powerhouse, much less attain its greater political aspiration, the ROK understands that it must develop its indigenous technological prowess. Said one Korean analyst, "I don't think we have design technology, just production technology."[121] It is the gap between the actual state of the ROK economy and the projected targets that worries planners in Seoul and pushes them to develop a more capable arms industry.

With changes in the global political climate, however, Korean options to this end are diversifying. On October 28, 1992, the ROK and Russia initialled a technology transfer agreement spanning a range of technologies, including electronics and aerospace.[122] Russia would benefit from Korean manufacturing capabilities that represent a quantum leap over its current practices. Korea would be able to exploit not only the vast trove of inexpensive raw materials as well as the untapped market for low cost producers; it would also gain access to a storehouse of expertise in a variety of fields in which the ROK is deficient, e.g., aerospace and systems engineering.

There are certain limitations in this teaming arrangement. Nonetheless, the agreement achieves a very important goal in Korea's objectives in its offset/ defense production stimulation goals: increased political leverage internationally that can be utilized in Korea's approach towards regional affairs. In conjunction with the provision of massive loans to the former Soviet Union (including one for $3 billion in 1989), Korea's economic policies provide a potential hedge against the ultimate impacts of US withdrawal, including what it sees as increased security vulnerability with regards to China, Russia and possibly Japan. Similarly, Korean efforts to expand economic ties with the PRC — including increased Korean exports to China and conclusion of several economic pacts covering shipping, aviation, taxation and fisheries — were aimed not only at broadening the range of economic relations (and exploiting the vast potential of the Chinese market), but also were part and parcel of the Nordpolitik policy of Roh Tae-Woo.[123] Economic relations between the two states served as the foundation for the eventual establishment of diplomatic relations as well. Relations with China, in turn, were aimed at further stabilizing the Korean peninsula as a whole, as North Korea's patrons were wooed through economic incentives.[124] A more conventional manifestation of Korea's interest in diversifying its options is the country's negotiations with France for a joint defense technical assistance agreement, and its interest in technology transfer packages involving the European Fighter Aircraft.[125]

Taiwan, on the other hand, represents an altogether different situation. Whereas the Korean strategy is framed by a desire for a regional role — and therefore is driven as much by political-diplomatic factors as by purely technological-economic considerations — Taiwan's posture is influenced by more narrowly defined considerations of security — namely, its ability to defend itself against the PRC. Thus, what Taiwan has focused upon is the acquisition of a foreign aerospace corporation, civil or military, in order to ensure that, even in the event of total isolation, it could produce aircraft on its own to ensure control of the skies. This is hardly surprising, in light of Taiwan's ambiguous diplomatic standing; nor is Taiwan's analogous response of developing an indigenous arms industry in order to safeguard its arms supply.

This is not to suggest that the ROC is not interested in developing a civil-oriented aerospace industry. Unlike the Korean case, however, the Taiwanese appear to be following almost a dual-track approach. Thus, Taiwan's support of domestic industry has not been geared explicitly around its defense production strategies. Instead, Taiwan has pursued more than one approach in its efforts to introduce advanced technologies into its economy to stimulate economic growth and strengthen the industrial base.

10.4.2   Economic Role of Offsets

It is clear that both states are highly motivated by the desire to become even more potent economic competitors, not only of the United States, but also of Japan. By teaming with Russia, Korea has strengthened its leverage against Japan by threatening to gain access to a market Japanese businesses covet, while developing alternative sources of technological inputs to offset Japanese reluctance to transfer advanced technologies. Both results strengthen Korea's negotiating stance with Japan (and, for that matter, the United States and other Western nations as well). For Korean economic planners, such potential benefits outweigh the possibility of more dire results: Russia may prove to be an economic and technological black hole for Korea and other investors. Despite the likelihood of such an outcome, access to Russia remains a central goal for supplementing existing Korean relationships.

Similarly, both Korean and Taiwanese decision-makers have approached European firms for advanced technologies with which to seed their economies. European firms, eager to establish a foot-hold in the lucrative, but traditionally American, markets of East Asia as well as to reduce costs by moving production off-shore, have shown a marked willingness to provide those same technologies. Thus, Taiwan has secured an agreement with Aerospatiale to produce test components. The ROK, meanwhile, is now producing pylons for the British Aerospace Hawk light attack/training aircraft.[126]

US defense industry analysts generally assume that European producers are less concerned about the long term competitive impact of technology transfers, and therefore are more likely to offer generous offset deals to break into these markets at the expense of American producers, who see themselves constrained by policy and political pressures in their offset negotiations. If such is the case, then one reasonably can assume that alternatives for both Korea and Taiwan will multiply in the future (or at least as long as the present excess production capacity and stockpiles of weapons remain in global markets).[127]

It is unclear, however, just how successful these efforts will be. In the first place, the very expense and dimensions of these programs could prove to be their undoing. The KFP program alone, for example, will cost at least $4.2 billion, on top of $10.8 billion in force structure improvements spent from 1985 to 1990. Additional related expenditures, as of mid-1990, could force the government to commit another $23.6 billion through 1995. All this occurs at a time when Korea's continued growth no longer is a certainty.[128] Similarly, the Ching-Kuo fighter program cost Taipei some $10 billion dollars in program development costs. The F-16 and Dassault Mirage 2000-5 programs are likely to incur at least an additional $12.75 billion, significant amounts even to a country with sizable capital reserves.[129] Indeed, these costs have led leaders in both countries to consider greater emphasis on commercial prospects — with foreign partners to share the risks — over military programs for economic development, as indicated by the Taiwan-McDonnell-Douglas tryst.[130]

This is compounded by South Korean and Taiwanese shortcomings relative to Japan, their putative model. This is most marked in the relative lack of depth in the South Korean and Taiwanese economies of both human and economic resources essential to developing their respective economies into world pacesetters. In both countries, there are deficiencies in both categories even for achieving the far less ambitious goal of creating a sophisticated defense infrastructure. This shortfall of sufficiently trained personnel would appear to be a nearly insurmountable constraint, at least for the foreseeable future.

While Korea, for example, views the F-16 deal as a turning point in its efforts to advance its industry through US technology transfers there is still only a very limited R&D budget. This makes replication of imported systems and components and their replacement with domestically developed alternatives (key elements in Japan's indigenous equipment and technology development programs) far more problematic. Lacking government and private sector research and development investments to further industry knowledge and understanding of advanced systems, it is doubtful if Korea can duplicate Japanese success in the near future, even in those areas where Korean domestic industries may be relatively competitive with US industry. As one Korean defense analyst notes (perhaps with some exaggeration), "It's like university students and junior high school students studying science together. Even if the United States transfers 100 per cent of its technology, we could only absorb about 5 per cent."[131]

Similarly, it is unclear whether Taiwan's industry and government will be able to absorb successfully the technology transfers it assumes will flow from past deals. In many ways, Taiwan is better positioned to develop its overall technological base (as well as defense technological base). In light of its large capital holdings — and despite the absence of large corporate combines — Taiwan has a sufficient technological base to launch limited national projects. In that regard, the IDF displays both the potential and limitations of Taiwanese defense industries. The very fact that it was shepherded successfully from design to prototype to initial operating capability serves as a signal of what the Taiwanese approach of relying on a multitude of small companies, coupled with aggressive national investment, can achieve.[132] The final product, however, fell short of the mark (one Taiwanese industrialist derisively suggested that "IDF" stands for "I don't fight.").[133]

The limited technological success of the IDF indicates that Taiwanese industry already could be at the saturation point in terms of its ability to absorb additional technology. This is compounded by the need to preserve military surge capacity while maintaining a civilian base, forestalling maximum exploitation of the available human and technological resources, and preventing a shift from military production to joint commercial facilities that would enhance the cross-fertilization of military and commercial know-how.[134] In addition, the government still lacks a comprehensive agenda that articulates specific goals and objectives behind the range of projects under consideration, other than the hope to build its aerospace capabilities. The absence of focused objectives, some observers feel, will impede the development of a comprehensive strategy, à la Japan, that would promote targeted development of key sectors.[135] (In examining Asian defense industries, Japanese defense contractors themselves note the importance of stimulating commercial sectors sufficiently to ensure recipients for technology transfers and spinoffs from military programs. Many of those same observers predict a greater shift to commercial projects from military programs in the near future.)[136] Even Korean President Kim Yong-Sam, in discussing the global "technology war," has noted the importance of formulating a more comprehensive technology management strategy for the post-Cold War era that links defense and commercial technology development.[137]

Finally, the very success of the Japanese model of aggressive negotiations with key industrial and political allies, and comprehensive implementation of a national vision which is itself supported by thorough and specific plans for stimulation of various segments of the key sector, means that Western nations will have greater reason to look at Taiwan cautiously; nations will not be as blithe in their transfers of technology as the United States was with Japan during the 1950s and 1960s. Western experience with the Japanese model has ensured that technologically advanced states will be far more wary in their licensing and co-production agreements. In conjunction with the end of the Cold War, which removed the political urgency of offset policies and technology transfer, the era of generous offset policies was over, at least with regards to the United States. Countervailing this caution, however, are the simple economics of excess capacity that force defense dealers to look to promising markets for new sales.

10.4.3   Policy Implications

United States' policies governing military offsets to South Korea and Taiwan have centered on loss of sensitive technologies to unfriendly third countries and the stimulation of potential competitors in military and/or commercial production. Several other policy and business implications emerge from present and anticipated trends in offsets to these countries as well as other Asian nations in general. They center around three major issue areas.

Offsets and the development of effective defense forces — We have noted that both Taiwan and South Korea are interested in promoting the development of indigenous defense research, development and production capabilities in part due to the fear of US military withdrawal from the Asia/Pacific region. At issue in this response, however, is the question of whether such policies further undercut political support in the United States for US deployments in the region, thereby making such concerns self-fulfilling predictions. We have argued elsewhere for the need to continue the US presence in Asia.[138] Policymakers in affected countries, weapons and technology purchasers, and defense firms themselves, must address the implications of their sales and licensing activities in the region in this context. Aggressive marketing behavior in one respect could contribute to regional security problems if arms purchases and licensing arrangements lead to perceptions in the West that the need to station forces for regional stability is no longer warranted due to the size of local military forces. Should such a development take place before either country has capable military forces and sufficient domestic production capacity, however, it could leave one or the other more vulnerable to local security risks than currently is noticeable. (By the same token, straightforward arms purchases by Korea and/or Taiwan provide the US with additional reasons to support those regimes.)

An additional concern is that unfocused diversification of suppliers for Korean and Taiwanese systems could lead to such a disparity in equipment compatibility that it would undermine defense capabilities. This argument often is used by US producers to justify continued relations, but it does contain a measure of truth (even while appearing self-serving). Even when equipment is purchased from single sources such as the United States, compatibility problems are immense. When vendors multiply, those problems only become more complicated.

US and European interests and competition in Asia: competitive and proliferation implications — It is clear that the United States and many European nations have different attitudes toward licensing advanced weapons technology to Taiwan and Korea. In part, this is due to differing perceptions of local development capabilities (as well as those that come from different positions in the markets; European producers may be more aggressive and generous in their licensing offsets because they want to make more headway in Taiwanese and Korean markets). This also can be attributed to divergent views on the security impact of such transfers. US firms perceive European companies as being less concerned over the loss of technology to unfriendly powers. Without entering into debate over the effectiveness of technology transfer controls, we will note for now that to a certain degree technological diffusion is inevitable. A single nation — or group of nations — will find it difficult if not impossible to monopolize all militarily relevant technologies. Moreover, technologies identified with major power status — automobiles, nuclear weapons or semiconductors — inevitably will be the target of concerted development efforts. Targeted technology control regimes may have been successful in denying or restricting access to the most highly advanced and critical military technologies to unfriendly powers. Attempting to deny access to all advanced technologies in the name of preserving the few truly critical items, however, is dubious.[139]

Similar arguments can be made when discussing the commercial impact of technology transfers and offsets. The more important point, however, is the underlying infrastructure and indigenous absorption capabilities of technology transfer recipients themselves. The comparison of the "little tigers" to Japan, for example, is highly flawed. Neither South Korea nor Taiwan, at present, constitutes the same degree of economic competitiveness embodied within a Japan that possesses not only first rate technology diffused throughout its economy, but a depth of economic, human and research resources that the ROK and ROC are still in the process of developing. Moreover, as noted previously, Tokyo benefited from a far more relaxed trade and technology transfer environment than either Seoul or Taipei are likely to witness, due in part precisely to the Western experience with Japan. Therefore, while not discounting competitive concerns as out of hand, we are not inclined to be overly concerned with the economic impact of military technology transfers and offsets on commercial and broad economic development (company-to-company licensing arrangements in commercial sectors, however, might be another matter).

From a policy perspective, the more important consideration is whether the United States and European nations, by pursuing competitive sales efforts in Asia, are unwittingly contributing to the potential for a regional arms race. The constraints that minimize the potential for either Korea or Taiwan to compete extensively with Western nations in third country military markets also reduce the likelihood of either nation becoming a regional military threat. However, other nations in Asia may be less sanguine about the long term implications of these trends and, accordingly, could devote greater resources to military assets, thereby contributing to regional instability and tensions. At least one major report on the spread of defense production capability and regional arms races has concluded that expanded offsets to other nations produce dubious benefits for the US defense industry as a whole while contributing to "a dangerously armed world."[140]

In response to competitive sales pressures from European firms in Asian markets, the new Clinton administration has announced its support for US defense companies in international markets (and it should be noted, of course, that the United States is the largest seller of arms in the world without such support). Deputy Secretary of Defense William Perry has indicated that "we should not only be willing to sell equipment to foreign countries, but [be] willing to help [industry]. The government should be willing to help [sales] in certain limited ways provided that we can assure sales [do] not risk proliferation of weapons of mass destruction, particularly nuclear technology, and we are not aggravating an unstable region in which regional wars are likely."[141] That posture — a step toward more active support for industry in contrast with the "hands off" approach characterizing earlier administrations — leaves sufficient room for US defense companies to sell and license their technologies to Asian nations, Korea and Taiwan in particular. Despite encouragement from Perry for defense firms to diversify into commercial fields, short term pressures are such that defense marketeers will focus on immediate defense related sales prospects over long term, and more dubiously attainable objectives of diversification.

Effectiveness of offsets in building local defense industries — As presently pursued, offsets to Korea and Taiwan have had limited impact in fulfilling larger plans for becoming self-sufficient producers across a range of systems (much less becoming global players in high tech industries). This apparent failure could be attributable to overly ambitious plans by central governments, as well as a measure of naivete in understanding the dimensions of domestic resources needed to fully exploit such transfers. There is no doubt that domestic capabilities have grown in both Taiwan and Korea as the result of technology licensing, production buybacks and other forms of offsets to these nations. However, offsets have not resulted in anything approaching the creation of global competitors in a vast range of systems (not disregarding successful export sales to date by either country in commercial areas), nor are they likely to in the immediate future.

This does not suggest that virtually any and all Western technology should be divulged to Korea or Taiwan without fear of the potential consequences. Structuring future offsets to move from finished product assembly backwards to component design to conceptual R&D would allow the maximum preservation of technological leads for Western nations, while garnering political capital and hard sales from cooperation. Few developing states or newly-industrialized countries can absorb or fund the entire infrastructure required for the effective exploitation of an entire industrial sector. As important, however, preserving R&D is essential in order to retain a thorough understanding of the trajectory of technological developments. Nowhere is this more important than in the area of military industries, in light of the likely consequences in the event of failure to retain cutting edge military technologies. As many military technologies, however, are now spun-on from the civilian side, rather than the reverse process, preserving R&D capabilities in military industries frequently means promoting dual-use technological research.

Such a measured, controlled use of offsets (and technology transfer programs in general) is far more likely to produce optimal patterns of trade and industrial development with the more developed economies of Taiwan and South Korea, and with such longer-term prospects as members of the Association of Southeast Asian Nations (ASEAN). At the same time, it is also less likely to garner negative reactions among the recipient states, maximizing the political as well as economic benefits to be gained from such programs.

10.5 Conclusions

A major lesson of recent technological development in the military arena is that states that have determined that their national security is at stake will commit significant resources in order to attain the weapons they view as necessary to preserve that security. Offsets have played a major role in the development of the military-industrial complexes of the countries examined, although not to the extent that either hoped. They have contributed to the sophistication of these one-time Third World economies, but their impact on economic development and growth remains debatable.

Offsets by themselves are insufficient to overcome structural deficiencies within the economies in question. The human resources constraints in both countries, coupled with limited technological capabilities, have prevented greater expansion of the two nations' overall levels of economic development to degrees that transfers of technology alone cannot yet overcome.

It is in this regard that much of the Western concern that both the ROK and the ROC may soon become economic behemoths along the lines of Japan are overstated. Japan, at the end of the Second World War, although devastated, nonetheless retained sufficient sophistication within its infrastructure that, upon the infusion of sufficient capital, it could be rejuvenated. Both South Korea and Taiwan, on the other hand, have been compelled to develop their current technological levels from far lower bases. While their accomplishments over the last two decades are all the more astonishing for the degree of advancement, nonetheless, there are inherent limitations in such economies.

This is not to suggest that the ROK and the ROC do not represent potential economic challenges to the United States and the West in the future; both have made dramatic economic progress, and their respective growth in international trade indicate their commercial capabilities. Indeed, the near-exponential growth in technological capabilities and standards in both economies would warn against too complacent an attitude. It does not pay, though, to overestimate their capabilities.

At the same time, unrestrained offsets raise serious policy and security issues that must be addressed before resulting in conditions similar to those in the Middle East in earlier decades. It is not in the best interests of Asia or the West to contribute to unrestrained growth in military production in the Asia/Pacific region, even though certain legitimate security concerns remain for both South Korea and Taiwan. Failure to address the policy impact of these programs could undercut their short term benefits while making their long term consequences intolerable.

Appendix I[142]

The Korean aerospace industry is dominated by three corporations: Samsung Aerospace, Korean Air, and Daewoo Heavy Industries.

Samsung Aerospace — Samsung Aerospace was founded in August, 1977 as Samsung Precision Industries. The group has focused on the production and overhaul of engines. The company assembles the GE J85 engine, as well as CFM56, LM2500 and F404. It is currently engaged in the co-production of the

PW4000 turbofan, with Pratt & Whitney. Samsung is also engaged in the manufacture of wing and fuselage components. It has produced and exported both of the latter, as well as stringers for use in large commercial aircraft. One of Samsung's main export contracts involves the production of 5,000 fuselage stringers for Northrop, for incorporation into Boeing aircraft. It is also under contract to produce stringers, doors and crown frames for the Boeing 747 and 747 passenger liners. In addition, it is engaged in building engine nacelles, and other components for McDonnell-Douglas, Lockheed, Grumman and MBB.

Samsung is also a 2 per cent participant in the development of the Pratt&Whitney 4000 engine for large wide-bodies airliners. In the helicopter area, Samsung is supplying the airframes for the Bell 412 and 212 models. In other aerospace areas, Samsung developed a successful rocket propulsion system for the Kooryong multiple rocket launcher. It is also the partner with Thomson-CSF for the Pegasus mobile SAM system.

The company also is exploring a joint venture with the ex-USSR. Central Aviation Hydromechanics Institute on glass fibres and other types of composite materials for aircraft.[143]

Korean Air — Korea Air's aerospace division was established in 1976, at Chinhae. It includes the Korea Institute of Aeronautical Technology as its R&D branch. Its plant has a floor space of some 2 million square feet. Among the contracts being undertaken there are wing-tip extension and flap-track fairing production for the Boeing 747. In addition, it is under contract with Douglas Aircraft Company and Hawker De Havilland for sheet metal assemblies for the nose caps and bonded panels. In addition, Korean Air has been responsible for the assembly of F-5 fighters for the ROKAF.

Korean Air is responsible for licensed production of the MD-500 helicopter, and currently supplies main rotor blades and fuselage parts to McDonnell Douglas Helicopter. It is also engaged in the licensed assembly of UH-60P Black Hawk helicopters as well as their GE T700-701C engines.

Daewoo Heavy Industries — Daewoo's first advanced aircraft contract was in 1944 with General Dynamics to supply fuselages, cockpit panels and ventral fins for the F-16. Since then, it has delivered part assembly sections for the Boeing B-737 and B-767, as well as the B-767SUD airframe assembly. It has been awarded the contract as well to build the wings and pylons for BAe Hawks (possibly in addition to those destined for the ROKAF), the nose compartment and tailcone for the Hawker de Havilland Dash 8 commuter aircraft. Had the US not cancelled the aircraft, Daewoo would have supplied 125 wings for the P-7 maritime patrol aircraft (the projected successor of the P-3). The company is also committed to providing fuselages and other components for the Dornier 328.

In the helicopter area, Daewoo will provide the hub assembly for the Bell 212 and 412 as well as the nose module and lower structures of the Westland Lynx. It will also participate in the construction of the H-76 Eagle HX utility helicopter and the BO-105 LOH/CB. Daewoo also is engaged in the production of the H-76 helicopter, in a 50-50 joint venture with Sikorsky/United Technologies believed to be worth at least $200 million annually. Daewoo Heavy Industry is responsible for parts and components manufacture, as well as early assembly. Daewoo Sikorsky then completes assembly and also test flies the resulting aircraft. It is also co-developing a new light helicopter, the KH-101 and KH-121, with MBB.

Daewoo also is engaged in aerospace R&D, which is believed to absorb some 3 per cent of sales revenue.

Other Corporations — The Sammi group, which manufactures steel for the defense industries, has entered into a joint venture with Agusta Aerospace of Italy for the assembly of SF-600 light planes, A-109 helicopters and S-211 trainer jets.

Hyundai Precision and Industrial Corporation is considering establishment of a sister company dedicated to the aerospace area. Hyundai in 1989 assembled a BK-117 helicopter, and is believed to be interested in developing private helicopters. It also has acquired technology from Japan's Kawasaki Heavy Industries.[144]

Appendix II

Presidential Statement on Military Offsets Policy, April 16, 1990

"The President announced today his Policy on Offsets in Military Exports. This responds to the requirement under the FY 1989 National Defense Authorization Act, Section 825, 10 U.S.C. Sec. 2505.

The President stated that the United States Government is committed to the principles of free and fair trade. Consequently, the United States Government views certain offsets for military exports as economically inefficient and market distorting.

Mindful of the need to minimize the adverse effects of offsets in military exports, while ensuring that the ability of US firms to compete for military export sales is not undermined, the President has established the following policy:

- No agency of the US Government shall encourage, enter directly into, or commit US firms to any offset arrangement in connection with the sale of defense goods or services to foreign governments.

- US Government funds shall not be used to finance offsets in security assistance transactions except in accordance with currently established policies and procedures.
- Nothing in this policy shall prevent agencies of the US Government from fulfilling obligations incurred through international agreements entered into prior to the issuance o this policy.
- The decision whether to engage in offsets, and the responsibility for negotiating and implementing offset arrangements, resides with the companies involved.
- Any exception to this policy must be approved by the President through the National Security Council.

The President also noted that the time has come to consult with our friends and allies regarding the use of offsets in defense procurement. He has, therefore, directed the Secretary of Defense, in coordination with the Secretary of State, to lead an interagency team to consult with foreign nations with a view to limiting the adverse effects of offsets in defense procurement. This interagency team will report periodically on the result of these consultations and forward any recommendations to the National Security Council."

Source: Office of Management and Budget, Offsets in Military Exports (Washington, D.C.: US Government Printing Office, April 16, 1990), pp. 23–24.

Appendix III

Economic Data: Republic of Korea and Republic of China (Taiwan)

Background Information
(all data for 1991 unless otherwise indicated)

	ROK	ROC
Population	43.0 million	20.5 million
Annual growth rate (%)	0.9%	1.1%
Nominal GDP (US$)	$264.9 billion	$175.7 billion
Nominal per capita GDP (US$)	$6154	$8590
Major exports	Chemicals (3.3%) Manufactured goods (52.4%) Machinery/transport equipment (37.8%) Metal manufactures (4.0%)	Textile products (20%) Electrical machinery (21%) Plastic articles (8.7%)
Major imports	Machinery/transport equipment (34.3%) Food/live animals (5%) Chemicals (11.6%) Mineral fuels/lubricants (12.4%)	Crude oil (5%) Capital goods (16%) Consumer goods (11%) Ag/indus raw materials (67%)
Major trading partners	US Japan Hong Kong Germany Canada	US Europe Japan Hong Kong

Selected Economic Indicators: Republic of Korea and Republic of China

	Consumer Price Index		Wholesale Price Index	
	ROK	ROC	ROK	ROC
1989	119.92	106.1	103.17	94.9
1990	130.21	111.4	107.47	94.3
1991	142.77	116.2	113.26	94.5
1992*	153.45	121.2	117.90	92.3
1993*	163.45	125.7	122.50	94.6
1994*	173.42	129.9	127.03	96.8

Base year: ROK: 1985 = 100; ROC: 1986 = 100
*Forecasts

	Nominal GDP (US $billions)		Real GDP (US $billions)	
	ROK	ROC	ROK	ROC
1989	212.97	146.86	223.59	149.72
1990	244.04	157.01	244.05	157.01
1991	282.97	175.71	264.63	168.52
1992*	306.39	207.03	283.39	180.70
1993*	348.36	235.17	304.58	193.74
1994*	407.36	275.61	327.43	207.03

	Gross Domestic Product	
	ROK	ROC
1989	118.70	104.7
1990	131.35	108.7
1991	145.53	113.1
1992*	158.48	116.5
1993*	168.75	120.7
1994*	178.85	125.0

Base year: ROK: 1985 = 100; ROC: 1986 = 100
*Forecasts

	Exports of Goods/Services		Imports of Goods/Services	
	ROK	ROC	ROK	ROC
1989	105.27	86.8	90.14	86.8
1990	110.66	89.0	95.83	88.9
1991	114.61	89.4	99.17	86.4
1992*	120.91	85.2	106.71	81.7
1993*	128.53	87.1	113.64	83.4
1994*	136.93	89.3	121.60	87.5

Base year: 1985 = 100
*Forecasts

	Trade Balance		Current Account Balance	
	ROK	ROC	ROK	ROC
1989	4.60	16.21	5.06	11.38
1990	−2.00	14.93	−2.17	10.87
1991	−6.98	15.69	−8.73	12.01
1992*	−5.91	13.55	−7.23	7.05
1993*	−5.23	11.05	−4.77	4.99
1994*	−5.58	9.55	−4.19	3.35

Note: FOB-FOB basis in US$billions

	Unemployment Rate (per cent)	
	ROK	ROC
1989	2.56	1.57
1990	2.44	1.66
1991	2.29	1.52
1992*	2.43	0.75
1993*	2.48	0.05
1994*	2.51	−0.28

*Forecasts

	Manufacturing Wage Rate (US$)	Annual Change (%)	Manufacturing Wage Rate (US$)	Annual Change (%)
	ROK		ROC	
1989	3.25	36.3	3.63	25.8
1990	3.71	14.0	4.09	12.5
1991	4.18	12.8	4.54	11.2
1992*	4.70	12.3	5.39	18.6
1993*	5.18	10.3	6.07	12.6
1994*	5.69	9.8	7.07	16.5

*Forecasts

	Unit Labor Cost (US$)	Annual Change (%)	Unit Labor Cost (US$)	Annual Change (%)
	ROK		ROC	
1989	169.03	22.2	104.12	3.2
1990	186.31	10.2	107.35	3.1
1991	204.47	9.7	105.94	−1.3
1992*	213.86	4.6	109.16	3.0
1993*	229.14	7.1	110.44	1.2
1994*	234.81	2.5	111.97	1.4

Base Year: ROK: 1895 = 100; ROC: 1986 = 100
*Forecasts

	Productivity	Change (%)	Productivity	Change (%)
	ROK		ROC	
1989	127.37	2.2	121.5	5.6
1990	135.01	6.0	127.0	4.6
1991	142.13	5.3	133.8	5.3
1992*	147.89	4.1	140.6	5.1
1993*	154.40	4.4	147.9	5.2
1994*	161.36	4.5	155.3	5.0

Base Year: ROK: 1985 = 100; ROC: 1986 = 100
*Forecasts

	Manufacturing Index	Change (%)	Manufacturing Index	Change (%)
	ROK		ROC	
1989	119.63	0.0	118.96	3.1
1990	130.31	8.9	118.12	−1.9
1991	138.90	6.6	126.67	7.3
1992*	144.85	4.3	132.30	4.5
1993*	150.06	3.6	138.97	5.1
1994*	156.68	4.4	145.71	4.9

Base year: ROK: 1985 = 100; ROC: 1986 = 100
*Forecasts

Endnotes

1. The authors would like to thank the following individuals for their comments and other inputs to this chapter: Arthur Alexander, Samuel Dash, Robert Downen, Alex Gliksman, Larry Niksch, Kazuo Ohmura, and Gregg Rubinstein.

2. For example, the most recent white papers of the Japan Defense Agency are cautious about potential instability in the former Soviet Union, and signs of continued militancy by North Korea and the People's Republic of China (See Japan Defense Agency, **Defense of Japan 1991** (Tokyo: Japan Times Co., Ltd., 1991), **Defense of Japan 1995** (Tokyo: Japan Times Co., Ltd., 1995), and Barbara Wanner, JEI Report, No. 33B, August 28, 1992, p. 4.) The Republic of Korea sees potential threats in the emergence of Japanese military power, in addition to continued threats posed by China and North Korea. (See Ministry of Defense, **Defense White Paper 1991–1992** (Seoul: Ministry of Defense, 1992)). Taiwan — and much of the Western world — remains concerned about possible attempts by the PRC to forcefully reunite Taiwan with the mainland (for example, see "Containing China," **The Economist**, July 29, 1995, pp. 11–12).

   For additional discussion of Asian perceptions of the threat environment, see Michael W. Chinworth and Dean Cheng, "The United States and Asia in the Post-Cold War World," **SAIS Review**, Vol. 11, No. 1, Winter-Spring 1991, pp. 73–91; Kiichi Saeki, "Post-Cold War Asia-Pacific Security," **Journal of Japanese Trade and Industry**, Vol. 12, No. 3, June 1, 1993, pp. 46–47; Korea Institute for Defense Analyses, **The Korean Journal of Defense Analyses** (various issues, particularly Vol. 4, No 2, Winter 1992, special issue on nuclear security); and, Research Institute for Peace and Security, **Asian Security 1994–95** (London: Brassey's, 1995) and earlier volumes.

3. We will define offsets broadly in this chapter to include licenses, production offsets, buybacks of spare parts, coproduction and any financial, technological or manufacturing consideration offered in return for a purchase of an advanced weapons system from abroad. Our definition, however, does not include barter, countertrade, or business development offsets such as development of tourism facilities in return for arms purchases because they have not been a regular feature of offset agreements with Korea and Taiwan.

4. In this article, we will use the terms Republic of Korea, Korea and South Korea interchangeably, as well as Republic of China, ROC and Taiwan interchangeably. In addition, we will refer to both entities as separate states for practical purposes, recognizing the diplomatic and legal considerations that otherwise might dictate against such usage.

5. Susan Carey, "Korean Companies Seek Broader Role in Aerospace," **Asian Wall Street Journal Weekly**, August 31, 1992, p. 12.

6. Kim Il Sung died on July 8, 1994.

7. Asia's apparent sensitivity to the issue might have been heightened precisely because of the parallels between the former Georgia governor cum president Jimmy Carter and his political successor, Bill Clinton. "Editorials React to U.S. Defense Spending Cuts," Foreign Broadcast Information Service, FBIS-EAS-93-025, February 9, 1993, p. 43, quoting **Korea Times** editorial of February 9, 1993; "Link to Asian Security Viewed," Foreign Broadcast Information Service, FBIS-EAS-93-025, February 9, 1993, p. 43, quoting **Korea Herald** editorial of February 9, 1993.

8. The Nixon doctrine contained three main principles: 1) the United States would honor its treaty commitments; 2) the U.S. would continue extending its nuclear umbrella to important allies; and, 3) the U.S. would provide aid and military assistance to Asian allies, with the expectation that those countries would be more responsible for manpower needs in meeting local defense needs. The Ford administration subsequently attempted to mitigate the impact of that policy by reaffirming U.S. troop commitments in Asia, particularly in South Korea. See William E. Berry, Jr., "Republic of Korea," Chapter 12 in Douglas J. Murray and Paul R. Viotti, eds., **The Defense Policies of Nations: A Comparative Study** (Baltimore and London: The Johns Hopkins University Press, 1989), p. 407–409; U.S. Department of State, **Department of State Bulletin**, Vol. 61, No. 1574, August 25, 1969, p. 143; Report to Congress, Richard Nixon, "U.S. Foreign Policy for the 1970s: "A New Strategy for Peace," February 18, 1970.

9. Dr. Dong Joon Hwang, "Industry: Into a New Era," **Jane's Defence Weekly**, November 16, 1991, p. 965.

10. Berry, p. 408–409. Candidate Carter's ideas were promulgated in Policy Review Memorandum 13 and Presidential Decision 12 in May 1977. The plan called for a draw down of all 32,000 troops in Korea over a four to

five-year period, retaining air and naval support. Less than one combat battalion ultimately was removed from Korea due to opposition in Korea and the U.S. Congress.

11. The Korean government remains quite clear on the perceived linkage between the need to stimulate domestic defense industries and the possibility of a U.S. withdrawal from the peninsula, noting that "the ROK is faced with the issue of US troop reduction or withdrawal in the 1990s, and the ROK-US military relationship is expected to undergo some changes. Under this situation, the ROK has no alternative but to continue its efforts to develop its own defense industry, which is a cornerstone for self-reliant defense." Republic of Korea, Ministry of National Defense (Seoul: Ministry of National Defense, 1989), **Defense White Paper 1989**, p. 163.

12. Kim Nak-Hieon,"Korea Starts to Fly High," **Asia Technology**, August 1990, p. 36.

13. David Silverberg, "Seoul Shifts Emphasis to Private-Sector R&D," **Defense News**, November 25, 1991, p. 10.

14. "Major Hurdles Seen for Korean Aerospace Development," **Pac-Rim Defense Marketing**, Vol. 1, No. 10, November 26, 1990, p. 1.

15. Terrence Kiernan and David Silverberg, "Technology Control Issues Cloud U.S.-S.Korea Relations," **Defense News**, September 7, 1992, p. 36.

16. Machmud Banjamin, "South Korea's Aerospace Industry," **Asian Defence Journal**, December 1990, p. 82.

17. The Ministry of National Defense (MND) has attempted to mitigate these shortages in the short term by allowing selected defense companies to utilize up to 15,000 designated military personnel annually in plant production. See Ministry of National Defense, **Defense White Paper 1991–92** (Seoul: Ministry of National Defense, 1992), p. 245.

18. Dr. Paik Young Hoon, President, Korea Industrial Development Institute, "ROK-US Defense Industry Cooperation: Past Achievements and Future Tasks." Speech before the Fourth Annual ROK-US Defense Industry Conference, July 16, 1990, San Francisco, California; Berry, **The Defense Policies of Nations**, p. 411; U.S. Congress Office of Technology Assessment, **Arming Our Allies: Cooperation and Competition in Defense Technology**, OTA-ISC-449 (Washington, D.C.: U.S. Government Printing Office, May 1990), p. 112.

19. Dr. Dong Joon Hwang, "Industry: Into a New Era," **Jane's Defence Weekly**, November 16, 1991, p. 967.

20. Hwang, "Industry: Into a New Era," p. 967; U.S. Congress, Office of Technology Assessment, **Global Arms Trade: Commerce in Advanced Military Technology and Weapons**, OTA-ISC-460 (Washington, D.C.: U.S. Government Printing Office, June 1991), p. 134–135. In at least some cases, most notably the sale of M-16 rifles, these arms exports have been in direct contravention of American wishes, one of the reasons for long-term American concerns about its military technology relationship with the ROK.

21. Korean participation in the Gulf War, including the dispatch of medical and air transport units, was predicated in part on the assumption that such an "investment" would "bear fruit" in the post-war period. See, for example, Pak Mu-chong, **The Korea Times**, February 1, 1991, p. 2, in FBIS-EAS-91-022, February 1, 1991, pp. 27–28.

22. Hwang, "Industry: Into a New Era" p. 965.

23. U.S. Congress, Office of Technology Assessment, **Global Arms Trade**, Chp. 8: "The Defense Industry of South Korea," p. 131–132.

24. U.S. Congress, Office of Technology Assessment, **Arming Our Allies**, p. 112.

25. Republic of Korea, Ministry of National Defense, **Defense White Paper 1989**, p. 166; U.S. Department of Defense, Office of the Comptroller, **National Defense Budget Estimates for FY 1993**, p. 137.

26. Kim Chae Su, Managing Director, Samsung Aerospace Co., Ltd., " ROK-US Cooperative Programs: KFP and HX." Speech before the Fourth Annual ROK-US Defense Industry Conference, July 16, 1990, San Francisco, California.

27. See Appendix for additional details on these three companies.

28. Banjamin, "South Korea's Aerospace Industry," p. 80.

29. The total cost for the program was revised to $4.2 billion in 1990 and rose to $5.2 billion by early 1993, despite shifting to the "less expensive" F-16. See Terrence Kiernan, "Lockheed Reassures Koreans on KFP," **Defense News**, February 22–28, 1993, p. 11.

30. Kim Chae Su, July 16, 1990 speech.

31. Korean officials initially determined that the balance of cost versus tech-
    nology gains made the F/A-18 more attractive, but U.S. demands for a cap
    on offsets minimized these potential benefits (See **Wing Newsletter**,
    "Korean Air Force Selects McDonnell Douglas F/A-18," Vol. 23, No. 1,
    January 3, 1990). The U.S. government estimated the value of the F/A-18
    package at $3.45 billion in 1990 (U.S. Department of Defense, "Korean
    Fighter Program Fact Sheet," February 7, 1990).

    An alternative explanation has been suggested that remains under investi-
    gation at this writing. As part of a larger reform of the military, the Korean
    government is looking into allegations that bribery of high officials in the
    previous regime by General Dynamics led the Ministry of National
    Defense to side with the F-16. See Terrence Kiernan, "South Korean
    Officials Investigate F-16 Purchase," **Defense News**, Vol. 8, No. 17, May
    3–9, 1993, p. 1, 44.

32. David F. Bond, "South Korea to Buy 120 F-16C/Ds, Reversing Plan to
    Order F/A-18s,"**Aviation Week and Space Technology**, April 1, 1991, Vol.
    134, No. 13, p. 30; Shim Jae Hoon, "Air Pressure," **Far Eastern Economic
    Review**, April 11, 1991, p. 12; Leopold, "S. Korean Modernization," p. 22;
    J.R. Wilson, "Fighting for a First," **Jane's Defence Weekly**, December 7,
    1991, pp. 1120–1122, and J.R. Wilson, "Korea Scrambles Fighter in Time,"
    Interavia Aerospace Review, February 1992, p. 48. Other technology
    transfers and offsets sought by Seoul included provision of a BVR missile
    (e.g., Sparrow or AMRAAM), an improved performance engine, ASPJ and
    LANTIRN — thus making the F-16s the equivalent of Block 50 level.

33. "New Korean Budget Paves Way for Budding Aircraft Industry," **Defense
    Marketing International**, Vol. 14, No. 17, August 21, 1992, p. 2.

34. Banjamin, "South Korea's Aerospace Industry," p. 82.

35. Wilson, "Korea Scrambles Fighter in Time," p. 48. The Martin Lockheed
    position on these issues is unclear at this writing, although there were no
    indications by Lockheed that it would have any less of a commitment to
    these objectives with its assumption of the program from General
    Dynamics.

36. David Silverberg, "S. Korea Banks on Technology," **Defense News**,
    November 25, 1991, p. 3.

37. Damon Darlin, "Technology Transfer Issue Snags U.S.-Korea Accord on
    Fighter," **Asian Wall Street Journal Weekly**, May 14, 1990, p. 3.

38 Wild Weasels are dedicated electronic warfare aircraft tasked with killing enemy SAM platforms.

39. David Saw, "Security in an Era of Change — The Republic of Korea," **Military Technology**, November 1991, p. 25.

40. James Heitz Jackson, "Exports: A Vicious Circle?", **Jane's Defence Weekly** (International Edition), May 5, 1990, Vol. 13, No. 18, p. 872.

41. The ROK press has suggested, however, that the FXX time-frame would be about 2010. "New Korean Budget Paves," p. 2.

42. The status of such assistance is in doubt with the sale of GD's aircraft division to Lockheed, however. Saw, "Security in an Era," p. 25. Lockheed's subsequent merger with Martin Marietta further clouds the situation.

43. This is believed to be based on the Nike-Hercules SAM, which the United States had provided the ROK during the 1950s and 1960s. In addition, it is believed that the State Arsenal Pusan may have developed an improved version of the Honest John rocket, but it is unclear what the status of that system is. Mike Howarth, "Defending the Republic of Korea," **International Defense Review**, February 1986, p. 195.

44. Saw, "Security in an Era," pp. 17–18.

45. Steve Glain, "Seoul Turns to Europe for Arms as Pentagon Guards Technology," **Wall Street Journal**, May 6, 1993.

46. Carey, "Korean Companies Seek Broader," p. 1.

47. Of that output, $177 million was exported, however. Carey, "Korean Companies Seek Broader," p. 12.

48. Carey, "Korean Companies Seek Broader," p. 12.

49. Carey, "Korean Companies Seek Broader," p. 12.

50. "Defence Industry Develops," **Jane's Defence Weekly**, August 8, 1992.

51. Saw, "Security in an Era," p. 16.

52. Author interviews with Hyundai executives, Seoul, Republic of Korea, May 1990.

53. Christopher F. Foss, "South Korean KIFV Family Detailed, **Jane's Defence Weekly**, January 11, 1992, p. 42.

54. Howarth, "Defending the Republic," p. 195.

55. "BMY Combat Systems Wins Howitzer Contract," **Asian Defence Journal**, September 1990, p. 114. In addition, the ROK appears intent upon gaining access to advanced ammunition technology, including Extended Range FB-Base Bleed rounds, for its 155mm systems (which include a large number of towed guns as well).

56. Robert Karniol and Joris Janssen Lok, "Atlas Is 'Chosen' in KDX Controversy," **Jane's Defence Weekly**, July 3, 1993, p. 7.

57. "Naval Forces Expanding," **Jane's Defence Weekly**, November 16, 1991, p. 969.

58. According to press reports, South Korea plans to deploy seven diesel attack submarines by 1997. The subs have a cruising range of 7,500 miles and a crew of 39. See Terrence Kiernan, "S. Korean Navy Eyes New Fleet of 7 Subs," **Defense News**, Vol. 8, No. 21, June 7–13, 1993, p. 12.

59. "South Korea's Torpedo Programme Falters," **Jane's Defence Weekly**, July 3, 1993, p. 13.

60. "$200 Million Matra Mistral Order for South Korea," **NATO's Sixteen Nations**, 1, 1992, p. 87.

61. George Leopold, "S. Korean Modernization to Test U.S. Relations," **Defense News**, September 30, 1991, p. 22; Steve Glain, "Seoul Turns to Europe for Arms as Pentagon Guards Technology," **Wall Street Journal**, May 6, 1993.

62. Thalif Deen, "South Korea's Growing Industrial Strength," **Jane's Defence Weekly**, July 29, 1989, p. 162.

63. Kiernan and Silverberg, "Technology Control Issues," p. 36. The Korean government is clear in intentions to expand business in overseas markets, declaring that "to overcome limited domestic demand and defense budget constraints, the defense industry has no alternative but to turn to overseas markets. By actively attracting repair and maintenance orders from abroad, local defense industries have attempted to enhance their operation rates." Republic of Korea, Ministry of National Defense, **Defense White Paper 1989**, p. 167.

64. Col. So Byung Min, Defense Industry Bureau, Ministry of National Defense, Republic of Korea, "Technological Cooperation Between the ROK and US Defense Industries and the Government's Role." Speech before the Fourth Annual ROK-US Defense Industry Conference, July 16, 1990, San Francisco, California.

65. Young-Ok Ahn, "The Impact of Technology Transfer on National Security and Economic Development," in National Defense University, **Economics and Pacific Security: The 1986 Pacific Symposium** (Washington, D.C.: U.S. Government Printing Office, 1987), pp. 130–144.

66. Republic of Korea, Ministry of National Defense, **Defense White Paper 1992** (Seoul: Ministry of National Defense, 1992), p. 209, 211.

67. Republic of Korea, Ministry of National Defense, **Defense White Paper 1989**, pp. 167–168.

68. "Major Hurdles Seen for Korea," p. 1.

69. Berry, **The Defense Policies of Nations**, p. 412.

70. Col. So Byung Min, Defense Industry Bureau, Ministry of National Defense, Republic of Korea, "Technological Cooperation Between the ROK and US Defense Industries and the Government's Role." Speech before the Fourth Annual ROK-US Defense Industry Conference, July 16, 1990, San Francisco, California.

71. Yu Yong-won, "British Planes in the Sky, German Submarines in the Sea — Korea's Weapons Sources Diversify," **Chugan Choson**, April 22, 1990, p. 34, in FBIS-EAS-90-089, May 8, 1990, p. 22.

72. Kiernan and Silverberg, "Technology Control Issues," p. 36.

73. Dr. Paik Young Hoon, President, Korea Industrial Development Institute, "ROK-US Defense Industry Cooperation: Past Achievements and Future Tasks." Speech before the Fourth Annual ROK-US Defense Industry Conference, July 16, 1990, San Francisco, California.

74. Dr. Paik Young Hoon, speech, July 16, 1990.

75. Col. So Byung Min, speech, July 16, 1990.

76.. Jee Man Won, "Where Should the Korean Military Go?"

77. Hwang, "Industry: Into a New Era," p. 967.

78. Kiernan, "S. Korea Aims," p. 29.

79. Korean analysts note that Japan has spoken of the potential "boomerang" effects of technology transfers to Korea in a vein similar to American concerns over creating "second Japans." See Young-ok Ahn, "The Impact of Technology Transfer on National Security and Economic Development," in National Defense University, **Economics and Pacific Security: The**

1986 Pacific Symposium (Washington, D.C.: U.S. Government Printing Office, 1987), p. 143.

80. Kiernan and Silverberg, "Technology Control Issues," p. 46.

81. Terrence Kiernan, "S. Korea Aims to Energize Industry," **Defense News**, November 4, 1991, p. 29.

82. Terrence Kiernan, "Seoul Courts Europe Arms Makers," **Defense News**, March 9, 1992, p. 4.

83. Giovanni de Briganti, "France Promises Asian Arms Sales; China's Ire Looms," **Defense News**, Vol. 8, No. 20, May 24–30, 1993, p. 1.

84. "IDF Fighter Program Provides Catalyst for Advanced Manufacturing Capability," **Aviation Week and Space Technology**, April 27, 1992, p. 39.

85. "Develop Advanced Weapons and Establish a Three-Dimensional Defense System", Chung Kuo Shih Pao, February 18, 1992, p. 9, in FBIS-CHI-92-038 February 26, 1992, p. 61.

86. "Develop Advanced Weapons and," p. 61.

87. Stanley W. Kandebo, "Taiwanese Fighter's F125 Powerplant to Begin Accelerated Cycle Program," **Aviation Week and Space Technology**, April 27, 1992, p. 42.

88. Bill Sweetman, "GE Aims Engine at Taiwan's IDF," **Jane's Defence Weekly**, November 2, 1991, p. 803. The F125/TFE1042 has a 0.45:1 bypass ratio, weighs 1360 pounds, can develop 6060 lb. of dry thrust. GE's proposed upgrade would increase dry thrust to 8000 lb, improving the thrust:weight ratio of the IDF (which currently is outclassed by the new MiG-29s of the PLA Air Force).

89. "Kokubo Kara, Keizai Yusen e," **Nihon Keizai Shimbun**, October 11, 1992.

90. Edmond Dantes, "Taiwan's Military Build-UP", **Asian Defence Journal** February 1993, p. 20.

91. Ibid.

92. U.S. Congress, Office of Technology Assessment, **Global Arms Trade**, p. 128.

93. David Hughes, "Taiwan to Acquire Patriot Derivative," **Aviation Week and Space Technology**, March 1, 1993, p. 61; Barbara Opell and David

Silverberg, Taiwanese May Soon Coproduce Patriot," **Defense News**, Vol. 8, February 22, 1993, p. 1.

94. "Taiwan Unveils 'Brave Tiger'," **Jane's Defence Weekly**, June 30, 1990, p. 1283.

95. Anthony Leung, "Charting the Taiwanese Sea Lanes," **Military Technology**, March 1992, p. 32.

96. Leung," Charting the Taiwanese," p. 32.

97. Julian Baum, "Steel Walls," **Far Eastern Economic Review**, July 9, 1992, p. 11.

98. Leung, "Charting the Taiwanese," p. 35.

99. Julian Baum, "Prepare to Surface," **Far Eastern Economic Review**, Vol. 156, No. 5, February 4, 1993, p. 10.

100. Julian Baum, "Prepare to Surface," p. 10.

101. Paul Lewis, "Weapons May Seal Taiwan Sub Buy," **Defense News**, March 1–7, 1993, p. 3, 29.

102. That leverage was indicated by the fact that the Netherlands had to adjust its policies restricting arms sales to Taiwan in order to allow such extensive technology transfers. A worsening outlook at the time for general employment at Dutch shipyards also was said to be a contributing factor. See Giovanni de Briganti, "Dutch, Germans May End Taiwan Arms Ban," **Defense News**, November 30, 1992, Vol. 7, No. 48, p 1, 2.

103. Baum, "Steel Walls," p. 10.

104. "Taiwan Missile Efforts Bolstered by Raytheon," **Aviation Week and Space Technology**, March 8, 1993, p. 20. For a regional comparison, see Raytheon's dealings with Japan on the Patriot and its licensed production agreement with the Japan Defense Agency, in "Patriot and Air Defenses," Chapter 3, pp. 67–95, in Michael W. Chinworth, **Inside Japan's Defense: Technology, Economics and Strategy** (New York: Brassey's (US), Inc., 1992).

105. Julian Baum, "A Foot in the Door," **Far Eastern Economic Review**, September 17, 1992, p. 12.

106. David Hughes, "Taiwan to Acquire Patriot Derivative," **Aviation Week and Space Technology**, March 1, 1993, p. 61; Barbara Opell and David

Silverberg, Taiwanese May Soon Coproduce Patriot," **Defense News**, February 22, 1993, p. 1.

107. Baum, "A Foot in the Door," p. 13.

108. Baum, "A Foot in the Door," p. 13. Lockheed, at this writing (prior to its merger with Martin Marietta), has responded with a modest $60 million off-set package proposal. Barbara Opall, "Lockheed Proposes Offset in Taiwan F-16 Buy," **Defense News**, Vol. 8, No. 17, May 3–9, 1993, p. 3, 44.

109. Chris Brown, "Douglas Venture Kickstarts Taiwan," **Interavia Aerospace Review**, January 1992, p. 38.

110. There were also reports that TAC was interested in acquiring the Convair division of General Dynamics, the chief contractor for the MD-11, in order to boost its aircraft assembly and construction background. See Chris Brown, "Douglas Venture Kickstarts Taiwan," **Interavia Aerospace Review**, January 1992, p. 38; "IDF Fighter Program," p. 40.

111. Jeremy Mark and Susan Carey, "With British Aerospace Accord, Taiwan Resumes Effort to Boost Aircraft Industry," **Asian Wall Street Journal Weekly**, September 28, 1992, p. 3.

112. David E. Sanger, "Overtures to Asia Pose Risk for U.S. Aerospace Industry," **The New York Times**, November 18, 1991, p. D1.

113. One of six private sector investors is affiliated with the Japanese trading company Mitsui & Co., Inc. Some U.S. critics of the deal saw it as a Trojan horse by which Japanese industry could gain a stronger foothold in the U.S. aircraft industry. "Taiwanese Premier Orders Review of MacDac Deal," **Defense Marketing International**, Vol. 3, No. 25, December 13, 1991, p. 1.

114. U.S. General Accounting Office, "Issues Raised by Taiwan's Proposed Investment in McDonnell Douglas," GAO/NSIAD-92-120, February 1992.

115. "Fly British," **The Economist**, September 26, 1992, p. 33.

116. Jeremy Mark, "Collapse of McDonnell Deal Prompts Taiwan to Focus on Developing Aircraft-Parts Industry," **Asian Wall Street Journal Weekly**, August 3, 1992, p. 17.

117. Paul Proctor, "Taiwan, Britain to Push RJ Buildup," **Aviation Week and Space Technology**, October 5, 1992, p. 36.

118. Paul Proctor, "Taiwan, Britain to Push, p. 36.

119. Mark and Carey, "With British Aerospace Accord," p. 3.

120. Julian Baum, "Prepare to Surface," p. 11.

121. Carey, "Korean Companies Seek Broader," p. 12.

122. "South Korea Turns to Russia to Help Build Competitive Aerospace Industry," **Aerospace Daily**, Vol. 164, No. 30, November 13, 1992, p. 240; "Seoul, Russia Agree on Technology Cooperation," FBIS-EAS-93-105, June 1, 1993, p. 20. South Korea also will establish three or four research institutes in Russia by the end of 1993 as part of a broad technology cooperation agreement. In addition, technical personnel exchanges will commence: 200 Russian researchers will reside with Korean firms, universities and research institutes during the first year of the agreement. That number will expand to 250 in the second year. A total of 79 Russian technology development projects will be transferred to South Korea for commercialization. Conversion of Russian military plants to civilian facilities also will take place under the agreement. Western firms of course, have similar opportunities. See Daniel Sneider, "Russians Team With West Firms," **Defense News**, Vol. 8, No. 22, June 14–20, 1993.

123. "Seoul Stresses Economic Cooperation With PRC," FBIS-EAS-90-010, January 15, 1993, p. 30.

124. The teaming of Korea and Russia also allows the ROK to compete more effectively in the political arena against Japan. By leapfrogging Japan's technology transfer policies, as well as insulating itself from potential constraints imposed by the United States, Seoul effectively can declare economic independence from both Tokyo and Washington, thereby removing itself further from the shadow of its two economic patrons. In light of generally negative Korean perceptions of Japan — stemming from economic frictions relating to their trade imbalance, Japanese technology transfer policies, and historical grievances — the political message implicit with this step is very clear: if Korea cannot gain the acquiescence of its major technological and political patrons, it is prepared to pursue alternative approaches.

It is reasonable to assume that in this more fluid environment, Japan also is fully cognizant of the military applications and implications of its transfers of high technology to other nations with relatively advanced manufacturing and development capabilities. Korea's concern over Japan as a military threat in the region is fully reciprocated on the part of Japan toward Korea. See, for example, Ted Holden, Laxmi Nakarmi, and Bruce Einhorn, "How Japan Keeps the Tigers in a Cage," **Business Week**, August 17, 1992, NO. 3279, pp. 98 ff.

The posture of the South Korean government is a longstanding one. See a discussion of attitudes toward global and regional technology transfers in Young-Koo Cha, "Technology Transfer in the Pacific Basin: A Korean Perspective," in National Defense University, **Pacific Regional Security: The 1985 Pacific Symposium** (Washington, D.C.: U.S. Government Printing Office, 1988), pp. 161–177.

125. Giovanni de Briganti, "France Promises Asian Arms Sales; China's Ire Looms," **Defense News**, May 24–39, 1993, p. 1; Edmond Dantes, "British Industry Seeks Wider Customer Base in Asia, **Defense News**, May 13, 1991, p. 10.

126. Paul Proctor, "Pacific Rim Aerospace Companies Expand Ties to European Aircraft, Engine Firms," **Aviation Week and Space Technology**, Vol. 133, No. 10, September 3, 1992, p. 81.

127. Steve Glain, "Seoul Turns to Europe for Arms as Pentagon Guards Technology," **Wall Street Journal**, May 6, 1993.

128. "South Korea Seeks Strengthened Military Before Expected U.S. Force Withdrawal," **Aviation Week and Space Technology**, Vol. 132, No. 22, May 28, 1990, p. 26.

129. Paul Beaver, "Taiwan Keeps Fighter Aircraft Options Open," **Jane's Defence Weekly**, January 16, 1993, p. 14.

130. "Kokubo Kara, Keizai Yusen e," **Nihon Keizai Shimbun**, October 11, 1992.

131. Atsushi Komori, "'Kokusan' de, Sangyo Kodoka," **Asahi Shimbun**, November 11, 1992.

132. Carey, "Korean Companies Seek Broader," p. 12.

133. Atsushi Komori, "'Kokusan' de, Sangyo Kodoka."

134. "Venture May Divert Funds from IDF," **Aviation Week & Space Technology**, September 28, 1992, p. 23.

135. "Taiwan Seeks to Build Aerospace Industry," **Wall Street Journal**, November 6, 1989, p. B-81.

136. Atsushi Komori, "Miyu Tenkan no Michi o Yokei," **Asahi Shimbun**, December 7, 1992, p. 13.

137. "Kim Yong-Sam Urges Linking Defense, Industrial Technology," Foreign Broadcast Information Service, **Daily Report: East Asia**, FBIS-EAS-93-111 (June 11, 1993), p. 23.

138. Michael W. Chinworth and Dean Cheng, "The United States and Asia," pp. 73–91.

139. For a broader discussion of technology control regimes, see National Academy of Science, **Balancing the National Interest: U.S. National Security Export Controls and Global Economic Competition** (Washington, D.C.: National Academy Press, 1987).

140. U.S. Congress, Office of Technology Assessment, **Global Arms Trade**, p. 13–16.

141. David Silverberg, "Perry Backs Limited Aid to Boost U.S. Arms Exports," **Defense News**, Vol. 8, No. 21, June 7–13, 1993, p. 24; editorial, "Guarantee the Loans," **Defense News**, June 21–27, 1993, p. 18. It is difficult to avoid commenting on the irony of this situation as well. Just as the U.S. government is attempting to economize on federal expenditures through DOD procurement budget reductions, it also will be increasing export subsidies for the very firms impacted by these reductions.

142. Information included in this section is derived primarily from "Major Hurdles Seen for Korean Aerospace Development," **Pac-Rim Defense Marketing**, Vol. I, No. 10, November 26, 1990, pp. 1–4; Machmud Banjamin, "South Korea's Aerospace Industry," **Asian Defence Journal**, December 1990, p. 80; and, Kim Nak-Hieon, "Korea Starts to Fly High," **Asia Technology**, August 1990, pp. 36–37.

143. Chu Ho-Sok, "ROK Aviation Industry Ready to Take Off," **Maeil Kyongje Sinmun**, August 29, 1991, p. 12, in FBIS-EAS-91-194, October 7, 1991, p. 41.

144. Chu Ho-Sok, "ROK Aviation Industry Ready to Take Off," p. 40. For additional information on specific contracts and/or their dates of completion, see Machmud Banjamin, "South Korea's Aerospace Industry,"**Asian Defence Journal**, December 1990, pp. 83–84.

Chapter 11

From Offsets to Industrial Cooperation: Spain's Changing Strategies as an Arms Importer[1]

Jordi Molas-Gallart
Science Policy Research Unit
University of Sussex, Brighton, UK

11.1 Introduction

In July 1984, Spain and McDonnell Douglas Corporation signed the most important offset deal ever agreed by Spain and a foreign corporation or government. Spanish firms had secured licensed and co-production agreements before,[2] as in the purchase of US F-5 fighter aircraft in the mid-1960s, but had never entered an offset programme of this magnitude.[3] Lacking experience in handling big offset programmes, the Spanish administration found itself having to manage an offset worth $1540 million (in 1981 US dollars). To address this situation a new office was created: the *Gerencia de Compensaciones* (Offsets Management Office) would be responsible for managing the F-18 programme as well as any other offset agreements that followed. Later, the office changed its name to "Gerencia de Cooperación Industrial" (Industrial Cooperation Management Office). I will argue that this change in name reflects a transformation in the acquisition and compensation policy followed by the Spanish government. From enthusiasm about offsets in the early and mid-1980s, the emphasis shifted in the early 1990s towards other ways of obtaining industrial and technological benefits when importing military equipment. Although offset deals remain an important aspect of Spain's arms importing policy, other "compensation" formulae, like foreign investment for joint ventures set on Spanish soil, are gaining preeminence. Besides, international co-operation is increasingly favoured as the means of acquiring highly complex and expensive arms systems. It may seem contradictory that while US sources expressed concern about the allegedly too prodigal offset deals that US defence companies had granted foreign clients, a main beneficiary of such an apparently lavish approach was shifting its purchasing policy away from offset agreements. The present chapter will attempt to clarify the causes behind this apparent paradox.

11.2   The 1984 Offset Deal for the Purchase of 72 F-18S from the US

11.2.1   Background

In June 1983 Spain agreed to purchase 84 F-18s from the US company McDonnell Douglas Corporation (MDC). Although talks on the compensation package had already been going for several years, spanning at least three defence ministers and two administrations, the offset agreement was not signed until one year later.[4] MDC committed itself to provide offset deals to the value of 1.8 billion 1981 US dollars. As the number of planes to be bought was later reduced to 72, the offsets were proportionally reduced to 1.54 billion dollars.[5]

Offset deals were becoming a common occurrence in the world defence markets. The compensation package became a factor, important as any other, in determining purchasing decisions. Firms like McDonnell Douglas and General Dynamics established whole departments specialised in negotiating and then managing offset agreements. In contrast, the importing countries often had little or no experience in the administration of offsets. That was the case in Spain, where the Offsets Management Office was quickly established after the agreement was signed. It was expected that the experience acquired could then be applied to negotiating and managing future offset agreements. Soon, the Offsets Management Office was overseeing a myriad of smaller compensation programmes. There is little doubt that the experience provided by the F-18 programme has been crucial in developing Spanish abilities as an informed customer of big weapons systems.

The economic goals that buyers pursue when signing offset agreements are well-known and will not be repeated here. Suffice to say that the positive effects on the Spanish defence industrial and technological base of such a programme were constantly highlighted by officials in industry and the Ministry of Defence. The importance of the F-18 programme for the Spanish defence industry and defence industrial policy has to be understood against the political and economic background at the time when the contract was signed. Spain's defence industry had emerged from Franco's dictatorship and the years of democratic transition in a state of decline. When, in the early 1980s, governments were able to start turning their attention to defence and defence industrial policies, they pursued a modernising strategy. First, the government expected that supplying the armed forces with advanced equipment could help "professionalise" a body characterised by decades of political interference and prove, to a sceptical military, that the democratic government (specially the left-wing administration that came to power after the elections in October 1982) took national defence seriously.

Second, it was hoped that the domestic industry could play an important role in this modernisation process, thus providing incentives for the development of high technology industries, in which Spain was clearly deficient. Foreign assistance was needed to place Spanish defence industry at a technological level comparable with that of neighbouring countries like Italy. In the early 1980s Spain's access to multinational joint development and production programmes was limited: Spain's NATO membership was still pending from a referendum and she was consequently absent from other major international arms cooperation fora. It was only through operations linked to the purchase of foreign defence equipment that Spain could attempt to upgrade the technological level of its defence industries.

It was not the first time that Spain had used defence imports to prop up its ailing defence industry. From the mid-1960s to the early 1970s, three major arms production programmes consolidated the three major (state-owned) Spanish defence firms.[6] Partly because of the economic crisis and political turmoil, no major defence procurement programmes were started in the second half of the 1970s. The F-18 programme came as a spur to the development of Spain's defence firms in the aerospace and electronics sectors. The offset deal was the most important project that the Spanish defence industry had entered for many years and, as we will see, helped some firms establish a foundation in some defence technologies upon which they have since continued to build.

Yet, as important as this economic rationale is, political considerations bear heavily on the Spanish interest in obtaining offsets for its big defence programmes. The purchase of 72 F-18s raised considerable opposition. An investment of well over $2 billion to buy US-made fighter planes was not a popular measure when unemployment rates were nearing 20% of the active population. In this context the offset deal became a cornerstone of the government's effort to justify the purchase to the sceptical Spanish public. Arguing that offsets covered 100% of the total value of the programme, it followed that the purchase was even helping to create employment and it did not have any negative influence on the battered Spanish commercial balance. Besides, the offset would help Spanish firms to break into the American market and, even more important, would involve the transfer of technologies essential for the development of Spain's "high-technology industries". After the contract was signed, and while MDC could keep and even better its yearly offsets targets, the evolution of the deal was accorded a high profile. Often the *Gerencia de Compensaciones* would distribute to the press assessments of the progression of the programme, including sectoral information, geographical data, and lists of the main beneficiaries. However, such dissemination of results dwindled as MDC started to fall behind its commitments.

11.3   The F-18 Offset Programme: Main Traits

In July 1984 the Spanish government and McDonnell Douglas signed the offset agreement linked to the purchase of 84 (later to be reduced to 72 planes) F-18s planes. MDC committed itself to place offsets for a total value of 1.8 billion 1981 dollars (proportionally reduced to 1.54 later) with Spanish firms over a period of 10 years, extendable for up to three more years. One of the objectives established was to

"offer to the Spanish industry in the aerospace and electronics sectors co-production opportunities in manufacturing, assembling, testing, repairs and revision of the aircraft, and to initiate and foster programmes for the development of Spanish industries in the broadest possible number of areas, helping and developing new industries including technology transfer."

The offsets were divided in four groups:

Group A ("designated offsets"): Work, items or services to be carried out, manufactured or assembled by Spanish firms on the planes to be bought by the Spanish Air Force. This includes all operations that would involve the transfer of capacities enabling Spanish firms to carry out maintenance, repairs and revision on these planes.

Group B ("aerospace co-production offsets"): Work to be carried out by Spanish firms on F-18s for the export market or other aerospace activities.

Group C: "indirect offsets" involving the use of defence-relevant technologies excluding those in the aerospace area.

Group D: indirect commercial offsets, including Spanish exports, investments in Spain including technology transfers, and sales derived from the latter.

McDonnell Douglas offered a list of potential offsets in groups A and B from which the Spanish government could choose. MDC estimated the value of this package as 40% of its total commitments. In any case, and whatever the Spanish final decision on the offsets initially offered by MDC, the contract established that a minimum of 40% of the offsets was to involve "technologies typical of developed countries", and a minimum of 10% had to involve technology transfers to Spanish-owned or controlled companies.[7] There were no pre-established upper or lower limits for the type of offsets, except that tourism related offsets could not exceed 10% of the total, and groups A and B (offsets directly linked to the manufacture of the F-18) had to account jointly for at least 17% of the total. Yet the achievement of this latter target was a shared responsibility between MDC and the Spanish government. When subcontracting F-18 work to Spanish firms under the offset agreement, the costs to MDC should not be higher than those it would incur when subcontracting to its normal suppliers. Consequently, the Spanish government has to pay for the additional costs that domestic firms may incur. That the commitment to a minimum investment in direct offsets involved both parties should not come as a surprise: being at the earlier stages of their learning curves, Spanish firms were bound to be less efficient than established equipment suppliers. It then falls on to the Spanish government to make up for the extra costs. To this end, the Spanish government put aside 100 million 1981 US dollars to finance eventual additional costs. Given the floor established for offsets in groups A and B, the amount committed for additional costs could total up to almost 40% of the value of the aerospace-related offsets subcontracted to the Spanish industry.[8]

Despite these eventual extra costs, the Spanish government showed special interest in maximising the amount of aerospace-related offsets during the negotiation process. Although local assembly was finally ruled out because of the excessive expense involved, Spain insisted on obtaining offsets in aerospace equipment, materials, avionics, and simulators. Group B offsets, guaranteeing Spanish work in 50% of all F-18s destined to the export market, were specially attractive. That other countries would buy F-18s with Spanish components was not only important for the technological development of the fledgling Spanish aerospace components industry, but could also provide grounds to praise the development of the Spanish defence-related firms, particularly if the extra costs incurred and paid by the Spanish government were not granted similar notoriety.

The offsets were to be executed over a period of 10 years, with MDC commitments growing as the years passed. As reflected in Table 1, for the last three-year period the level of commitments exceeds by 60% the amount to be spent during the first three-year period that ended in 1987. One reason for this progression in the level of commitments might have been the need to undertake the necessary groundwork to carry out such a complex commitment; it can be assumed that the efficiency of the organisations will improve as time passes, hence the increasing commitments. Yet, a significant plus of this arrangement was that MDC completed and even outstripped its projected commitments during the first

Table 1: McDonnell Douglas Projected F-18 Offset Commitments (1983–1993) — Revised Commitment 72 Planes

	Period Ending	Offset Commitment 1981 $ (thousands)
Period 1	31 Dec 1984	47000
Period 2	31 Dec 1987	403000
Period 3	31 Dec 1990	450000
Period 4	31 Dec 1993	643000

years of implementation, when public scrutiny was at its greatest, immediately after what had been a much contested purchase.

At the time of signing the contract, McDonnell Douglas assured the Spanish government that, according to its own research, it had identified potentially eligible offsets to a value of 4.4 billion 1981 USdollars: that is, almost three times the size of its eventual commitment. Yet despite these assurances, implementation became fraught with difficulties. Managing the whole scale of the programme became a very complex task, Spain did not accept many proposed offset operations, and, eventually, MDC started to fall behind its projected commitments. The next section will discuss the problems that have appeared in the implementation of this agreement and how these might have tarnished the image of the whole project.

11.4   Programme Implementation

The F-18 offset deal included a wide range of operations and was, in principle, open to contributions in any area of Spanish technological development. Because of such flexibility, this sort of deal has been described in the literature as the best kind of offset agreement for purchasing countries.[9] In principle, it allowed the Spanish authorities to establish, to a certain extent, some sectoral or regional priorities. However, during its implementation several problems constraining such flexibility surfaced.

Table 2 presents the sectoral distribution of the offsets received under the F-18 programme to the end of March 1994. Interestingly, defence offsets[10] account for only 28% of the total value of the F-18 offset programme, down

Table 2: Sectoral Distribution of F-18 Offsets — Up to 31st March 1994

Sector	Share of Offsets
Defence	28.42%
Chemicals & Pharmaceuticals	17.54%
Iron & Steel	12.46%
Foodstuffs & Consumer Goods	8.75%
Electronics & I T (Civil)	8.07%
Investment & Technology (Civil)	4.55%
Shipbuilding	3.90%
Capital Goods	3.80%
Others	12.51%

Source: Data supplied by the *Gerencia de Cooperación Industrial*.

from 35% in December 1988. Despite the interest of the Spanish negotiators in obtaining direct offsets involving substantial technology transfers, the final configuration of the F-18 programme has been biased in favour of indirect commercial compensation. This relatively low and falling presence of defence offsets is explained both by the difficulties faced by the US defence industry, and by the limited capacity of Spain's military-related industry to absorb a high volume of direct offsets. It can be argued that, for instance, such limitations were implicitly recognised in the offset agreement when the minimum value for aerospace offsets (including also indirect offsets) was established at a meagre 17%. This was a low figure if we consider that it is one of the fields in which the Spanish negotiators were most eager to obtain offsets.[11]

Regarding indirect commercial offsets (Group D), Table 2 shows a significant concentration in a few industrial sectors. Chemicals and pharmaceuticals,[12] iron and steel, foodstuffs, and electronics account for well over one half of the total indirect offsets. With the exception of electronics, they are "traditional" industrial sectors in which the Spanish economy is relatively strong. This sectoral distribution is not surprising when a large portion of these indirect commercial offsets involve additional exports of Spanish goods. While technology transfers can, and often will, benefit sectors in which Spain does not have much of a commercial advantage, such "trade-oriented" offsets will necessarily benefit industries able to supply products that the export markets can absorb.

In short, the sectoral distribution of the F-18 offsets programme has largely been defined by the existing industrial capabilities. The potential flexibility to establish sectoral priorities in the allocation of offset operations is largely constrained by the existing domestic capacities, such constraints being tighter the larger the offset programme. There will always be a limited degree of flexibility for the receiving country to set sectoral priorities and use the offset as a tool of defence industrial policy; the Spanish case shows, for instance, how local capabilities in fields like simulators and automated test beds were introduced through the F-18 offset programme. These are qualitatively very important operations, but in terms of volume are much smaller than the bulk of indirect commercial offsets.

In terms of regional distribution, there is a high concentration of offsets in those regions that would be the "natural" receivers of such work in the absence of any offset distribution policy of a regional nature. In other words, the regional distribution of offsets is largely determined by their sectoral allocation; there are no signs of a regional policy being implemented on the back of the offset agreement.

As Table 3 shows, the province of Madrid appears by far to be the main receiver of offsets. The major reason for the pre-eminence of Madrid is that it

Table 3: Geographical Distribution of Offsets — Up to 31st March 1994

Region	F-18 Programme % of all offsets	All Programmes % of all offsets
Madrid	59.9	64.4
Andalucia	13.4	11.9
Basque Country	7.6	7.3
Catalonia	7.1	6.4
Valencia	6.5	4.8
Asturias	4.1	3.2
Others	1.4	2.0

Source: Data supplied by the Gerencia de Cooperación Industrial.

receives most defence offsets;[13] Madrid is the only area in which the defence offsets outweigh indirect commercial compensations. The remaining regions are mainly receivers of indirect "civilian" offsets. Andalucia, the Basque Country and Catalonia have all received more indirect offsets than Madrid, with Andalucia being the most important recipient.[14]

The concentration of offsets in Madrid has been growing over the years, alongside the increasingly defence-oriented nature of Spain's offset policy. This concentration results in a clustering of technologically significant offsets in the province.[15] This is not surprising; the aerospace and electronics firms that receive most of the direct offset work have their headquarters and most of their research and production facilities in Madrid.

There is also a noticeable concentration of offsets at the firm level. Table 4 shows the 10 firms that have received the largest share of offset activity. Two defence-related firms, CASA and INDRA,[16] account for 30% of all offsets and the 10 firms in Table 4 account for almost 50% of the total value of F-18 offsets. This concentration exists despite the large number of firms that have partici-pated in one or more offset agreements: 413 by the end of 1993. Therefore there must be a large number of companies participating in very small offset opera-tions, particularly in the commercial fields. To select and oversee these small operations requires a substantial administrative effort.

Compared with the proliferation of small firms that receive some offset work, in the defence area such activity is extremely concentrated, with only two firms, CASA (aerospace) and INDRA (electronics), accounting for over 90% of the F-18 defence offsets.[17] Because defence-related offsets have been more important from a technological point of view, such concentration of defence off-sets is very significant. First, it means that there has been very limited diffusion

Table 4: The Industrial Beneficiaries of F-18 Offsets to 31 March 1994

| Firm | Offsets Received | | Sector |
	Million Ptas.	%	
Casa	50502	16.96	Defence
Indra	42138	14.15	Defence
Ertisa	16525	5.55	Chemical
Union Naval de Levante	9120	3.06	Shipbuilding
Pro.Quimicos del Mediterraneo	7393	2.48	Chemical
Asturiana de Zinc	5308	1.78	Iron & Steel
Amper Programas	5234	1.76	Defence
Santa Barbara	4618	1.55	Defence
Repsol Petroleo	3845	1.29	Chemical
Scott Iberica	3078	1.03	Chemical

Source: Data supplied by the *Gerencia de Cooperación Industrial*

of defence-related technological capabilities obtained through the F-18 deal. Second, while the Offsets Management Office has to invest large amounts of time and effort in overseeing the indirect commercial offsets, its main interest resides in areas dominated by a few firms and institutions. Indirect commercial offsets thus appeared as the main cause of an onerous management overhead, and would henceforth be avoided if at all possible.

The importance of aerospace and electronics firms, as recipients of offset activity, is not accidental. Besides being the defence areas in which Spain is most dependent on imports, offsets in these fields can offer the Spanish defence-related industry assistance in areas that the Ministry of Defence considers most critical, including microelectronics and related technologies (like simulation, software, radars, and testing and maintenance equipment), and new materials (specially ceramics and composites). To mention only two examples, offset deals helped CASA develop its skills in the manufacture of composite structural components for aircraft, and the electronics firm CESELSA (now subsumed in the electronics conglomerate INDRA) establish an important presence in the field of simulators and automated test beds.

The implementation of the F-18 offset programme has been besieged by another set of problems linked to the management of such a big and "flexible" programme. As McDonnell Douglas submitted projects for approval to the Spanish Offset Management Office on a one-by-one basis (the contract established that the suitability of projects had to be agreed between both parties), the Office was soon overwhelmed by hundreds of projects of widely varying size, and had to decide whether they conformed to the conditions required to be accepted as genuine offsets. Not that this decision was easy; for instance, for commercial offsets the transactions proposed had to result in a net increase for Spanish exports to the United States or a net decrease of Spanish imports. Therefore the Offset Management Office had to decide, for each proposed commercial offset, whether it would amount to a net gain in the balance of trade or would just divert already existent trade flows. Besides, the proposed operations could be (and were) in any sector. Eventually, many proposals were not accepted. By December 1986, the total value of rejected proposals amounted to 23% of the total proposals in the commercial area. For defence-related offsets the proportion of "rejected" proposals was even higher: 41% of the total value of the defence-related offset proposals submitted. Eventually, by the end of March 1994, a total of 7759 applications had been processed, of which 1190 (15%) had been rejected amounting to a 31% of the total value of the projects submitted (see Table 5).[18]

After a project is accepted the Management Office has to calculate its "offset value". To this end, it has to check the information received from the participating Spanish companies, evaluate the help they are receiving from the US company "providing" the offset, assess the growth of the normal trade flows that the new offset has caused, calculate the Spanish value added that the new operations involve, and translate this value into 1981 US$.[19] The problem of selecting and assessing the applications and administering the whole programme is compounded by the large number of proposals that McDonnell Douglas has presented to the Spanish authorities.

Notwithstanding the large number of rejections, MDC initially managed to keep the offset programme progressing at a good pace. In the initial years the offset contracts granted surpassed the goals set in the agreement. In 1987, for instance, the offsets realised exceeded by 51% the commitments for that year.

Table 5: Situation of the F-18 Offset Programme as at 31st March 1994

Total Commitment:	**1543 M$ 1981**	
Credited:	**1259 M$ 1981 (81.6% of total commitment)**	
	Number	**Value**
Proposals Submitted:	7759	2617 M$ Current
(of which) approved:	6543 (84%)	1760 M$ (67%)
" under consideration:	26 (0.3%)	38 M$ (1.5%)
" rejected:	1190 (15%)	818 M$ (31%)

Source: Data supplied by the *Gerencia de Cooperación Industrial*

Yet in 1988 the yearly surplus was down to 4.3% of the commitments for that year, and from 1989 MDC started to fall short of the planned yearly payments. The surplus that had been accumulated in the first five years of the programme was rapidly eroded; by the end of 1991 the **total** realised offsets were trailing projected commitments by almost 6%. In 1991 the offset contracts accounted for only 45% of that year's projected commitment. When the programme reached its projected closing date by the end of December 1993 the default accumulated had reached 18% of total commitments. Out of a target of 1981 US $1543 million, the total credited offsets amounted $1265 million.

Despite the promising start, MDC proved increasingly unable to comply with its offset commitments. This is partly due to the fact that annual commitments increased as the programme progressed. The growing obligations have coincided with the international economic crisis of the early 1990s and the fall in demand for the defence industries. There have been increasing difficulties in finding additional markets for Spanish products, and the contraction in the defence markets is shrinking the base on which defence offsets can be offered to Spanish companies. Although Spain's preference for group B offsets continues (as shown by Spain's interest in making components for the F-18s sold to Finland in 1992), the participating US companies are hard pressed to keep for themselves as high a portion of this work as possible. To allow Spanish companies to participate in the manufacture of F-18 components, no matter how small this participation, would not go down well in the US when defence firms are shedding thousands of jobs.

The offset agreement stipulated the possibility of a three-year grace period for MDC to fulfil its commitments; this period started on 1st January 1994. The first months of 1994 saw the culmination of the negotiations between MDC and the Spanish authorities to determine the offset projects that would be carried out over this three-year period ending on 31st December 1996. It is expected that the agreements signed in early 1994 will cover all the remaining MDC obligations. What is significant about this batch of offsets is that they are all direct defence offsets, aimed mainly at increasing the capability of Spanish firms and the Spanish Air Force to maintain the F-18s over its complete life-cycle.[20] The projects that Spain proposed were the result of an analysis undertaken, over a period of some two years, in anticipation of the foreseeable failure by MDC to fulfil all its commitments by the end of 1993. The main objective was to put an end to further "commercial" offsets and to concentrate instead on defence compensations, targeted mainly at diminishing Spanish dependence in weapons system maintenance and support. This is in line with the overall direction of the offset agreements that Spain has entered over the last years: the main emphasis is in obtaining direct defence offsets. As we will see below, the F-18 programme with its large volume of indirect, non-military, mainly commercial compensations has become an, admittedly very large, exception to the many offset agreements signed by Spain.

11.5 Main Outcomes

After all the implementation problems, there is little doubt that the programme has had beneficial effects. It can hardly be questioned that it brought to Spain a substantial workload in different areas of the economy and that, in consequence, there was a job creation effect. Exports to the US of defence and civilian products under the offset agreement helped to assuage the negative effects on the trade balance of the import of the F-18 fighters. Some offsets programmes involved the training of industrial and Air Force personnel[21] and others have helped Spanish defence-related firms to homologate their products in the international markets.

Yet these results have been obtained at a cost. Apart from the administrative difficulties that we have discussed in some detail, there is the question of the "cost premium" paid for offsets. As mentioned above, a system was implemented to help Spanish receivers of direct offsets (Groups A and B) to keep their prices within the market prices MDC expected to pay for these components from its normal suppliers. In a nutshell, the difference between domestic and "market" costs was covered by Spanish public funds. The F-18 has been the only offset programme to implement such a system.

In this section, three main problems with the implementation of the F-18 US-Spanish offset agreement have been identified. First, there is the administrative ordeal of having to review thousands of applications for offsets and apply regulations that may be subjected to different interpretations.[22] Second, the ambiguous basis on which the criteria and the procedures for selection are established cause doubts about the eligibility of some operations. By 1989, the Spanish administration acknowledged that they had difficulties assessing some of the offset proposals, and the opposition questioned in Parliament the eligibility of some selected projects.[23] The third problem lies in the long span of time over which the offsets will be distributed; as the Spanish case shows, the programme can fall victim of economic circumstances impossible to foresee when signing the contract.

It can be argued therefore, that smaller offset contracts offer clear advantages over long term massively complex agreements. In fact, most of the programmes that the Offset Management Office administers are much smaller than the F-18 programme. Some of these programmes are direct agreements to co-produce or jointly develop specific components for inclusion in the systems acquired by the Spanish Armed Forces. Unlike the F-18 offset agreements such co-production agreements are much more narrowly targeted and do not develop over such long periods of time. In fact, many of them could not be called "offset agreements". Strictly speaking an "offset agreement" is a high value counter-trade[24] operation with a long period for the completion of the contract.[25]

11.6   Other Offset Deals

The weight of the F-18 agreement within the total population of offset deals that Spain signed as an arms importer can be appreciated from Table 6. This single agreement accounts for more than two-thirds of the total value of all offset agreements, and almost one-half of the value of outstanding offset obligation as at the end of 1993.

Although it is by far the most important, the F-18 offset agreement is one of many managed by the Offsets Management Office. By December 1986, the Office administered 40 projects; by the end of 1993 this number had grown to 72.

As shown in Table 7, about two-thirds of the number of offset deals have been signed with US firms and these include the most important deals in terms of their economic value.

The massive difference between the F-18 and other offset programmes can also be seen in Table 8; this provides details of the most important offset pro-grammes signed during the 1980s. It shows that the largest deals have been signed with US firms. The second most important deal after the F-18 was less

Table 6: The Number and Value of Offset Agreements Signed by Spain for Imports of Defence Material over the Period 1983–1993

	Number of Offset Agreements	Total Offset Volume (M.Ptas.1993)	Offsets Pending (M.Ptas.1993)
Offsets Signed	72	516,000	143,000
F-18 Offset	1	354,000	65,000

Source: Elaborated from official data provided by the Secretary of State for Defence to the Spanish Congress Defence Commission on June, 21 1994. Cortes Generales, *Diario de Sesiones del Congreso de los Diputados, V Legislatura, Comisión de Defensa,* sesión núm. 14 21 Junio 1994.

Table 7: Offset Agreements Linked to Spanish Arms Imports 1983–1993

	US	Europe	Total
Total number of Deals	46	26	72
Completed Deals	19	7	26

Source: Elaborated from official data provided by the Secretary of State for Defence to the Spanish Congress Defence Commission on June, 21 1994. Cortes Generales, *Diario de Sesiones del Congreso de los Diputados, V Legislatura, Comisión de Defensa*, sesión núm.14 21 Junio 1994.

Table 8: Spain's Most Important Offset Programmes in the 1980s

Programme	Offset Value	% Total Programme	Non-defence Offsets	Duration Years	Vendor
EF-18	1543 M$1981	100	Yes (72%)	10	US
AV-8B (Harrier)	130 M$	100	Yes	?	US
Lamps MK-III	36 M$	30	Tec.Transfer	6	US
Roland		67	?	?	France
Harpoon	20 M$	20–50	<20%	?	US
Chinook	44 M$	50	Tec.Transfer & Ind. Invest.	8	US

than one tenth its size; the offset for the purchase of 8 AV-8B ("Harriers") to McDonnell Douglas amounted to $130 million (in current terms).[26] The remaining programmes are all moderate in size and are dwarfed by the dimension of the F-18 agreement. The F-18 offset deal is also exceptional because of its very high percentage of indirect non-defence offsets. There has clearly been a trend towards more accurate targeting of offset programmes, even when this was done at the price of lower returns in absolute terms. For instance, the Roland offsets package, despite only being for 67% of the total contract value, has been crucial in developing Spanish capacities in missile manufacturing, a field that Spain was eager to enter. The F-18 agreement is also different inasmuch as it was rare, at that time, to find 100% offset deals.

The modest presence of European firms among Spanish offset partners contrasts with the European orientation of most international arms development and production programmes in which Spain has expressed interest. However, the trend toward cooperation with US companies will not disappear just because Spain's enthusiasm for a particular form of offset is waning. In some very important instances, Spain has chosen US firms for acquisition programmes and future development projects instead of competing offers from European joint programmes. The most recent and relevant example of such a trend is the purchase of Hughes TOW 2-B anti-tank missiles. Spain had, at a previous stage, joined the European programme TRIGAT, but finally decided to withdraw and buy US TOW missiles. As part of the deal, Hughes has agreed to rescue the troubled Spanish state-owned firm ENOSA (a firm involved in vision and optical systems), and to create a joint firm (Gyconsa) with the Spanish electronics holding INDRA. Gyconsa is a systems engineering company responsible for the Spanish TOW programme and for developing a new electro-optically guided short range anti-tank missile for the late 1990s (MACAM-3). This is probably the best and most important example of the new strategy, which uses purchasing programmes to draw foreign partners into Spanish firms with a view to maintaining the partnership for future developments and programmes.

11.7   Changing Strategies: From Offsets to Industrial Agreements

When, in 1984, Spain decided to buy 12 Harriers AV-8B from McDonnell Douglas, it did so under an offset programme. When, in the early 1990s, Spain was considering the modernisation of the same aircraft and the procurement of a further 8 Harriers in more advanced versions, the institutional arrangement for this purchase were very different: Spain would participate in a joint development and production programme that would also involve the United States and Italy. The shift from plain purchase with offsets to partial joint development and production is a significant one. Although the amount of business generated for the Spanish firms is similar,[27] the programmes are managed in a different way. While offsets must be approved by the Offset Management Office, and they are agreed after the procurement decision has been made, joint development and production involves the direct participation of industry from the early development phase. Hence when final procurement decisions are made, the tasks that will be contracted to Spanish companies will have been, by and large, defined. Theoretically, this allows the Spanish firms to interact more closely with their "senior" partners. Negotiations on workshares involve directly the participating firms, and the corporations from the smaller countries bear the brunt of the responsibility to ensure that they can have access to meaningful tasks. In joint projects, the responsibilities for the development programme are usually shared, implying a deeper involvement of the junior partners from the early stages of development and production.

In this new situation the task of the Offset Management Office was substantially redefined, and its name accordingly changed. The re-labelled Industrial Cooperation Management Office sees its new broader role as to offer institutional support to the Spanish firms negotiating with their foreign "senior" counterparts, and to put in place mechanisms to guarantee that Spain receives a "juste retour" for its imports of military systems.

Spain's move from offsets to other forms of cooperation became progressively clearer in the early 1990s. This move was not unique to Spain; for instance, Greece was shifting away from offset agreements towards other forms of cooperation, specially joint ventures, as early as in 1987. In the mid-1980s, Spain started to participate vigorously in several international development and production programmes.[28] Although some highly publicised failures have led to a measure of scepticism among industrialists, some government officials, and the press, international development and production programmes mark a new phase in Spain's policies as an arms importer and in the internationalisation of its defence industrial base. Even when the participation of a small partner in a joint project is marginal and agreed as a form of compensation with the main (foreign) producer, there are significant differences with offset deals in at least two respects. First, the tasks to be developed by the small partner are agreed before the purchase (which is not always feasible in offset agreements), and are usually "direct" in that they relate to the specific arms system being object of the transaction. Second, there is no need to oversee a large number of offset applications to determine whether they conform to the agreement. Therefore management is less cumbersome, although not devoid of protracted negotiations as countries and firms strive for control of those tasks that they find more rewarding from a technological point of view.

When joint programmes involve genuine joint development, small partners become more deeply involved in research and production, and gain better control over the evolution and characteristics of the programme than in an offset agreement. Yet the main difficulty for small countries with an intermediate technological level, is to find areas in which its industry may be able to provide a meaningful contribution to the joint programme. One of the rôles of offset agreements can be to provide the basis on which a country can start developing "niche" expertise in defence-related areas that will later allow it to participate in joint development and production programmes. Joint development and production may then be interpreted as a further step in the process of internationalization of the domestic industry. For instance, up to a certain extent, the Spanish move from offsets to international cooperation has been supported by the experience gained in the F-18 and other previous offset programmes. Spain's main contribution to the co-operative programme to develop and produce the Harrier

II Plus aircraft revolves around the appointment of CESELSA as the prime contractor for the simulators and automated test beds. These are areas in which CESELSA developed most of its expertise through the F-18 offset programme.

The role of offsets in Spanish defence procurement has subsided due to the undeclared but emerging policy of using acquisition programmes to draw foreign partners into domestic companies. Its most important example so far has been the arrangements accompanying the sale of TOW anti-tank missiles to Spain by Hughes. The sale of TOW missiles to Spain came at a cost for Hughes. As part of the deal, Hughes has bought a 49% share in the state-owned ENOSA and in the newly created Gyconsa. Similarly, following the sale of communications equipment to the Spanish Army, Thomson CSF has become a shareholder in the domestic assembler of such equipment, Amper Sistemas. Another Thomson subsidiary took a 40% share in a new venture involving the Spanish firms Bazán and INISEL, whose first goal has been to supply underwater electronics systems to the Spanish Navy.

At times, foreign firms have invested in Spanish ventures related to joint international development and production programmes, specially the European Fighter Aircraft. For instance, Rolls-Royce is a major shareholder in Industria de Turbo Propulsores (ITP), the Spanish partner in Eurojet, the consortium in charge of developing and producing the EF2000 engine. Also, Lucas Aerospace launched a joint venture with CASA to form the "Compañía Española de Sistemas Aeronáuticos, S.A." (CESA), a firm specialising in the production of hydraulic components for aerospace applications. The company also participates in the EF2000 programme.

In all these cases the foreign shareholder does not control the company but has, nevertheless, a substantial stake in it (usually between 30 and 49 per cent). So far, the Spanish authorities have been reluctant to relinquish control of key activities in the defence field to foreign owners. Hence the substantial, yet minority stakes, through which foreign firms are allowed to access the Spanish market.

Although these operations are linked to a single transaction, the participation of foreign companies in the ownership of Spanish firms brings about the promise of a longer commitment to the Spanish industry. After the foreign firms have sunk substantial investments to modernise and improve the Spanish firms, it is to be expected that they will try to maintain their presence in Spain to make their initial investment more profitable.

The Spanish authorities are specially interested in the technological and marketing skills that foreign companies can bring to their Spanish associates. For the foreign partners these operations often entail sizeable investments against promises of additional purchases. That foreign firms are ready to risk investments in a market like the Spanish, that is anything but growing, is a reflection of the difficult situation in which arms exporters find themselves. US companies, like Hughes, may be attracted to these ventures not only by the moderate size of the Spanish markets, but also by the opportunity they offer to establish a bridgehead in Europe for fear of the emergence of a closed European defence market. That Spain has used the "buyers market" to prop up the technological level of some of its ailing defence related industries should not come as a surprise.

11.8   Conclusions

Since signing the F-18 offset agreement, the Spanish defence industry and its international surroundings have changed beyond recognition. It is not surprising then that the ways through which Spain has sought to improve this industry, when driven to purchase defence equipment abroad, have also evolved. Spain has used an increasing variety of methods to draft technological and marketing skills in support of its defence firms. Offset agreements were the first of them. Later, with a more qualified defence industrial base, with membership of international defence organisations, and with a more competitive international defence market that strengthened its bargaining power as a purchaser, Spain managed to obtain other compensating arrangements.

Although offsets have never been fully abandoned as a way of securing industrial benefits when importing arms, other avenues are now available that avoid many of the problems with offsets. The F-18 example shows the difficulties encountered in the management of big, long-term, flexible offset programmes. Uncertainty over the ability of the contracting company to fulfil its commitments, difficulties interpreting complex and at times vague clauses, and the effort necessary to deal with thousands of proposed offset operations are the most obvious obstacles in the implementation of an offset agreement. Clearly, smaller offset programmes are easier to administer, but are usually narrower and more difficult to control and to adapt to changing circumstances.

The success of other arrangements, like compelling foreign sellers to take a stake in domestic firms, remains to be seen. The long term benefits of foreign participation in domestic defence companies may not accrue if the foreign investor does not see its efforts rewarded by a flow of sales to the armed forces. Already, Hughes has made its disappointment with the poor results of its Spanish investment publicly known. The unavoidable clash of interests between domestic firms and foreign sellers then moves from the highly formalised and structured environment of the offset management offices, to the more fluid market relations between firms and between them and their buyers. Foreign firms may press the Ministry of Defence to maintain a flow of orders for their Spanish ventures in the knowledge that if such custom is not forthcoming they can always withdraw from Spanish industry. Their Spanish partners will be more interested in assuring that the promised transfer of technologies and marketing skills takes place, and that the involvement of the foreign partner improves the firm's access to the notoriously difficult export market.

In this context, we expect the policy of using arms imports to "attract" foreign investors to continue. Together with international joint production and development programmes, they will be the main tools used to capitalise on defence imports to improve the technological capabilities of the Spanish military-related industries. This is not to say that offsets are a thing of the past. Although their relative importance is diminishing, Spain has accumulated important experience in negotiating and managing offset agreements. Because the Spanish administration feels it is learning to extract better offsets than before, the offset option will remain an alternative to consider in almost any weapons transaction. Yet, with the preference given to other forms of "compensation" like international cooperation, or direct foreign investment in Spanish defence production, offsets will probably be increasingly limited to small transactions. A small operation may not justify an international programme, or a foreign direct investment in Spain, and will not suffer from the main drawbacks of large offset agreements that characterised the F-18 programme. In other words, offsets are here to stay as one element of the Spanish arms purchasing policy. However, the main policy thrust has moved away from offsets, and towards other forms of obtaining industrial compensations when importing arms. These new forms (joint development and production, foreign direct investment) invariably entail more intricate patterns of international interaction, in which firms are playing an increasingly important role.

Endnotes

1. The author acknowledges the assistance received from Antonio Rodríguez and the Gerencia de Cooperación Industrial when writing this chapter.

2. Offsets may include co-production agreements, but also other sorts of countertrade deals. They are different from mere co-production agreements in that they have to reach a preset value and are implemented over long periods of time.

3. Its only relevant precursor was the 20% offset agreed for the purchase of 30 Mirage III fighter aircraft from France in 1968.

4. Later on, one of the defence ministers involved in the negotiations, Agustín Rodríguez Sahagún, recriminated his successors for having accepted conditions he had previously rejected. Cinco Días (Madrid), 26 April 1989.

5. Although both official Spanish sources and MDC declared the offset agreement to cover 100% of the value of the transaction, this direct relationship is not explicitly established in the official agreement.

6. Jordi Molas-Gallart, **Military Production and Innovation in Spain**, Chur: Harwood Academic Publishers, 1992, pp. 49–50.

7. The system to assess the value of technology transfers is not clearly determined in the initial agreement. This offered four vague alternatives: the "just value" of the technological licence transfer, its value to the Spanish company, the highest of the former, or any other mutually agreed value.

8. No information is available on the extra costs eventually incurred; yet additional costs of more than 30% over the contract values are likely. Part of these extra costs would later be recouped by the State in the form of additional tax income and social security contributions.

9. Grant T. Hammond, **Countertrade, Offsets and Barter in International Political Economy**, New York: St. Martin's Press, 1990, p. 43.

10. These refer to Groups A, B, and C as described above.

11. By the end of 1993, aerospace offsets reached 31%, well beyond the established floor.

12. The weight of pharmaceuticals within the "chemical & pharmaceutical" sector is very low.

13. This explains why, for all programmes, the concentration in Madrid is even bigger: the presence of direct offsets is lower in the F-18 programme than in the other ones.

14. Andalucia and the Basque Country are also areas receiving direct defence offsets: the aerospace firm CASA has a couple of plants in Andalucia, and the aircraft engine components firm ITP has its main manufacturing centre in the Basque Country.

15. Indirect commercial offsets are far from having the technological content of direct offsets; they have included for instance the US purchase of Spanish paper pulp, the US import of Spanish wire for tires, and the construction of a cruiser.

16. CASA and INDRA are respectively the leading aerospace and defence electronics companies in Spain.

17. This is why, despite the fact that defence only accounts for 28% of the total offset, CASA and INDRA lead the list of major offset receivers.

18. Including all other offset programmes, the total number of applications processed by 31st March 1994 exceeded 9000.

19. Antonio Rodríguez, "**Los programas de compensaciones asociados a las adquisiciones de material de defensa**," in *Economía Industrial*, January–February 1987, p. 88.

20. One of the objectives is to make the Spanish firm Industria de Turbo Propulsores (ITP) capable of performing full maintenance on all the GE equipped Spanish military aircraft. Besides, once complete, these projects will mean that no further payments in the form of royalties or the like will be owed to US firms.

21. Although the chapter concentrates on the offsets received by industry, the Spanish Air Force has also been an important receiver, above all of training and technology transfer, related mainly to the operation and maintenance of the aircraft.

22. To tackle the problem of interpretation two mechanisms were implemented. First, some points in the agreement were further clarified in the minutes of a series of meetings between the Spanish Offset Management Office and MDC that followed the signature of the contract. Minutes and offset agreement conform a single contractual body. In the second place, in every routine quarterly meeting between the Gerencia and MDC, new minutes are signed gathering the criteria and procedures followed to assess offset applications; such criteria are used as guidelines for future similar applications.

23. Cinco Días (Madrid), 26 April 1989.

24. Countertrade exists whenever an export operation is contractually linked to a "compensating" import.

25. Luis Jiménez, "**Las transacciones por compensación en el comercio internacional: los acuerdos 'Offset'**", *Revista de Aeronáutica y Astronáutica*, no. 576, December 1988, pp. 1354–1358.

26. Most of the offset contracts signed with Spain are specified in current dollars. US inflation over the period of application will erode the real value of the offset obligation.

27. Partners in international projects have a share of the production work equivalent to their share of the purchase of the final system.

28. Jordi Molas-Gallart, "**Spanish Participation in the International Development and Production of Arms Systems**" *Defense Analysis* 6 (December 1990): pp. 351–365.

Chapter 12

US — Swiss F-5 Transaction and the Evolution of Swiss Offset Policy[1]

Bernard Udis
Department of Economics
University of Colorado at Boulder, USA

12.1 Introduction

After the conclusion of World War II Switzerland passed through a series of dependencies on other countries for military aircraft. Britain and France were the major suppliers. The Swiss first purchased the DeHavilland Vampire and later produced under license the DeHavilland Venom. The Hawker Hunter was also purchased from Britain. It was assembled in Switzerland after refurbishment and modernization in the United Kingdom (UK). In mid-1961 the Swiss Parliament made a decision to fund the acquisition of the French Dassault Mirage III aircraft under license.

The Mirage III project proved quite disappointing for a variety of reasons[2] which resulted in substantial cost overruns[3] and technical difficulties. This project had been set up with a fixed budget, which the Swiss government was unwilling to expand. Consequently, the original goal of acquiring one hundred aircraft was unmet and fifty-seven were actually acquired. The Mirage III experience (still described in some Swiss circles as a "debacle") led to the reorganization of the Swiss military procurement system. In 1968 a new civilian-controlled organization, the Defense Technology and Procurement Agency (GRD for the initials of the German words) was established to handle procurement matters.[4] Shortly thereafter, in response to a perceived need for a ground attack aircraft a competition was encouraged among interested suppliers and the finalists appeared to be the A7G "Corsair" of LTV Corporation of the US and the French Dassault Mirage "Milan" — a follow-on version of the Mirage III with improved air-to-ground capabilities. After a lengthy competition, the GRD announced a decision to buy neither aircraft.[5] This left a void in the Swiss arsenal which was temporarily addressed by the purchase of additional Hawker Hunters.

By the early 1970s it was clear that the Swiss had reached a critical point in developing a policy to acquire modern weapon systems — particularly aircraft. While at that time the Swiss mechanical and engineering industry was widely

321

acknowledged to be of high quality, the aerospace industry was lagging far behind that of neighboring countries and also behind the other armed European neutral — Sweden. The postwar experience indicated an unwillingness on the part of the government to provide the financial support which would have been necessary to develop and sustain an advanced domestic aircraft industry with an indigenous design capability. The challenge was to obtain modern military aircraft in such a way as to acquire repair, maintenance, and modification capability for the life cycle of the weapon system and to counter the political charges that "defense francs" were leaving the country when foreign military equipment was purchased. Continued production at home under license of increasingly sophisticated aircraft in small numbers appeared no longer viable — either economically or technically.

12.2   The F-5 Case

The apparent answer was to be found in ordering foreign military equipment but requiring offset commitments as a form of additional *quid pro quo*. By 1975 the Swiss government was considering the acquisition of modern military aircraft and in June of that year agreed to buy the F-5 E/F aircraft from the Northrop Corporation of the United States through the US Defense Department under its Foreign Military Sales program. What turned out to be the first of two orders was designated Peace Alps I and comprised seventy-two aircraft. It carried an offset obligation of at least 30% of program value which was to be conducted on a "best efforts" basis with no penalties for failure to meet the target percentage. A relatively brief and simple Memorandum of Understanding (MOU) was signed by the defense ministers of the two countries in early July of 1975. The document was designed to set the framework for the offset commitment which was to be borne essentially by the principal contractors, Northrop and General Electric (GE), with a back-up role for the US Department of Defense. The Department of Defense also agreed to (a) waive the cost of import duties in evaluating solicitations from Swiss industry and provide duty-free entry certificates, (b) give special consideration to Swiss industry tenders to bid on a competitive basis, (c) seriously attempt to have technical data necessary for production made available to Swiss contractors at reasonable cost, (d) ensure that necessary export licenses for the preparation of bid packages were made available and (e) provide a waiver of US buy national laws and rules.

In turn, the Swiss Federal Military Department agreed to aid Swiss firms in making their capabilities and products known to possible American buyers, in coordinating the efforts of Swiss industry in responding to US offers, and in accommodating US requirements for handling classified information.

The agreement was effective for eight years and provided for monitoring by project officers of progress toward meeting the objectives of the MOU on at least an annual basis. In addition, government and industry representatives from both sides were to meet every two years to review progress as well. Of particular importance was the portion of Paragraph 3 that provided for US Department of Defense augmentation of industry efforts to meet offset commitments if it appeared that private efforts alone would fail to meet offset goals by the expiration of the MOU.

During the first several years of the project, progress toward meeting offset commitments was slow. This was a common complaint in Switzerland expressed by government and industry officials. In retrospect observers on both sides agree that a combination of inexperience and naivete contributed to the early delays and disappointments. The main US contractors, Northrop and General Electric, were still learning their way through the offset maze and still trying to identify Swiss firms whose cost and quality characteristics made them attractive partners in offset ventures. In addition, in a series of cautionary observations, GE warned that it would take a long time to develop the toolings and skilled labor necessary to qualify Swiss firms to participate in producing engine parts.

Many Swiss firms, on the other hand, initially called upon US firms with a "here I am" attitude, expecting an order to be forthcoming almost automatically on the grounds of their nationality. There was also a rather widespread belief in Swiss industry that the Pentagon would direct subcontracts to Swiss firms. Thus, disappointments were frequently encountered by such firms unaware that their offers had to meet stringent quality and price standards, and that their managements must demonstrate a willingness to compete for contracts.

Swiss industry, not surprisingly, found the paperwork associated with selling to the US military confusing and burdensome. Some Swiss government officials also complain that US government procurement personnel and industry purchasing agents were not aware of the waiving of the Buy American Act by the US — Swiss Memorandum of Understanding. An early lesson learned was that each Swiss bid had to bear the statement "Entitled to Buy American Act Waiver". The Swiss fought to have the MOU published in the US *Defense Acquisition Regulations*. Swiss firms unsuccessful in their quest for orders from American contractors occasionally complained to the GRD and to the press with stories of unfair competition and protectionism.[6]

Much time was spent in steering committee meetings with representatives of Swiss industry determining the nature of the offset package and identifying those firms which would participate in the program. A central role was played by the trade association known by the initials of its German name — VSM, the Union of Swiss Machine Industries, which initially monitored offsets for the GRD. The Swiss pressed for emphasis on aerospace work. In the past many smaller subcontractors had survived largely by manufacturing foreign aircraft under license. Since the F-5 was not to be produced under license, the survival of such firms was felt to depend upon their receipt of offset work. However, after detailed surveys of Swiss industry by the principal contractors, it was concluded that major participation by such firms in the direct production of the F-5 or its engines was not a viable option. Final assembly was to be conducted by the Swiss Federal Aircraft Factory (F+W) at Emmen and this consisted of the bulk of *direct* offsets on the aircraft. Thus, purchases of Swiss products from non-aerospace manufacturing industries would count in fulfillment of the offset commitment.

Even though *indirect* offsets (sales by Swiss firms not involving the F-5 aircraft) dominated in the F-5 project — accounting for approximately 85–90% of the offset commitment — to qualify for offset credit, the sales had to be made by Swiss firms which either were involved in defense work or could be. Thus, the sale of commercial items by a Swiss firm with a defense division was viewed as strengthening the entire firm and hence qualified for offset credit. The focus was not to increase the general welfare of Switzerland through reductions in unemployment (usually very low) or improvements in the balance of payments but rather upon assisting firms that would have received the orders had the weapon system been produced in Switzerland.[7] Such firms could become producers of items the Swiss military department would buy in the future. A paper by a one-time Swiss Armaments Chief emphasized that protection of the defense industrial base was a major goal of the offset program.[8] This is further indicated by the exclusion of such service industries as banking, insurance, and tourism from the list of Swiss industries with which transactions would count toward fulfilling offset obligations. High ranking GRD officials have described their offset policy as "armament policy, not economic policy" and as an "alternative method of pursuing goals of self sufficiency and maintaining readiness." (private conversation).

Another consideration in the MOU dealt with the issue of "additionality" or "causality". Thus Paragraph 4 (B) noted that in any computation of offset credits, "the primary test will be a mutual accord as to whether or not a given sale occurred as a result of efforts arising from this offset agreement." In the words of a high ranking Swiss Defense official, "We don't want to rebaptize established business relations as offsets. Some foreign firms look like archaeologists trying to find ancient transactions with Switzerland ..." which might quality for offset credits.

It is interesting to note that while ultimately both General Electric and Northrop were successful in meeting their offset obligations, the methods employed reflected the basic differences between the two firms. General Electric is a much larger and diversified company of which the GE engine division is only a relatively small part (accounting for under 10% of total corporate sales during the Peace Alps period). Thus GE was able to meet almost all of its offset commitments within the parent corporation. Northrop, on the other hand, was forced to go out to F-5 subcontractors on several tiers as well as to recruit assistance from outside the F-5 project entirely in order to fulfill its commitments. Such efforts were successful and Northrop amassed an impressive record in providing marketing assistance to Swiss firms. Northrop's marketing skills and influence aided the sale of Swiss light aircraft abroad. However, in aircraft and related sales, self-imposed limitations by the Swiss occasionally caused a problem. In furtherance of Swiss neutrality, substantial legal obstacles existed to the export of military equipment. This led to a continual problem of defining what objects qualified as "military". Light trainer aircraft could be armed and transformed into light ground attack aircraft. GE originally considered having Swiss firms machine turbine blades but encountered obstacles because of its inability to meet a Swiss government requirement for certificates of end use to ensure that Swiss-made parts didn't end up as part of lethal systems in areas of conflict. While this requirement was subsequently eased, provision of parts and equipment for third country sales which were such a significant part of the offset success in the F-16 deal with Belgium, Netherlands, Norway, and Denmark were thus largely ruled out by Swiss law.

Despite such obstacles, Northrop demonstrated creative approaches to meeting its offset commitments. It went to some lengths to spread awareness of the quality of Swiss equipment and materials. For example, it purchased Swiss machine tools to demonstrate their high quality and installed Swiss roofing materials on Northrop buildings. During the later years of the project, Northrop also facilitated a three-way trade among firms in Switzerland, Spain and Australia in partial fulfillment of its offset commitments to the latter two countries under the terms of their F-18 purchases.

Offset officials at Northrop noted the importance of viewing offsets as more than a device to serve the customer's purposes, and recognizing that they can serve the seller's strategic interests as well. Both Northrop and GE continued their dealings with Swiss firms after the completion of their formal commitments under the Peace Alps programs. Officials of both firms explain that a major reason for such transactions was their discovery of reliable suppliers in Switzerland.[9]

As noted above, however, the F-5 offset program was slow in gaining momentum and the US Defense Department found itself obliged to intervene to insure that the official offset commitment was attained. In part this involved expanded direct purchases and attempts to encourage other US Government acquisitions of Swiss products. Substantial frustration resulted from head-on encounters with trade restrictions other than the Buy American Act (See note 10). This contributed to a Pentagon decision to abandon this increasingly awkward role. On May 4, 1978, Deputy Secretary of Defense Charles Duncan signed a memorandum which effectively placed full responsibility for meeting any further offset commitment upon the US firm which had agreed to such conditions, removing the US government from any back-up role. This significant change in US offset policy was a direct consequence of the Swiss F-5 Program.

In October of 1980 an Amendment to the earlier Memorandum of Understanding was signed by the Defense Secretaries of the two counties providing for the purchase by the Swiss of "approximately 40 F-5 aircraft over and above that quantity covered by the basic ... MOU." The actual number of additional F-5 aircraft acquired was thirty eight. Paragraph 2 of the Amendment described its purpose as extending "the period of time during which Swiss industry will be allowed to compete with US industries for DoD contracts," with reciprocal access to Swiss Government defense contracting by US industry.

Paragraph 5 implicitly recognized the impact of the Duncan Memorandum. While the US Government commitments agreed upon under the original MOU would continue for the time period originally specified — eight years — no additional obligations would apply to the US Government in attaining additional offset goals associated with the subsequent F-5 purchases. However, the US Department of Defense agreed, upon the completion of its obligations under the basic MOU, to continue to provide the five trade-opening provisions originally accepted, albeit on a case-by-case basis (waiver of cost of import duties in evaluating defense solicitations, provision of technical data to Swiss contractors at reasonable cost, provision of export licenses, provision of duty-free certificates, and provision of waivers of buy national and balance of payments restrictions).[10]

The amendment, although signed in October 1980, was not to become effective until July 1983. It would remain in effect for four years — until mid-1987. This second purchase of F-5 aircraft became known as Peace Alps II. Of particular interest is the fact that this amendment to the original MOU dealt only with governmental responsibilities with no mention of particular firms or offset obligations. Such specific details were contained in separate agreements between the Swiss Government and the major contractors — Northrop and General Electric. The offset goal was raised to fifty per cent and a penalty for failure to meet the goal, liquidated damages, was included in the Northrop agreement. The penalty became moot as the offset goal was over-achieved. Indirect offsets also dominated transactions during Peace Alps II and their industrial distribution is shown in Table 1. F+W (Emmen) remained responsible for the bulk of assembly operations. Some components for the F-5 continued to be manufactured in Switzerland and there was some buyback of parts for the US Air Force T-38 trainer.

Table 1: Industrial Distribution of Indirect Offsets Received by Swiss Firms During Peace Alps II

	Percent
Aerospace	48
Machinery and Machine Tools	24
Precision Instruments and Tools	8
Electronics	4
All Others	16
Total	100

Source: Swiss Embassy, Washington, DC

Summary statistics of orders received in Switzerland under the F-5 offset program are presented in the Table 2. Data are presented separately for both parts of the Peace Alps Program and by principal source of such orders: Northrop, General Electric, and the US Department of Defense. Of interest is the decline in the US Defense Department's share of total offsets from 35.4 per cent in Peace Alps I to 10.9 per cent in Peace Alps II. To some extent this is a reflection of the influence of the Duncan memorandum of 1978 which was in full effect during Peace Alps II. On the other hand it should be noted that while

Table 2: Status of Orders at Program Conclusion in June 1987
Swiss Offset Program — Peace Alps I & II*

	Department of Defense	General Electric	Northrop Corporation	Total US$
Peace Alps I Status at conclusion, July 1983	77,747,712	48,385,427	93,634,573	219,767,712
Peace Alps II Status at conclusion, June 1987	33,309,574	62,072,225	210,088,483	305,470,237
Total for Peace Alps I & II	111,057,286	110,457,652	303,723,011	525,237,949

Source: Swiss Embassy, Washington, DC

* For purposes of comparison, the contract values in current dollars for the Swiss purchases were $340 million for Peace Alps I and $280 million for Peace Alps II. These figures do not include the value of missiles and spare parts which were purchased later.

this rule eliminated DoD's role as guarantor of offset commitments by private firms it did not prohibit continued purchases from abroad by DoD when such purchases were viewed as beneficial to US national security. Thus the $33.3 million of DoD purchases from Swiss industry during Peace Alps II fall into that category and represented orders to Swiss industries which were eligible for offset credit.

In retrospect, the Swiss F-5 deal appears to have had some unmistakably positive aspects. Switzerland was able to continue the modernization of its Air Force while Swiss financial goals were attained and US and other foreign firms became more aware of the capability and quality of Swiss industry. The F-5 offset deal also led to economies of experience which facilitated the negotiations and organization of the subsequent Swiss purchase of the US McDonnell-Douglas F-18 military aircraft, in which Northrop and General Electric also play significant roles. It clearly advanced Swiss technology. Thus, Pilatus established a numerical control facility as part of the F-5 offset program which later received forgings from Northrop to machine for the F-18, prior to the Swiss decision to purchase the F-18. Such work was banked as offset credits for the subsequent project. The Swiss are also still producing rudders and elevators for F-5s sold under the Pentagon's Foreign Military Sales (FMS) program. There are still substantial numbers of F-5s flying in the air fleets of many countries and the Swiss are one of the few sources of parts for those aircraft. This puts such Swiss producers in a potentially attractive position. Also, as noted earlier, Swiss aeroengine firms have had an active role in producing parts for the GE CFM-56 passenger jet engine. Technological spinoffs into Swiss industry can also be seen as contributing to the possibility that Swiss firms may participate more actively in joint European projects as Switzerland moves closer to the European Community.

A retrospective view of the F-5 transaction, however, shows mixed results within Swiss industry. Producers of major defense systems are seen by knowledgeable observers as having profited little. However, many firms producing parts for US defense goods profited well. Their employment grew and they were able to establish and maintain a presence in the US market as they broadened their clientele. Swiss producers of machine tools, instruments and parts also did quite well. However, Swiss observers note that such successes were temporary as they led to US Congressional retaliation via the establishment of additional nontariff barriers. Swiss machine tool producers have been frequent targets of such actions.

While there are some Swiss firms disappointed in their experience under the F-5 project, the Swiss government has used offsets since 1976 reflecting the view that offsets have, on balance been beneficial for Switzerland. In the words of an official of the GRD "offsets are still a politically effective tool in keeping Swiss defense appropriations flowing and they helped the F-18 project receive parliamentary and popular approval."

This same official noted that there were losers during the F-5 project both in the US and Switzerland but that such firms were unable to prove their competitiveness. In his opinion winning Swiss firms did not underbid or "dump" but rather won on price and performance criteria. US contractors benefited from uncovering high quality suppliers previously unknown to them. Thus, GE purchased twenty 5-axis Swiss milling machines and claimed that "they had never seen such quality ... with reworking cut from 20% to 2%."

Concerning the F-5 as a weapon system, Swiss defense officials insist that they knew what they were buying when they decided to acquire it and they are very happy with it. In no sense is the F-5 viewed as a "lemon." Informed GRD officials point out that the F-5 was less expensive than the newer and more capable F-16 and that some saw the possible acquisition of the F-16 (then becoming a standard aircraft among smaller NATO member countries) as beset with political obstacles growing out of Swiss neutrality policy. Should the Swiss become interested in a midlife upgrading of their F-5 aircraft, several options are available to them. For example, Northrop has developed a series of upgrades to the F-5 aircraft that improve its avionics capabilities and alter its cockpit to mimic that of the F-16. This system of improvements converts the F-5 into a lead-in trainer for the F-16. A Canadian firm, Bristol Aerospace, has developed similar F-5 upgrades that alter its cockpit to resemble that of the F-18. This serves as a lead-in trainer for the Canadian CF-18 and ostensibly could play a similar role in the Swiss transition from the F-5 to the F-18.[11]

12.3   Swiss Offset Policy

The most commonly encountered view of offsets among traditional economic theorists is negative. The typical explanation for such hostility is the belief that since offsets most often change the results that would be encountered in an environment of free markets, they must therefore be trade diverting and welfare reducing. Swiss economists are not unlike their colleagues elsewhere in this respect — especially in such Swiss government departments as Commerce and Treasury. Such departments, however, have little influence in weapons acquisitions. Thus, as an official of the GRD put it, "Commerce disapproves of offsets and they can stand back with clean hands while we must dirty ours in actually dealing with offsets." On theoretical grounds, Swiss defense officials emphasize the absence of competitive markets for advanced weapon systems and doubt the wisdom of denying themselves access to measures which they believe will strengthen the nation's defense.

Consequently procurement executives in the GRD have been instructed by the Minister of Defense "to insist on full economic compensation of funds spent abroad for major military equipment.[12] This compensation may be accomplished via direct participation (licensed production or co-production), or indirect participation which enables Swiss firms to sell their products and services to defense contractors and the US Department of Defense for work unrelated to the weapon system being acquired by Switzerland. While other rigid rules don't dictate the precise form of the compensation (offset), all major weapon system purchases by Switzerland since 1976 have been so compensated.[13] With few exceptions most Swiss military work is performed in military divisions of firms also producing civil products. Thus, even indirect offsets of a non-military character may still help sustain firms which constitute part of the Swiss mobilization and industrial base.

A former Swiss Armament Chief has identified the benefits of licensed production or co-production as follows:

"— simultaneous training of maintenance personnel during final assembly of equipment in Switzerland
 — acquisition of production technology and skills
 — upgrade and retrofit capability
 — in-country spare parts and logistics support
 — maintenance of mobilization base
 — reduced dependence on foreign sources
 — Swiss industry involvement and employment"[14]

The Swiss goal in indirect participation or offsets is to gain equal access to foreign procurement offices and to contracts for goods and services not directly related to the military products being purchased by the Swiss. Here the objective is to obtain entry into new markets abroad for firms in the Swiss mobilization and industrial base. Agreements in the offset context are often aimed at penetrating markets previously protected by company or government imposed restrictions and barriers such as "buy national" laws. In the Swiss case the most frequent forms of indirect offsets have been the purchase of Swiss goods, provision of marketing assistance to Swiss firms, licensing of technology, R&D collaboration and various forms of training.[15]

Following the successful conclusion of the F-5 project in 1987 the two governments negotiated a new Memorandum of Understanding which took effect on November 1, 1988. This MOU provides for mutual access to the defense markets of each party together with a waiver of "buy national" preferences and import duties for military products. The agreement has been extended several times and its current expiration date is December 31, 1997. A continuing source of frustration to the Swiss has been the continued application of US statutory and regulatory restrictions on DoD procurement that are not subject to the waiver. These restrictions on the foreign sourcing of specific products such as precision instruments, hand and machine tools, forgings, castings, and precision elements have denied opportunities to Swiss industry.[16] While the Swiss have sold some military products to the Pentagon, one that appeared to represent a significant penetration of the US defense market, the Air Defense and Anti-Tank System (ADATS) which the US Army had selected for use in its Forward Area Air Defense System (FAADS) was subsequently cancelled, ostensibly for technical reasons.

Of particular interest is a sentence in the Amendment to the MOU which extended it to the end of calendar year 1997. This Amendment, which became effective February 5, 1990, states that:

"The Governments agree to discuss measures to limit the adverse effects of offsets on the defense industrial base of each country."

This language is responsive to section 82J(C)(2) of the National Defense Authorization Act, Fiscal Year (FY) 1989 (102 Stat. 1918) as amended by the similar act for FY's 1990 and 1991 approved November 29, 1989. The actual act reads as follows:

"In negotiating or renegotiation of any memorandum of understanding between the United States and one or more foreign countries relating to reciprocal procurement of defense equipment and supplies or research and development, the President shall make every effort to achieve an agreement with the country or countries concerned that would limit the adverse effects that offset arrangements have on the defense industrial base of the United States ..."

A former US Executive Branch official concerned with offsets has described this congressional requirement as "absurd" since a) "who could possibly sign up to the last clause," and b) "such instructions violate separation of powers and are known to be frivolous by the authors who use such to get in digs which can later be used politically because the public isn't that sophisticated." In fact, there have been no discussions between the Swiss and US governments over the "adverse effects of offsets" since the parties have perceived no such effects. This is a good example of how the Executive Branch finesses an unenforceable instruction.

12.4   Swiss Parliamentary Attitudes Toward Offsets

The use of offsets has been accepted by the Parliament despite the belief that offset arrangements add to the cost of weapons compared to the option of buying from the supplier on an off-the-shelf basis. The aforementioned presumed advantages have convinced the Swiss Parliament that a cost premium of ten per cent or less on direct offsets (coproduction) is a reasonable price to pay for a well-designed offset program. If the premium exceeds ten per cent, the deal must be evaluated on a case-by-case basis. This informal rule of thumb policy has been in effect since Peace Alps II and it was operative in the more recent Swiss decision to purchase the US F-18 military aircraft under terms of a 100 per cent offset agreement.

Nevertheless, an impartial observer of the operation of the 10% rule must add some *caveats*. A nagging question concerns the accuracy of the cost estimates. For example, much of the assembly work is done at the Federal Aircraft Factory at Emmen which employs some seven hundred employees. There exists at least the possibility of "creative accounting" which might keep the reported increment of costs over those of an off-the-shelf purchase below the 10 per cent level. This point is not raised to suggest deliberate distortion but rather to emphasize the complexities of applying anything approaching a precise form of benefit-cost analysis to offsets. Hartley, calling upon public choice theory reminds us that "Government decisions are likely to be the result of actions by various agents and interest groups in the political market, acting in their own self-interest and seeking to influence policy in their favour."[17] Recognition of this fact explains why knowledgeable US observers have characterized much that transpires in the offset area as "smoke and mirrors."

12.5   Current Swiss Offset Policy

The 10% cost differential rule of thumb still applies as a criterion on direct offsets (coproduction). Thus the Swiss recognize that offsets are not "free." Offsets now are firmly implanted in Swiss military procurement and there is little chance of their being abandoned anytime soon. The prevailing view is that they provide a unique means to attain important Swiss armament objectives.

The Swiss have raised minimum contract values below which they will not insist on offsets. Thus, while earlier all contracts valued at more than 10 million Swiss francs required offset provisions now that requirement no longer applies to purchases below 50 million francs. This change in policy was made in the early 1990s and was motivated by the goal of reducing the burden of administrative costs on relatively small contracts.

The procedure for accounting for offsets has also been changed to ease the administration of offset programs. Thus, previously the Swiss government contacted Swiss firms subsequent to the receipt of a claim from a US (foreign) company to confirm a transaction eligible for offset credit. Now Swiss firms must sign a statement attesting to the fact that a foreign purchase was made as part of an offset deal.

Another change deals with the required offset percentage of contract value. As noted previously, the offset goal increased from 30% during Peace Alps I to 50% in Peace Alps II. In the current F-18 project the offset goal has been established at 100%. As a GRD official observed, "The going offset percentage has been increasingly climbing and we Swiss didn't wish to be left behind."

Endnotes

1. Sources of material in this section consist essentially of interviews conducted among government, industry, and trade association officials in the United States and Switzerland and with Swiss diplomatic representatives in the United States. The meetings in Switzerland were held in May 1977 and the more recent ones in May of 1989 and 1991. The author wishes to acknowledge his gratitude for the generous and frank comments of all the participants — Swiss and American. For a variety of reasons, maintaining the anonymity of sources is the standard approach in this type of paper. However, the depth of knowledge in this area of one person and his apparent unlimited patience and willingness to share it demands recognition. I refer to Werner Kaelin, representative of the Defense Technology and Procurement Agency at the Swiss Embassy in Washington, whose generous assistance is gratefully acknowledged. Any remaining errors of fact or interpretation are the complete responsibility of the author.

2. Many of the problems with the Mirage III resulted from an over-ambitious effort by the Swiss to integrate a Hughes Aircraft avionics system and "Falcon" missile system into an adequate French aircraft, which was not designed to operate with such systems.

3. Anticipated program costs for the Mirage III grew from approximately 43–48 million Swiss Francs in 1961 to 356 million francs in 1964. Schwartzenberger, Oats, **Operation Zero: Switzerland Searches for a Combat Aircraft**, p. 5. The English translation of the Moser book (see notes 4 and 5) was privately reproduced in 1973.

4. The information in the text on the number of Mirage III aircraft acquired and the establishment of the GRD are taken from an English translation of Moser's book, by a then-LTV official, Schwartzenberger, *op. cit.*, pp. 5 and 9.

5. This surprising decision is analyzed in a book by a Swiss journalist, Moser, Sepp, **Operation Null:Die Schweiz Sucht ein Kampfflugzeug**. Zurich: Flamberg-Verlag, 1973. Apparently the highest ranking officers of the Swiss military were unable to heal a split over the mission and capabilities which the new aircraft was expected to perform and meet. The Corsair A-7 was a subsonic ground attack aircraft while high ranking Swiss officers were arguing for the acquisition of a supersonic fighter. Other factors also contributed to the infamous "null" decision.

6. The flames were fueled when the major Swiss producer of power plant equipment, Brown-Boveri, originally low bidder to supply electric drives for components in the Clinch River, Tennessee power generating plant of the Tennessee Valley Authority saw its victory rapidly disappear when the director of the Energy Research and Development Administration awarded the contract to GE. The Swiss claim that US officials estimated an excessively high cost escalation rate for Brown-Boveri; added US customs duties; and a 6% per cent penalty under the terms of the Buy American Act in order to drive the total Swiss price above the GE bid. More than sixteen years later this event is still brought forward as an example of US duplicity.

7. Thus, the Swiss government provided financial aid to the aircraft firm Pilatus as it invested in heavy milling machines and numerical control machine technology. In addition, near the conclusion of Peace Alps I and through the remainder of the subsequently expanded F-5 project, Swiss aeroengine firms produced parts for the GE CFM-56 engine used on the Boeing 737 passenger aircraft.

8. Wittlin, Felix M., **"Swiss Industry Participation in Foreign Arms Procurement,"** *NATO'S Sixteen Nations*, Special Edition on Common Defense, 1989, pp. 71–73.

9. However, the likelihood that the Swiss would continue their aircraft modernization efforts and their willingness to "bank" some fraction of such purchases toward future offset commitments probably also contributed to continued US purchases following the completion of offset commitments under the F-5 Program.

10. It should be noted that "buy national preferences" in the United States affect government purchases only and operate much like a tariff. This preference traces to the Buy American Act of 1933. The Defense Department has adopted a policy under the Act of giving a fifty per cent preference margin to domestic producers while other government agencies offer a six per cent preference to American suppliers (or twelve per cent if the item is produced

by a "small" firm). However, a large number of outright restrictions and prohibitions on the purchase of foreign goods and components by defense agencies now exist. (For a recent study of such trade barriers, see *The Impact of Buy American Restrictions Affecting Defense Procurement, A Report to the United States Congress by the Secretary of Defense* (Washington: Department of Defense, July 1989)). The impact of waivers of Buy American Preferences such as those continued in the US-Swiss Memoranda of Understanding on such restrictions and prohibitions is not unequivocal.

11. Dornheim, Michael A., "**F-5 Cockpit Mimics F-16 with Northrop Upgrades**," *Aviation Week and Space Technology*, Vol. 139, No. 22 (November 29, 1993), pp. 56–57.

12. Wittlin, *op. cit.*, p. 72.

13. *Ibid.*

14. *Ibid.*

15. *Ibid.*

16. *Ibid.*, p. 73.

17. Hartley, Keith, **The Economics of Defence Policy**, London: Brasseys, UK, 1991, p. 62.

Chapter 13

The UK Experience with Offsets[1]

Stephen Martin and Keith Hartley
Centre for Defence Economics
University of York, York, UK

13.1 Introduction

Although not unique, the UK's experience of offsets is unusual. The UK is a substantial exporter of arms and thus domestic manufacturers frequently incur offset obligations when selling overseas. The UK also imports defence equipment, largely but not exclusively from the US, and typically invites offset proposals from potential suppliers. British industry is thus in the unusual position of both giving and receiving substantial amounts of offset work, and this duality makes the UK an attractive subject for a case study of the impact of offsets. Most other countries are typically importers of defence equipment and thus only receive offset work. The US is different again being largely a seller of arms and thus only gives offset work.

In the US, both sub-contractors and labour unions have claimed that offsets reduce domestic employment opportunities, transfer technologies, and create potential competitors in world markets.[2] These claims have led to calls for Congress to limit the amount of offset work that US firms can offer. Conversely, recipients of offset work in many countries often claim that such work would have been won by domestic manufacturers anyway, that it is invariably low technology (metal-bashing) print to order work, and that it does little to enhance domestic technological capabilities and thus the economy's international competitiveness. Given that UK manufacturers both give and receive offsets, their experience offers a rare opportunity to compare the alleged effects of offsets.

However, the UK has a substantial indigenous defence manufacturing capability and this might colour the attitude of UK industry towards offsets. In many countries, without such an extensive indigenous capability, the procurement choice will usually be between alternative imported systems, each with its own offset. Because such imports bring work for domestic firms, offsets are seen as a 'good thing'. In the UK, the availability of a domestic product means that the procurement choice is often wider, and that the choice is either the domestic option or an import with offset. In these circumstances, the offset option, because it typically means less work for UK manufacturers than that brought about by the domestic product, might be seen as a 'bad thing'. Thus firms in countries with similar offset requirements might still have very different attitudes to offsets depending on the level of indigenous capability.

There are very few economic evaluations of offset programs, not least because of the considerable problems associated with such an exercise. First, there is little, if any, routinely published data. Hence the analyst is reliant on the goodwill of those in industry and government to discuss such matters. Second, offsets are big business and are thus commercially sensitive. In an era of high unemployment, vote conscious governments are sensitive to the charge of spending large amounts of tax-payers' money on products that generate few domestic jobs. One response to this is to cite the number of jobs created by offset work. Nevertheless, governments remain vulnerable to criticism of the efficacy of their offsets policy which is thus a politically sensitive issue. Third, those involved with offsets in both industry and government have vested interests. Consequently, it is sometimes difficult to disentangle fact from fiction.

This last problem can, to some extent, be ameliorated by comparing the impact of incoming and outgoing offset work. Given that the same firms will be both receiving and giving offset work, and assuming that offset requirements do not vary widely from one country to another, then it is to be anticipated that, say, the employment and technology effects should be similar for both types of offset. From the analyst's point of view, the major advantage of the fact that UK industry both gives and receives offset work is that it permits such a comparison to be made.

The purpose of this chapter is to outline the major issues associated with offset, as seen from a UK perspective, and to review the relevant evidence. Given these findings, likely future policy developments are discussed.

13.2   The Defence Committee's Investigation into the Boeing Offset Agreement

In the 1970s, with the growth of unemployment and the ever-increasing costliness of defence equipment, purchasers sought domestic industrial benefits when buying off-the-shelf, foreign designed equipment. By the end of the decade, the UK had a similar policy and the first purchase to attract an offset was the Harpoon missile. However, until the mid-1980s, UK purchases with offset were relatively small and attracted little public attention. In 1986–8, however, the UK Government simultaneously awarded a $1,1500 million contract to Boeing for the supply of seven airborne warning and control system (AWACS) aircraft and cancelled the troubled rival indigenous Nimrod project. To reduce the adverse impact on the UK's defence industrial base of such a decision, Boeing had offered a 100% offset and claimed that this would lead to 40,000 man years of work for British industry spread over a five-year period. The MoD broadly agreed with Boeing's claim, believing that the job losses resulting from the cancellation of the Nimrod project would be equalled, if not exceeded, by job gains from the offset. When the contract was finally signed the offset was to be 130% of the purchase price, to be fulfilled over an eight-year period.

The existence of an offset commitment to the UK by a foreign contractor does not guarantee that orders will be placed with UK firms. The aim is to get UK firms onto the bidders list which, in the large US market, is viewed as a substantial benefit, as adequate competitions can often be run between internal suppliers without the need to consider potential European sources (ie the offset is a way of entering the US market). However, UK firms will only win the order if their product is competitive in terms of price, quality and delivery.

To be eligible as offset, the MoD requires that the work must meet a number of criteria:

a. it should consist of orders for defence products and services, or orders for high technology products for civil application

b. it should be 'new' work, placed as a result of the offset agreement and consist of products not previously purchased, products purchased from new suppliers, or represent a significant increment to existing levels of business

c. the work should contain as large a proportion of high technology orders as possible which encourage UK companies to consolidate and advance their capabilities, broaden their product base or improve their competitiveness; and

d. that orders should be placed over a period not exceeding that of the delivery of the foreign contractor's equipment.

However, in 1988 press reports about the Boeing offset alleged:

a. that low technology work was being counted as offset;

b. that some of the offset work would have been placed with UK contractors irrespective of the offset agreement ie it was not new work generated by the offset; and

c. that the volume of offset work was lower than anticipated and that, as a result, few jobs were being created and/or sustained.

These claims prompted an investigation of the workings of the AWACS offset agreement by the Parliamentary Defence Committee. They took evidence from Boeing, UK industry, and the MoD, and their report provides one of the few detailed investigations of the impact of any offset.[3]

13.2.1 New Work

The requirement that offset work should be new work, generated by the offset, is a particularly difficult one to enforce as it would seem impossible to judge whether industry would have won a contract without the offset agreement. This difficulty is exacerbated by the fact that Boeing annually places large amounts of work with UK suppliers e.g. in 1987 Boeing placed contracts worth almost $1 billion with British industry. Thus, there quickly emerged the issue of whether follow-on contracts should be offset eligible. MoD agreed that 60% of the value of purchases involving follow-on work to contracts that Boeing had placed with UK suppliers before 6 November 1988 (the date Boeing submitted its best and final offer price for the AWACS aircraft) could be counted as offset credit. The Defence Committee commented that there was a strong argument for disallowing these contracts as offset credits and considered the imposition of a 40% discount as extremely favourable to Boeing. Certainly, both the Society of British Aerospace Companies and the Defence Manufacturers Association thought that much offset approved work was not new business.

13.2.2 High Technology

Work meets the MoD's technology requirement if it is of a similar technological standard to that contained in the AWACS. Clearly, there will be some low technology work on AWACS (e.g. aircraft galleys) and thus contracts for the supply of similar items will be acceptable towards the offset. Indeed, such work would be needed for Nimrod. However, the Defence Committee expressed the hope that such low technology work should not come to constitute a significant proportion of approved offset work.

The AWACS offset agreement permitted contracts for work on new Boeing commercial aircraft to count as offset credit and, in particular, for 35% of the value of any purchase of Rolls-Royce engines to be counted towards the fulfilment of Boeing's offset obligation up to a maximum of $800 million. The Defence Committee made two points about this. First, that this permitted over one-half of the offset obligation to be met by the purchase of civil aerospace products when the offset was designed to compensate defence manufacturers for the cancellation of Nimrod. Second, that the purchase of Rolls-Royce engines to go in civil aircraft is not in the gift of Boeing (as the airline selects the engines it requires) and, therefore, considerable doubt is cast on the idea that these purchases occurred as a result of the offset.

When negotiating the offset agreement with Boeing, the MoD wanted as much work as possible to be on the AWACS system itself. Such work would be the equivalent, in terms of quality, of the high technology work lost on the

Nimrod project. However, the scope for Boeing to offer such direct offset work was limited because the AWACS aircraft was already in production and most of the AWACS supplier sources were already well established. Thus most of the offset (about 95%) was necessarily indirect which, the MoD argued, was not a matter of concern providing that it meets the necessary offset criteria.

13.2.3 Job Implications

Boeing's offset obligation was financial, and its fulfilment was measured in terms of the value of approved offset work; the agreement does not set a target for jobs to be created. However, the apparent potential of the offset programme to provide at least as many jobs as would be lost in the cancellation of the Nimrod programme was a strong argument in favour of the Government's decision to purchase the AWACS system. The Defence Committee commented that it should therefore have been an important test of the effectiveness of the offset programme that it created the expected employment. Initially, the MoD made no attempt to monitor the number of jobs created. However, the Defence Export Services Organisation (DESO), which administers UK offset policy, did remedy this after the Defence Committee expressed surprise that monitoring had not been undertaken from the beginning of the offset programme.

Based on company responses, the estimated UK employment benefits of the AWACS offset programme are summarised in Table 1. Admittedly, the employment figures are based on the period July 1988 to December 1990 and omit the periods from November 1986 to June 1988 and from January 1991 to May 1992. Nevertheless, two aspects of the results are interesting. First, 38% of the respondents claimed no employment impacts. Second, since the start of the job monitoring exercise, the net number of jobs sustained is 1279 and the net number of jobs created is 113, a grand net total of 1392 jobs (in those companies that responded to the survey). If the figures in Table 1 are expressed in job years and are adjusted to allow for non-respondents, the maximum total of jobs sustained and created is 2151 job years. These data cover 30 months of the AWACS offset although the full programme lasted 67 months. Grossing up the figure of 2151 job years so that it relates to all 67 months of the programme yields a figure of 4804 job years. Even using the higher figures, the actual numbers are considerably below the original Boeing claim of 40,000 man years of work over 5 years (equivalent to some 20,000 man years over the 2.5 years of the job monitoring exercise). However, an MoD statistical analysis of the offset orders showed a total of 37,500 man years of work sustained in UK industry — a figure close to the Boeing estimates.[4] The substantial discrepancy between the Boeing/MoD estimates and the company responses (in Table 1) remains to be explained and

Table 1: Employment Impacts of the AWACS Offsets

Period	No. of companies consulted	No. of non-responses	No. of companies claiming no effect	No. of companies saying job sustained	No. of companies saying job created	Total number jobs sustained [1]	Total number of jobs created
July–Dec 1988	107	25	30	45	7	790	12[2]
Jan–June 1989	108	28	33	40	7	536	6[2]
July–Dec 1989	106	22	34	42	8	698	97
Jan–June 1990	67	10	17	35	5	573	4[2]
July–Dec 1990	56	9	19	27	1	706	0
Overall response	444	21%	38%	54%	8%	1279	113

Notes:
(1) Each total contains the same 500 jobs at one company plus the same 6 jobs at two other companies: hence net number is 1279.
(2) Each of these totals contains the same 3 jobs created at one company: hence the net number of jobs created is 113

Source: HCP 218.[6]

casts doubts on the claimed employment benefits of the offset programme. Possible explanations include the discrepancy between jobs and man-years estimates, the difficulty which companies encounter in trying to estimate employment impacts, the need to ensure that all estimates are for full-time equivalents, and the reliability of company responses. Alternatively, the difference could reflect the fact that the MoD counted a too high a proportion of offset sales as new business, whereas companies believed that new business was only a fraction of the total offset. One expert believed that genuinely new business was typically 25% to 40% of an offset, with a maximum of 50%. MoD's position is to claim that the success of offset agreements can only be measured in financial terms.[5]

13.3   Other Studies of UK Offsets

It is against this background that the authors undertook two studies of offsets.[7] The first focused on offsets associated with UK imports of defence equipment, while the second examined the impact of offsets when UK firms exported their products. With regard to the first study, DESO supplied details of the 18 leading UK companies which had undertaken most of the offset eligible work since the mid-1980s. These companies were approached at the end of 1992 and a questionnaire was used as the basis for a semi-structured interview about the impact of offsets. Four of the firms were part of the same company and a single response covered the group's activities. Another firm returned three copies of the questionnaire, with each response reflecting the experience of a different business within that company. Three firms declined to participate in the study and another three firms could find no trace of having undertaken offset work (despite being on the MoD/DESO list of companies)! This yielded 10 completed questionnaires for analysis.

Although the sample is small in terms of the number of firms interviewed, these companies accounted for just over 88% of the gross output of the UK's aerospace industry in 1991. Moreover, given that these firms have undertaken most of the offset work, one might, if anything, anticipate a biased response in favour of the policy. In the absence of any data, the survey approach is the only method of obtaining insights into offsets and testing hypotheses about new business, profitability, technology, etc.

Before outlining the survey results, the reader might find it useful to know how the MoD executes its offset policy. The foreign prime contractor (e.g. Boeing) will submit to DESO the values and dates of purchase orders that it has placed with UK firms and which it wishes to claim towards its offset obligation. DESO will then write to the UK firm and ask it to verify this information. DESO will also enquire whether the contract:

a. introduces new technologies or enhances the firm's competitiveness;
b. represents new business or a significant increment to existing business;
c. involves high or low technologies; and
d. involves civil or defence work and, if the former, whether the technology involved could be said to be of benefit to the defence field.

Depending on the respondents answers to these questions, DESO will allow anything between zero and 100% of the amount claimed by the foreign firm. If the latter is dissatisfied with the outcome of this process, it can re-submit contracts for approval and negotiate with DESO over the amount allowable. Ultimately, however, DESO's decision is final. One consequence of this procedure is that UK firms, as distinct from the prime contractor, will not know for certain which contracts are actually counted by MoD as offset work although they will, of course, know which contracts are being claimed towards an offset obligation. This lack of information only serves to increase the difficulty of ascertaining the impact of UK offset policy.

13.4 Survey Results

The survey asked questions about bidding for and undertaking offset work, the importance of offset work to firms, its profitability, the reasons for their success in obtaining offset work, and the benefits of offsets. Initially, questions were asked about bidding for and obtaining offset work. Table 2 presents a summary of firms' responses to these questions. The large disparity in the size of the firms responding to the questionnaire presents a problem. If one simply looks at the number of firms giving the same response to a question then this will tend to give more weight to the (larger number of) small firms in the sample. Alternatively, if one weights each firm's response by its share of aerospace output then this will give more weight to the (relatively few) large firms. The compromise adopted is to report both indicators for each question.

Half of the respondents had been knowingly invited to bid for offset work and the same firms had knowingly bid for such work. However, nine of the ten

Table 2: Survey Responses About Bidding for and Obtaining Offset Work

	Yes		No	
	Number of responses	Output of UK aerospace industry (%) in 1991	Number of responses	Output of UK aerospace industry (%) in 1991
Has your firm ever knowingly been invited to bid for offset work?	5	61	5	39
Has your firm ever knowingly bid for offset work?	5	61	5	39
When bidding for work, do you always know whether the purchaser will claim it towards an offset obligation?	1	<1	9	>99
Has your firm ever undertaken work which the buyer claimed towards an offset obligation?	8	>99	2	<1

respondents did not always know whether the purchaser would claim contracts for which it had bid as offset work. Of these respondents, two of the small firms believed that they had not undertaken any work which the buyer claimed as offset.

Firms were asked to indicate the percentage of their turnover in 1991 that was offset work. Responses varied from less than 1% to 35% and these are summarised in Table 3. As the Table indicates, there is a considerable difference between the responses of small and large firms. For all five small firms, offset work accounted for over 5% of turnover yet for the large firms this figure was, in all cases, less than 5%.

Offset contracts might be more profitable than other work if UK firms, knowing that foreign suppliers have to meet an offset obligation, seek to capitalise on this by slightly increasing their profit margins. Alternatively, UK firms might cut their profit margins on offset work as a way of entering the sizeable US market. However, all respondents reported that offset work was equally as profitable as other work.

Four firms had undertaken direct offset work for Boeing on the AWACS, two had done work for McDonnell Douglas on the Harpoon missile, and one had done work for Boeing on the Chinook update. A very small proportion of firms' offset sales involved items to be included directly in the equipment which gave rise to the offset obligation. Four firms (accounting for over 60% of UK aerospace output in 1991) reported that this figure was less than 5% and another two (accounting for over 20% of industry output) said that it was zero. Two firms did not know what this figure was likely to be.

Firms were asked to rank, in order of importance (from 1 = most important to 5 = least important), five reasons why the respondent thought that foreign firms placed offset work with them. Table 4 summarises these responses. Here, we were interested in the effect of the purchaser's offset obligation. One (albeit large) firm put the purchaser's offset obligation as the most important reason.

Table 3: The Importance of Offset Work to Firms

Offset work in 1991 as percentage of turnover	Number of respondents	Output of UK aerospace industry 1991 (%)
<1	2	78
1–5	1	19
5–10	2	1
10–15	2	1
>15	1	1

Four firms thought that the offset obligation was the least important reason. Five of the eight firms cited their product quality as the most important reason why foreign firms placed offset work with them. To obtain an overall indicator of the importance of the offset obligation, an average ranking for each reason is reported in the penultimate column. This gives equal weight to all firms' responses and confirms the impression that the offset obligation is the least important reason why UK firms won offset contracts. Of course, it is possible to argue that the rankings of large firms should be given greater weight than those of smaller firms and hence the average ranking reported in the last column of Table 4 weights each firms' ranking by its share of total aerospace output. As a result, the offset obligation becomes a much more significant reason why UK firms won offset work.

Respondents were also asked to estimate the percentage of their offset eligible sales that they believe they would have won in the absence of the purchaser's offset obligation. There are obvious problems of bias in such a question. Six firms responded that they would have won all of these sales, one firm did not have any idea, and another, one of the large firms, believed that it would not have won any of these sales.

Six firms thought that none of their offset work had brought new technology into the firm. One firm was unable to give a figure but thought it to be minimal. Another firm thought it small and certainly less than 5% of all their offset eligible sales. We also interviewed a US firm that was awarding offset work to UK industry. This US respondent argued that it was placing R&D work with UK firms but only those who were willing to accept fixed-price contracts. This

Table 4: UK firms' beliefs about why foreign firms placed offset work with them

| Reason why foreign firm placed offset work with UK company | Frequency with which reason achieved ranking | | | | | | average | |
	1	2	3	4	5	n/a	a	b
Because of:								
the purchaser's offset obligation	1	—	1	2	4	—	4.0	2.6
the price of your product	3	2	2	—	1	—	2.3	2.4
the quality of your product	5	2	—	—	1	—	1.8	3.2
work you already do for the buyer	3	1	—	1	2	1	2.7	3.2
other reasons	3	1	—	—	1	3	2.0	1.6

Note: See text for details of how the average ranking for each reason was calculated.

respondent said that UK sub-contractors could not expect cost-plus R&D contracts when it, the prime contractor, had committed itself to supply goods to its clients on the basis of a fixed price contract.

Another criticism of offset work is that it is typically of short-duration ceasing on completion of the American firm's offset obligation (not least because the firm might have offset obligations elsewhere and thus needs to transfer work out of the UK). Conversely, the work might continue if the US buyer is seeking to bank offset credits in the anticipation of incurring an obligation in the UK at some later date. One (small) firm said that follow-on work had been generated and four other firms (three of them small) expected the work to continue with or without the offset. One small firm said that the work was only short-term. One of the large firms was unable to offer an opinion while another said that direct offset work was short term whereas indirect offset was not.

Another benefit claimed for offsets is that it can improve the competitiveness of those undertaking such work. This might come about through a contract to develop a new product or through winning work which involves the installation of new production techniques. Alternatively, such sales, particularly in the large US market, might increase learning economies and thus reduce unit production costs. On all three counts, the competitiveness of the UK firm would be improved. However, we found it difficult to find any substantial evidence to support these claims. Six firms said that offset sales had not improved their competitiveness while one, a large firm, said that any improvement to their competitiveness had been small.

Overall, these results offer a broader picture of offsets than that coming from the Defence Committee's report. Nevertheless, the underlying message is very similar. Although offsets do appear to offer some benefits, UK industry believes that these are quantitatively quite small and certainly appear to fall far short of the massive benefits which one might have anticipated from a $1.5 billion programme of new work. This is confirmed when one recalls that the firms in the survey were those who (according to MoD) had benefited most from offset work. This is not to say that offsets *per se* do not work; rather that current policy does not achieve all that it might. This is a theme that we return to later.

Of course, it is always possible that firms will be responding to enquiries about incoming offset work strategically; that is, responding in a such a way as to achieve the desired policy response. One way to analyze this possibility is to examine whether outgoing offset work has a similar, but opposite, impact on UK industry to incoming work. This prompted the dispatch of a questionnaire to all 49 members of the British Defence Manufacturers Offset Group (BDMOG) in early 1993. Responses covering 35 of these members were received. Two respondents declined to participate in the study and in five cases a single response covered more than one member (eg different divisions within the same firm were members of the BDMOG). This yielded 26 responses and, of these, two further firms were also excluded from the analysis as one was not involved in defence markets while another produced solely for the UK market. Thus the final result was 24 questionnaires for analysis from firms who accounted for almost 90% of UK defence exports in 1991.

As Table 5 reveals, the 24 survey responses came from a variety of firms whose defence exports in 1991 ranged from zero to goods and services worth hundreds of millions of pounds. Of these 24 firms, 12 had been a contractor for a military export sale that had involved an offset since 1 January 1985 and 7 had been a sub-contractor assisting a prime contractor to fulfil its overseas offset obligation since 1 January 1985. Larger firms are more likely to been involved with offset, both as a contractor and as a sub-contractor assisting another firm to meet its offset obligations.

Those (12) firms that had, since 1985, exported defence equipment involving an offset were asked to supply details about any one of these export sales which the respondent considered to be typical of exports with an offset. One firm was unable to supply the detailed information which we required. Of the 11 sales for which details were supplied, 8 were for aerospace products and all of the contracts were signed between 1986 and 1992. The contract values ranged from £2 million to £350 million, with a contract duration ranging from 6 months to 10 years. The average contract value was £64 million and had a mean duration of just over 4 years. The value of the offset associated with these contracts ranged from £0.7 million to £200 million and the time allowed for its

Table 5: Size Distribution of Survey Respondents

Value of defence exports in 1991 (£m)	Number of respondents to survey	Number of firms that have been:	
		contractor for military export with offset since 1985	sub-contractor assisting prime with offset since 1985
0–10	9	1	1
10–20	4	3	—
20–40	2	2	1
40–80	2	—	—
80–160	2	1	—
160–320	2	2	2
over 320	3	3	3
Total	24	12	7

fulfilment ranged from 18 months to 10 years. The average offset value was £41.5 million and just over 5 years was allowed for its fulfilment.

To examine whether UK jobs were being exported in order to meet offset obligations, respondents were asked to estimate the number of additional employee-years of work that would have been generated by the sale for the firm's domestic operations in the absence of any offset requirement. Seven firms replied that the offset would have no impact on the volume of work. The other estimates ranged from a loss of 50 to 350 employee-years with the total loss being some 626 employee-years. In other words, whilst the value of offsets was relatively large (over £640 million), the adverse employment impacts were trivial.

Concern has also been expressed by sub-contractors in the US that primes attempt to meet their offset obligations not by transferring work from their own factories but by taking work from their sub-contractors and placing this with firms in the country where the offset obligation has been incurred. Clearly, offset obligations can be met from a variety of sources (eg prime/sub-contractors, domestically or overseas) and respondents were asked to indicate the approximate percentage of the offset obligation which was expected to have been met by these different sources. Table 6 details the responses to this question.

Table 6: Who Fulfils the Offset?

| | Percentage of offset obligation met by: | | | | |
| | Vendor's operations | | Vendor's sub-contractors | | |
Offset	Domestic	Overseas	Domestic	Overseas	Other firms
1	5	0	5	0	90
2a	75	25	0	0	0
2b	50	25	15	10	0
3	100	0	0	0	0
4	0	0	100	0	0
5	5	0	95	95	0
6	100	0	0	0	0
7	100	0	0	0	0
8	100	0	0	0	0
9	100	0	0	0	0
10	5	0	7	88	0
11	0	100	0	0	0

Note: the figures for 2a relate to the specific offset under discussion. However, in the opinion of the respondent this is atypical of offsets and thus the data for 2b relate to offsets in general as far as this firm is concerned.

Five of the respondents indicated that their domestic operations would be meeting all of the offset obligation. Three respondents suggested that it would largely be met by their sub-contractors while another claimed that the offset obligation would be met neither by themselves nor by their subcontractors but by other firms. Using one firm's estimate that one employee-year would be taken from its UK sub-contractors for every £70,000 worth of offset, then the offsets associated with the 11 export sales in this study will cost UK sub-contractors some 479 employee-years of work. Adding this figure to the number of employee-years of work taken from the vendor's own factories, yields a total loss to British industry of some 1105 employee-years of work. This is hardly a staggering figure when it is recalled that the total value of offsets for the sample is some £456 million! Moreover, such job losses can be viewed as part of the price of obtaining export business which, in turn, supports employment in the UK (i.e. UK firms would not have obtained the foreign order without an offset package).

As Table 7 demonstrates, offsets can be met in a number of ways and the actual method chosen will often depend on the type of economy where work

Table 7: How is the Offset Obligation Met?

	Percentage of offset obligation met by:						
Offset	Co-production	Licensed production	sub-contractor production	overseas investment	technology transfer	counter-purchase	other
1	5	5	20	5	5	60	0
2a	0	0	0	70	5	25	0
2b	0	20	40	0	5	35	0
3	0	0	0	0	20	80	0
4	0	50	0	0	50	0	0
5	0	0	100	0	0	0	0
6	20	0	80	0	0	—	70
7	0	0	10	0	20	0	0
8	0	0	100	0	0	0	0
9	0	0	0	0	100	0	0
11	0	0	24	0	0	76	
All	2	3	16	36	7	33	2

Notes:
(i)   The figures for offset 2a relate to the specific offset under discussion. However, the respondent argued that this is atypical of offsets in general and the data for 2b relate to offsets in general;
(ii) The omission of data for offset 10 is because the respondent was unable to answer this question.

has to be placed. For example, it will be easier to provide production work for the aerospace industry in those countries with a well developed industrial base. Conversely, overseas investment and counterpurchase might be the only way of fulfilling an obligation if the purchaser's economy is predominantly agricultural and/or based on oil. Of the total offset obligations (£403.3 million), overseas investment and counterpurchase each provided about one-third of the total offset requirement, although the fact that overseas investment was only used in one other offset (and even in this case only accounted for 5% of the obligation) suggests that the sample data might exaggerate its importance.

Concern has also been expressed that offsets can play an important role in eroding the international competitiveness of a domestic industry by transferring technology and know-how to foreign companies who then proceed to compete with the original suppliers in international defence markets. Survey respondents were asked whether the offset had led to, or was expected to lead to, any technology transfer. Seven firms replied affirmatively and one further firm said that, although no technology transfer was associated with the offset under discussion, offsets did typically lead to such transfers. These eight respondents were asked whether this transfer of technology had improved, or was likely to improve, the competitiveness of the respondent's rivals and five firms replied affirmatively. Two of largest firms both replied in the negative — one pointed out that where possible it was yesterday's technology which would be transferred or that if it was to be current technology the firm would seek to retain control of it by establishing a joint venture company in the foreign country in which it had a majority stake.

Evidence was also sought on two further areas of controversy in the offset literature. One of the supposed benefits for firms with an offset obligation is that through the need to place work with firms in the foreign economy it will discover new, lower cost, sources of supply. However, recipients of offset work have claimed that it is typically short-term work and that once a prime contractor has fulfilled its offset obligations it will transfer such work elsewhere — perhaps to a firm in another country where it has outstanding offset obligations.

In six of the eleven offset sales the respondents said that the offset obligation had led to the discovery of new, lower cost, sources of supply and in all six cases the intention was to continue to do business with new sources once the offset obligation had been fulfilled. Respondents pointed out that offset work was likely to be short term when the supplier was uncompetitive but the purchaser needed to place work there to fulfil the offset obligation.

The results of these two surveys suggest that incoming and outgoing offset work have broadly similar albeit opposite impacts. As far as exports are concerned it would seem that offsets are having only a minimal impact on UK employment levels despite the substantial sums involved. Similarly, although there are substantial sums of incoming offset work, the impact on domestic employment levels is also surprisingly low. There appears to be relatively little technology transfer and neither types of offset seems to have any significant impact on the international competitiveness of the UK economy. Both the surveys and the Defence Committee's report give the impression that although from a financial perspective offsets often involve significant sums, in terms of jobs, technology and international competitiveness, their impact is considerably smaller. The fact that outgoing offset work is having little detrimental effect on the UK economy will be welcome news, although the corollary of this, that incoming work is having little positive impact, will be of more concern.

13.5 Implications for Policy

It is not difficult to reconcile the size of the AWACS offset with its relatively small impact on the real economy reported by British firms. First, Rolls-Royce is unlikely to believe that it sold civil aero-engines to foreign airlines as a result of Boeing's offset obligation. However, Boeing was able to count up to $800 million worth of civil engines towards its offset obligation. Second, Boeing was able to count 60% of follow-on work for contracts placed prior to purchase of AWACS towards its offset obligation. Again, British industry, with good reason, might well have considered that such work would have been won irrespective of the offset and thus would not include the employment effects of this work in their survey responses.

It is unlikely that any future vendor of equipment to the MoD would be able to count aero-engines or follow-on work against its offset obligation. Of course, it might well be that the Rolls-Royce engines were allowable against Boeing's obligation in order to boost the size of the offset and thus make the cancellation of the UK's own Nimrod programme more politically acceptable. Apart from the aero-engines and follow-on work issues, respondents expressed concern about UK offset policy. Although there was a general dislike of offsets and support for the Government's position of discouraging the use of offset as an instrument of defence procurement, firms argued that a stronger offset policy was necessary to ensure that British industry was not disadvantaged by the practices of other countries towards non-indigenous procurement. Respondents wanted a 'level playing-field' and there was a feeling that the MoD should require offsets from all countries which demand offset from UK industry.

Particular criticism was made of the fact that the UK did not normally seek offset from WEAG countries and yet these countries invariably required offsets when purchasing from UK manufacturers: Table 8 outlines some of the WEAG

Table 8: Examples of WEAG offset requirements

Nation	Offset requirement
Belgium	Mandatory 100% of contract value; high technology work
Denmark	Mandatory 100% of contract value; defence related and work of similar technology to that of the product purchased.
Netherlands	Mandatory 100% of contract value; to be direct offset and of similar technology to product purchased.
Norway	Mandatory 100% of contract value; work to be of similar technology to that of product purchased with penalties for non-performance.
Portugal	Mandatory 100% of contract value and 60% to be defence industry related. Penalties for non-performance.
Spain	Expected 100% of contract value. Work to be of similar technology to goods purchased.

Source: Survey respondents.

nations' current offset demands. Firms also argued that the MoD's value threshold (£10 million) should be considerably lowered and that, like other nations, UK policy should include penalties for non-performance. One respondent pointed out that the MoD had placed a series of contracts over a matter of months with a firm in one of the WEAG states. Each contract was just under the threshold but together they totalled a sum far in excess of £10 million. The survey respondent had recently made a sale to the same WEAG country and, as a consequence, had incurred an offset obligation which was of a similar value to that of this country's sales to the MoD. Whereas the UK firm now had to place work in the overseas country, the foreign vendor of equipment to the MoD was under no such obligation to place work in the UK.

Finally, there is the issue of the cost of an offset compared with an off-the-shelf purchase and who pays this premium. Typically, defence ministries (including the UK MoD) insist that no premium is paid for the offset. However, the cost and price premia reported by respondents to the survey of UK exporters (see Table 9), suggest that offsets are not costless and that typically the buyer bears most of this cost. If similar cost and price premia apply to UK imports with offset, a sensible way to proceed would seem to be to seek a number of quotes from any potential foreign vendor, reflecting various offset levels e.g. at 0%, 50% 100% and 150%.[8]

Table 9: Cost and Price Premiums Imposed by Offsets (Compared with an Off-the Shelf Sale)

Firm number	Contract value (£m)	Cost premium associated with offset (%)	Percentage of cost premium added to contract price
1	120	>0	100
2	350	8	100
3	2	60	100
4	30	15	100
5	23	5	100
6	50	35	0
7	18	?	?
8	4.5	0	n/a
9	19	3.5	0
10	52.6	0	n/a
11	38	3	100
Mean	64.3	14.4	75
Median	30	5	100

13.6 Conclusion

Despite the difficulties associated with research into offsets, the picture to emerge from this chapter is a coherent one. Although large financial sums are often involved, the real impact of offsets, in terms of jobs, technology and international competitiveness, is likely to be much smaller. For the UK as an exporter of defence equipment this is, obviously, a reassuring finding. However, as a potential importer with offset, it casts doubt on the ability of current offset policy to compensate UK industry, in anything other than a most marginal way, for the purchase of a foreign system in preference to a domestic option. Moreover, there is a clear disparity between the UK's offset require-ments and those imposed on UK suppliers by WEAG states. This suggests that a review of policy might be timely. Moreover, any such review could consider the implications of the fact that offsets are not costless and hence that, for future defence purchases, various quotes might be sought reflecting different levels of offset.

Endnotes

1. This chapter resulted from a research project funded by the ESRC (grant No. R000233146). The authors are grateful to all those who contributed to the surveys.

2. OMB, **Impact of Offsets in Defense-Related Exports**. Office of Management and Budget, Executive Office of the President, Washington DC, 1987 and OMB, **Offsets in military exports**. Office of Management and Budget, Executive Office of the President, Washington DC, 1990.

3. HCP 286, **The Working of the AWACS Offset Agreement**. House of Commons, Defence Committee. London: HMSO, 1989.

4. HCP 394, **Statement on the Defence Estimates 1991**. House of Commons, Defence Committee, London : HMSO, 1991, p. 61.

5. HCP 218, **Statement on the Defence Estimates 1992**. House of Commons, Defence Committee, London : HMSO, 1992, p. 19.

6. *Ibid.*

7. For full details see Martin S. and Hartley K., UK Firms' Experience and Perceptions of Defence Offsets, **Defence and Peace Economics**, 1995, forthcoming and Martin S. and Hartley K., Defence Equipment, Exports and Offsets: The UK Experience. **Defense Analysis**, 1995, forthcoming.

8. Hall P. and Markowski S., On the normality and abnormality of offset obligations, **Defence and Peace Economics**, 1994, vol. 5, no.3, pp. 173–188.

Chapter 14

US Offset Policy

Bernard Udis and Keith E. Maskus
Department of Economics
University of Colorado at Boulder, USA

14.1 Introduction

In this paper we review in detail the evolution of US offset policy. While this history is complicated it may be characterized broadly by two observations. First, the United States, through the activities of its defense contractors, is largely in the role of offset provider because its firms are net international suppliers of military systems. This means that the US government has not had to develop much in the way of an offset policy covering its own defense procurement, though we argue that there is such a policy in implicit terms. More importantly, US policy has been aimed at regulating international conditions for providing offsets and at either helping or not interfering with American firms. Second, there is significant uncertainty, even in theoretical terms, about whether foreign offset demands have damaged US military, economic, or political interests. This fact has led to an ambivalent US policy, which might fairly be described as benign, albeit somewhat confused, neglect. We describe how political concerns are mounting in the United States about offsets, suggesting that additional efforts will be mounted to place restrictions on their use.

14.2 Background and Definitions

A significant problem in the economic analysis of offsets and the establishment of national policies to deal with them, derives from the breadth of current definitions. The meaning of the term has varied during the post-World War II period and while the mechanisms have remained largely unchanged, their goals and purposes have varied widely.

Thus, through the 1950s the United States was

> ... not overly concerned with economic interests vis-à-vis its European allies ... nor was the United States particularly concerned with the economic costs incurred in maintaining forces in Europe. Indeed the US balance-of-payments deficit on military account was considered yet another positive mechanism of assisting European recovery. Rather the United States urged its NATO allies to expand their military forces as *their* contribution to the Atlantic Alliance and provided more than $10 billion in military grant aid (through the Military Assistance Program) to assist them in this task. (italics added)[1]

In other cases the recipients paid for the equipment.

The primary motivation for such weapons transfers was to assist in providing a counter to any possible Soviet thrust into Western Europe. The same objective underlay US aid for the restoration of European defense industry. In furtherance of this objective, by the late 1950s direct transfers of military equipment were being replaced by licensed production of American weapons. Early candidates for such licensed production included the F-86 and F-104 fighters, the M113 Armored Personnel Carrier, and several utility helicopters.

Joel Johnson has described this period as one with significant and long-lived implications for the US.[2] This production assistance program was administered in the Defense Department by an office which reported to the Undersecretary for International Security Affairs. First identified as the Office of Programming and Control it later became the Office of Military Assistance. It evolved further into the current Defense Security Assistance Agency in 1971. Its function was to help allies secure and/or produce weapons for their defense, "not to sell American products".[3] Johnson also explains the early role of US defense firm officials involved in these programs as assisting the Europeans in assimilating US weapons and technology. He sees this as establishing a mind set which became fixed in the subsequent outlook of US firms toward Europe.

By 1960, economic conditions had changed. European prosperity was widespread and the US was facing a balance-of-payments deficit. President Kennedy put forth a 14 point program in 1961 designed to correct the situation. One of his recommendations called for efforts to reverse the imbalance in US military outlays abroad by urging financially capable allies to buy newer US weapons.[4] According to Bare, this proposal had two objectives: force improvement for military purposes, and reduction of the US payments deficit through larger purchases of weapons from the United States.[5]

In July, 1961 the US and West Germany signed the first of seven so-called "offset" agreements, designed to minimize the impact on the American balance-of-payments of maintaining US military forces in Germany. German procurements from the US offset roughly 80 per cent of the balance-of-payments costs of maintaining US forces in Germany.[6]

The similarity of these earlier measures to current offset practices is emphasized by such additional measures as:

... increased non-military government procurement in the United States, special financing agreements for some of these purchases and for the loans, establishment of a fund to promote German investment in the United States and, in the 1972–1973 agreement, German financing of a program to rehabilitate troop facilities used by American forces in the FRG (Federal Republic of Germany). This last measure introduced a new concept to the agreement — budgetary relief.[7]

By the late-1960s and early 1970s a subtle change had occurred in the approach of European governments toward acquiring American weapon systems. Objectives began to appear in addition to the acquisition of attractive equipment well designed to meet defense needs. Such additional objectives included:

- the economizing of scarce foreign exchange to protect a nation's balance-of-payments position;
- technology transfer to the buying industry or perhaps more broadly diffused throughout industry in the buying country;
- investment by the seller in the industry of the buying nation, and perhaps the buyback of some of the output resulting from the investment; and
- the provision of an argument to counter political complaints that domestic tax revenues leak out of the country if it orders military equipment from abroad, thus benefiting foreign industry, and workers.

Two important early cases of US offset sales occurred in 1975; the purchase by Switzerland of F-5 military aircraft from Northrop, and the purchase by a consortium of Belgium, the Netherlands, Norway, and Denmark of the F-16 fighter from General Dynamics. These two transactions were among the first major sales of US military equipment linked to offset obligations and they had significant implications on future US offset policy. While the US government was involved in both transactions, there was a significant difference in the role which the US government agreed to play in the two cases. Specifically in the Swiss F-5 case, the US Department of Defense agreed to act as guarantor for the offset commitments entered into by the major US prime contractors — Northrop and General Electric. Thus, if these two firms were unable to successfully complete their offset obligations under the contract (initially set at 30 per cent) within the life of the contract — originally set at eight years, the US Defense Department agreed to enter and take action to make up the difference. No such government role was envisioned in the F-16 sale to the four smaller NATO states.

The F-5 offset program in Switzerland was slow in gaining momentum and the US Defense Department found itself obliged to intervene to insure that the official offset commitment was attained. In part, this involved expanded direct purchases and attempts to encourage the acquisition of Swiss products by other US government agencies. Substantial frustration resulted from direct encounters with trade restrictions other than the Buy American Act.[8] This contributed to a Pentagon decision to abandon what had become an increasingly awkward role. On May 4, 1978, Deputy Secretary of Defense, Charles Duncan, signed a memorandum which effectively placed full responsibility for meeting any further offset commitments on the US firm which had agreed to such conditions, removing the US government from any back-up role. This significant change in US offset policy was a direct consequence of the Swiss F-5 program.

Through the late-1970s and 1980s the incidence and magnitude of offset goals both grew and in the spring of 1994, offset goals set at 100 per cent or more of the purchase price were not unusual.

14.3 Recent Developments Regarding Offsets in Equipment Sales[9]

Recent US offset policy, (or perhaps, more accurately, offset history since a coherent policy doesn't exist), has been marked by numerous statements critical of the phenomenon by economists in the Departments of Treasury and Commerce, and by a small number of members of Congress. The former oppose offsets on theoretical grounds as constituting impediments to competitive markets and therefore leading to trade distortion and welfare reduction. The latter usually express concern for the economic interests of firms and employees in their districts or states. They believe these firms or employees pay the costs of production work being transferred abroad, or suffer "spoiling" of their markets when US prime contractors agree to buy from foreign suppliers (in the case of indirect offsets).

Efforts to limit or abolish offsets have been frustrated by a troublesome fact of life: the lack of jurisdiction by the US Congress over the behavior of foreign firms and foreign governments. American firms competing with foreign firms for orders outside the United States would be placed at a severe competitive disadvantage if prohibited by US law from offering offset deals while their competitors experience no such limitations. This leads to the anomalous condition of US prime contractors resisting ostensible offers of help from their government.

14.3.1 Reporting Requirements

With very few exceptions, the product of US offset policy consists of a series of reports on the economic effects on the US economy of offsets awarded in military exports and/or several reports on negotiations concerning such offsets. Section 309 of the Defense Production Action (DPA) of 1950 (50 U.S.C. 2099) as amended in 1984 (P.L. 98-265) and 1986 (P.L. 99-441), required a series of annual reports on offsets in military exports. In response to this law, a group of documents containing interesting and valuable information was issued annually from 1986 through 1990. They were produced by an inter-agency group chaired by the Office of Management and Budget. In addition to tracing domestic and international developments in the area of defense offsets, they include case studies of US military aircraft and missile sales to other countries.[10]

This Act expired on October 10, 1990 and with it, the requirement for the report. Thereafter, the Act was twice revived and allowed to expire, and finally revived again on October 29, 1992, retroactive to March 1, 1992. While considerations other than offsets played more significant roles in this strange sequence of expirations and recoveries, when the DPA returned, so did the offset reporting requirement — but with interesting differences. Now the Secretary of Commerce was designated as (1) responsible for the preparation of the report, and (2) responsible to function as the President's Executive Agent for carrying out the requirements of Section 309. It should be noted that this shifted the responsibility for the preparation of the annual report on the impact of offsets away from the Office of Management and Budget which had aroused the ire of Congressional critics with its conclusions that the impact of offsets on the US economy and defense technology base had been relatively minor.

In addition, the revised DPA charged the Secretary of Commerce with the responsibility to issue regulations covering the reporting on offsets agreed to in sales of defense items by US firms to foreign buyers. During the subsequent eighteen months, neither the requisite Executive Order nor the regulations concerning industry reporting on offset agreements required of the Commerce Department had appeared. Finally, on April 26, 1994 the **Federal Register** carried proposed regulations to cover the "new" reporting requirements. They were put forward by the Bureau of Export Administration of the US Department of Commerce and provided a 30-day submission period for written comments from interested parties.[11] This long delay in a response from Commerce in meeting its obligations suggests that offset matters do not represent a high priority of the Clinton Administration. A reluctance on the part of the Administration to undertake actions which might threaten export sales in the high technology area may explain this foot-dragging on possible restrictions on offset sales.

Section 825 of the National Defense Authorization Act for fiscal year 1989, as amended by the similar acts for fiscal years 1990 and 1991, contains a requirement that whenever a US firm contracts to sell weapons systems or other defense-related items abroad, and the offset deal exceeds $50,000,000, the firm must notify the Secretary of Defense of the proposed sale in accordance with regulations to be prescribed by the Secretary of Defense in consultation with the Secretary of Commerce. (This paragraph is identified as Section S2505 (c) of Chapter 148 of Title 10, US Code, as amended by Sections 821 and 824.)

No such regulations have ever been prescribed. In the words of a former executive branch official associated with offset matters, DoD has simply "stonewalled" on this issue, arguing that this information probably will be reported in any event when firms apply for licenses to ship arms under the terms of export control regulations or when foreign governments arrange to purchase armaments under the Foreign Military Sales (FMS) program of the Defense Security Agency. It might be added that such information may also be collected under the terms of the new "Feingold Amendment," which is discussed below.

14.3.2 Efforts to Control Offsets

Despite the suggestions in the initial OMB reports that offsets have had limited impacts on the US economy, many in Congress and in some Executive Departments remain unpersuaded. The Congressional language in Section 825 of the National Defense Authorization Act, fiscal year 1989 (Public Law 100-48; 102 Stat. 1517) made it clear that concern was growing among legislators that the use of offsets threatened US technology loss, economic costs, and potentially weakened the US defense industrial base. Section 825 mandated a series of reports (published in 1990, 1991, and 1992 and very much abbreviated compared to the economic impact reports previously mentioned) that present information on the progress of negotiations concerning offsets in military exports. The President was directed to initiate negotiations with offset-demanding countries purchasing defense equipment from the United States to secure an agreement to limit the "adverse effects" of such offsets on the respective defense industrial bases of each country. Further, in negotiating or renegotiating Memoranda of Understanding which attempt to lower barriers to defense trade through the reciprocal waiver of Buy National Acts, the President was directed to make every effort to "limit the adverse effects that offset arrangements have on the defense industrial base of the United States".[12]

The United States has signed general Memoranda of Understanding with twenty-one nations. Of these, nine contain language committing the parties to consult for the purpose of limiting the "adverse effects of offsets". Four others are in the process of being negotiated while the remaining eight are more recent MOU's which have not yet come up for renegotiation. A US Defense Department official concerned with this matter noted that while discussions have, in fact, taken place with the representatives of several of the nations whose MOU's contain the above clause, they have "essentially been of the fact-finding variety". They have aimed at determining what such offset policies (if any) require and what the philosophy of the government is on the general topic of offsets. He also noted that there were also discussions on offsets with other NATO members during negotiations on the NATO Code of Conduct (see below).

Another DoD official commented that if a country has overriding political goals that are viewed as advanced by offsets, "no amount of talking by the

United States is likely to change that". Of particular interest is the effort by the Netherlands when renegotiating its MOU with the United States to add words calling for consideration of the adverse effects of "other Buy National initiatives."[13] The final agreement includes words to the effect that the two governments "intend to discuss measures to limit the adverse effects of offsets *and other regulations* on the industrial base of each country" (italics added). Apparently other countries have shown interest in similar wording.

Other portions of Section 825 called for the establishment by the President of a comprehensive offset policy in connection with contractual offset arrangements dealing with defense equipment [S2505(a)]; the protection of the US defense industrial base and the financial position of US firms from damages resulting from technology transfer to foreign countries or firms under offset arrangements [S2505(b)(1)]; the waiver of paragraph (b)(1) under certain cases of national security (b)(2); and an appeals procedure for US firms damaged by such waiver (b)(3).[14]

An Executive/Legislative Branch disagreement transpired when congressional actions in 1988 required a new presidential policy statement concerning offsets. After fifteen months, the Bush Administration released a statement on April 16, 1990 which essentially restated the Duncan Memorandum, to the effect that the US government would not fulfil the role of guarantor of offset commitments incurred by private American firms.

Although Congress is the driving force behind efforts to control offsets, there was one interesting case of the Executive Branch attempting to limit the magnitude of an offset percentage negotiated in sales efforts by US firms. In the summer of 1989 the Republic of Korea was engaged in negotiations for the purchase of a new military aircraft. The competition had narrowed to two US aircraft: the F-16 of General Dynamics and the F/A-18 of McDonnell-Douglas. While early in the negotiations, the Koreans had presented a demand for a 30 per cent offset level (their usual requirement), they later raised their demand to a level approaching 60 per cent. In addition there were signs that the heavily competing US firms might advance offers to 100 per cent. In an unprecedented and somewhat puzzling step, the acting director of the Defense Security Assistance Agency of the Department of Defense sent an identical letter to the chairmen of the two American firms, which appeared to oppose an offset level in excess of 30 per cent. In somewhat obtuse language, the letter concluded, "… we are not prepared to support a sale which includes an offset offer which exceeds the amount determined after final discussions between our two governments".[15]

This attempted intervention was justified in the letter by reference to Section 825 of the Defense Department Authorization Act of 1989. On the face of it, the government of the Republic of Korea and the two American firms acceded to the perceived message in the letter by limiting the offset level to 30 per cent. It would appear that this supported the conventional view that intervention to limit offsets could work if the competitors were of the same nationality and thus subject to the pressure of their common government. In fact the matter is more complex because the final decision of what specific items will receive offset credit and on what terms, remains in the hands of the buying state. While South Korea agreed to a 30 per cent offset level, its control of the details enabled the South Korean government, in effect, to extract a level of purchases by the seller which substantially exceeded 30 per cent. Here again one sees the futility of an attempt by a single government to control offsets.

Another American Executive Branch action relevant to the offset issue is the so-called NATO Code of Conduct. A US proposal of March 1990 called for negotiations within NATO to consider a more open alliance-wide market for weapons coupled with the gradual elimination of offsets. Not much progress has been achieved toward this objective despite the approval of a text in April 1993 by the Council of National Armaments Directors and its transmission to the North Atlantic Council for approval. In the opinion of a well-informed former US Executive Branch official, the Code of Conduct will achieve little, even if it is finally adopted, "because the words subordinate progress on the reduction of offset to achievement of other conditions that have little chance of success".[16] The same author attributes the lengthy negotiation process to the reluctance of smaller NATO members to forego the advantages of offsets on their purchases, problems associated with agreement on language covering technology retransfer, and general uncertainties concerning the future of NATO.

An analysis of US government actions on offsets since the late-1970s shows a consistent dichotomy in approach between the Congress and the Executive Branch with the latter more reluctant to intervene to restrict offsets. This divergence in attitude is clearly illustrated by a comparison of Congressional and Executive Branch "findings" on offsets. The congressional comments are contained in the National Defense Authorization Act, FY 1989, (approved September 29, 1988) as amended by the similar acts of FY1990 and 1991 (approved November 29, 1989). The following quotation is taken from Section 825(a): "Congress makes the following findings:

a. Many contracts entered into by United States firms for the supply of weapon systems or defense-related items to foreign countries and foreign firms are subject to contractual arrangements under which United States firms must agree:
    i.   to have a specified percentage of work under, or monetary amount of, the contract performed by one or more foreign firms;

ii.   to purchase a specified amount or quantity of unrelated goods or services from domestic sources of such foreign countries; or

iii. to invest a specified amount in domestic business to such foreign
countries.

Such contractual arrangements, known as 'offsets', are a component of
international trade and could have an impact on United States defense industry
opportunities in domestic and foreign markets.

b.   Some United States contractors and subcontractors may be adversely
affected by such contractual arrangements.

c.   Many contracts which provide for or are subject to offset arrangements
require, in connection with such arrangements, the transfer of United States
technology to foreign firms.

d.   The use of such transferred technology by foreign firms in conjunction with
foreign trade practices permitted under the trade policies of the countries of
such firms can give foreign firms a competitive advantage against United
States firms in world markets for products utilizing such technology.

e.   A purchase of defense equipment pursuant to an offset arrangement may
increase the cost of the defense equipment to the purchasing country and
may reduce the amount of defense equipment that a country may purchase.

f.   The exporting of defense equipment products in the United States is important to maintain the defense industrial base of the United States, lower the
unit cost of such equipment to the Department of Defense, and encourage
the standardized utilization of United States equipment by the allies of the
United States."

Such alarmist "findings" by the Congress stand in stark contrast with the
following observations in the fifth annual report by the Office of Management
and Budget on offsets in defense trade.[17]

Overall ... it is clear that military export sales, net of their associated offsets, to the extent that they
have measurable effects, result in positive impacts on the US economy as a whole and to the defense
sectors in particular.[18]

The effects of offsets on total US employment are minor. That is to say, military sales abroad with
contractually required offsets are likely to increase domestic employment by somewhat more ...
than would comparable sales without offset ... largely because offsets are a substitute for (but are
less labor intensive than) the imports that would replace them to finance the foreign sales ...

... such offsets are inefficient ... these inefficiencies, however, are reflected more in the distribution
of US employment across industries than in the level of total employment ... relative to normal
trade, offsets reduce employment in industries in which the US and the purchasing countries have a
comparative advantage and increase employment in industries in which both ... have a comparative
disadvantage ...

Independent of their effect on total US employment, the magnitude of the distortions (and therefore inefficiencies) introduced by offsets is positively related to the degree of their concentration in industries in which the US has comparative advantage.[19]

... in industrial sectors affected by defense sales and offsets, there was a very small positive net effect on total US imports and exports. There was a corresponding drop in trade in other sectors, a small appreciation of the dollar, and no net effect on the US trade balance. Instead the main effect ... was on the distribution of trade among sectors.[20]

... some of the controversy over offsets has resulted from the fear that offsets in the form of direct investment and technology transfer would lead to the creation or expansion of new industries abroad.... While this may take place from time to time, the major effect ... (is) to strengthen existing competitors and expand their markets ...[21]

The most recent instalment in this conflict began in the spring of 1994. As usual, the offset-related material is embedded in an omnibus bill hardly devoted to the topic of offsets — in this case the State Department Authorization Bill. Section 732 dealing with Reports Under the Arms Export Control Act is amended to require that:

Each such numbered certification shall contain an item indicating whether any offset agreement is proposed to be entered into in connection with such letter of offer to sell ... and a description from such contractor of any offset agreements proposed to be entered into in connection with such sale. (As enacted into law, a complete description of the offset agreement will only be required if requested by the Senate Foreign Relations Committee or the House Foreign Affairs Committee.)

No United States supplier of defense articles or services sold under this Act, nor any employee, agent, or subcontractor thereof, shall, with respect to the sale of any such defense article or defense service to a foreign country, make any incentive payments for the purpose of satisfying, in whole or in part, any offset agreement with that country.

... the civil penalty for each violation of this section may not exceed $500,000 or five times the amount of the prohibited incentive payment, whichever is greater.

It is still too early to know the full implications of these amendments, particularly how widely the prohibition on "incentive payments" will be applied. To some extent, the answer depends on the frequency of direct payments to third parties *in the United States* in order to secure offset fulfilment. If the practice is widespread such incentives may soon be shifted to beneficiaries abroad.[22] However, it is clear that for the first time, Congress has entered into regulation of the substantive side of offsets. In addition, a new group of congressional committees, those dealing with foreign relations/affairs, has been brought into the subject of offsets.

The sponsor of these amendments was Senator Russ Feingold of Wisconsin. His involvement resulted from an action taken by Northrop Corporation under its offset agreement negotiated under the terms of the F/A-18 sale to Finland.

Northrop had offered to pay part of the transportation cost involved in a proposed sale of paper-making machinery by a Finnish company (Valmet Corporation) to the International Paper Company of Selma, Alabama. According to a Northrop official, their proposed payment to a shipping company subsequently would have been charged to the Finnish government as offset administrative costs (see below) but Senator Feingold saw it as a "bribe" to the potential US buyer. After a determination by the US General Accounting Office that the deal would have been legal,[23] Senator Feingold, speaking on the floor of the Senate, described the situation as falling "between the cracks of ... the Anti-Kickback Act [and] the Foreign Corrupt Practices Act ...".[24]

The Senator's motivation is easier to understand when one learns that the Finnish firm was in competition for the Selma sale with a company in the Senator's home state of Wisconsin. The sale was finally secured by the Wisconsin firm — the Beloit Corporation subsidiary of Harnishfeger Industries — after it lowered its price for the paper-making equipment.

This case also involved an unsuccessful attempt by the Secretary of Commerce to have the Secretary of Defense consult with the Government of Finland on the matter under the terms of the bilateral Memorandum of Understanding between the United States and Finland.[25]

Another constituency in the United States is now being mobilized to oppose offsets in defense trade. This group is that which advocates strict arms control and sees offsets as a major contributor to the proliferation both of armaments and arms-making technology. An example of this position is found in the publications of the Federation of American Scientists, an essentially pacifist organization. The January/February 1994 issue of their publication "F.A.S. Public Interest Report" is devoted to this topic.[26] It is difficult to predict what success this effort will attain, but if a sufficient number of groups with their own particular dissatisfactions with offsets manage to ally themselves into a unified group whose goal is severely to limit or prohibit offsets, they may acquire sufficient political power to convert offsets into a significant domestic political issue.

In late June, 1994 a new report by the US General Accounting Office (GAO), which is Congress' investigative arm, attacked the practice of nations purchasing US weapons with American aid grants and then demanding offsets on such purchases. The study dealt with weapons trade between four nations that receive significant arms aid, Israel, Turkey, Egypt, and Greece, and their US suppliers. While the firms were not named in the report, in order to protect proprietary information, press treatments identified the likely companies as McDonnell-Douglas, General Dynamics, Lockheed, United Technologies' Pratt and Whitney engine division, and the engine division of General Electric.

The GAO study examined a sample of $11.6 billion in sales, of a total of $60 billion in US weapons sales to the four countries, over the last two decades. The required US offsets amounted to about 41 per cent of the contract amounts. While the GAO report limited itself to examining the use of offsets when a foreign nation uses US grant funds to purchase American defense goods, Representative Cardiss Collins of Illinois, chairwoman of the House Subcommittee on Commerce, Consumer Protection, and Competitiveness (of the House Energy and Commerce Committee), which requested the study, commented that offset agreements "are hurting our country and taking jobs away from the United States." A Wall Street Journal story noted that Representative Collins and her Subcommittee were "scrutinizing arms sales with an eye toward tougher limits on offsets."[27] Industry spokespersons who defend the general concept of offsets have largely opposed the demand for offsets by US aid recipients as a form of "double dipping." However, they are inclined to interpret Representative Collins' statement as a trumpet call signifying the arrival on the scene of yet another champion of domestic industry and foe of the offsets concept. This development signifies a further spread of concern over offsets among Congressional committees.

14.3.3 Change in Rules Governing the Recovery of Offset Administrative Costs

US firms incur costs in administering offset terms which they have agreed to as part of a sales contract. Historically their ability to recover such costs has hinged, in part, on the nature of the general contract. If it was negotiated as a straight commercial deal between a foreign government and an American contractor, the likelihood of recovering such costs depended upon the talent of those representing both parties during the period of the contract negotiations and the policies of the buying governments.

Buyers interested in securing US weapon systems have the option of buying under terms of the Foreign Military Sales (FMS) program of the US Department of Defense. Under this program the US government via its Defense Security Assistance Agency acts as intermediary between the foreign government and US defense contractors, purchasing the desired equipment under its own procurement regulations and then transferring it to the foreign buyer. Certain governments, particularly those with limited experience in buying sophisticated equipment, prefer to use the FMS route which ensures that the weapon systems acquired meet US military standards. While FMS rules permit producers up to a 3 per cent administrative charge, these have historically **not** included offset administrative costs as an allowable cost.

In July, 1991 a change was introduced by the Defense Department which now allowed offset administrative costs to be recovered under FMS contracts provided the Letter of Offer and Acceptance (LOA) contained a note with certain specific information. The nature of the note was carefully detailed in the regulations. It had to:

a. i.   Specifically address offsets;
    ii. Advise foreign governments that the price of contracts awarded in support of the LOA might include administrative costs associated with implementing the foreign purchaser's offset agreement with the contractor; and
    iii. Include a statement that the US government assumes no obligation to satisfy or administer the offset requirement or to bear any of the associated costs.
b. Offset administrative costs must be reasonable and readily identifiable ... and their estimated level must be included in foreign military sales pricing information provided to the foreign government as early as possible, but before submittal of the LOA.
c. Some examples of offset administrative costs —
    i.   In-house and/or purchased: organizational, administrative and technical support, including offset staffing, quality assurance, manufacturing, purchasing support; data acquisition; proposal, transaction and report preparation; broker/trading services; legal support; and similar support activities;
    ii. Off-shore operations for technical representatives and consultant activities, office operations, customer and industry interface, capability surveys;
    iii. Marketing assistance and related technical assistance, transfer of technical information and related training;
    iv. Employee travel and subsistence costs; and
    v.   Taxes and duties.[28]

After complaints by the industry and other sources, the Department of Defense issued a proposed new rule with request for public comments.[29] Industry response has been favorable.[30] In the proposed revision all references to a note in the LOA informing the foreign government that "the price of contracts awarded in support of the LOA may include administrative costs associated with implementing the foreign purchaser's offset agreement with the contractor ..." have been deleted. At the time of this writing in the late spring of 1994, the expectation among informed sources is that the proposed revision will be adopted.

14.3.4   Offset Policy on Civilian Sales

Given the spread of offset requirements into civil trade, it may be useful to note that a United States government policy on countertrade in non-military exports was developed within the Executive Branch and put forth in a guideline document on July 29, 1983. For whatever reason, this document was classified and never publicly released. However, it was summarized by the Department of Commerce in a 1992 publication, as follows:

The policy prohibits US agencies from promoting countertrade and states that, although the US Government views countertrade as generally contrary to an open free-trading system, it will not oppose participation by US companies in countertrade transactions unless such activity could have a negative impact on national security. Consistent with this policy, US agencies may provide advisory and market intelligence services to US businesses and advise US businesses that countertrade goods are subject to US trade laws, including quotas.

In addition, US agencies are to review applications for government export financing for projects containing countertrade/barter on a case-by-case basis, taking account of the distortions caused by these practices. The policy states that the United States will continue to oppose government-mandated countertrade and should consider raising its concerns about such practices with relevant governments and in multilateral fora. Finally, the policy urges US agencies to exercise caution in the use of their barter authority, reserving it for those situations that offer advantages not offered by conventional market operations.[31]

Section 2205 of the Omnibus Trade and Competitiveness Act of 1988, approved August 23, 1988, provided for:[32]

a.   the establishment by the President of an interagency group on countertrade to be chaired by the Secretary of Commerce with representatives from such departments and agencies as the President deem appropriate (In Executive Order 12661, Section 2–101, dated December 28, 1988 the President designated as members of this committee the Secretaries of Commerce, State, Defense, Treasury, Labor, Agriculture, and Energy, the Attorney General, the Administrator of the Agency for International Development, the Director of the Federal Emergency Management Agency, the US Trade Representative, and the Director of the Office of Management and Budget — or their designated representatives.)

b.   the review and evaluation of
   i.   US policy on countertrade and offsets in light of current trends in international countertrade and offsets and the impact of those trends on the US economy;
   ii.   the use of countertrade and offsets in US exports and bilateral US foreign economic assistance programs; and

iii. the need for and the feasibility of negotiations with other countries, through the Organization for Economic Cooperation and Development and other appropriate international organizations, to reach agreements on the use of countertrade and offsets; and

c. the making of recommendations to the President and Congress on the basis of the review and evaluation.

According to Eisenhour, no such reports have ever been published due to interagency disputes.[33]

Section 2205 also provided for the establishment within the International Trade Administration of the Department of Commerce of an Office of Barter whose functions were:

d. i. to monitor trends in international barter;

ii. organize and distribute information relating to international barter useful to business firms and other organizations and individuals including commercial opportunities for barter transactions beneficial to US enterprises;

iii. notify Federal agencies with operations abroad when it would be beneficial for the Federal Government to barter government-owned surplus commodities for goods and services purchased abroad by the Federal Government, and

iv. provide assistance to enterprises seeking barter and countertrade opportunities.

The Office of Barter primarily exists to provide information to US industry on barter opportunities and plays no role in the formulation of offset policy. Of some significance is the fact that it is located in a different part of the Commerce Department than the group responsible for offset reporting and weapons trade.[34]

14.4   US Military Offset Policy (as Buyer)

One informal US military procurement policy has a bearing on the offsets issue and should be noted. For years it has been a central procurement practice to require a North American source for all major weapons systems purchased by the US military. While certain American government officials insist that this is a national security matter and thus has nothing to do with offsets which they believe to be economically motivated, all do not agree.[35] The opinion of most foreign observers is that such a requirement is indistinguishable from a standard offset requirement and that the motive is irrelevant. This requirement continues to provide ammunition for those who charge the US with inconsistency when it assumes an anti-offsets stance.

14.5   US State Offset Policies

Another interesting point on offset policy in the United States relates not to the federal level of government but to the state level. Beginning at the turn of the decade, the State of Maryland began to insist that offset credit be provided to it for state purchases abroad from countries requiring offset credits on their own purchases. Maryland reserves the right to assign offset credits granted on its foreign purchases to American firms based in Maryland with the specific details to be worked out between the US firm and the supplying nation. In addition, the states of Missouri and New York have established similar programs but they are not yet fully functional. Ohio, Washington, and Arizona also are exploring the possibility of taking such action.

14.6   Assessing US Offset Policy

To this point, we have reviewed the particulars of US offset policy in substantial detail. Two outstanding characteristics of US policy emerged. First, because US defense contractors are largely suppliers of military equipment, the US government has been predominantly faced with developing a policy regarding the provision of foreign offsets. Second, in doing so the United States has displayed a marked ambivalence about the issue. On the one hand, US authorities have, in the past, worked actively to assist American firms in acquiring foreign contracts subject to offset. More recently, however, the government has preferred not to get involved heavily in setting details of how American firms compete internationally. Indeed, such a hands-off policy is consistent with the US tradition of *laissez faire*. On the other hand, there are undeniable concerns that the demands for offsets on the part of foreign procurement authorities may damage US interests in certain dimensions. Thus, the government has imposed numerous reporting requirements and has pushed for some international rationalization of offset policies. Overall, however, there is no coherent US policy on offsets.

In an important sense, of course, the absence of policy represents the choice not to intervene, thereby leaving the field largely open to foreign governments. In that context, it is interesting to assess briefly the implications of this situation for the United States. This is a complicated situation and we only touch on various issues here.[36] The main point of this review is that there is substantial uncertainty about how offsets influence American interests. This fact points to the importance of further study of both the directions and importance of the various effects.

There are four groups of issues surrounding global offsets that concern US policymakers. The first is the impact on certain American security objectives. It has been a long-standing US goal to increase interoperability of weapons systems among its allies. Offsets may tend to force subcontractors in many nations to employ technologies for producing parts that are consistent with the final weapons (e.g., fighter aircraft) of the most successful prime contractors. To the extent that this is true, there is some convergence of aircraft types and subsystems. The United States also has an interest in expanding the range of military suppliers available. It is clear that American prime contractors, through the offset process, have become increasingly aware of the significant technical capabilities of smaller firms in Western Europe and elsewhere. The subsequent introduction of these suppliers into the American procurement process has provided a greater range of choice and competition. Of course, to the extent that this has disadvantaged US subcontractors there could be increasing concerns for both military and political reasons. There seems to be little consensus of opinion in the United States about the extent of this latter effect. Finally, as a military matter, the US government may wish to limit transfer of sensitive technologies and it is conceivable that offset requirements make control of this process more difficult. The demise of COCOM (The Coordinating Committee on Multilateral Export Controls) in the Spring of 1994 will probably stir fears of technology loss. It is worth noting, however, that new export control procedures are currently under international review that may ease such concerns.

A second area of interest relates to economic objectives. In general, because the United States is primarily an offset supplier, the issues are the obverse of those detailed for offset-demanding nations.[37] The primary issue is the effect of foreign offsets on US employment. In an earlier section we reviewed the evidence put forward by the Office of Management and Budget,[38] which argued that the impact was negligible or even positive. In economic terms, OMB's arguments are sensible, because they are based on the presumption that market distortions such as offsets influence the interindustry (or interfirm) structure of employment but not the aggregate level. Moreover, at the time of OMB's latest analysis, military offset obligations that may have displaced American employment in defense contractors remained a fairly small proportion of domestic and foreign military sales. However, we note that since that time offsets have grown in frequency and magnitude and the domestic demand for military contracts has declined due to defense downsizing in the United States. It is conceivable that the sensitivity of American employment in the defense industry with respect to foreign offset demands has increased since 1990. This issue clearly bears further study.

There are other important economic objectives that may be influenced by offsets. To the extent that co-production requirements reduce output in US manufacturing facilities there may be a deleterious impact on economies of scale, raising the costs of procurement. Counterbalancing this problem are the possibilities that foreign input suppliers are more efficient than domestic ones and that foreign offsets may substitute for declining demand for military goods from the US government. Further, there may be substantial economies of scope that are generated by international operations and production sharing. Offsets likely enhance the process of international technology transfer, which is desirable from the standpoint of maximizing the return from military R&D. Some might argue that permitting technology transfers under offsets may enhance the pace of overall technology transfer, as any associated commercial technical spillovers from military technologies would be more likely to accrue to foreign countries than they would otherwise. This could represent a competitive disadvantage for US firms that would, in the absence of offsets, enjoy the fruits of the spillovers more rapidly than their international rivals.

A third general issue regards political problems from offsets. Overwhelmingly this relates to the impacts of foreign offsets on regional economic activity and employment. We have noted one such instance for a Wisconsin firm that was able to exert sufficient political pressure to win a contract that would otherwise have been lost to an offset, though the firm also had to lower its price in order to gain the order. Clearly, such problems underlie Congressional interests in placing limits on foreign offsets, as we have described.

The fourth area is perhaps least appreciated, but nonetheless potentially significant. There are concerns about the impact of offsets (and, more generally, barter and countertrade) on the international trading system. At their core, offsets should be understood as extensive forms of commercial regulation involving requirements for direct foreign investment, production, trade, and technology transfer. In that sense, offsets are in the domain of trade-related investment measures (TRIMs). Like other TRIMs, offsets must be analyzed in the decidedly second-best world of imperfect competition, scale economies, and government policy distortions. There is no clear theoretical case that TRIMs reduce economic efficiency and welfare. However, TRIMs are often so arbitrarily applied and complex that they seem almost surely to interfere with rational business decisions. Concern about this led to the inclusion of TRIMs in the Uruguay Round, where a set of disciplines has been negotiated over their use.[39] Among other things, these accords will ban the use of domestic content regulations and export performance requirements because these regulations directly distort trade. It remains to be seen whether and how offset requirements will be covered by these new disciplines.

In a related vein, substantive negotiations in the Organization for Economic Cooperation and Development and, in the near future, the new World Trade Organization will concern themselves with economic regulations that affect the conditions for competition. Elements such as antidumping procedures and anti-monopoly regulations will be scrutinized for potential harmonization and ratio-nalization. Again, offsets may be viewed as fitting squarely into this domain and procurement officials will need to keep abreast of those developments.

14.7 Conclusions

Readers of this paper who live in countries governed under the Parliamentary system may find many of the details related above somewhat puzzling. Certainly much of what appears to be continuous conflict between the Legislative and Executive branches of the US government, regardless of which party is in power, is explained by the absence of discipline within the American political system.

In addition to competition for power and influence between the several branches of government, there is a similar competition between such Executive branch agencies as the Departments of Defense and Commerce and the Office of Management and Budget. These pursuits of political influence have led to a con-fusing tangle of laws and policies which are, at the least, overlapping and con-tradictory. When the divergent interests of principal defense contractors and smaller subcontractors and other suppliers are included the stewpot boils all the more. The time is overdue for a comprehensive review of legislation, executive orders, and other regulations dealing with offset policy but such a development is unlikely without a courageous act of leadership on the part of the President and the Congress.

Endnotes

1. Bare, C. Gordon, "**Burden-Sharing in NATO: The Economics of Alliance**," Orbis, Vol. 20, No. 2, Summer 1976, p. 418.

2. Johnson, Joel L., "**The United States: Partnerships with Europe**," in Ethan B. Kapstein, ed., *Global Arms Production: Policy Dilemmas for the 1990s* (Lanham, Maryland: University Press of America), 1992, p. 107.

3. *Ibid.*, p. 108.

4. US House of Representatives, Committee on Armed Services, **US Military Commitments to Europe**, 93rd Congress, 2nd Session, 1974, p. 53.

5. Bare, *op. cit.*, p. 418.

6. *Ibid.*, p. 419.

7. *Ibid.*, p. 420.

8. It should be noted that "Buy National Preferences" in the United States affect government purchases only and operate much like a tariff. This preference traces to the Buy American Act of 1933. The Defense Department has adopted a policy under the Act of giving a 50 per cent margin to domestic producers while other government agencies offer a six per cent preference to American suppliers (or 12 per cent if the item is produced by a "small" firm). However, a large number of outright restrictions and prohibitions on the purchase of foreign goods and components by defense agencies now exist. [For a recent study of such barriers, see the United States Department of Defense, **Impact of Buy American Restrictions Affecting Defense Procurement, A Report to the United States Congress by the Secretary of Defense**, (Washington, D.C: Department of Defense, July, 1989).

9. We wish to acknowledge our debt to Mr. John Howard Eisenhour formerly of the Institute for National Strategic Studies at the National Defense University for his generous assistance in sharing his encyclopaedic knowledge of the evolution of US offset policy.

10. These include sales of F-16s to Belgium, the Netherlands, Denmark, Norway, and Greece; Patriot missiles to West Germany and the Netherlands; AWACS aircraft to the U.K. and France, and F/A-18s to Canada, Australia, and Spain.

11. Two responses in particular are worthy of noting; from the US Defense Department and the Aerospace Industries Association of America, Inc. In the first, Kenneth S. Flamm, Principal Deputy Assistant Secretary of Defense expresses substantial dissatisfaction with the content of the proposed rule and the manner in which it was produced. He recommends "that Commerce withdraw the proposed rule and convene an interagency group to draft a new, coordinated rule." Among other complaints, Secretary Flamm lists "the significant paperwork burden that the rule would impose on the defense industry, (citing) the proposed rule's requirement for considerable additional reporting, twice yearly, on all transactions taken to implement offset agreements ... (and) an unnecessary retroactive reporting burden".

In calling for the withdrawal of the proposed rule and the drafting of a new coordinated rule, Flamm also suggests that the interagency group "consider the question of whether the Administration should seek repeal of the various statutory offset reporting requirements" (Flamm, Kenneth S., Principal Deputy Assistant Secretary of Defense, letter to Sue Eckert, Assistant Secretary for Export Administration, US Department of Commerce, dated May 24, 1994).

In addition, Joel Johnson, Vice President, International, of the Aerospace Industries Association of America also focused his dissatisfaction with the proposed new rule on the additional paperwork burden which it would impose upon industry. He also expressed concern over definitions and categories of data which "go well beyond what is needed to prepare a report for Congress". In his opinion, "Every offset is different, and trying to add negotiated numbers involving technology transfers, training, production, services, risk equity ventures, and sales of unrelated goods, will produce numbers that will be singularly uninformative. Commerce would learn far more about terms, trends, and effects of offsets by meeting once a year with five to ten offset managers from the forty or so companies that account for most US offset obligations, than it will through broad collection of data."

Finally, Johnson expressed concern that the data being collected focus largely on offsets with little attention to "the sales which precipitated the offset ... (their) support (of) US foreign policy interests ... (their) strengthening) the US industrial base and (lowering) unit costs of equipment to the US armed forces" (Johnson, Joel L., Vice President, International, Aerospace Industries Association of America, Inc., letter to Brad Botwin, Director, Strategic Analysis Division, Office of Industrial Resource Administration, US Department of Commerce, dated May 23, 1994).

12. Office of Management and Budget, **Offsets in Military Exports, April, 1990**, Washington, D.C: US Executive Office of the President, July 16, 1990, p. 87.

13. See note 8.

14. *Ibid.*, pp. 85–86.

15. US Defense Security Assistance Agency, letters of August 8, 1989 from Glenn A. Rudd, Acting Director to Stanley C. Pace, Chairman and Chief Executive Officer, General Dynamics Corporation, and John F. McDonnell, Chairman and Chief Executive Officer, McDonnell-Douglas Corporation

16. Eisenhour, John Howard, **Offset: The Political Dimension of Countertrade**, unpublished manuscript, 1994, p. 65.

17. Office of Management and Budget, *op. cit.*

18. *Ibid.*, p. 43.

19. *Ibid.*, pp. 53-54.

20. *Ibid.*, pp. 54-55.

21. *Ibid.*, p. 59.

22 **"US Government Enacts New Offset Curb, Reporting Mandate"**, *Countertrade Outlook*, Vol. XII, No. 10 (May 30, 1994), pp. 1–5.

23. Eisenhour, *op. cit.*, p. 55.

24. **Congressional Record** (Washington, D.C.), January 26, 1994, p. S117.

25. Letter from the Secretary of Commerce to the Secretary of Defense dated April 1, 1993, and from the Secretary of Defense to the Secretary of Commerce dated July 16, 1993. Excerpts from both letters appear in Eisenhour, *op. cit.*, p. 55.

26. "F.A.S. Public Interest Report," **Journal of the Federation of American Scientists (FAS)**, Vol. 47, No. 1, January/February 1994.

27. Jeff Cole, **"Report Assails Defense-Sector 'Offset' Deals,"** *Wall Street Journal*, June 22, 1994, p. 3. See also John Mintz, **"GAO Report Critical of Military 'Offsets',"** *The Washington Post*, June 22, 1994, p. F-4.

28. **Code of Federal Regulations**, Vol. 48, Chapter 2, (Parts 201 to 251) especially, Part 225.7303 "Cost of doing business with a foreign government or an international organization," Revised as of October 1, 1993, pp. 203–204.

29. **Federal Register** Vol. 59, No. 72, April 14, 1994, Proposed Rules, pp. 17756–17757

30. For example, in response to the request for public comments, Joel Johnson, Vice President, International, of the Aerospace Industries Association of America observed that the proposal "removes an unnecessary irritant in our relations with potential customers, and treats those costs in the same way as other accounting differences between a sale to the US government and a sale to a foreign government. Furthermore, just as a customer must expect to pay for any nonstandard feature he requires on the equipment, he must expect to pay for costs associated with offsets, which are a cost the contractor must incur that would not be involved in a normal sale to the US government" (Johnson, Joel L., Vice President, International, Aerospace Industries Association of America, Inc., letter to Ms. Alyce Sullivan, Defense

Acquisition Regulations Council OASD (A&T) DP (DAR) the Pentagon, dated June 1, 1994).

31. Verzariu, Pompiliu, **International Countertrade: A Guide for Managers and Executives** (Washington, D.C: US Department of Commerce, International Trade Administration) August, 1992, p. 4.

32. While the following material is keyed to specific parts of the law, the wording has occasionally been altered to facilitate understanding.

33. Eisenhour, *op. cit.*, p. 43.

34. *Ibid.*

35. For example, in July of 1987 David G. Wigg, then Deputy Assistant Secretary of Defense, Policy Analysis, in testimony before a Congressional Committee observed:

   Even the US has an offset policy of sorts in that we require that there be a domestic production capability for each critical weapon system or component that we purchase from any foreign source except Canada (because they are considered part of the US industrial base) (US House of Representatives, **Countertrade and Offsets in International Trade**, Hearings before the Subcommittee on International Economic Policy and Trade, of the Committee on Foreign Affairs, June 24 and July 10, 1987).

36. Udis, Bernard and Keith E. Maskus, **"Offsets as Industrial Policy: Lessons from Aerospace,"** *Defence Economics*, Vol. 2, 1991, pp. 151–164.

37. *Ibid.*

38. Office of Management and Budget, *op. cit.*

39. For an analysis of the options, see Maskus, Keith E. and Denise R. Eby, **"Developing New Rules and Disciplines on Trade-Related Investment Measures,"** in Robert M. Stern, ed., *The Multilateral Trading System: Analysis and Options for Change* (Ann Arbor: University of Michigan Press), 1993, pp. 449–472.

Chapter 15

The Business of Offset: A Practitioner's Perspective
Case Study: Israel

Alon Redlich & Maison Miscavage
International Technology Sourcing, Inc., Chicago, Illinois

15.1 Introduction

This chapter is written by practitioners of offsets, members of the management team of International Technology Sourcing, Inc. (ITS). A strategic planning and offset advisory firm headquartered in Chicago, Illinois, ITS represents US defence firms facing the challenges of offsets throughout the world. As a complement to their offset operations, the company also caters to the international business planning and overseas technology investment needs of leading civil-sector international corporations, including various Fortune 100 companies. Since its establishment in 1986, the company has conducted projects in 12 countries, identifying, evaluating, and pursuing numerous advanced technology ventures. ITS also provides advisory services to the US government regarding binational technology co-operation initiatives aimed at the commercialisation of defence technologies.

The company's offset services are particularly geared towards devising, pusuing and executing indirect offset strategies. As the chapter discusses, it is ITS' belief that while meaningful indirect offsets can bring enormous benefits to procuring nations, they can also benefit contractors. A country with a significant technology base, for instance, may hold business opportunities which can be tapped and leveraged through offsets that would be of tremendous interest to the contractor even outside of their role in fulfilling offset obligations. Additionally, innovative indirect offsets limit the challenges a contractor might encounter in the process of pursuing direct activities.

When this chapter was written (early 1995), the company was engaged in investigating offset strategies and pursuing indirect offset fulfilment projects in a variety of countries, such as the UK, Australia, the UAE, Finland, Israel, Switzerland, India, and Malaysia. ITS fully recognises how and to what extent offsets can negatively impact free trade. However, the authors are of the opinion that if pursued appropriately, offsets can, in principle, be a mutually beneficial activity for both parties. This chapter will present some of the authors' observations on the current offset environment, and major trends companies should consider when mapping out offset strategies. It also discusses some of the guiding philosophies of International Technology Sourcing regarding offsets, and attempts to demonstrate why, if executed properly, offsets are not necessarily a burden to companies but can instead be a tool for creating partnerships that benefit both client country and contractor.

This chapter will illustrate the authors' methods of pursuing and executing offsets by briefly reviewing a recent campaign they supported in Israel. From 1991 to 1994, ITS was retained by a major US aerospace firm to assist in the development and implementation of an offset strategy for a major fighter aircraft acquisition by the Israeli Air Force. Lockheed, with the F-16, and McDonnell Douglas, with the F/A-18 and (after a shift in policy by the US government) F-15, were the airframe manufacturers competing for the tender. The engine competition was between Pratt & Whitney and General Electric of the US. We hope that this brief review of the company's involvement in this campaign will provide some insights into how ITS approaches an offset assignment, and how technology-based ventures and other modes of co-operation can play an important role in fulfilling offset obligations in a mutually beneficial manner.

The chapter is divided into three sections. The first section presents the philosophy and principles ITS adheres to and uses to guide its offset services. A review of the current offset environment follows this, identifying some of the major trends in the today's offset world. The final part of the chapter discusses the company's recent involvement in Israel, and describes the manners in which it worked with the client company and Israeli authorities to identify, evaluate, present and pursue mutually beneficial offset opportunities. This part of the chapter includes a summary of the guidelines and goals of Israel's offset program (referred to as Industrial Cooperation), and a brief overview of the Israeli environment and how specific features within it relate to offset activities. While the authors have made every effort to provide meaningful insights into this campaign, for reasons of confidentiality the identities of certain parties, specific ventures, and results of this initiative will not and cannot be discussed.

This chapter is written in tribute to our clients and the numerous entities throughout the world with whom we have worked over the years. It is due to them that we have had the opportunity to participate in some very exciting initiatives pursuing technology-based business ventures, and support the development of strategic plans in connection with major government procurements.

15.2   An Offset Philosophy

The most basic, and also the most crucial, challenge facing offset activities is how to reconcile the interests of the purchasing country and those of the supplying foreign contractor. That the positions of these two parties, while generally perceived as diametrically opposed with regards to offsets, can in fact be reconciled is the fundamental tenant driving our company's offset services.

As observers and active participants in offset-related activities in various countries, we are witness to shifts and changes in the way contractors and governments pursue offsets. In campaigns over the last number of years, the contractors and the governments interests have been too often at odds. On one side, governments are attempting to reap as much benefit as possible from the transaction, e.g. augmenting their defence manufacturing base, employment, technology transfer, exports, and other concerns. Contractors, however, are aggressively seeking to sell their product(s) while keeping the costs of doing business to a minimum. The necessity of accomplishing these goals has become especially poignant for contractors now that they are faced with a post-Cold War world, and the accompanying diminished demand for defence equipment.

At first look, it may seem that this conflict of interests cannot be resolved. It is unfortunately with this opinion that the two parties often approach their offset operations. Too many bright and capable people in both camps see themselves in purely adversarial positions, and focus not on working together, but rather on finding ways to outsmart each other.

In light of this animosity between defence contractors and governmental offset authorities, the authors of this document submit that significant changes must be brought about in the offset environment. Governments must recognise that the abilities of contractors to provide subcontracting opportunities, technologies, employment, etc. to foreign countries are limited. And in the long run, continued aggressive demands by foreign governments are not in their best interests. High offset demands will inevitably increase the costs of the systems sold, and may even bring about legislation limiting the ability of contractors to provide meaningful offsets in the future. Indeed, the US government has been sending signals that it may attempt to regulate the practice. In parallel, contractors need to appreciate the expectations and actual needs of their client governments to impact their country's economy as a way of compensating for the substantial transactions offsets are associated with. While these expectations may be unreasonable at times, we feel there is validity to the request that for transactions of such magnitudes, some very tangible benefits should be brought to the country and that the contractor's capability to deliver these benefits should be a significant part in the decision making formula for large-scale procurements.

The task at hand — to positively impact the economy of the purchasing country — is a challenging one for both government authorities and foreign contractors. ITS has witnessed time and again that even when defence contractors are committed to benefiting and impacting the client country, they are still faced with very substantial obstacles. For example, few governments have developed their offset mechanisms to the point where they present specific opportunities in their country that are relevant to the defence contractors. Too often, the focus is one-sided: "what can the contractor do for me?" versus, "what can we successfully do together?" Frustrated by unrealistic expectations and lacking any promising opportunities related to their core businesses and primary capabilities, at times contractors find themselves forced to entertain proposals not at all related to their core business interests, and actually at odds with management directives. Proposals are sometimes submitted with the recognition that their only purpose is to appease the demands of the given government's offset authority. Obviously, in the long run this benefits neither party.

As the demands put on them by offset authorities in various countries increase dramatically, as will be described later in this chapter, this conflict between contractor and client nation will only become more acute. Already, thoroughly disconcerted by the challenges of pursuing and conducting offsets, some companies both in America and Europe are considering strategies that assume full payment of liquidated damages in lieu of fulfilling their offset obligations. Such an approach is clearly counterproductive for all parties. The client country not only loses the opportunity to strengthen its industrial and technology base, but also ends up paying an inflated price for the procured equipment, since companies will frequently include the liquidated damage penalty in the price of the contract. Yet, by taking this approach the contractor also puts himself in a losing situation. First, the long-term interests of his client are not served. This may hurt the contractor's prospects in future competitions in that country. Secondly, given the intimate nature of the international offset community, the contractor will quickly earn a reputation for not pursuing valid industrial co-operation activities and damage his prospects for sales in other nations as well.

Many take it for granted that the interests of client country and contractor will always be in conflict. However, it is a conviction of the authors that, approached properly, this dispute can be mediated and resolved favourably for all concerned. While offsets clearly benefit the client country, they can be a used as a unique business tool to also serve the contractor's interests. Pursued appropriately, offsets can enhance a company's international reach, leverage the ability of innovative foreign technologies, diversify manufacturing locations, and encourage the corporation to pursue strategic alliances with entities in the target country.

Offsets are here to stay. Recognising this, International Technology Sourcing believes that they should not necessarily be looked at as a burden, but as a tool which can bring about activities of strategic value for contractors and client governments alike. This notion, that both parties, foreign defence contractor and client country, can reap substantial benefits from offset fulfilment activities is the cornerstone of ITS' approach to offset.

The formula ITS uses to turn this idea into reality is rather straightforward: conduct an in-depth assessment of the strengths and needs of the defence contractor, and a thorough analysis of the target country environment. Looking at the company, ITS will assess its international business development thrusts, manufacturing and distribution strategies, availability of technology, and gaps within its strategic technology matrixes. Simultaneously, ITS assesses the target country, reviewing and analysing the priorities of its government, its decision makers and their respective agendas, its industrial infrastructure, technology infrastructure, gaps in national technology matrixes, etc. With the results of these in-depth assessments, ITS conducts a detailed correlation analysis that identifies, in very specific terms, how the needs and gaps of one party can be impacted by the strengths of the other. The results of this analysis serve as the foundation for the offset strategy developed hand-in-hand with the client company.

Using this strategy, International Technology Sourcing enables contractors to offer the offset authorities of a given target country a "basket of opportunities" relevant to their needs and at the same time in the contractor's interest. These opportunities, resulting from the correlation analysis described above, will typically yield positive responses from the offset authorities, who are unaccustomed to analytical approaches. They will also generate positive feedback from the company's senior management, which usually frowns upon offset initiatives unrelated to the company's core businesses. While this is indeed a time-consuming, complex task, it yields tangible, specific opportunities for **mutual benefit**.

It should be emphasised that to a great extent, the ability of offset executives to generate projects that can meaningfully impact the client country and the contractor depends on their ability to mobilise internal resources for the offset campaign. Put more simply, offset executives must motivate colleagues in different parts of the company to do business in the target country. To that end, offset executives should work hand-in-hand with their business development, R&D, and technology colleagues when looking into the potential client countries and identifying opportunities for mutual co-operation. In a way, offset executives are an extended marketing arm of a targeted country. They function as brokers, bringing together parties from their company and supplier base, and relevant entities in the targeted country. And offset executives must go beyond finding opportunities; at times they need to act as venture capitalists and investors, motivating parties in their own company by funding some of the initial investigatory activities and/or a substantial portion of the initial investment.

Meaningful offset proposals can play an important role in a country's selection of a product, perhaps not necessarily winning a campaign but certainly playing an instrumental role in a loss if they fail to stand up to the expectations and demands of government offset groups. This is because they can provide some very real economic benefits. But for the contractors, offsets can also be highly beneficial, enhancing a company's international reach, gaining them access to innovative foreign technologies, diversifying manufacturing locations, and encouraging the corporation to pursue advantageous strategic alliances in new markets. But to reap these benefits, contractors and purchasing countries must abandon the adversarial relationship they have too often adopted over the past several years, and focus on working together to realise the long-term mutual benefits of the unique partnership offset creates. It is the conviction of the authors that, while challenging, the task at hand is attainable through an approach and methodology as that described above.

15.3   The 1990s Offset Environment

Offsets first played a role in government procurement contracts as early as the 1950s. Since then, and particularly over the past five to ten years, the nature of offset business and the expectations countries hold for offsets have changed tremendously. What started as an gesture of goodwill and a manageable incentive on the part of contractors, has inflated to, at times, a critical component in procurement tenders. Under certain circumstances, offset proposals may seriously impact the outcome of the competition and even determine the profitability, or lack thereof, of major campaigns.

Three major trends have emerged in offset transactions over the last several years as the importance of offset has magnified:

- The typical level of commitment has greatly increased, and shows no signs of dropping or even plateauing. Governments that ask for a given level of offset now regularly see contractors offer well above, as much as double or greater, that measure.
- Indirect offsets have the potential to grow significantly in importance. Direct opportunities are increasingly difficult for contractors to offer because of the current strains on the defence industry. Additionally, governments have realised that offset can be wielded as a real development tool for their industrial infrastructure and their economy as a whole. Several Gulf states, for example, perhaps realising this later point have expressly stated little or no interest in direct opportunities.
- Lastly, the governments of countries on the supply side of the offset equation are paying more attention to the practice. This is especially true here in America, where talk of regulating offsets is mounting.

Those considering regulating the practice should be advised that offsets are here to stay. They are not a sweetener, to be thrown on the table in the final minutes of negotiating to bring a deal to a close, nor are they vehicles for corruption to be discussed behind closed doors only. They are a prominent and important part of the international business world. As offsets play a greater role than ever in arms transactions, they have also grown in importance in civil-sector procurements. Telecommunications companies are a prime example of commercial entities that have had to learn the offset trade over the past dozen years, as the fall of the Soviet Union, the opening of China, and other factors have given these companies opportunities for huge sales abroad. Offsets are a necessary part of their transactions with these and similar nations.

15.3.1   The Offset Explosion

Offset commitments/obligations of an extremely high percentage of contract value, which we will define as 100% or equal to the value of the contract itself, are not new to the offset environment. Perhaps the first such agreement was made in 1982 by McDonnell Douglas Corporation in exchange for a Canadian Government order of F/A-18s. But it is only since the opening of the current decade that such substantial obligations have become commonplace. For example:

a.   A consortium led by the UK's Westland has announced it will make an offset commitment of no less than 375% if it wins the UK's attack helicopter tender. The contract is worth roughly £2 billion. The UK does not require any set percentage of defence contracts to be fulfilled through offsets, but does ask that contractors bring benefit to the nation's defence industry.
b.   Raytheon has proposed a $1 billion commercial venture to the Kuwaiti government to offset the sale of a Patriot Missile System. The system is valued at just over $300 million — making the offset worth 333% of the contract value. Kuwaiti's offset law requires foreign contractors, civil and defence, to make an investment of 30% of contract value.
c.   Thomson-CSF made a 300% offset commitment to Austria for the nation's purchase of AS 1.1 billion in air defence radar from Thomson. Austria explicitly asked for a 300% commitment when it announced the tender. Interestingly, only about 20% of the offset value is in direct initiatives.
d.   Boeing Corporation recently completed a 130% commitment to Britain to offset the UK's purchase of several AWACS aircraft.
e.   General Motors recently committed to a 115% offset agreement with Canada to compensate for an order of light armoured reconnaissance

vehicles (LAV-Reece) for the Canadian Forces. The value of GM's contract is over C$600 million. Most of the offsets will be in the form of fabrication of the vehicle and the building of subassemblies.

Percentages of contract value are not the only way to measure how increasingly demanding the offset environment has become. For example, as with offset programs in other nations, the United Arab Emirates is asking companies to make direct investments into the country's economy that create new businesses. But the Emirates guidelines place a very significant qualifier on this request: that any ventures prove profitable within a certain number of years, to a certain amount of dollars. If these goals are not met, the contractor is considered at default on its obligations, regardless of the financial and time commitments it may have made to the enterprise, and is subject to a penalty of up to 8.5% of its unfulfilled commitments.

What accounts for the offset escalation? One factor is unquestionably the shrinking defence environment, prompting contractors to seek export orders more aggressively than previously. Offsets offer companies a way to compete beyond the products themselves. A good offset offer may not entice a country to purchase an inferior product, but it certainly may sway a decision between two pieces of equipment of equal calibre. However, countries are also demanding more than previously. A number of nations, particularly in the Middle East, have drawn up their first offset guidelines over the past few years. Others, such as Australia and Norway, have recently reworked old policies. Most of these new guidelines are quite demanding.

There is always a chance that governments, particularly the US, will decide that offset offers and obligations are escalating to harmful levels and attempt to limit the practice. But barring such action and considering these trends from both contractors and offset authorities, it is highly unlikely that current requested or offered percentage levels will drop.

15.3.2   A Greater Role for Indirect

The traditional way for companies to fulfil offset obligations has been through direct offsets, in the form of subcontracting, coproduction, and licensing. These will continue to be a significant factor in offset agreements. However, direct obligations have become a very challenging and controversial task in the current defence environment. Also, more and more often countries are expressing interest in indirect offsets, presumably because of their potential to develop a nation's industrial base and catalyse an economy as a whole.

This is not to say that direct offsets will not continue to play anything less than a very important role in most offset proposals. On the contrary, some governments make it clear that they are only interested in direct opportunities, or at least offsets which will benefit their defence industry in general. The UK, for example, as mentioned does not explicitly demand offsets yet does consider them, and states that the primary criteria for judging offset proposals is the value they can bring to the British defence industries. Australia asks for very specific benefits out of offsets, and exclusively in its defence sector. The nation expects to gain certain capabilities for its defence industrial base for every procurement, and explains these to the bidding contractors.

However, defence contractors have entered an extremely difficult period in which to fulfil direct offset demands. On a short-term, practical level companies are forced to export jobs. From a long-term, strategic perspective, companies are at times obligated to share highly valuable technologies and, in doing so, create their own future competition. While these considerations have always challenged contractors trying to meet direct obligations, the current downsizing of the defence environment has made these issues more volatile than ever. For example, America is expected to lose nearly 3 million defence-related jobs from the time that the high level of defence expenditures in the 1980s began to decrease, to 1997. In the US aerospace sector alone, hundreds of thousands of jobs have been terminated. Just over the last four years, six large aerospace contractors have cut their operations in California, America's most aerospace-dependent state, by over 100,000 jobs. The number of major military aircraft builders has contracted to five today (one of these, Rockwell, is currently without a contract for any aircraft) from eight as recently as 1990. Defence companies are in no position to be perceived as helping foreign competition or shipping jobs abroad.

The requests for sharing valuable technologies are by no means limited to those for parts or subsystems. Fully industrialised and developing countries alike have often made it clear they want offsets to hand them the capability to manufacture procured systems in their entirety. For example, Turkey asked for — and received — an F-16 plant. If the US F-16 manufacturing facilities close soon, as is slated to happen, Turkey will become the world's sole F-16 supplier. Both Indonesia and Malaysia are aggressively using offsets to build indigenous aerospace industries as well.

Indonesia provides an excellent example of a contractor creating his own competition by agreeing to direct offset obligations. Recently Indonesia sold a number of CN-635 short-range transports. This sale for Indonesia's Industri Pesawat Terbang Nusantra (IPTN) comes as a result of an offset agreement by the company with Construcciones Aeronautics SA (CASA) of Spain for co-production of the aircraft — confirming that CASA has succeeded in making a competitor for itself.

Yet at the same time that contractors are experiencing great difficulties with meeting direct offset demands, a number of countries are bringing out guidelines asking primarily for indirect opportunities. Some of the Gulf states provide a good example of this trend.

For instance, the UAE offset program, established in 1991, makes no requests for direct offsets, instead stressing project profitability, technology transfer, and the growth and diversification of the nation's industrial base. The Saudi offset program, while initially laying a good deal of importance on developing an indigenous defence industry, has changed course and now makes indirects the higher priority. On the whole, offset programs in the Middle East, except for Israel, have been of either a civilian or a dual-use nature (such as the formation of aircraft maintenance companies).

In the future, the most important forms of indirect offset fulfilment will be technology transfer and direct investment, as opposed to the barter and countertrade that have traditionally characterised indirect schemes. The role for barter and countertrade may not be over — witness Malaysia's recent payment to Russia for 18 MiG 29s in the form of palm oil — but on the whole such transactions have a more limited role to play in the modern offset business. The Norwegian and Finnish governments, for example, forbid companies to use raw materials purchases for offset credit. (Part of the reason Malaysia may have allowed accepting the palm oil as an offset was that these MiGs came at an exceptionally low price. The venture may also open up new markets for the commodity, which Malaysia produces in very substantial quantities. Of course, note that palm oil is not the only offset in the deal; Russia offered to set up a joint venture with the Malaysians for maintenance and logistics support for the MiGs, and other offset schemes for this transaction are pending.)

Another reason that indirects may take a greater share of the offset environment is that contractors are realising the potential value of fulfilling obligations through third-party companies. A contractor can help a foreign company establish a presence in a country the contractor has offset obligations in, and tie the investments of that company to its offset contract. In this way, a contractor earns credit for the money and effort that the third party spends setting up operations. However, while more companies are seeking third-party fulfilment scenarios, offset authorities have become increasingly uncomfortable with the practice. They are currently working to define the levels of credits to be awarded for such activities, and the requirements for proof of causality they will seek in such scenarios from the foreign defence contractor.

15.3.3 Government Attention

As offsets have gained in scope, governments on the supply side of the offset equation have shown increased interest in the business. While much of the attention that offsets have received is negative, the need for exports seems to be counterbalancing some of this sentiment.

The magnitude of offset proposals today has caused many parties to argue that offsets have escalated out of control, and call for government regulation. The GATT treaty now being evaluated, for instance, contains a provision prohibiting GATT signatories from imposing, seeking, or considering offsets for government procurement transactions. Developing countries would be allowed to negotiate exceptions. However, if this provision would actually discourage countries from engaging in offset remains to be seen. Many nations do not impose any sort of offset requirement, or even ask for offsets — yet it is understood that any contractor who wants to do business there must present a substantial offset proposal on a "voluntary" basis.

The US government has traditionally frowned upon the practice of offsets. However, this has not impeded the offset efforts of US defence contractors, because despite any misgivings the government ultimately left the decision of whether to offer offsets or not in the hands of contractors.

This lack of involvement may change in the years ahead. The US government is sending signals that it may be considering imposing limitations and regulations on the practice of offset. In December of 1994, for example, the US government announced that American companies must begin reporting any single offset obligations in excess of $5 million against defence-related exports, and any individual offset transaction for which they receive credits equal to or greater than $250,000. The reporting will be administered by the Bureau of Export Administration (BXA) of the US Department of Commerce, which will be responsible for compiling an annual report to Congress on the impact of offsets. Many observers of offset activities see in such initiatives an alarming sign of government involvement in offsets, and warn that such efforts to control the freedom of American defence contractors to offer substantial offset proposals will drastically effect the ability of defence contractors to export their goods, and, by definition, have an enormous negative impact on the health and stability of these companies.

One US government attempt to regulate the offset business recently passed — but to the relief of contractors, was dropped soon afterward. In 1991, the DOD decided to require US arms sellers to notify their buyers in Letter of Agreements that the administrative costs of offset programs might be included in a system's sale price. As soon as the requirement appeared, it created a problem for a US contractor. McDonnell Douglas, on the verge of winning a sale of helicopters to the UAE, suddenly found its sale in jeopardy because the UAE government refused to sign a Letter of Agreement with McDonnell Douglas as long as this new clause was included. Perhaps realising that regulating offsets might do more harm than good to US contractors, and hence to the DOD, the Pentagon dropped the rule in 1994.

Acknowledging the importance of offsets to the defence industry would seem more in step with the activities of other governments with regards to offsets. Britain, for example, in the fall of 1994 established an Offset Advisory Service in an effort to help British defence contractors improve their penetration of developing and newly industrialised markets, especially in the Middle and Far East. These regions are assumed to be purchasing the bulk of all defence exports for the next several years. The French MOD has in the past assumed responsibility for portions of the offset commitments of the country's defence contractors (though the Ministry recently stated that it may discontinue this notably high level of involvement).

But regardless of governmental standpoints on the practice, defence contractors' need for support in devising, pursuing and executing offset agreements is more critical than ever. As discussed above, most nations will likely continue to expect very substantial benefits from offset, and their expectations may rise even beyond the currently very high levels. Yet simultaneously, contracting defence-related sales world-wide will continue to limit the means for contractors to meet these demands. It is our opinion that one way for contractors to address the difficulties of offsets is by taking advantage of the increasing role for indirect offsets. Through indirect initiatives, a defence contractor can resolve the several problems stemming from direct offset, still bring value to the client country, and also significantly benefit the company itself through indirect offsets rooted in the transfer, development, and exploration of technologies. We hope that the next section will help illustrate how this process works in practice.

15.4   Peace Fox VI/Peace Marble IV Competition

At the end of January 1994, the Israeli Ministry of Defence officially announced that it had chosen to purchase 20 McDonnell Douglas F-15I fighter aircraft. The order was predicted to cost over $2 billion, and would provide the Israeli Air Force (IAF) with only slightly modified versions of the USAF's F-15E, currently the most technologically advanced fighter in the US Air Force (USAF) arsenal. Five more aircraft were later added to the order.

Thus ended the IAF's latest fighter aircraft procurement. The primary competitors for the tender were airframe manufacturers McDonnell Douglas and Lockheed Corp. (which acquired General Dynamics, the rival to McDonnell Douglas when the competition began in 1992), and engine makers Pratt & Whitney (P&W) and General Electric (GE) of the US. That the final victor of the competition was the F-15 and McDonnell Douglas (MDC) came as somewhat unexpected. At the outset of the two-year performance evaluation and decision-making process, the aircraft being considered were the Lockheed F-16 and the F/A-18 from McDonnell Douglas. The Israelis had expressed interest in the F-15E, but at the time the plane was not approved for export by the US government. The Pentagon upgraded the choices of fighters available to Israel shortly after the country signed a historic peace agreement with the PLO September 13, 1993. The Israeli MOD announced shortly afterwards that it would choose the slightly modified version of the E that had been approved, the F-15"I".

The tender, called Peace Marble IV and Peace Fox VI, respectively, by Lockheed and MDC was of crucial importance for both the aircraft and engine manufacturers. To all four companies, it was considered a "must-win" sale. This importance stemmed from a variety of factors. One is the reputation and image of the IAF. The Israeli air command is considered to be among the best (many would argue that it is the best) in the world. For this reason, many other countries closely watch IAF procurements and consider the purchase of a system by the IAF as a very important vote of confidence in that piece of equipment, with implications for their own future acquisitions. Hence winning an air-related competition in Israel is of substantial significance to any defence firm. Furthermore, the order was to be rather large. Sales of such magnitude have become increasingly rare since the end of the Cold War, and thus more crucial than ever for contractors. Another factor that made the Peace Marble IV/Peace Fox VI competition critical was both contractors' interests in keeping assembly lines open. The F-15E program had already been terminated when the sale was approved (though McDonnell Douglas' other entry, the F/A-18, in its E/F derivative, will be produced for several years to come for the US Navy), and the F-16 was entering its last year of production for the USAF. Any future US production of these aircraft depended on foreign sales. Lastly, both the USAF and US Navy had an interest in the outcome of the sale. Any overseas sales of the F/A-18 or F-16 would allow the contractors to spread fixed production costs over that many more aircraft, reducing the per-unit cost of those systems to the US armed forces, as well as to other foreign customers.

In early 1992, ITS was approached by one of the four primary contestants for the tender. Offsets were expected to play an important role in the competition, and the company was seeking our support in developing meaningful offset proposals to present to the Israeli offset authorities. The company recognised that of the three critical components for a win — the system itself, the price, and the offset package — the last is the most flexible element and most under the control of the company, and thus more open to inventive and creative approaches. To that end, they retained ITS' services. After detailed briefings by the client company, we embarked on a thorough analysis of the Israeli environment identifying and evaluating numerous offset scenarios to best support the campaign. We were to investigate possible indirect opportunities, while the contractor's in-house offset team would develop direct proposals. In addition, ITS was asked to provide a detailed "theatre of operations" analysis and help develop the strategic plan that would guide the company's offset activities.

15.4.1 Israeli Offset Guidelines: Priorities and Thrusts

The Israeli government refers to its offset policy as Industrial Cooperation. This name describes fairly accurately what Israel wants from offsets. The primary goal of Israel's offset program is to encourage foreign and Israeli firms to not only work together, but to establish very close, long-term working relationships.

The reasoning behind this stems from the characteristic condition of Israeli firms and Israeli capabilities in general. While often technically sophisticated, most Israeli companies have limited access to global markets and need the value that can be generated from strategic partnering with industry leaders. With a few prominent exceptions such as Israel Aircraft Industries (IAI), Tadiran, Elbit, and the like, the partnering that can come about as a result of offset obligations can be of immense value to most Israeli companies. It is the intent of Israel's Industrial Cooperation Authority, the Israeli government agency that administers offset agreements in Israel, that offset commitments be leveraged and utilised by linking Israeli companies with foreign industry and technology leaders. It is expected that Israeli companies will net subcontracting opportunities, R&D work, technology transfer, investment, and global market access and exposure. There are certainly other issues in Israel that the government feels offsets can address, some of which we will mention below, such as the Israeli defence sector's financially strapped condition and the massive influx of Russian immigrants that has followed the fall of the Soviet Union. But that these issues are important to developing offsets is due to current circumstance, rather than any philosophical foundation of the Industrial Cooperation policy. The classic premise behind Industrial Cooperation remains helping Israeli companies grow and bringing wealth to the country through partnering them with appropriate foreign firms.

It is important to note that central to the theme of Israel's Industrial Cooperation is that activities pursued under the banner of offsets be truly beneficial to both parties. While numerous offset authorities around the world may use this terminology, few are truly committed to the concept. Our experience indicates that while Israeli authorities can at times be demanding, the demands are to encourage contractors to search for genuine and profitable opportunities with Israeli partners. The Israeli offset authority, the Industrial Cooperation Authority, recognises that its role and contribution to Israeli industry is not in the extraction of opportunistic and short-term projects, but rather in the creation of long-term relationships between foreign and Israeli companies. And indeed, an analysis of offset activities in Israel indicates that numerous offset-driven initiatives have led to long-term, strategic co-operation agreements maintained long after any offset obligations have been satisfied.

The Industrial Cooperation Authority (ICA), a small body within the Ministry of Industry & Trade, was established as an interdepartmental agency to initiate, monitor and co-ordinate the industrial co-operation agreements origi-nated by government trade. ICA also monitors industrial co-operation activities created through private-sector trade. Actual industrial co-operation agreements are made with the relevant government agency for the tender in question. ICA does not approve or disapprove projects, but is responsible for monitoring the progress of offset agreements. The ICA operates its central office in Tel Aviv, and has two branch offices with full-time staff in the US and Europe.

The guidelines for Industrial Cooperation are fairly loose compared with those of many other nations, and even lenient in some respects. For example, Israel has no liquidated damages clause, and asks for 35% (or more) of the con-tract value to be equalled in offset purchases, a rather reasonable request in com-parison with many countries. Israel does not request any specific direct/indirect split, or ask that particular industries get benefits. Yet the loose and open nature of the Industrial Cooperation policy suits the country's well-known demand for excellent and timely offset proposals by allowing it flexibility in what it can ask, and how it may deal with contractors. The period over which a company's' offset obligations to Israel must be completed is negotiable; however, it is usually three years. 20% of the obligation is expected to be completed in the first year of imple-mentation, and 40% in each of the two subsequent years. In large scale transac-tions the period of performance may be extended to as much as 7 to 10 years.

Specific offset-related initiatives credited against a contractor's obligations are termed Industrial Cooperation Benefits (ICBs). The relative value of various ICB possibilities, as stated in the Industrial Cooperation guidelines, is as follows:

- Direct Subcontracting and Purchase of Industrial Goods and Engineering Services: Such procurements will be credited at 100% of the purchase value.
- Research and Development: Credit for purchases of R&D services from Israeli firms will be negotiated, but will never fall under 100% of the pur-chase price. Purchase from Israeli companies of development work that leads to new production in Israel will be credited at 100–200%.

- Investment in Capital: Direct investment will be credited at a rate of up to 200% of the amount invested.
- Transfer of Technology and Industrial Proprietary Rights: These will be credited relative to the added value of export orders such transfers bring about, for up to four years.
- Co-Production and/or Co-Marketing: Credit for such arrangements will be negotiated.
- Software: Software development in Israel is encouraged, and companies will receive 150% in credits of the value of software development tasks performed in Israel.
- Transportation: Such services purchased from Israeli companies, excluding the delivery of goods to Israel, are limited to 10% of the total offset commitment.
- Third Party Transactions: Credits for third-party transactions are limited to 50% of the total IB commitment, and will be credited with a value from 50% to 100%.

Since ITS' involvement with the Peace Marble IV/Peace Fox VI campaign, the Israeli government has introduced a major change in the country's offset policy. Instead of requesting offsets, the Israeli government will now require offsets with its purchases by law. Legislation for this is pending in the Knesset.

Details on changes to the Industrial Cooperation policy were not available at the time of writing. However, the change is not expected to greatly affect large defence contractors pursuing offset business in the country. Israel has long been a very important market for these companies, and one in which they always proposed aggressive offset proposals despite the fact that offsets were not enforced by law. In bringing Industrial Cooperation into law, the Knesset is primarily targeting the many civil-sector companies, some European, several Japanese, selling to Israel that have continually refused to enter into offset agreements.

15.4.2   Implementing the ITS Methodology

An article published during the campaign highlighted the importance of seeking indirect opportunities. The February 15–21, 1993 edition of Defence News said that the companies for this tender had created a "spiralling offset competition ... prompting industry calls for US government intervention to prevent a loss of US jobs and businesses." All companies involved had by then been negotiating offset packages with Israel for over a year. One of the companies was said to be preparing to offer both parts manufacture and final assembly of its system. Another was indicating that it would make an opening proposal of a 70% offset commitment, which was expected to rise significantly by the final stages of the competition. Such large and potentially challenging direct offers and the publicity that follows them are the types of challenges ITS and our client companies hope to avoid through indirect initiatives.

The project goal, as defined by the company's senior management and ITS principles was "to provide the company a competitive edge over rival companies by ensuring the review and submission of meaningful and timely offset fulfilment proposals positioning the company to emerge as the aggressive front runner, understanding and addressing the challenges and opportunities in the Israeli environment. Furthermore, to enable the company to submit a 'basket' of offset fulfilment proposals that are timely, significant, and of national interest to Israel, while also fitting the company's technology and business thrusts."

As a prerequisite to developing the basket of opportunities, ITS conducted an 8-month long analysis of the Israeli theatre of operations. The purpose of this analysis was two-fold: to ensure that the projects included in the basket of opportunities addressed the most important needs and priorities of the Israeli environment, and thus would be welcomed by the heads of the Israeli Industrial Cooperation Authority and other decision makers; and second, to provide an in-depth briefing to the company's senior management and campaign team, ensuring a high degree of clarity regarding various critical factors in the Israeli environment.

Guiding the selection of projects to be included in the basket of opportunities was an assessment of the Israeli government's criteria for evaluating offset proposals. It was the assessment of ITS that aggressive indirect initiatives would generate very positive responses from the Israeli authorities, who, based on previous campaigns, learned to already expect subcontracting, assembly and other direct offset opportunities from US aerospace firms. Indirect initiatives allow a contractor to drastically expand the menu of opportunities from which it can choose, enabling it to benefit to a greater extent from the supply of innovation and technology in the target country. (This is of course true only in countries such as Israel, various European nations, etc. which enjoy a strong industrial and technology infrastructure.) Furthermore, as discussed above, fulfilling offset obligations through indirect initiatives alleviates some of the pressure to provide subcontracting and other direct initiatives.

As described at the beginning of this chapter, ITS approaches offset as a tool to address strategic needs and critical gaps in a company's technology matrix. Prior to embarking on any in-country work, ITS worked closely with the client company to define priority areas and gaps in the company's technology arsenals. The fundamental notion was that if Israel could provide solutions to any of the needs identified, numerous organisations within the company would consider doing business in Israel regardless of the company's offset needs there.

As in all of ITS' projects, a dedicated team was assembled to execute this two-year assignment. The ITS project team consisted of three groups: a think tank consisting of high-level ex-government, military, and industry leaders; a team of "hunters"; and a stand-by team of evaluators specialising in different technology areas. The think tank was charged with reviewing and assessing larger, strategic issues and providing insights to ensure sensitivity and understanding towards the various players in the Israeli environment. The "hunters" were tasked with executing the field work necessary to locate the most valuable opportunities and projects relevant to the company's needs and priorities. The evaluators were responsible for assisting ITS' internal team in evaluating the technology and business promise of the various projects identified.

ITS' methodology calls for the teams to execute enormous in-country efforts, reviewing and assessing literally hundreds of entities and opportunities. Equipped with the need lists generated in the beginning of the process, ITS canvassed the Israeli environment. Over a 16-month period the ITS team held face-to-face meetings with hundreds of entities from various industry, research, and academic circles in the State of Israel. The purpose of this field work was to conduct the correlation analysis, matching the priority areas of the client and potential sources of technology and innovation in Israel. The theatre of operations analysis also investigates priority subjects such as: country overview; employment and immigration; the defence environment; the current offset climate; IAF selection criteria; competitors' activities; and more. It was critical to provide the client company with both the "big picture" briefing, as well as the very specific details on opportunities and ventures for the implementation of the offset strategy.

15.4.3   The Israeli Environment and its Implications for Offsets

No offset proposal should ever be considered "generic," a formula that can be offered from country to country in exactly the same form. It is the conviction of ITS that offsets must be tailored to a country's specific environment. For this reason, it is crucial for a contractor to thoroughly understand the country to which it is selling. The contractor should be able to demonstrate a deep understanding of the industrial infrastructure, technology capabilities, labour force, economic goals and priorities, etc. of the country it is attempting to sell to, and understand the implications of these issues for what the contractor can realistically offer.

As one reviews the countries in which defence contractors need to participate in offset activities, it is fairly easy to make a distinction between those where offset fulfilment is a straightforward task, and those where it will be an enormously challenging and painstaking process. It is our assessment that Israel is a good place to do offsets. While not without challenges, Israel has built a sophisticated industrial and technological base that offers a great number of avenues and opportunities for contractors searching for offset fulfilment venues. In conducting the theatre of operation analysis, ITS focused on assessing the country's potential to supply innovative technologies and solutions to the client company, and on understanding major political, economic, and social issues that would influence the offset strategy to be pursued. The team also conducted a thorough assessment of Israel's Industrial Cooperation guidelines, and put together case studies of the offset strategies pursued in previous large-scale defence procurements in the country. Some of the priority issues that offset scenarios could address are discussed below.

15.4.3.1 Technology Environment

Israel is unique. In less than 50 years, the nation has developed from a primarily agrarian economy into a small, fully industrialised nation. Israeli companies have become important players in a number of niche markets, and Israel is now recognised as a world-class centre for research and development in several high-tech fields, such as medicine, energy, agriculture, information technology, and defence. Over the last decade, the nation has sustained an annual 3 to 6% growth rate as measured by change in GDP. Inflation, currently at roughly 13%, may be higher than desired but is certainly a tremendous improvement over the triple-digit figures Israel struggled with in the 1980s. Exports from Israel have steadily risen for the past four years.

Israel has a population of approximately 5 million. But despite this limited labour pool, and limited natural resources, it has prospered. One of the most notable, and widely recognised, characteristics of the Israeli environment that has helped it to flourish is the skill level of the Israeli workforce. As much as 24% of the workforce is estimated to hold advanced technical and academic degrees; the per capita of engineers in Israel is higher than anywhere in the world. Despite their high level of expertise, however, labour costs for Israeli professionals are competitive, and generally less than for those with equivalent backgrounds in the US, Europe, Japan, and parts of SE Asia. The Israeli government provides numerous subsidies for R&D, further pushing down the cost of the country's engineers and scientific talent.

A major achievement of this labour pool has been the establishment of Israel as one of the world's high-tech centres. Israel's economy is becoming increasingly based on high-tech R&D and limited-run production work. Through utilizing state-of-the-art technology and focussing on "niche" markets, many

Israeli high technology companies have managed to make names for themselves. This strategy has been pursued by Elscint, a leader in medical diagnostics imaging; Sharplan, which supplies 30% of the US market for surgical lasers; Scitex, producer of highly innovative colour printing technology; Orbotech, which has a majority share in the world market for advanced automatic optical inspection systems for PCBs; ECI Telecom Ltd., a leader in digital communication equipment; and others.

Over the years, numerous foreign firms, including many American high-tech leaders, have placed substantial work in Israel. Some have established manufacturing facilities, distribution centres, and R&D laboratories. Intel, for example, which opened a design centre in Haifa in 1974, recently announced plans to build a $1.5 billion facility in Jerusalem, nearly doubling Intel Israel's current workforce of 1,250. The Israel Intel organisation was responsible for the architecture of the 386 chip, among other accomplishments. Israel is recognised as a centre of excellence for computer-related technologies, and Motorola, IBM, Digital, Hewlett Packard, and National Semiconductor have also elected to establish research and development centres there.

In addition to the knowledge base of the Israeli people themselves, the State has played an important role in building the nation's thriving high tech environment. The expertise of Israel's workforce has traditionally been complemented by very high amounts of government R&D spending. For example, current estimates put Israeli R&D at nearly 3% of GDP, a level equal to that of the US, and higher than that of either Japan or Germany. Under certain circumstances, the government will subsidise the salaries of scientists and engineers, and provide investors and foreign companies with significant financial incentives and tax holidays.

The implications of the above to our offset strategy were several. First, it stressed the advisability of investigating how the country's technological strengths could be leveraged to address some of the client's technology needs, an option which might not be relevant in other countries. Second, it encouraged the investigation of establishing an R&D centre in Israel as part of the company's "global centre of excellence" strategy. Third, it suggested that the client might benefit from the availability of matching grants and funding provided by the Israeli government.

15.4.3.2   Employment/Immigration

A review of the priorities impacting the Israeli environment indicated that employment and the impact of immigration were among the most important issues facing the Rabin government in 1992/93. With an influx of over 200,000 immigrants per year, and an unemployment rate of over 12%, Rabin faced an emerging liability of explosive proportions. Not only would this impact the upcoming elections, but massive unemployment among Russian immigrants might also put a halt to future waves of immigration, jeopardising the very foundation of the State of Israel as a refuge and home to Jews in need.

The addition of over a half million people to a country with a total population of only five million, in less than five years, presented tremendous challenges. But alongside the challenges came a unique set of opportunities. The Russian and other ex-Soviet immigrants were (and are) a highly educated group of people. 60% of the recent arrivals had higher education, and 15% had engineering or scientific degrees. Compared with the Israeli populous, among the immigrants were proportionately 12 times as many people with degrees in the natural sciences, 13 times as many engineers and architects, 4 times as many technicians, and nearly 6 times as many doctors. It has been said that successfully absorbing one million of the Russian immigrants would effectively double the value of Israel's human capital.

The immigration/employment issue had significant implications for the offset campaign. The proposals in the offset basket needed to target Russian immigrants and scientists, and to provide immediate employment opportunities. Rather than propose only long-term, large-scale industrial initiatives, the client company emphasised generating jobs within a very short period of time, using activities such as software development, contract R&D, etc.

15.4.3.3 Defence Industry Crisis

Israel's defence-industrial sector is a major driver of her economy, and the country's reputation for developing cutting-edge, highly effective weaponry and defence-related equipment is widely known. However, this reputation has come at a high price. Of Israel's expenditures on R&D, two-thirds are invested in defence. As a portion of GDP, spending on defence has stood at roughly 20% and higher. With a limited local market for defence products, the Israeli defence industry has always been highly dependent on exports.

The end of the Cold War very seriously affected the Israeli defence establishment, and by 1992 the sector had entered a true crisis. Spending as a portion of GDP had sunk to 10–12% of GDP from 20% and higher levels in under a decade. Compare this to the defence "drawdown" in the US, where defence spending has gone to between 3 and 4% of GDP from 5% over the same period and is still a major economic issue. Not only has Israel itself cutback on its demand for weaponry, but the lower global demand for military equipment has cut export opportunities for Israeli defence companies. Other difficulties such as cost overruns on strategic projects and under-utilised manufacturing facilities exacerbated the situation. Israel's defence industries were laying off thousands of workers. And as the defence industrial complex has long been a symbol of Israeli self-sufficiency and technical prowess, the issue was highly charged. Defence industry workers have organised large and violent demonstrations, for instance, protesting layoffs. The survival of the Rabin government was at stake, and it was well-known that the situation would impact the way the offset proposals would be evaluated.

The crisis was best evidenced in two of Israel's leading defence enterprises: Israel Aircraft Industries (IAI), and Israel Military Industries (IMI). IAI, Israel's largest industrial entity with 17,300 employees and $1.5 billion in sales, was still suffering from the trauma of the cancellation of the Lavi fighter aircraft. At the time, several setbacks had added to this blow. Boeing cancelled a $150 million contract to convert 10 747s from passenger to freight aircraft; a pending sale of IAI's Kfir aircraft to Taiwan and the Philippines fell through; and a successful bid by IAI to sell advanced, unmanned, miniature aircraft to the US DOD had been put on hold pending an appeal by a US manufacturer challenging the bid process. IMI was facing severe setbacks as well. With 1991 losses of $239 million, and a directive to release a full fourth of its 7,600 employees, the company faced tremendous employee unrest. Confronted with a 40% decline in export orders, and the need to close four of its 16 manufacturing plants, the company was in dire need of jobs and export orders.

The defence industry crisis seriously impacted our offset strategy. Recognising the importance of the country's defence industry to the nation, and fully aware of the fact that Rabin held not only the portfolio of Prime Minister but also that of Defence, we structured a basket of opportunities that addressed to a significant extent the needs of such defence entities. Whenever possible, extra effort was made to identify or create an opportunity to work with defence enterprises. Defence conversion opportunities were also an important part of our strategies to address this issue.

15.4.4   The Basket of Opportunities

Towards the end of 1992, ITS submitted a detailed basket of opportunities to the client company. This consisted of the results of the team's technology related investigations in Israel, which focused on six areas: manufacturing technologies; electronics and photonics, propulsion; aerospace subsystems; information technology; and materials and structures. Equipped with a detailed wish list relating the specific needs of the company, ITS worked closely with the Industrial Cooperation Authority and the Israeli government to identify relevant Israeli entities and assessed their potential contributions. Throughout the process, numerous delegations from the contractor travelled to Israel to meet with the companies highlighted in the basket of opportunities, and pursue discussions as to potential modes of co-operation. It should be noted that though the technology capabilities of the potential partners were extremely important, other factors such as the management teams of the companies, and their experience with international ventures, were no less crucial to this partnering process.

ITS complemented this technology-oriented work with a detailed review of Israel. Our presentations to the client included a detailed review of the top thirty-plus decision makers in Israel, an analysis of decision makers versus influencers, and careful descriptions of the priorities, goals, and "pet projects" of each. Furthermore, as said the theatre of operations analysis provided in depth assessment of Israeli government criteria for evaluating offset proposals, and set forth recommendations to the client company to function as criteria for its opportunity selection. This analysis also included a detailed mapping of the Israeli government, including the Ministries of Defence, Finance, Industry and Trade, and the relevant arms of the Israeli Defence Forces. The theatre of operations analysis was designed to set the stage for the company's pursuit of offset ventures in Israel. As in all campaigns, it was critical that both senior management and the project team feel confident in their understanding of the environment, and develop an appreciation for the unique circumstances of the given target country.

One of the recommendations ITS submitted was to carry a major technology seminar in Israel to facilitate communication and contact between relevant Israeli entities, and the technical, as well as the business development, representatives of the client contractor. Of the 340 Israeli entities reviewed up to that time, 110 were identified as possessing potentially valuable contributions and were invited to attend this seminar, which ITS orchestrated in mid-1993. The delegation from the client company consisted of 40 subject-matter experts from different divisions of the company. These individuals were interested in exploring how Israeli entities might assist them in better achieving their technological and business goals. Unlike other seminars, which tend to focus on what the local companies wish to sell, this seminar was structured to focus on what the client company wanted to buy: i.e., what are the strategic needs and issues the company needs to address and resolve. Though the seminar was obviously connected to the client's offset interests in Israel, it was conducted with the interest of finding business opportunities that the company would want to pursue regardless of any offset credit they might receive.

The technology seminar, combined with on-site facility visits, yielded over 100 potential opportunities for co-operation. The overall assessment of the team was that Israel is a hotbed of innovation and technology, and a country that should be monitored and assessed regardless of offset commitments. The success of the seminar also scored a victory for the client company's offset group.

Members of the client company recognised that by acting as a catalyst to bring representatives from numerous parts of the corporation to Israel, the need to develop offsets opened up opportunities that otherwise would have gone unnoticed, or still worse, gone to the competition. Of the 100 potential projects identified, over 30 were rated as top priority initiatives. Several were signed and executed towards the end of 1993, prior to any selection of the plane or the engine, due to their enormous relevancy and contribution to the needs of the company.

On the basis of the information gathered by the ITS teams, the client company was presented with a strategy recommending four basic thrusts for the company's offset activities in Israel. The first called for aggressively pursuing co-operation with government-owned defence entities, responding to the government's priority to address the defence industry crisis. The second called for the company to target strategic co-operation with leading Israeli high-tech companies, ensuring that the client company and its divisions benefit from business activities pursued in Israel. The seminar exemplified this thrust. The third recommendation was to develop added-value, people-intensive initiatives which would address Prime Minister Rabin's mandate to generate jobs immediately. Fourth, ITS recommended that the company team-up with in-country technology investment and holding companies to leverage its own investments with those of experienced local partners. This four-pronged strategy formed the basis for the basket of opportunities. Each recommendation was accompanied by a set of entities most suited to the needs of the client. Furthermore, ITS presented specific projects for the client company to carry out with each of the entities it recommended.

15.4.5   Procurement Selection Analysis

There was never a clear favourite between the F-16 and the F/A-18. The IAF was familiar with the Lockheed aircraft, already in possession of over 200, and the planes had performed well. Indeed, the plane had attained a special significance to Israelis because the IAF used it in numerous combat missions, including the successful surprise bombing of an Iraqi nuclear plant in 1981. Additionally, ordering more F-16s would provide savings in infrastructure, maintenance, and training costs. However, a sizeable contingent in the MOD and IAF backed the F/A-18. The aircraft uses two engines instead of one, giving it a possible survivability advantage; was perceived as more capable than the F-16 in night attack; and offered the advantages of fleet diversification. The contest between GE and P&W was viewed similarly; either engine was deemed up to the task.

However, the MOD appeared to be on-schedule in its decision-making process and nearing final determinations in the later part of 1993. But it then stalled over rumours that the US Administration would let Israel purchase the F-15E, a plane that the Israelis had expressed great interest in but that had never been available for export. Congress' approval of the F-15E for export to Israel paved the way for the IAF's acquisition of the aircraft.

Industrial co-operation initiatives are important to Israel. However, it is our assessment that offsets, as a rule, will not sway the decision of the IAF or any other branch of the Israeli military unless the various systems under consideration are perceived to be of equal value. Thus the choice of the F-15E/I.

A shift in strategic and operational priorities for Israel made the F-15I preferable over the F-16 or F/A-18. In the past, most of the IAF's procurements stressed interception and peripheral air superiority. However, the now low probability of a conventional war on Israel's borders and the introduction of missiles into the Middle East military balance transformed several basic tenants of national security. Israel would now have to be able to operate against long-range targets, countries such as Iran, Iraq, and Libya. And it might have to do so at night, and avoid detection in severe weather. The F-15I possesses night flying, all-weather, and long-distance strike capabilities at a higher level than that of either the F-16s or the F/A-18s originally offered.

Lockheed responded to the change in the competition, offering a thoroughly updated version of the F-16, the F-16ES. The F-16ES would have been a very capable aircraft, and substantially cheaper than the Eagle. However, the plane was still in the design stages, a fact that may have fundamentally weakened Lockheed's position.

The order was a major victory for McDonnell Douglas. It also sweetened a recent Saudi order for 72 F-15s (a procurement Israel protested). Of the two engine companies, Pratt & Whitney was selected to power the Eagle with the F-100-PW-229 engine. Israel's first F-15Is are to be delivered by 1996–97.

Over the three years in which ITS supported this offset initiative, we learned several important lessons. First, while of great importance for IAF procurements, offsets will not sway a decision to buy any particular system unless the various systems being considered are perceived to be of equal value. Second, we found Israel to hold great promise in diverse areas of technology, from expert systems for composite repairs and fibre optic lasers, to solid modelling/simulation technologies, to adhesive bonding, to multimedia/training, all activities highly relevant to most companies pursuing offset initiatives in Israel. Third, Israeli entities are enormously interested in co-operation with foreign companies, and very aware of the role and ramifications of offset obligations. Lastly, we developed an appreciation for the activities and support provided by the ICA, and have found them to be in principle open to innovative initiatives and uncommon methods for fulfilling offset commitments.

15.5   Conclusion

The ITS motto is "offset fulfilment through global technology initiatives". This chapter was written to provide a practitioner's insight into the current offset environment and demonstrate how technology initiatives can play a significant role in the formation and pursuit of offset strategies. It is our hope that the reader has gained insight into our company's philosophies and methodologies, and that the review of Peace Marble IV/Peace Fox VI has provided a tangible example of the philosophies and principles discussed in this chapter. As the demand for offset increases, so will the challenges of pursuing it. It is our sincere hope that fulfilment of offsets through technology initiatives will be adopted as a primary mode of fulfilment by both defence contractors and governments alike, paving the way to long-term, mutually beneficial relationships crossing geographic and national boundaries.

Chapter 16

Concluding Remarks

Stephen Martin
Centre for Defence Economics,
University of York, UK

The aim of this chapter is to identify any common themes that emerge from the case studies and the associated lessons that can be drawn for public policy towards offsets. Given that the analysis has focused on a variety of countries, often with very different defence, economic, industrial and political backgrounds, it might be anticipated that few, if any, such points would materialise. Indeed, given the various forms of offset (such as co-production, licensed production, direct and indirect offset) and the different policy objectives, the task of identifying any common themes might have proved an onerous one. On the contrary, though, there appear to be a number of findings which, whilst not readily apparent in all of the case studies, come through sufficiently strongly to warrant discussion.

Perhaps the first point to make — and one which applies to virtually all countries — is that the absence of a reliable and consistent body of data makes any evaluation of offset programmes incredibly difficult. Indeed, in some cases the only publicly available data was the financial size of the offset together with a very brief description of the type of work which was considered to be eligible towards the vendor obligation. This data deficiency is all the more surprising given the substantial financial sums that are often involved and the fact that the offset package has sometimes proved the decisive factor in a purchaser's choice of vendor. Indeed, the US is the only country where regular and rigorous attempts have been made to track the impact of offsets in terms of jobs, technology and international competitiveness. Here, of course, the focus is on the domestic impact of offsets associated with US exports, rather than that associated with US imports (which is the more relevant scenario for most countries).

Typically, the impact of a direct/indirect offset is measured in financial terms (e.g. $500 million over a five-year period) and, in these circumstances, the success or failure of the offset depends on whether the vendor meets its obligation within the specified time period. However, the usefulness of this approach towards the evaluation of any offset programme depends on whether the work which is eligible towards an obligation actually occurred as a result of the offset, or whether it merely reflected existing business relations. If it is the latter case, then the impact of any offset, no matter how large financially, is likely to be rather trivial.

Also relevant for the evaluation of any offset is information on the programme's cost. That is, how much more does the offset cost compared with an off-the-shelf purchase? Many, but not all, states seem wedded to the idea that offsets are free goods and are reluctant to publicly admit that an offset costs more than an off-the-shelf purchase. Once this is recognised, though, further issues arise concerning the cost effectiveness of the offset programme and whether there are any other policy instruments which could obtain similar benefits for a smaller outlay.

Aside from the lacuna of data, the case studies reveal a number of interesting themes. First, offsets have involved a learning experience for both the vendor and purchaser and, as with any new initiative, both parties probably made mistakes in the early days. Vendors might have underestimated both the cost and the degree of difficulty with meeting their offset commitments. Initially, offset agreements were often on a 'best endeavours' basis but, as a number of countries learnt, financial penalties for the non-fulfilment of offsets proved a better incentive than the much vaguer 'best endeavours'. Firms in a number of purchasing countries initially, and quite erroneously, believed that an offset obligation guaranteed them orders irrespective of their cost and quality performance and, when such sales did not materialise, it led to widespread disenchantment with offsets. Also, firms with an obligation would, understandably, seek offset credit for as many purchases as it could lay claim to, irrespective of whether they met the necessary criteria. Consequently, administering offset programmes, particularly large ones, proved an onerous task. Inevitably disputes will arise over whether work is new work, generated by the offset, or whether it reflects established business patterns. Similarly, there will be debate as to whether the work meets the necessary technological standards and, where there is no obvious market price, there might be difficulty attaching a mutually agreeable value to, say, technology transfers. These teething troubles are inevitable although experience suggests that they decline as both parties become more familiar with each other. The only way around many of these problems is to agree a package of offset work in advance rather than wait for the vendor to place work with domestic industry. However, this is simply not practical for, say, a $1 billion worth of indirect offset!

Second, there seems to have been a move away from rather general offset programmes with broad eligibility criteria, and towards more focused measures. This might reflect the recognition that offsets cost more than an off-the-shelf purchase and that purchasers wish to concentrate their scarce resources in specific areas rather than provide a general subsidy to all of industry.

Third, the time horizon of those seeking offset seems to have lengthened, particularly in countries with a developing defence industry. One of the criticisms of offset is that once a vendor has fulfilled its obligation it will transfer its business to another state where it has an outstanding commitment. To overcome this, many countries allow a firm to bank offset credit in anticipation of a future obligation and this provides an incentive for the firm to continue placing work with domestic manufacturers. Of course, many countries are seeking the production work that this can bring and so the banking arrangement is the appropriate response to this form of short-termism. However, developing defence industries often want more than just production work, with technological and marketing skills being particularly attractive. To induce foreign manufacturers to share these assets, a number of countries now seek to draw foreign firms into the domestic economy through either equity investments in existing domestic firms or the establishment of joint ventures. Both approaches provide the foreign firm with an incentive to continue to place work in the domestic economy and to share other skills as this increases the profitability of its overseas investment.

The interpretation of this move away from broadly defined short-term offset work and towards a more focused long-term investment strategy is, by no means, clear cut. It could be that it reflects what is perceived to be the failure of the former approach and that, as alleged, foreign suppliers cease placing work in the domestic economy once their offset obligation is complete. An alternative interpretation would emphasise the success of the offset strategy in laying the foundations on which future joint ventures could be built. By encouraging foreign firms to place work with domestic manufacturers, both parties become familiar with doing business with each other. The foreign firm is made aware of the capabilities of domestic manufacturers who, in turn, become aware of the cost and quality requirements for sales to the foreign firm. In this scenario, offsets force domestic manufacturers to become more efficient and, once this has occurred, make the foreign manufacturer more willing to invest in the local firm. The move away from offsets and towards joint ventures does not reflect the failure of the former; rather, the reverse. Of course, this form of offset is likely to be more attractive to those countries with a developing defence industrial base than to states that have less of a need for new technologies.

Finally, none of the country studies provide any evidence to suggest that offsets are likely to disappear in the foreseeable future. Certainly, the US has unilaterally sought to limit the size of offset that American firms can offer and Congress has passed a bill that limits the steps that US firms can adopt to fulfil any offset obligation. As part of a Code of Conduct for defence trade, the US has also sought multi-lateral agreement with its NATO partners to limit and eventually eliminate all offsets, which it views as a barrier to defence trade. However, since an initial draft in 1992, the Code of Conduct has made little progress towards being a more substantive document and thus the prospect for a mutual elimination of all offsets, within this forum at least, remains remote. Elsewhere, as long as purchasers continue to require offsets, and there is no reason why they should cease to do so, competitive pressures will force vendors to meet such demands.

Index

Each country's main entry (usually a complete chapter) is in bold. For the reader's convenience, particular areas of interest may also be included as a subheading.